Annette and Luc Vezin

The 20th-Century Muse

Translated from the French by Toula Ballas

Harry N. Abrams, Inc., Publishers

Contents

An Attempt to Revise a Simplistic View

Cherchez la femme, the investigator always advises in mystery novels. Look for the muse, suggests the biographer. By its mythological origin, a muse is a feminine noun. "Muse, the name of the nymph who inspired Numa. Every woman or every thing personified as a feminine type, considered as an inspiration," says the *Littré,* a nineteenth-century French dictionary.

But the muse who, in the twentieth century, inspired the creator, the writer, the painter, the filmmaker, the photographer, or the musician was not always a woman. It could have been a man, a color, or a memory. From New York to Tokyo and from Paris to Mexico, we have chosen to retrace the paths of twenty-four muses who have left their mark on creativity in the twentieth century. This is a deliberately restrained chronological approach, but one that justifies itself by the new dimension of the phenomenon. It is not that there are more muses today than yesterday—perhaps even the opposite may be true, as few contemporary artists openly admit to such sources of inspiration—but the nature of the muse has changed. Following the evolution of the status of women and their greater access to all the areas of creativity, the muse in the twentieth century is no longer the often passive figure whose name had been almost forgotten, like Dante's Beatrice, and who only retains her literary identity. She has become an active character who is conscious of her importance.

Above all, this role is not (is no longer?) a one-way street. A spark: Martha Fleischmann for James Joyce; a perfect model: Dina Vierny for Aristide Maillol; a patroness: Peggy Guggenheim for Jackson Pollock. Some participate in a creative game of mirror images, like Frida Kahlo and Georgia O'Keeffe, and others,

For me, woman is the representation of the eternal principle of creation. . . . I'll find another cliché tomorrow, but for today, does that one work for you?

—Federico Fellini

becoming memories, continued to inspire the creators after death, as Yoko did for Araki or Robert for his brother, Joseph Cornell.

In casting light on the muse who has contributed to the birth of a work, are we giving in to the temptation to reduce the mystery of creation to simple biography? The debate launched by the nineteenth-century French writer Charles-Augustin Sainte-Beuve was taken up by Proust in his essay "Contre Sainte-Beuve" ("On Art and Literature"), in which he wrote: "A book is the product of another me than the one that we manifest in our habits, in society, or in our vices." That idea is echoed today by the writer V.S. Naipaul. "Everything valuable that I have to say is found in my books," stated the 2001 Nobel Prize winner for literature while delivering a series of recollections on his childhood in Trinidad. So many examples have allowed the novelist to become the work and still be able to speak to the act of creating that work. For this volume we follow in the footsteps of filmmaker Jean-Luc Godard—who despite being miserly with biographical details himself confides in his book *Jean-Luc Godard par Jean-Luc Godard*, "I'm happy to know that Conrad traveled in first class and that his wife and children traveled in third"—and openly confess our weakness for biographies. In following the paths of the muses, who are sometimes friends, sometimes lovers, often creators themselves, and always inspirational, we will revise the simplistic view of their roles, in the hopes of giving the reader a renewed desire to read, to listen, and to see.

The Spark

"The light keeps me alive," wrote the poet René Char. An image, a scent, or a sound is sometimes enough to ignite a creative life. And so it was one night in January 1909 when the taste of a morsel of toasted bread dipped in tea must have led Marcel Proust to begin *À la recherche du temps perdu* (*Remembrance of Things Past*). The bread, transformed in *Swann's Way* into "one of those plump shortcakes called *petites madeleines*," became synonymous with the enduring light that lives on in the minds of artists. Less well-known but equally fruitful an inspiration was James Joyce's vision of a young girl on a beach in Ireland, a memory revived some twenty years later by his brief encounter with Martha Fleischmann, who would inspire some crucial episodes in *A Portrait of the Artist as a Young Man* and *Ulysses*. Even more stunning is the true story of Lillita, Charlie Chaplin's child-bride, who would end up, thanks to Vladimir Nabokov's novel *Lolita*, being the basis for a modern-day archetype.

Lou Andreas-Salomé
Friedrich Nietzsche
Rainer Maria Rilke

The Young Girl, the Eagle, and the Lion

From czarist Russia where Louise Salomé was born in 1861, to Nazi Germany where she died in 1937, Lou Andreas-Salomé—novelist, literary critic, and psychotherapist—was friends for a short time with the German philosopher Friedrich Nietzsche in 1882, then for longer with the German poet Rainer Maria Rilke and the seminal Austrian psychoanalyst Sigmund Freud, provoking a creative whirlwind with each encounter. According to one critic: "When Lou takes on a passionate attachment for a man, that man gives birth to a book nine months later."

"Lou is the daughter of a Russian general. She is twenty years old. . . . She is as shrewd as an eagle and brave as a lion, and yet still a very girlish child who perhaps will not live long." Writing alone in a house in the Tautenburg forest in Thuringia, Germany, Nietzsche lyrically described to his friend Peter Gast the one he was waiting for and the one who was late in arriving. But this abstract and romantic evocation mentioned nothing about her silvery blonde locks, her slightly turned-up nose, or her ready lips.

Louise Salomé was born in Saint Petersburg on February 12, 1861, in the official residence occupied by her parents across from the Winter Palace, the home of the czar. The family spoke German and French with each other, but the young Salomé grudgingly learned to speak Russian at school. When she was eighteen years old, she engaged in a bizarre student-teacher relationship with Henrik Gillot, a married Dutch Lutheran minister and father of two girls who preached in a small church on Nevsky Prospect, the city's main boulevard. For several months she visited him in secret, spending hours filling her blue notebooks with entries comparing Hinduism, Christianity, and Islam, the Old Testament and the Trinity, French theater and German poetry. Following her father's death in 1879, she revealed her secret and her mother, crazy with worry, summoned Gillot, who explained calmly that Lou was a genius and demanded the privilege of continuing her education. Things soon took a turn for the worse. Gillot asked for Salomé's hand in marriage—she was nineteen and refused, stunned by the proposal. Several days later she decided to leave Russia and enrolled in a university in Zurich to pursue courses in theology, philosophy, and art history. A brilliant and serious student, Salomé soon exceeded her energy, fell ill from mental and physical exhaustion, and was advised to seek respite in the sun of southern Europe. She left for Rome accompanied by her mother. One of her teachers, Professor Kinkiel, recommended her to his friend Malwida von Meysenburg, an important figure in the German feminist movement and a friend of Wagner and his then devoted disciple Nietzsche.

When Salomé arrived in Rome in the spring of 1882, she paid a visit to Malwida's salon and became acquainted with Paul Rée, a friend of Nietzsche's who soon wrote him to describe their encounter. Nietzsche's response on March 21 from Genoa, where he was staying, was surprising: "Greet this young Russian for me if you think it will do any good. I lust for such souls. Soon I will grab one for myself. Marriage is something different. At most I could agree to a two-year marriage and even that only because of what I have to do in the next ten years." Why speak of marriage when he didn't even know Lou? His friend Rée, who to all evidence was already madly in love with her, took the joke lightly. But was it a joke? Nietzsche was considering a ménage à trois, though a completely platonic one. "A study project," "a magnificent plan," "an inner circle" in which there would be long discussions about God and the world, good and evil. What better place to receive this future Trinity than Paris? For the modest Meysenburg, it would have been shocking to encourage this "salon." Unwittingly, however, she set the stage for this triple meeting.

Ménage à Trois

Salomé and Rée took long walks together in Rome and often stopped to sit in a side chapel of Saint Peter's Basilica. There they delivered great discourses on the nonexistence of God. One day Nietzsche appeared, walked straight to Salomé, and said: "From what star have we fallen together here?" Malwida, at whose home Lou and Paul lived, had told the philosopher where to find them. Lou recounted her first impression of this man of medium height, shy demeanor, and mysterious allure. "They were not the eyes of many shortsighted people, they did not stare or blink at you, or embarrass you by coming too close. They seemed rather like guardians and keepers of his own treasures, mute mysteries upon which no uninitiated glance was permitted to fall."

Nietzsche quickly understood that he had to distance himself from his friend Rée if he was to seduce Salomé. But he needed a chaperon in order to carry out his plan, so he wrote to his sister Elisabeth suggesting that she invite Lou to visit. He did not say he was in love but simply desired to "make a more precise judgment of her." Besides, the young lady was ugly, "but like all ugly girls, she has cultivated her spirit in order to be seductive." Finally, she was a pure spirit who "from her earliest childhood has worked hard to teach herself and has sacrificed everything for this goal." Elisabeth realized that her brother was in love.

Incipit tragoedia: "The tragedy begins here." *The Gay Science*, the book that Nietzsche had finished writing several months before meeting Salomé, ended with this aphorism in the original edition. A premonition it seems. They met up along the edges of the lake in Orta, north of Milan, and Lou left with him to visit Monte Sacro on the small island of San Giulio. In this landscape dotted with little churches and monasteries, they lingered alone for hours, prey to the whirlwind of their emotions. So what happened there? Without a doubt it was the revelation of a strong communion of ideas and feelings. "I owe to you the most beautiful dream of my life," recalled Nietzsche. "Whether I kissed Nietzsche on Monte Sacro, I do not know," wrote Salomé. Some time later they found themselves in Lucerne. Lou was friendly, Nietzsche asked her to marry him. She declined the proposal, speaking of friendship and of work. And she always included Rée. When they returned to the hotel, Nietzsche suggested that all three of them take a photograph. He arranged the scene in front of portrait photographer Jules Bonnet's camera. Using a wagon as the set piece, he had Lou kneel in the center of it and yoked Rée and himself to the cart with a rope held by Lou. She was transformed into a coach driver and, at Nietzsche's request, carried a riding crop embellished with a bunch of lilacs. The photograph was a great success—and a complete scandal. Nietzsche later wrote, "You're going to see women? Don't forget the whip." Six weeks passed. Bowing to Nietzsche's insistence, Lou agreed to visit him in Tautenburg in Thuringia, where he planned to spend the summer in the company of his sister Elisabeth. Lou's letter accepting the invitation delighted him. The completion of *The Gay Science*, after six years of effort, and Lou's imminent arrival filled him with joy.

The Summer of 1882

The two women met in Bayreuth where Lou had gone to hear Wagner, and departed together to meet up with Nietzsche. A solid antipathy was soon born between them. When they disembarked at the Dorndorf train station on August 7, 1882, Nietzsche was in great humor. It would not last long. Elisabeth immediately described to him Lou—whom she called the Russian, the Finn, or the Jewess—and her behavior at Bayreuth in the company of the Wagner clan, whose relations with Nietzsche had become strained. When they finally found themselves in private conversation, things improved. "I knew that once we would get to know each other—which we failed to do in the beginning because of the turmoil of our feelings—we would soon discover, beyond all the petty gossip, how deeply akin we are." But the misunderstanding persisted. Lou was not in love and Nietzsche "secretly desired something else," wrote Lou. They talked in the bedroom until late into the night. Nietzsche took her hand and kissed it. When Lou had a fever, he slipped letters under her door and spoke to her for hours standing in the hallway. Soon they were able to continue their walks together. "A beautiful day in the quiet pine woods, alone with sun rays and squirrels. . . . Talking with Nietzsche is very exciting, as you know. But there is a special fascination if you encounter like thoughts, like sentiments and ideas—we understand each other perfectly. Once he said to me in amazement, 'I think the only difference between us is that of age. We have lived alike and thought alike.' "

What did they speak about? As far as Elisabeth could tell—and for the most part, they avoided her presence—their conversations were shocking. They discussed sex, morality, and religion (how God was created by man, and how to live in a world without God). Lou considered taking notes but abandoned the idea because their conversations "ranged from the nearest to the most distant realms of thought and do not lend themselves to precise formulations." For his part, Nietzsche wrote to his friend Gast, "Every five days we have a little tragic scene." Heaven and hell occupied most of their discussions. Nietzsche encouraged her to write, even though he told her that the style of the first section of her essay on women was "horrible." But Lou wondered if Nietzsche wasn't wasting his time endlessly talking to her instead of working. In one sense he agreed and noted: "I must not live too long beside you." In her book *A Struggle for God*, published three years after her encounters with Nietzsche, Lou recalled this troubling closeness that blended intellectual and erotic exaltation. When Lou left Tautenburg, she gave him the poem "Hymn to Life" as a goodbye gift, in which the last lines announce the sufferings to come:

If you have no more happiness to give
Give me your pain.

When they parted, and Rée and Lou headed again for Berlin leaving Nietzsche on the platform of the Leipzig train station, they knew that their "Holy Trinity" had had its day. The break was abrupt for Nietzsche. But this thwarted love, this dream of perfect intellectual fusion with a woman young and full of energy inaugurated the most creative period in his life. Over seven years, from 1882 when he first met Salomé until the stroke that paralyzed him in January 1889, he wrote the key works of his oeuvre in a state of complete solitude. He then spent the last ten years of his life enclosed in madness, cared for by his mother and his sister, and he ignored all the attention that had suddenly caught up with him. But if the encounter with Lou proved to be philosophically fertile, the rupture plunged him into an unprecedented state of depression. Hoping for revenge against "the Russian," his sister Elisabeth launched into a vendetta, even attempting to obtain Lou's expulsion from Germany for moral turpitude. "For about a year there were stirred up in me the sorts of feelings that I denied with the best will in the world and that I believed controlled me in their basest forms: revenge and resentment," wrote Nietzsche to Gast. Revenge and resentment were two concepts contrary to the Nietzschean way of thinking and which Zarathustra would know to avoid.

Several months after Lou's departure, Nietzsche was the first to recognize that his encounters with her had been beneficial. In 1884 he wrote to his mother, "You may say what you like against this girl. . . . It still remains true that I have never found a more gifted and thoughtful person. And although we have never agreed any more than I have agreed with Rée, we were both happy after each half hour we spent together that we had learned so much. It is no accident that I have accomplished my greatest work in the past twelve months." If Lou's treachery had plunged him into despair, the writing of the first part of *Thus Spake Zarathustra* in several days at the beginning of 1883 inaugurated a new phase of creativity. Without diminishing the work, it is difficult not to see Zarathustra as the inverse image of a Nietzsche prey to jealousy, frustration, and abandonment. When Lou left, it had been to rejoin Rée with whom she shared an apartment in Berlin. As Zarathustra says, "He who is consumed by the flame of jealousy turns at last, like the scorpion, the poisoned sting against himself." Elisabeth declared that her brother was above carnal desires, a saint without sexuality. "Do I counsel you to chastity?" asks Zarathustra. "Chastity is a virtue with some, but with many almost a vice." And women, in Nietzsche's eyes, did not emerge from his unhappy love for Lou with increased stature. "Woman is not yet capable of friendship. Women still are cats and birds or at best cows."

Opposite: **In this photograph from 1880 Louise Salomé stands in her family home in Saint Petersburg, the perfect model of a serious and well-behaved young student.**

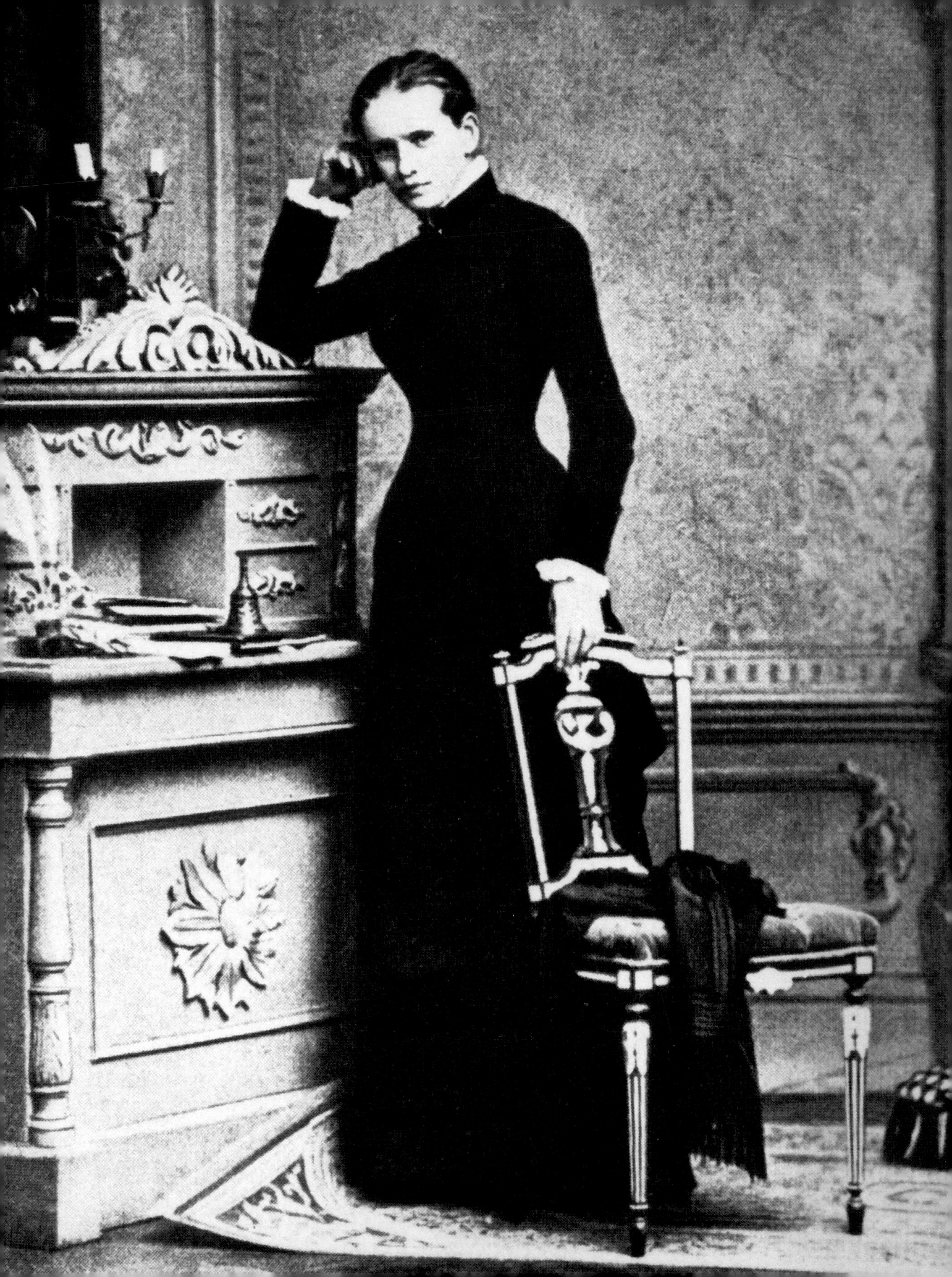

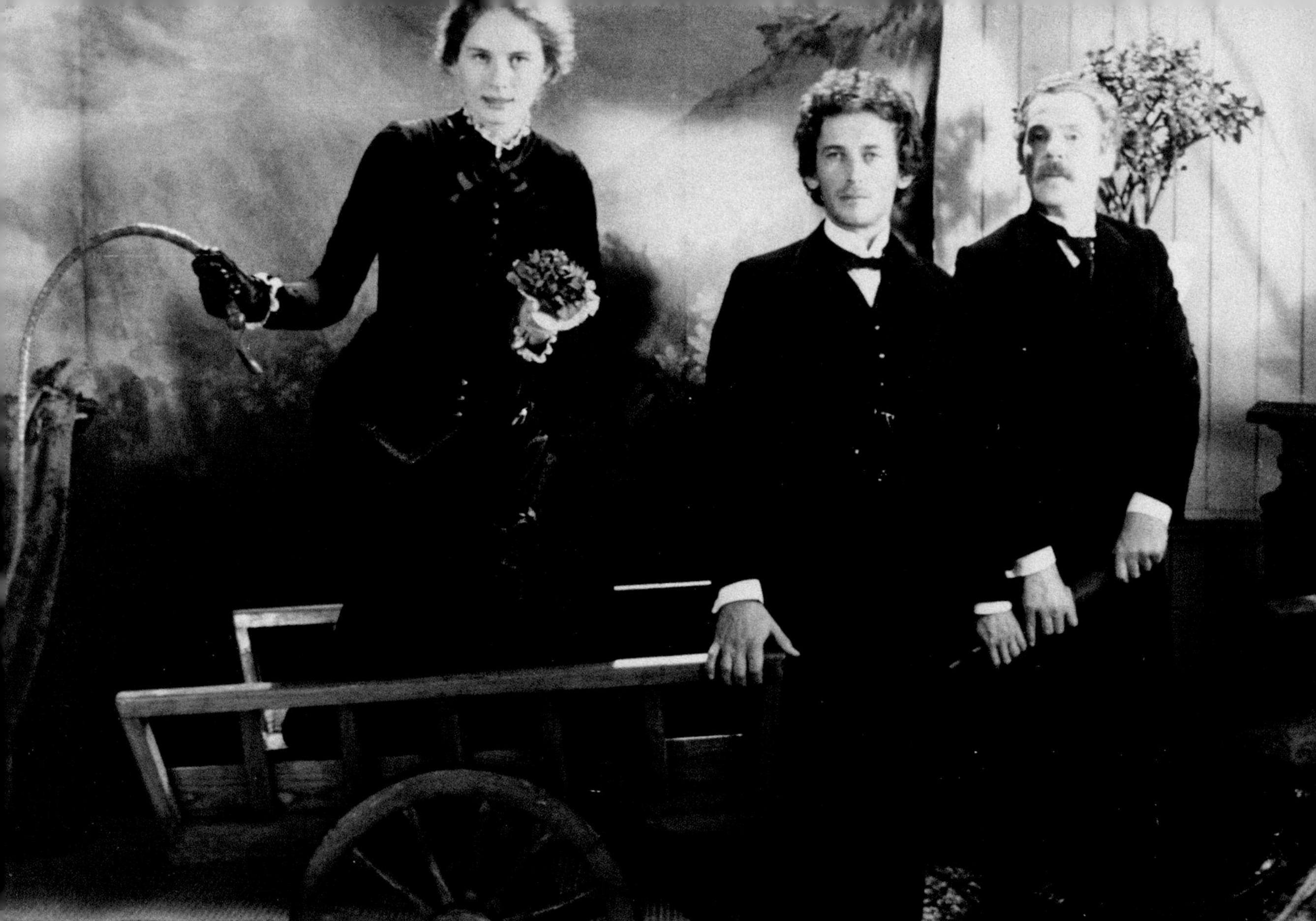

Opposite: **The Holy Trinity—as Friedrich Nietzsche nicknamed them—found themselves in front of photographer Jules Bonnet's camera in Lucerne in 1882. Lou Andreas-Salomé, Nietzsche, and Paul Rée posed for a photograph that would turn into a scandal. Lou's kneeling position, complete with whip in hand, had a connotation erotic enough to shock their contemporaries.**

Above: **This legendary scene was in Liliana Cavani's 1977 film, *Beyond Good and Evil*, starring Dominique Sanda, Robert Powell, and Erland Josephson. Same rural background, same wagon. Only Lou Andreas-Salomé's position has been slightly modified and the symbolism of the female flower reinforced by the bouquet in her other hand.**

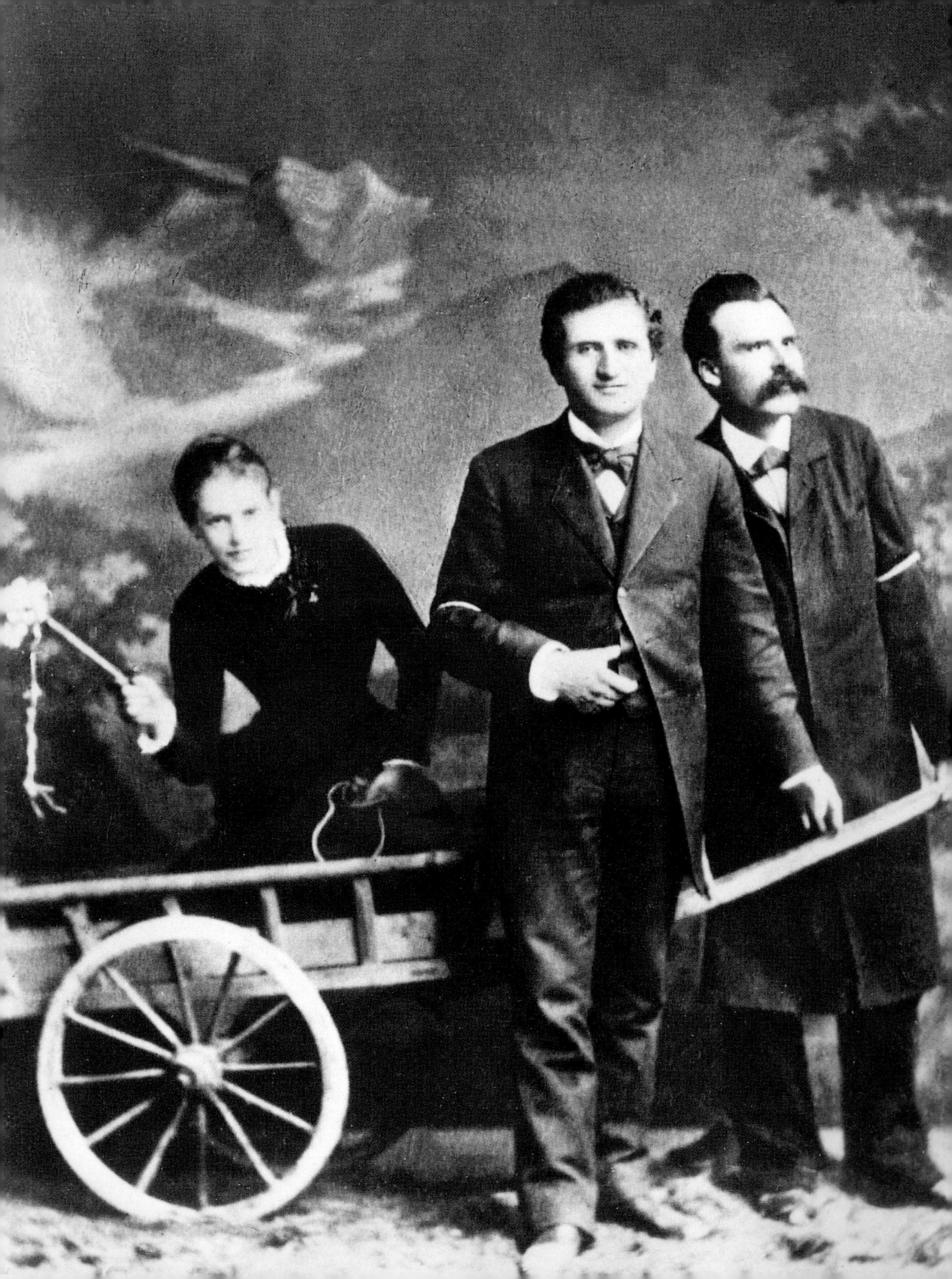

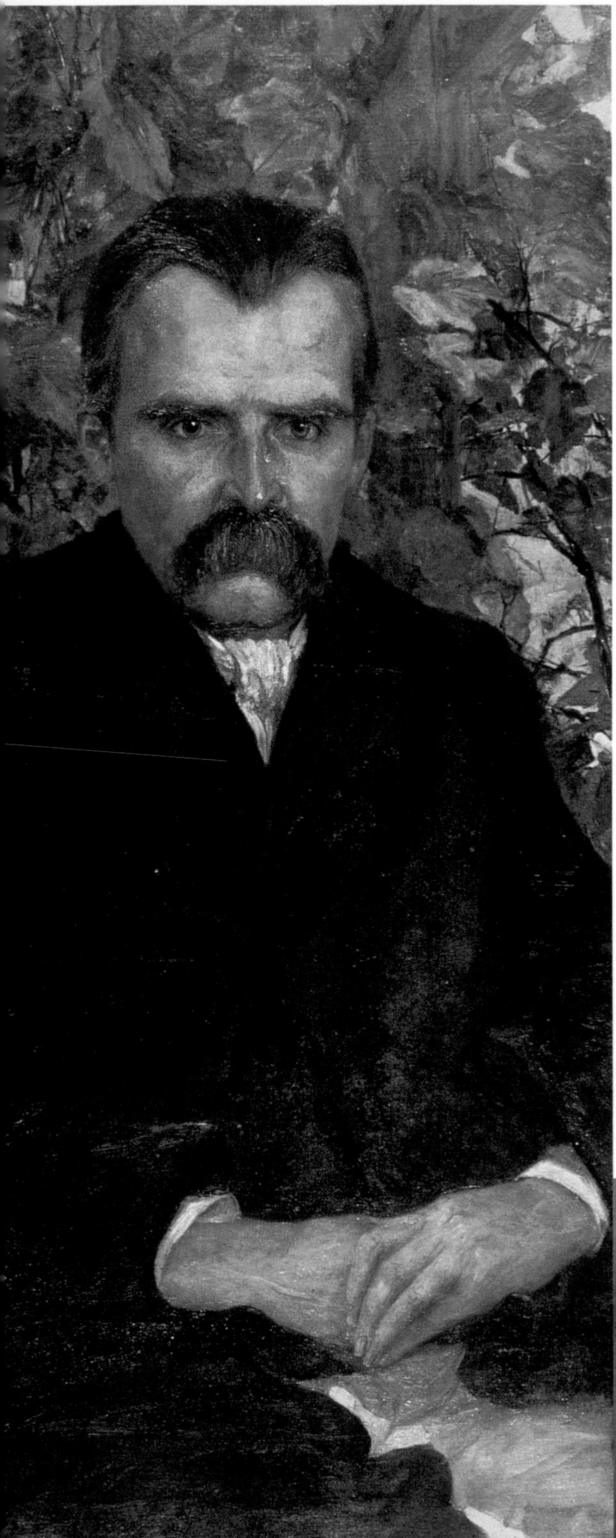

Left: **Years later a somber-looking Friedrich Nietzsche sat for painter Curt Stoeving around 1890–1900.**
Below: **Now a respected critic and writer, Lou Andreas-Salomé never saw Friedrich Nietzsche again after their break, but their names remained linked even in the mind of Sigmund Freud, with whom Lou would work. Here, an undated portrait of Salomé.**

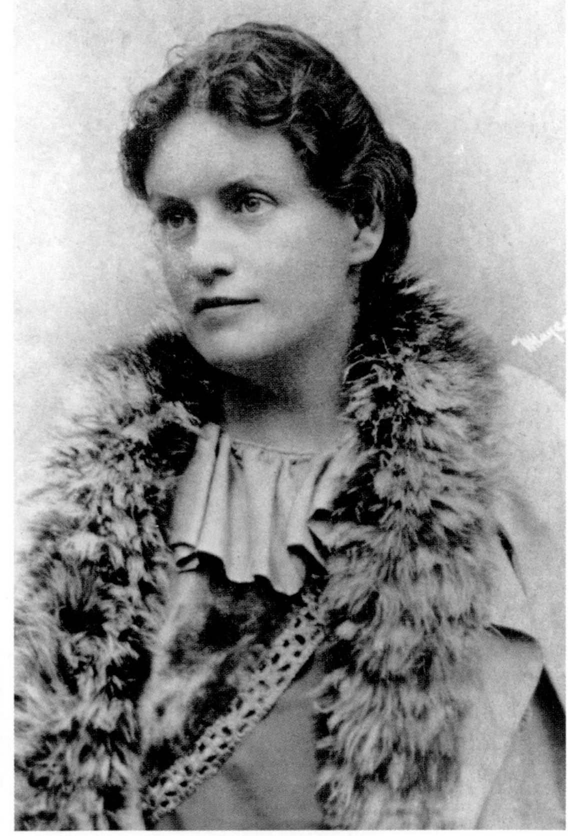

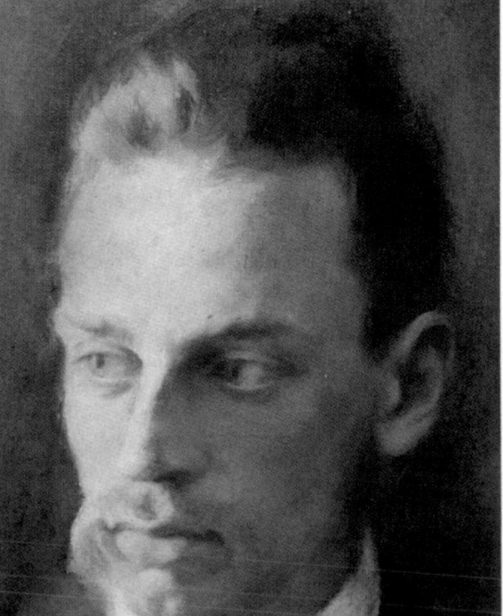

Left: **Rainer Maria Rilke painted by Helmuth Westhoff in 1901 (detail).**

Opposite: **A manuscript by Lou Andreas-Salomé annotated in Friedrich Nietzsche's hand.**

14.

Es könnte einmal eine Zeit kommen, in welcher nur noch kleine philosophische Denker große philosophische Gedanken haben könnten.

in welcher „der große Gedanke" einen Beweis dafür abgibt, daß sein Urheber ein kleiner Denker ist.

15.

(Vielleicht würde der ehrlichste Philosoph nicht bis zur Philosophie kommen.)

Der redlichste Philosoph würde vielleicht ~~nicht~~ bis zum „System" kommen dürfen

16.

Was den Denker über die Menge stellt, ist nicht so sehr ~~seine~~ die Geisteskraft als ~~seine~~ die ~~Geistes~~richtung sind (Geistes.

During their long walks in Tautenburg, Lou and Nietzsche discussed most notably her essay on women. For Lou, "pregnancy is the cardinal condition which has gradually, in the course of time, determined the character of women." Zarathustra writes, "Everything about women is a riddle. And everything about women has one solution—its name is pregnancy." The encounters with Nietzsche would be as productive for Lou. Her first book, *A Struggle for God*, written when she was twenty-three, was a publishing success. Her friendship with Nietzsche and the wicked rumors of frustrated passion gave her an aura of prickliness and authority. Lou would keep the experience of her intellectual intimacy with Nietzsche with her forever. In the eyes of Rilke, whom she would love, and of Freud, with whom she would work closely, she was inextricably linked to the philosopher. The rest of her life, from her paper marriage to the Persian-born Friedrich Carl Andreas, a linguist with the charm of a monk, to the 1901 death of Paul Rée, who drowned in the Inn River near a spot where he had often walked with Lou, further fed her legend. At thirty years old, Lou was part of the bohemian intelligentsia, had an established literary and critical career, and while she drew men to her she remained a virgin. She often reflected on this strange mix, and in her *Diary* she revealed that Rilke was her first lover. When they first met, Rilke had already published some poems under the name of René Maria Rilke. Lou encouraged him to write "more simply about simple things." His writing changed, became cleaner and more precise. With her advice he abandoned the somewhat affected French-sounding René for Rainer and found glory with his new name. After their split Rilke would write to her: "The process of transformation that took place in me in a hundred places at the same time emanated from the great reality of your being. . . . All this happened because I had the good fortune to meet you at the moment I was in danger of losing myself to the absence of form."

The Poet and the Psychoanalyst

Lou was fifty in 1911 when she was presented to Freud at the Weimar congress of the International Psychoanalytic Association. They spoke much about Nietzsche during the meeting, and Freud was impressed to have before him a living connection to the author of *Beyond Good and Evil*. He was amused also that Lou, only a few years younger than he, wanted suddenly to understand everything about psychoanalysis. But her intuitions and her attentiveness surprised him. In October 1912 she moved to Vienna for six months and worked closely with him. She attended his classes, and took his side against Alfred Adler, with whom Freud had split. What a strange spectacle to see this fifty-one-year-old woman calmly listening to accounts of the most uncouth sexual behavior, all the while taking notes or knitting. Her actions quickly became amusing to the participants who joked about the nonstop "mating" of Salomé's knitting needles. Called by Freud the "poet of psychoanalysis," Lou contrasted with him by her boundless optimism. Her credo was "Life is magnificent."

In the last years of her life as a recluse in her home in Hainberg near Göttingen, eroded by cancer, Salomé was under Nazi high surveillance. If this psychoanalyst friend of Freud's managed to escape real persecution, it was Nietzsche's shadow, a figure revered by the Nazis, that protected her. But Salomé now felt it was necessary to organize her estate. What would become of Nietzsche's letters so carefully guarded in a bank safety deposit box? And those of Rilke's? Ernst Pfeiffer, her companion in old age, was designated as the sole executor. Lou died on January 5, 1937. Contrary to her last wishes—she requested that her ashes be scattered in her garden, which was forbidden by German law—the urn was placed in her husband's tomb in the municipal cemetery of Göttingen. No commemorative plaque marks the place. Fifty years after their encounter, she finally responded to Nietzsche's ultimate injunction: "And now Lou, dear heart, sweep aside all the clouds in heaven!"

Bibliography

Andreas-Salomé, Lou. *Nietzsche*. Champaign: University of Illinois Press, 2001.

Martin, Biddy. *Woman and Modernity: The Lifestyles of Lou Andreas-Salomé*. Ithaca, N.Y.: Cornell University Press, 1991.

Pfeiffer, Ernest, ed. *Sigmund Freud and Lou Andreas-Salomé: Letters*. New York: W.W. Norton & Co., 1985.

Rilke, Rainer Maria. *Duino Elegies* (Bilingual Edition). Berkeley: University of California Press, 2001.

Martha Fleischmann
James Joyce

A Nausicaa for *Ulysses*

From his Catholic childhood on, James Joyce (1882–1941) worshipped the Virgin Mary and dreamed at one point of becoming a priest. But in 1898 the vision of a young girl on an Irish beach became for him the ideal of a pagan Mary, whom it was possible to adore without renouncing life or art. Twenty years later he came across this same type of female in the form of a Swiss lady of leisure, Martha Fleischmann. She would become the principal model for Gerty MacDowell, a central character in his novel *Ulysses*.

The platonic romance shared by James Joyce and Martha Fleischmann from December 9, 1918, to February 2, 1919, seems innocent enough. A few glances by the writer out the window at his Zurich neighbor, some words exchanged in the street, the sharing of an old collection of poetry, *Chamber Music*, a ceremony—a sort of ridiculous black mass—and that was basically it. There was an epilogue to this "non-affair": Martha, who was very ill—because of this situation she believed—went to see Joyce in June 1919 and threatened to kill herself with "violent gestures towards me," wrote the author to the painter Frank Budgen, his confidant in this matter. He managed to get out of this bad situation diplomatically and calmed her by returning all their correspondence. For the author, Martha represented the incarnation of a fantasy that was at the source of his creativity and the principal model for MacDowell in *Ulysses*.

"My first impression of you"

Who, then, is Martha? When Joyce met her, this thirty-three-year-old Swiss woman was the not very ardent mistress of an engineer named Rudolph Hiltpold. Her great problem in life seemed to be her father's modest background while, on her mother's side, she was descended from Bernese nobility. In his biography of Joyce, Richard Ellmann draws an unflattering portrait: "She spent her days smoking, reading romantic novels, and primping. She was vain and wished to be snobbish." But for Joyce there was "something frank and almost shameless in her allure." He praised "the softness and regularity of her features and the gentleness of her eyes." Martha was elegant, dressed and coiffed in the latest style; but while she was an attractive woman, she was no great beauty.

Their encounter, a mixture of the trivial and the sublime, is pure Joyce. On December 9, 1918, the writer was daydreaming at the window of his Zurich apartment when his attention was drawn to a woman pulling on a toilet chain in the building across the street.

"A day or so afterwards," recounts Richard Ellmann, "he was on his way home when he observed the same young woman walking ahead of him. . . . As she turned to enter her building he saw her face, and his own lit up . . . *'mit grösstem Erstaunen'* ('with great amazement'). For it appeared to Joyce . . . that he was seeing again the girl he had seen in 1898 by the strand, wading in the Irish Sea. . . ."

Joyce knew that there was nothing to it, but Martha's allure corresponded exactly to the young girl's he had seen twenty years earlier on an Irish beach and who had helped him choose the path of art over religion. The future writer, then in a full crisis of faith, named this kind of vision an "epiphany." The scene was the origin of a crucial episode in his first novel, *A Portrait of the Artist as a Young Man*, at the point when the hero, Stephen, questions his future: "A girl stood before him in midstream, alone and still, gazing out to sea. She seemed like one whom magic had changed into the likeness of a strange and beautiful seabird. . . . Her eyes had called him and his soul had leaped at the call. To live, to err, to fall, to triumph, to recreate life out of life!"

Twenty years later (or thirteen after the editing of *Portrait*), Joyce wrote to Fleischmann:

My first impression of you.
Here it is.
You were dressed in black, wearing a big hat with waving feathers.
The color suited you very well.
And I thought: a pretty animal.

"To recreate life out of life"—it was this desire to transform the trifling incidents of daily life and the words overheard in a Dublin bar into a Homeric epic that compelled Joyce to write *Ulysses*. But a lot of life would have to unfold before the fourteen-year-old visionary could become the author of one of the greatest novels of the twentieth century. The young tormented Irishman, a brilliant Jesuit student full of pretensions, who saw himself become the "poet of [his] people" would first have to suffer through often miserable exiles in Trieste, Zurich, and Paris. But it was Dublin that sealed his fate as a man. On June 10, 1904, James Joyce approached a tall "auburn-haired" girl on Nassau Street. She was originally from Galway in the west of Ireland and had come to work as an employee in a Dublin hotel. Her name was Nora Barnacle, which would lead Joyce's father to say: "She'll never leave him." He was not mistaken. Nora would give him two children, Giorgio (also known as George) and Lucia, making up the family who, according to Joyce, were the only people in the world he loved. But Nora stayed in the background of the writer's work, remaining a simple and naive wife to the point of making this surprising declaration one day to him: "Jim, I've never read your books, but I will do it one day; they must be good since they sell well." Nora would not be the inspiration for his novels, and Joyce would search long for the type of woman who incarnated the mysterious young girl on the Irish beach before finding her in Martha Fleischmann.

The Look of the Blind Man

When 1918 neared its end, he felt old and serene enough to launch into an affair, all while maintaining a certain detachment. Moreover he was sick; the preceding year he felt such a pain in his right eye that he lost consciousness in the middle of the street. Operated on shortly after, the eye was saved but Joyce suffered a loss of vision that left him in semi-blindness for the rest of his life. The writer had lost all illusions and, from his first encounters with Martha, he was aware that he had no hope of seducing her. This romantic adventure could only be an affair of a voyeur, even while the voyeur was in the process of losing his eyesight. The comedy of the situation could hardly have escaped the author of *Ulysses*.

"I had a fever yesterday evening, waiting for a sign from you," he wrote to Martha, whom he spied at the window. "But why do you not want to write even one word to me—your name? And why do you always close your shutters? I want to see you!"

One imagines with what pleasure the coquettish Martha surrendered herself to this game of hide-and-go-seek and seduction at a distance conducted by glances and clandestine letters. And fancy Joyce! And Joyce himself was enjoying living out an episode of *Ulysses* while finding material for another story.

In his novel the hero, Leopold Bloom, maintains a secret exchange of letters with a certain Martha Clifford, which he signs with the pseudonym of Henry, using a Greek "e"—an epsilon. In his letters to the real Martha, Joyce would amuse himself by using this same epsilon in his signature. It is not the only coincidence—and Joyce adored coincidences—between the two correspondences. In the novel, Bloom sends letters with stamps enclosed to Martha (Clifford), which angers her and, replying to the person she nicknames "my poor little naughty boy," she "wishes [she] could punish [him] for that." In December 1918, Joyce played the same little sadomasochistic game in writing to Martha (Fleischmann). "Have I offended? But *how*? I beg you to send me a line immediately. Here is an envelope all ready. . . . For the love of God send me a line."

A Nausicaa for *Ulysses*

Joyce was not satisfied merely to relive the already completed adventures from *Ulysses* with Martha Fleischmann. Thanks to her, he could pursue the very subject of his novel: the transcription of Homer's *Odyssey* as lived in one day by Leopold Bloom in Dublin. Martha Fleischmann would be the character of Nausicaa. In *The Odyssey* Ulysses finds himself thrown on a beach where Nausicaa, daughter of King Alcinous, is in the middle of washing her clothes in anticipation of her marriage. Once the washing is done, she plays ball with her companions. Their cries wake Odysseus who, wearing "a leafy branch to cover his manhood," comes out to encounter the young girls. Nausicaa wants to seduce Ulysses, but he leaves her to rejoin his wife, Penelope, in Ithaca.

The scene enchanted Joyce: "In Naxos an old man of fifty, maybe bald, with Nausicaa, a girl barely sixteen years old. What a lovely theme." He planned to perform the scene again with Martha and to write it in "a namby-pamby jammy marmalady drawersy (alto là!) style with effects of incense, mariolatry, masturbation, stewed cockles, painter's palette, chitchat, circumlocutions, etc. etc." Consider the chapter's opening line: "The summer evening had begun to fold the world in its mysterious embrace." Compare, one more time, the correspondence with Martha: "I imagine a misty evening to myself. I am waiting—and I see you coming towards me, dressed in black, young, strange and gentle. I look into your eyes . . ." the way Ulysses and Nausicaa would have looked into each other's.

On a Dublin beach Nausicaa was transformed into Gerty MacDowell, Martha the coquette's double: "There was an innate refinement, a languid queenly hauteur about Gerty which was unmistakably evidenced in her delicate hands and higharched instep." Gerty was a "votary of Dame Fashion" who found the accessory she was looking for—a certain hat—"at Clery's summer sales" and for whom underclothes were her "chief care." Joyce's also. When he finally arranged a rendezvous with Martha, he passed the evening discussing ladies' underwear.

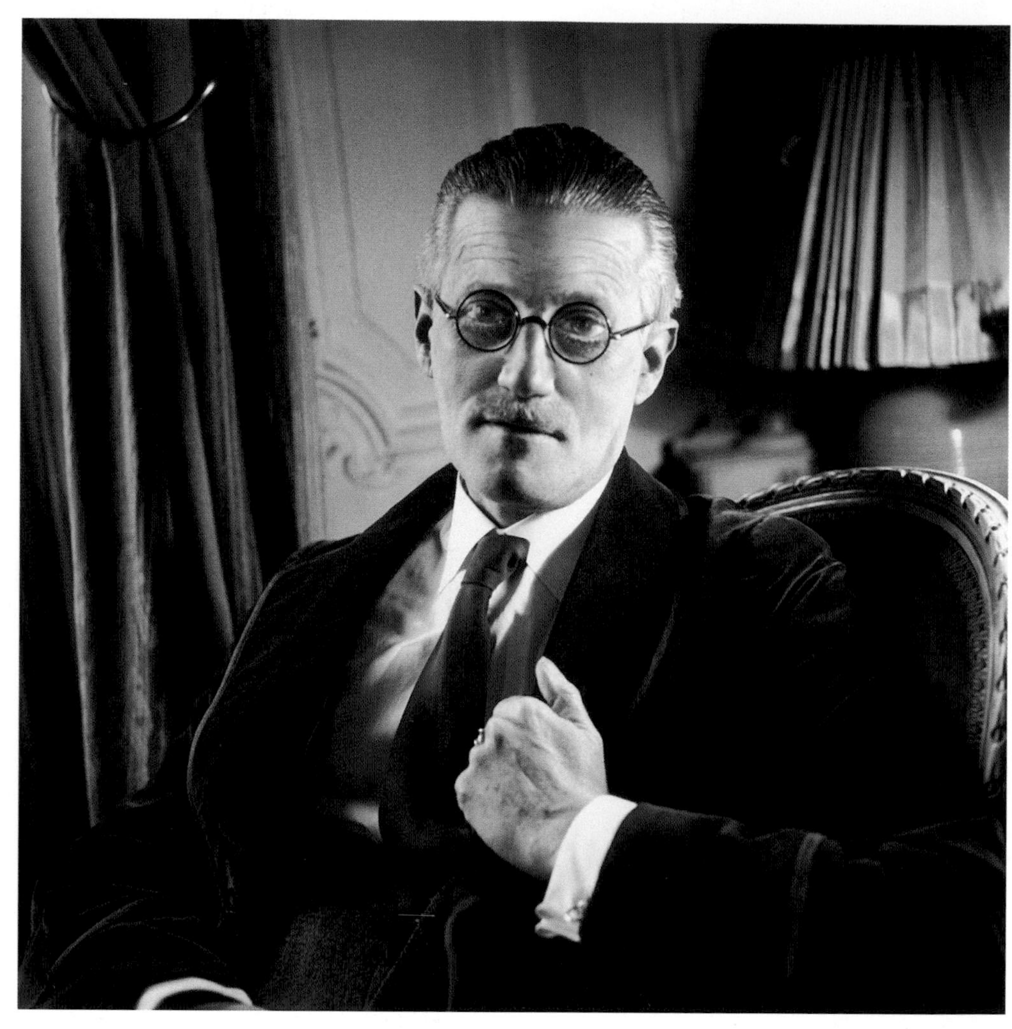

Above: **James Joyce in 1934. Fourteen years after its publication in France, *Ulysses*—considered obscene until 1934—was finally authorized for release in the United States.**

Opposite: **Martha Fleischmann had, according to James Joyce, "something frank and almost shameless in her allure" with "the softness and regularity of her features and the gentleness of her eyes." In Zurich from December 1918 to February 1919, he engaged in a platonic romance that would inspire an episode of *Ulysses*.**

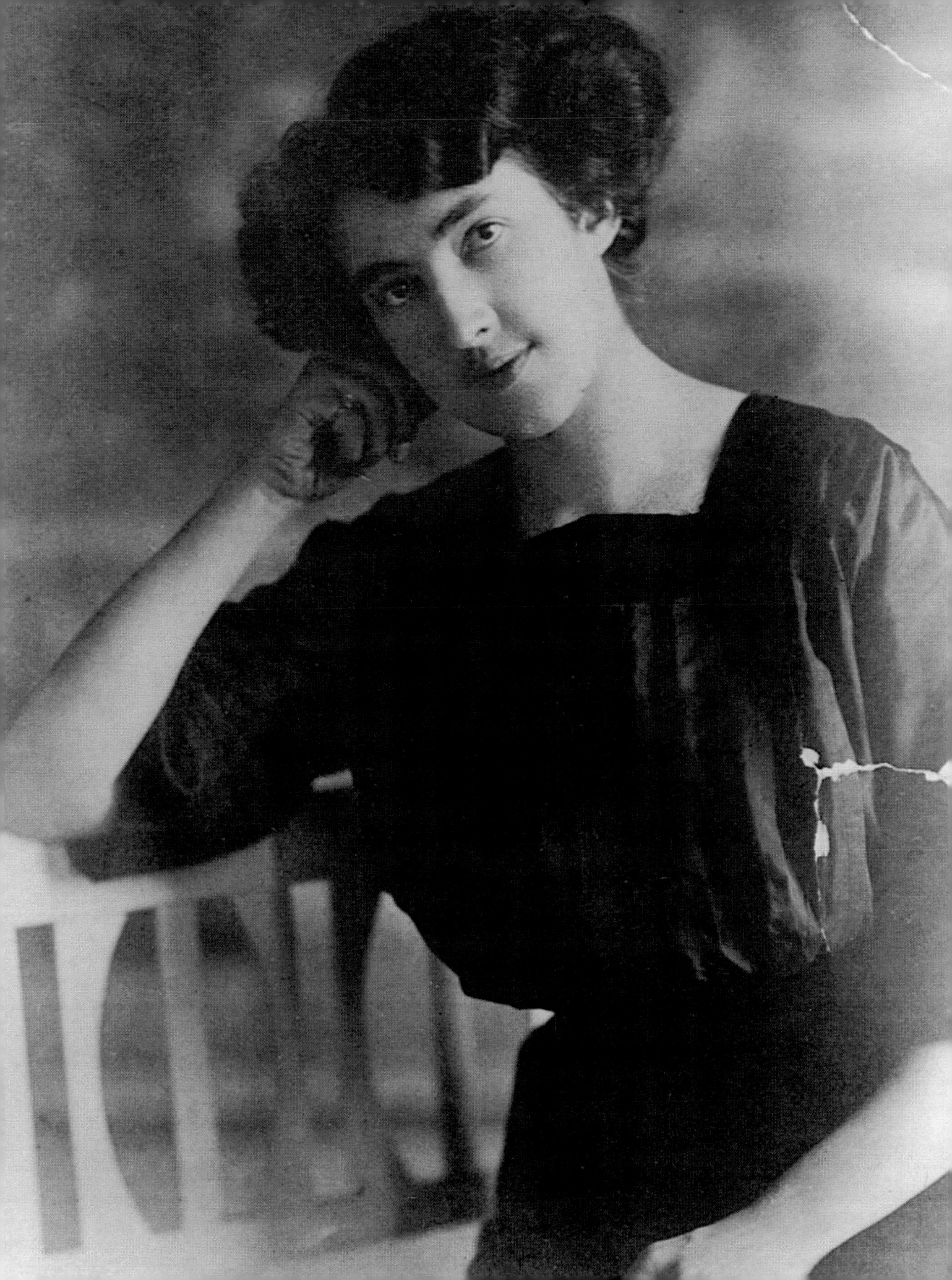

for my pressing season as hereinafter must they chirrywill immediately pending on my safe return to ignorance and bliss with my ropes of pearls for gamey girls the way you'll hardly know me. Is post purification we will and render social service, missus. Let us all ignite as aposcals and help our Jakeline sisters clean up the hogshole. Burn only what's Irish, accepting their coals. Write me ... cursorily for Henrietta's sake on the life of jewvries and the sludge of King Harrington's at its height running boulevards over the whole of it. Bear in mind by Michael all the provincial's bananas peels and elacock eggs making drawadust jubilee along Henry, Moore, Earl and Talbot streets. Luke at all the memmer manning he's dung for the pray of birds strewing the Castleknock road and the Marist fathers eleven out on a rogation stag party. Compare them caponchin trowbers with the Bridge of Belches in Fairview, east Dublin's favourite wateringplace and ump as you lump it. Stand on, say, Aston's, I advise you strongly, along quaith a copy of the Seeds and Weeds Act when you have procured one for yourself and take a good longing gaze into any nearby shopswindow you may select at suppose, let us say, the hoyth of number eleven, Kane or Keogh's and in the course of about thirty-two minutes' time proceed to turn aroundabout on your heehills towards the previous causeway and I shall be very cruelly mistaken indeed if you will not be jushed astowshed to see how you will be meanwhile durn well topcested with cakes of slush occasioned by the raush jam of the crosse and blackwalls traffic in transit. When will the W. D. face of our muckloved city gets its wellbelavered whitewish? Who'll disapperaguss Pape's Avignue or who'll uproose the Opian Way? 'Tis an ill wee blows no poppy good. And this labour's worthy of my higher. Do you know what, little girls? One of those days I am advised to positively strike off hiking for good and all until such time as some mood is made to get me an increase of automoboil and footwear as I sartunly think now, honest to John, for an income plexus that, that's about, the sanguine boundary limit.

Sis dearest, Jaun added, melancholic this time whiles his onsaturncast eyes in stellar attraction followed swift to an imaginary swellaw. O, the vanity of Vanissy! All ends vanishing! Personally, Grog help me, I am in no violent hurry. If time enough lost the ducks walking easy found them I'd turn back as lief as not if I could only find the girl of my heart's appointment to guide me by gastronomy under her safe conduct. I'd ask no kinder of fates than to stay where I am, leaning on my cubits, at this passing moment by localoption in the birds' lodging the pheasants among all well on into the bosom of the exhaling night, picking stopandgo jewels out of the hedges and catching brilliants on the tip of my wagger for them breezes zipping round by Drumsally

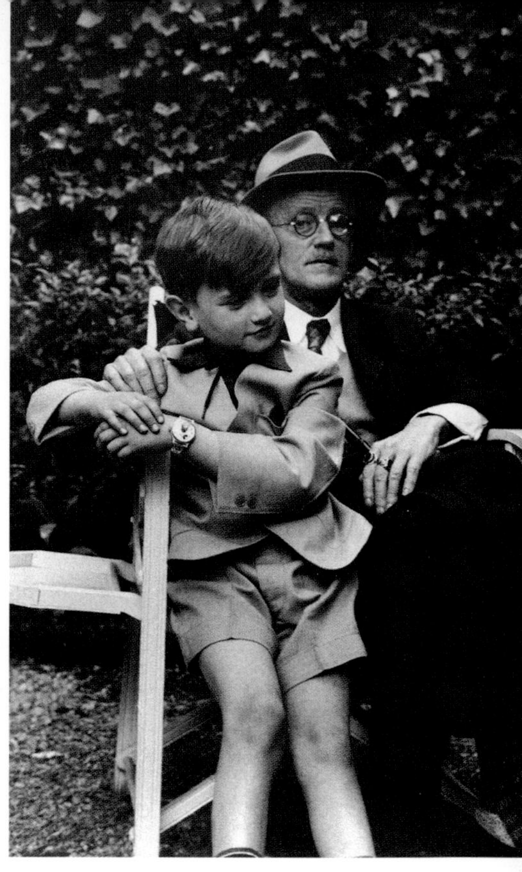

Left: **Reading proofs was a creative act for James Joyce. "There were five sets of proofs and he made innumerable modifications," said his printer. "The book grew by one third in proof," noted Richard Ellmann, Joyce's biographer.**

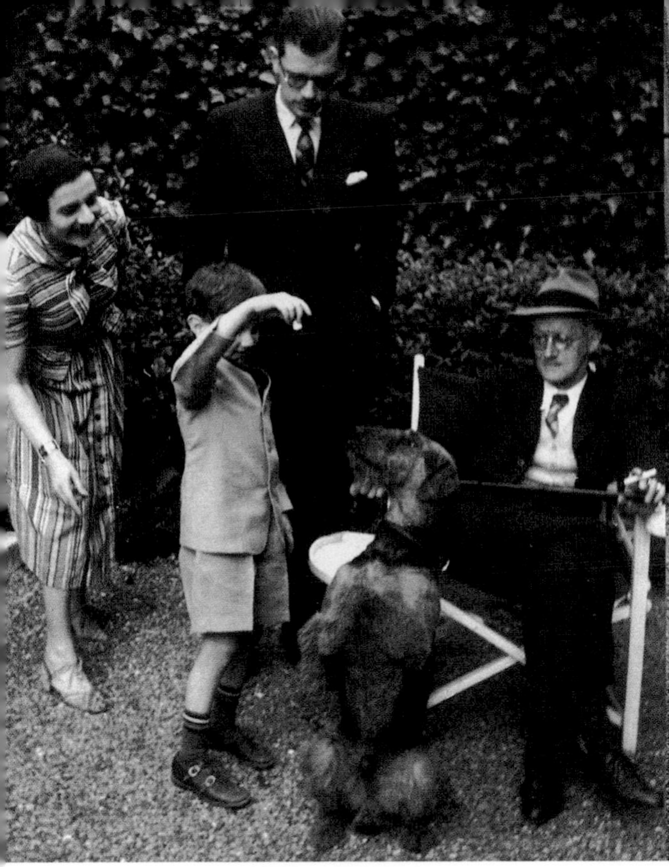

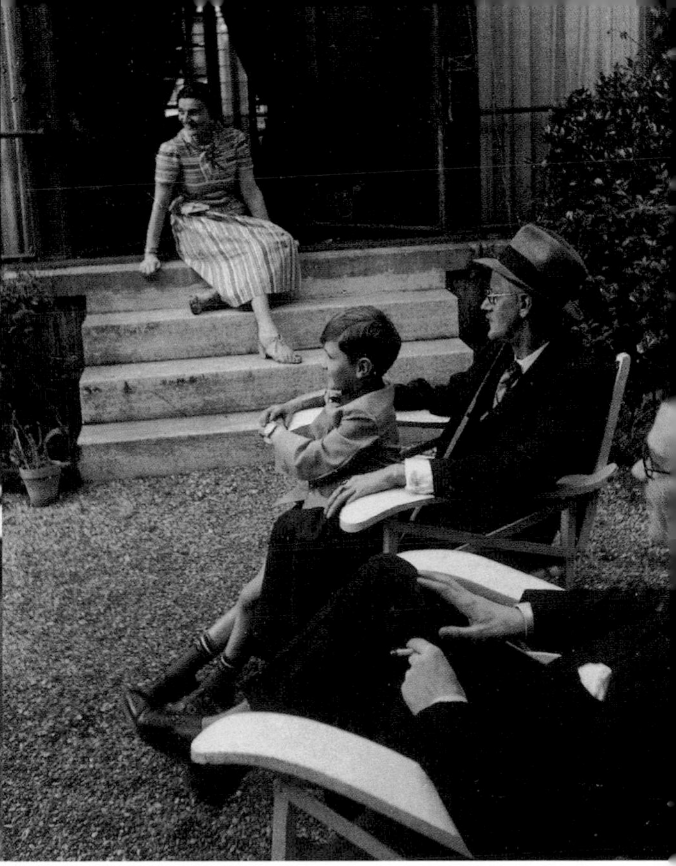

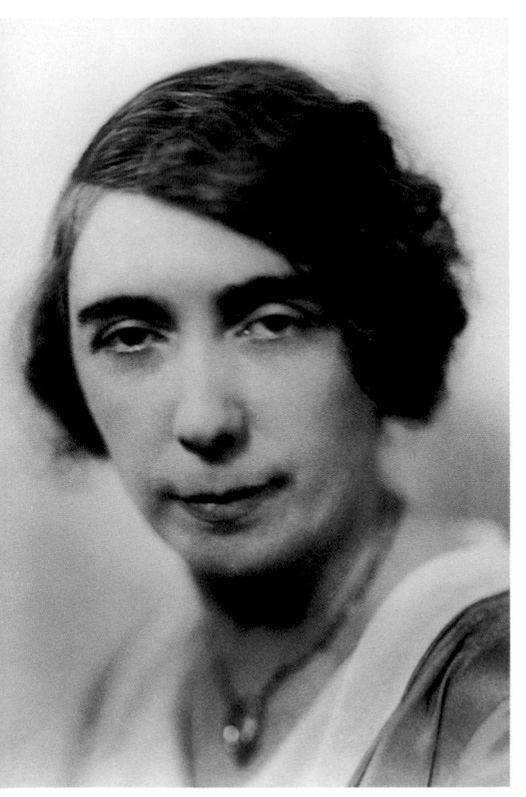

Left: **First spotted in Dublin on June 10, 1904, Nora Barnacle would become James Joyce's companion for life. She stayed in the background of the writer's work to the point of making this surprising declaration: "Jim, I've never read your books, but I will do it one day; they must be good since they sell well."**

Above: **For James Joyce, his family were the only people in the world he loved. In this series of photographs taken by Gisèle Freund, published under the title *Three Days with Joyce* (1990), he tolerated being photographed numerous times with his family. We see him here with his son Giorgio (also known as George), Giorgio's wife, Helen, and their son Stephen.**

But let us return to the beach scene in *Ulysses*. Gerty went there with two friends who were watching after their children. She kept to herself, seated on a rock. A little further down sat Leopold Bloom. Like Nausicaa's servants, Gerty's friends played with a ball that got away from them and rolled over to Bloom. He returned it with a reluctant kick, and the ball "stopped right under Gerty's skirt." Contact was established.

In the romance with Martha Fleischmann, the next—and final—stage was the "black mass." The event took place on February 2, the author's birthday, which coincided with Candlemas—the celebration of the presentation of Jesus in the temple, also called the Purification of the Blessed Virgin because the Virgin holds a candle. (Dates held great importance for Joyce; Bloom's odyssey in Dublin is supposed to unfold on June 16, the anniversary of his first meeting with Nora.) The writer organized this strange and ridiculous ceremony in Frank Budgen's studio, and asked him to paint a nude with a pair of ample buttocks while he went to a friend's home in search of a menorah.

The affair, such as it was, was his effort to, in effect, combine two peoples—the Irish and the Jews—who for him had a parallel destiny. That is why he wrote to Martha, "[in seeing you] I thought: a Jewess." Under the pretext of poor eyesight, he drew her into Budgen's studio to light the taper thereby exposing the nude painting. Later Joyce recounted to Budgen: "I have explored the coldest and the hottest parts of a woman's body." According to the painter's account, this did not mean that they had had a sexual rapport but that the writer only caressed her. Joyce thanked her with a postcard signed "[*Marias*] *Lichtmesse*," alluding to the candle held by Mary during Joyce's famous Candlemas-birthday.

In the episode from *Ulysses*, the writer was closer to the Homeric text than during his adventure with Martha Fleischmann. In *The Odyssey*, Ulysses hesitated a moment while debating whether to embrace Nausicaa's knees on the beach before deciding it was best "to stand apart and use honeyed speech." Bloom's reciprocal seduction of Gerty took place at a distance during the fireworks display that exploded above the sand. He allowed Gerty to adopt all sorts of positions on her rock, leaning ever further and further back better to see the rockets overhead and revealing her underclothes to Bloom, who took advantage of the spectacle offered him by this "little devil" to masturbate.

Then night fell and Gerty moved away. "She walked with a certain calm dignity characteristic of her but with care and very slowly because Gerty MacDowell was. . . . Tight boots? No. She's lame! O!" Martha Fleischmann also limped (although less noticeably than Gerty), as if to fill out even the smallest details of the role that Joyce had given her. He would take leave of her, but not without signing one last postcard: "Greetings from Odysseus to Nausicaa."

Fleischmann would reappear in Joyce's life one last time in February 1930. His eyesight had continued to deteriorate, and he reluctantly faced the umpteenth operation that he had been advised to undergo. Martha, alerted somehow to the situation, joined the supporters of the procedure by offering testimonials about the doctor's abilities. More than ten years after their adventure together, Nausicaa selfishly concerned herself with her voyeur's vision; she did not want Joyce to become blind . . . like Homer.

Bibliography

The Complete Works of James Joyce. CD-ROM edition. E-Codex Publications, Division of Insight Engineering, 1995.

Ellmann, Richard. *James Joyce*. New York: Oxford University Press, 1983.

Ellmann, Richard, ed. *Joyce: Selected Letters*. New York: The Viking Press, 1975.

Freund, Gisèle. *Three Days with Joyce*. New York: Persea Books, 1990.

Kathe (Helen Hessel) Henri-Pierre Roché and François Truffaut

Helen, *Jules et Jim*, Pierre and François

Helen Hessel lived under the sign of the trinity formed with Franz Hessel and Henri-Pierre Roché, two young men with clear literary ambitions who collected female conquests. Two carefree lives changed completely by their encounter with Helen. She would enter the annals of literature and cinema forever under the name of Kathe—the character in the novel *Jules et Jim* by Henri-Pierre Roché and the film by François Truffaut—as the mythical symbol of the free woman.

"I am, at seventy-five years old, all that remains of Kathe, the formidable heroine of the novel *Jules et Jim* by Pierre Roché. You can imagine the curiosity with which I have waited for the moment to watch your film on the screen. On January 24, [1962, the date of the film's release], I ran to the cinema. Seated in the dark room, dreading the veiled resemblances, the more or less irritating parallels, I was very quickly swept away, seized by your magical power and that of Jeanne Moreau to bring back a life that was lived blindly. That Pierre Roché was able to tell the story of the three of us while keeping very true to the unfolding events is nothing short of miraculous. But did you have the disposition, did you have the affinity to shed light on [the situation to the point of rendering palpable] the essence of our intimate emotions? From this point of view, I am your only authentic judge since the two other witnesses, Pierre and Franz, are no longer here to tell you 'yes.' Affectionately yours, dear Mr. Truffaut."

This letter, signed Helen Hessel and dated January 30, 1962, was a shock for François Truffaut. He responded immediately. "I was very happy to receive your letter, which I read with great emotion. I made *Jules et Jim* with profound respect because I have never loved a book as much as this one."

From Pierre and Franz to *Jules et Jim*

The Catherine (as Kathe was called) in Truffaut's film was originally named Helen Hessel. Helen Grund was her name as a young girl. Jules, that was Franz Hessel, and Jim, Henri-Pierre Roché. Franz resembled Jules, a round little fellow, and Henri-Pierre, whom everyone called Pierre, a lanky character, was the living portrait of Jim. Both Jules and Jim had literary ambitions like the people they're based on and, also like them, they collected female conquests. Two carefree lives changed completely by their encounter with Helen.

Born on April 30, 1886, in Berlin, the youngest child in a family of bankers and Prussian officers, Helen Grund moved to Paris to study painting. Naturally, the apprentice artist chose to live in the bohemian neighborhood of Montparnasse in the little Hôtel Odessa, and she would go out accompanied by two girlfriends. In the novel, Henri-Pierre Roché recalled their arrival this way: "Jules announced to Jim that there was a new shipment of girls from his country, Berliners this time. . . . There were three of them and they didn't miss a thing nor were they at a loss for words." In reality Franz Hessel made Helen Grund's acquaintance in the autumn of 1912 at the Café du Dôme, the meeting place for Germans in Paris before World War I. Franz spotted this little blonde compatriot with her sporty charm, went up and stood before her, saying: "Your eyes remind me of Goethe's in the middle of his life." They met again at a friend's home and, the Christmas of 1912, Franz asked Helen in a letter if she would include him "in her schedule." She replied that she didn't have one but that she would be delighted to see him more often. For six years this young German had shared everything with his French friend Henri-Pierre Roché, whom he met in 1906 at the Quat'z'Arts ball in Montparnasse. They were the same age and from similar backgrounds. Pierre was born in Paris in 1879 to well-to-do Protestants, Franz in 1880 in Stettin to a family of Jewish bankers. They were two partyers who remade the world and fell in love with the same women. Usually it was Roché who took the initiative and got the girl. Franz fell in love with her later. There was Marie, Franziska, Maga, Odile, Germaine, and so on. When the two weren't flirting, they traveled, visiting Greece and going ecstatic over the beauty of the bodies of statues, or striding along the streets of Munich, where Franz's family lived, or Paris, where Pierre made use of his innumerable relatives to act as mediator between collectors and artists. He introduced Picasso to Gertrude Stein, and Brancusi to his patron, the American collector John Quinn. All his life Henri-Pierre would make these kinds of successful introductions, all the while dreaming of literature. He began with short stories, completing a short work entitled *Jules*—a portrait of a pathetic creature who fled from women and committed suicide. Roché eventually gave up trying to publish the story, but he did not stop trying to write. For over forty years he scrupulously kept notebooks in which he recounted every day, in raw terms and in the tiniest details, especially his romances with women—women betrayed, seduced, loved, abandoned. But with Helen it was different.

Since Franz had known Pierre, this was the first time that he had fallen in love first and for good. He thought it useful to forewarn his friend: "Pierre, not Helen, not that one, I beg you." This very scene was transposed to the book and then to Truffaut's film:

> "Not that one, OK, Jim?
> Not that one, Jules, replied Jim."

Franz and Helen were married in May 1913 in Berlin and quickly returned to Paris. From the beginning the relationship did not seem easy between the placid Franz and the unpredictable Helen who could one evening, on a dare, jump into the Seine—another scene carefully repeated in the novel. At first Pierre kept his promise and did not interfere in their romance. Then in 1914, with the beginning of World War I, the trio were separated for five years. During these years, the couple's first child, Ulrich, was born, then Stefan. Franz left for the war on the Eastern front in order not to fight the French. On his return the couple struggled. Like Jules in the novel, Franz accepted Helen's other lives but she reproached him for not being jealous enough. It was amidst this tension that Pierre visited them in Munich, where they were living, and his visit marked the beginning of a long and tumultuous liaison between Pierre and Helen. Franz resigned himself to the situation in order to keep Helen; for Franz's sons, Roché was Uncle Pierre. Pierre, explaining his actions, confided to Franz: "It's as if I were loving you." Adding to the strained dynamic of this ménage à trois of sorts, Helen's own sister Johana also became Pierre's mistress. Roché already had the idea for a novel relating these intertwined affairs but, for the moment, he had his hands full with art brokerage dealings with the Swiss painter Paul Klee, and love affairs with Helen and two French women, Germaine, whom he would marry, and Denise, with whom he would have a son, Jean-Claude. Helen, for her part, also multiplied her lovers.

Pierre encouraged Helen to keep a journal like he did on which they could base a novel, but her vague attempts at writing would be confined to her chronicles of fashion—which were highly valued—that she wrote over ten years for the German newspaper *Frankfurter Zeitung.* Very clear about her literary abilities, Helen confided in 1921 to Pierre: "What is most important to me is a life that develops constantly in motion." Life with Pierre, however, would soon turn stormy. Then in 1933, in the middle of a scene more violent than ones that had preceded it, she threatened to kill him. They separated then forever, living for close to thirty years within a hundred yards of each other without ever meeting again.

During this time, Franz lived in Berlin, separated from his wife and children. He worked at a publishing house, translated Proust with Walter Benjamin, and published several books, even encountering a certain success with *Promenades* whose opening line is the exact reflection of his vision of life: "To walk slowly in a bustling street is a rare pleasure." The Nazis's arrival to power would soon ruin any such innocent pleasure. But Franz could not resolve to leave Berlin, and it was necessary for Helen to come and seek him out in 1938 and to repatriate him *in extremis.* At the beginning of World War II, he was, being a German, locked up in the infamous Les Milles internment camp in the south of France. When he was finally freed, he took refuge in nearby Sanary, which had become a center of German intelligentsia in exile. He died there of cardiac arrest in January 1941.

In Dieulefit in the Drôme region of France, Roché's life during the war was completely different. He had not seen Franz again after his final split with Helen, and learned of his death some time later. As an admirer of Marshall Philippe Pétain, head of the Vichy government in France, he was hired to revise the French national anthem, "La Marseillaise," in order to make it conform more to the spirit of the times and, in July 1941, was pleased to have read Adolf Hitler's *Mein Kampf.* But the memory of Franz reemerged regularly. He wanted to write their story, which he summed up as that of a friendship torn apart, finally, by a woman. "Helen was a double-edged sword that separated us. I would like to know what Franz really thought of our tripartite life and of Helen, that devourer of men." In March 1943 he noted in his journal that he "wrote the novel *Jules et Jim* with a resolute pen, and Franz played the main role." Jules was the title of one of his first stories, Jim was the nickname Helen had given him, and Kathe the diminutive of Helen's middle name. The novel was finished in September. It arrived in 1946 on the desk of publisher Gaston Gallimard, who gave it a favorable response. Roché won the Claire Bellon book prize but not commercial success. Many years later François Truffaut discovered the novel in a secondhand bookstore.

François Truffaut's Love at First Sight

Evoking *Jules et Jim*, Truffaut exclaimed: "From the opening lines, I fell in love at first sight with the writing of Henri-Pierre Roché." He was enthusiastic about this story of an amorous trio and dreamed of putting it on the screen with Jeanne Moreau, who was already a star, in the role of Kathe/Catherine, the wife of the "small and round Jules" and mistress to the "tall and thin Jim."

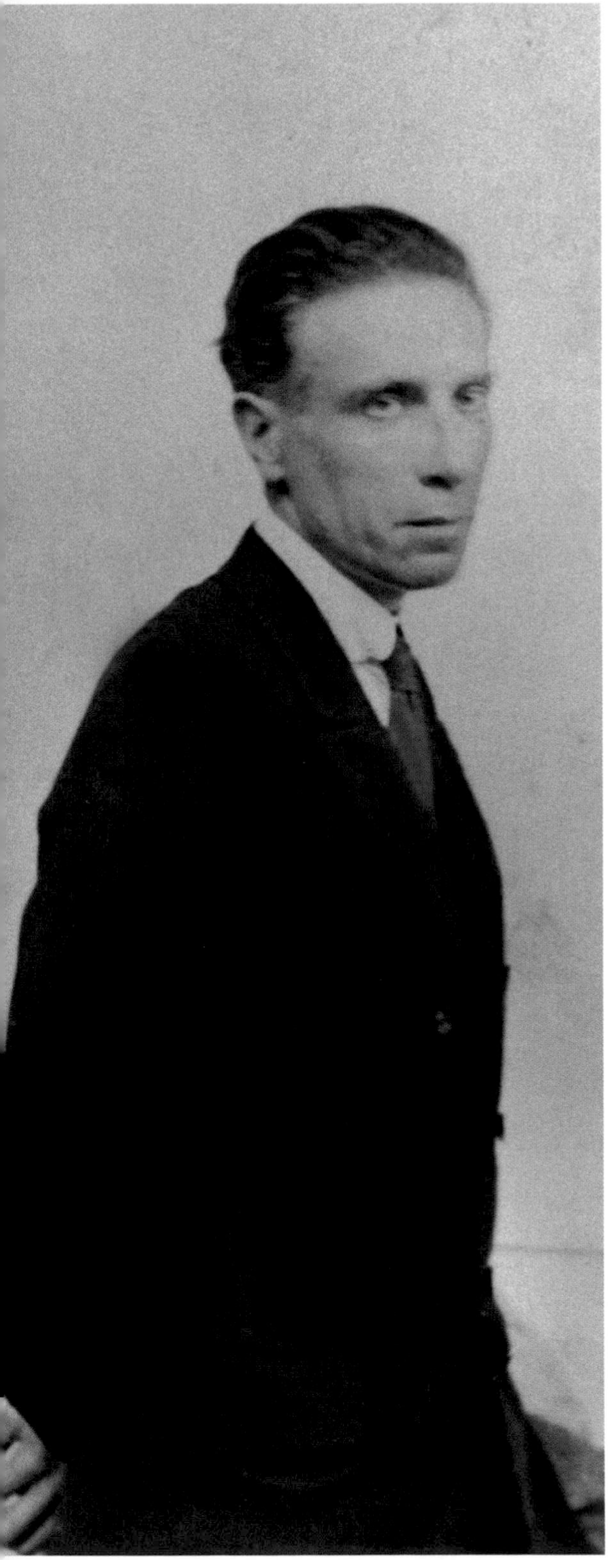

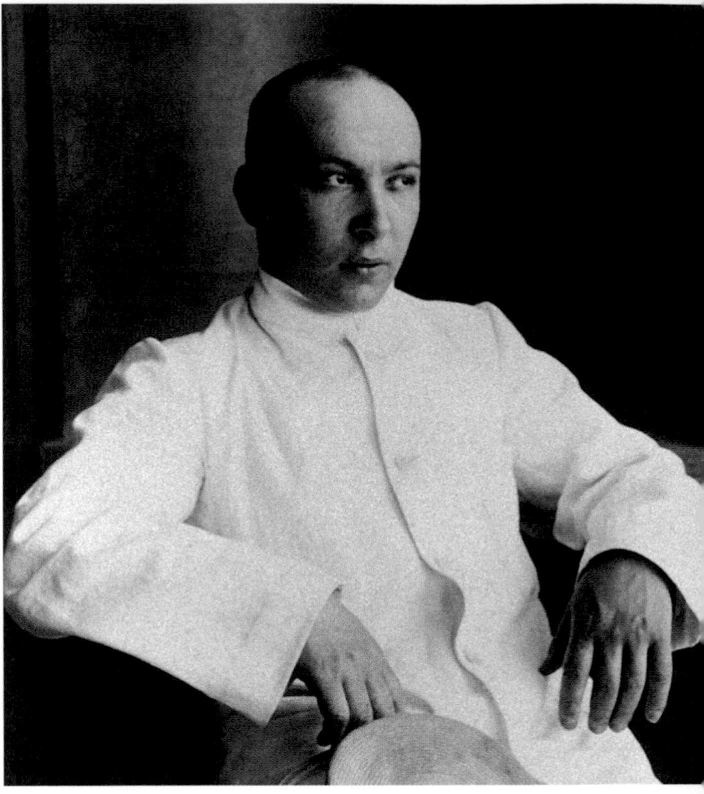

Left: **At an early age Henri-Pierre Roché abandoned the diplomatic career that his family had intended for him and broke off his engagement in England to dedicate himself to the pleasures of Parisian life. In a book dating from 1926, his mother, Clara Louise Roché, had written: "All men are absurd; once they find a woman to their taste, they imagine that they have the right to take her or borrow her as if she were an object."**

Above: **For the German-born Franz Hessel, Paris before World War I was like a new homeland. Nicknamed "Pudding" by the young English girls, he seduced Helen Grund with his round face and his childlike mouth.**

Opposite: **It was Franz Hessel whom Helen Grund married before the war but Henri-Pierre Roché with whom she later returned to live in Paris.**

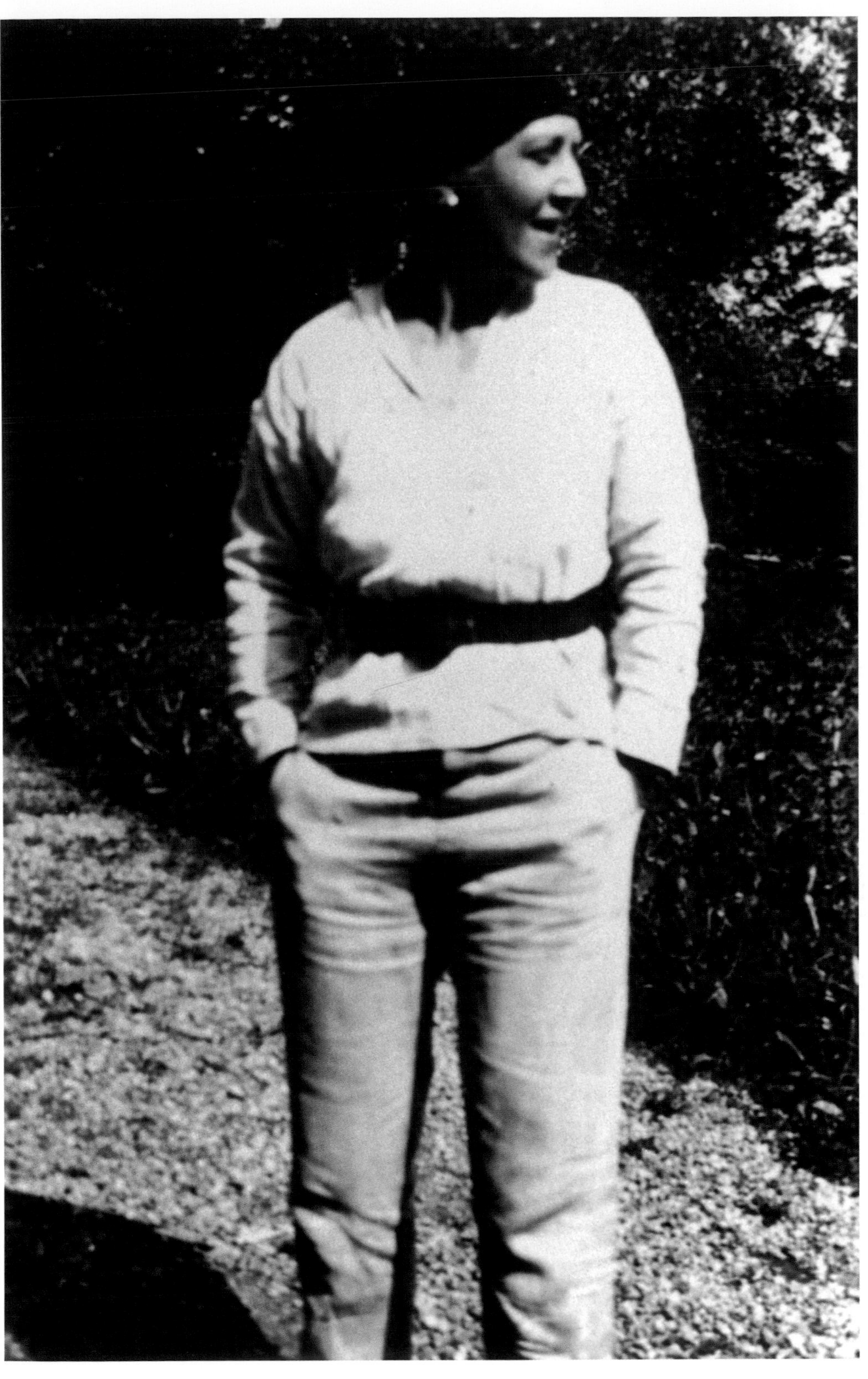

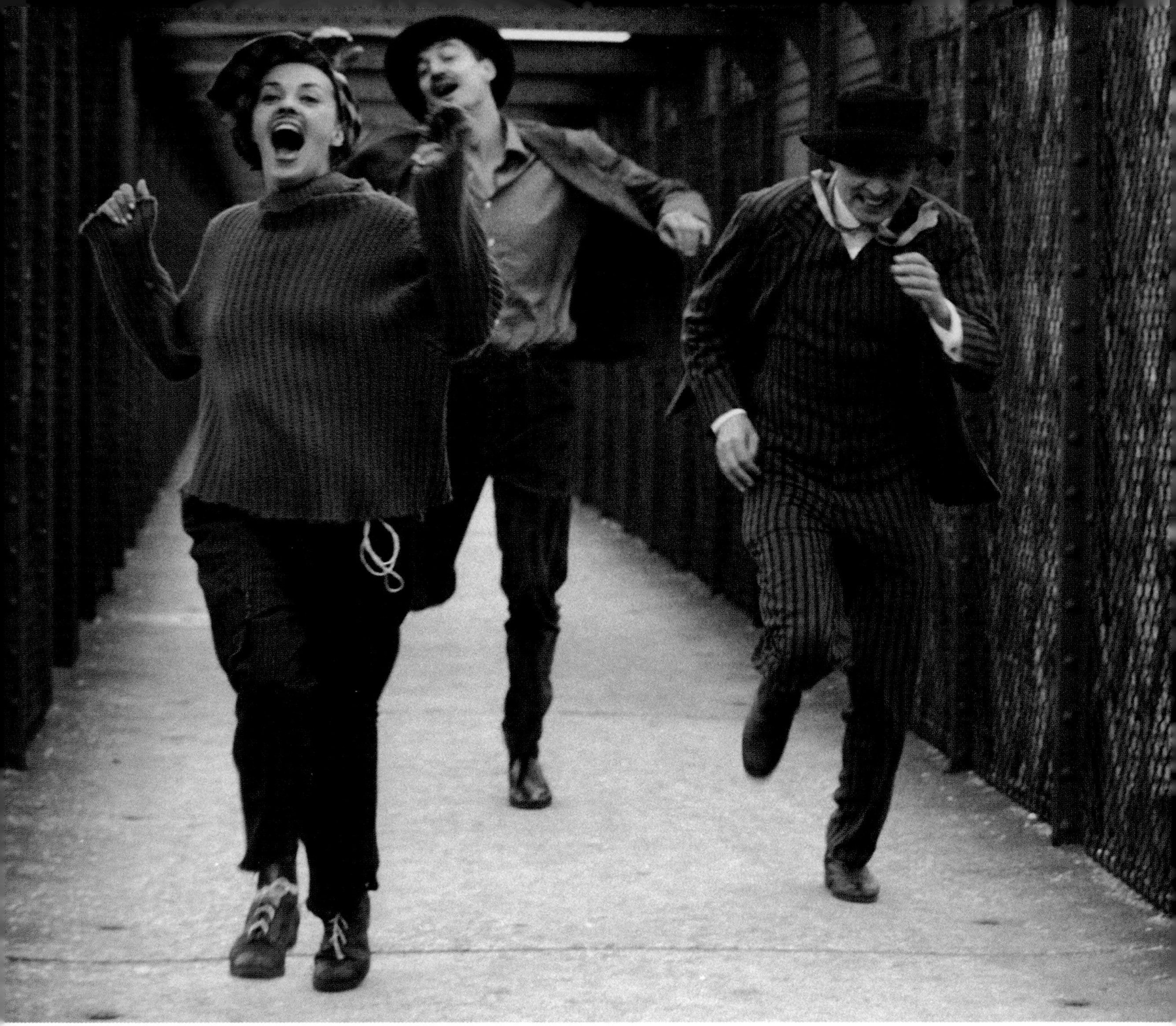

Above: **An amorous trio led by a boyish Jeanne Moreau is how François Truffaut gave life to *Jules et Jim* in 1962. Performed by Oskar Werner (Jules) and Henri Serre (Jim) it was also the first appearance on screen by Sabine Haudepin in the role of Catherine and Jules's daughter.**

Right: **Contrary to the title of the book and the film, the poster reveals that the central character was Kathe, played by Jeanne Moreau.**

Opposite: **A perfect moment shared between Jeanne Moreau and François Truffaut, who at the time was completely in love with the actress.**

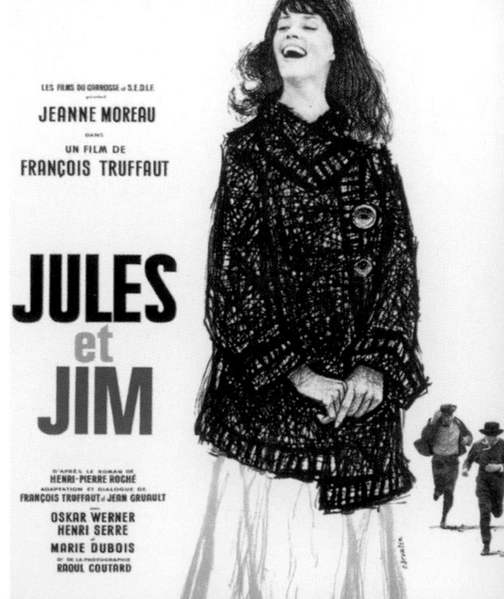

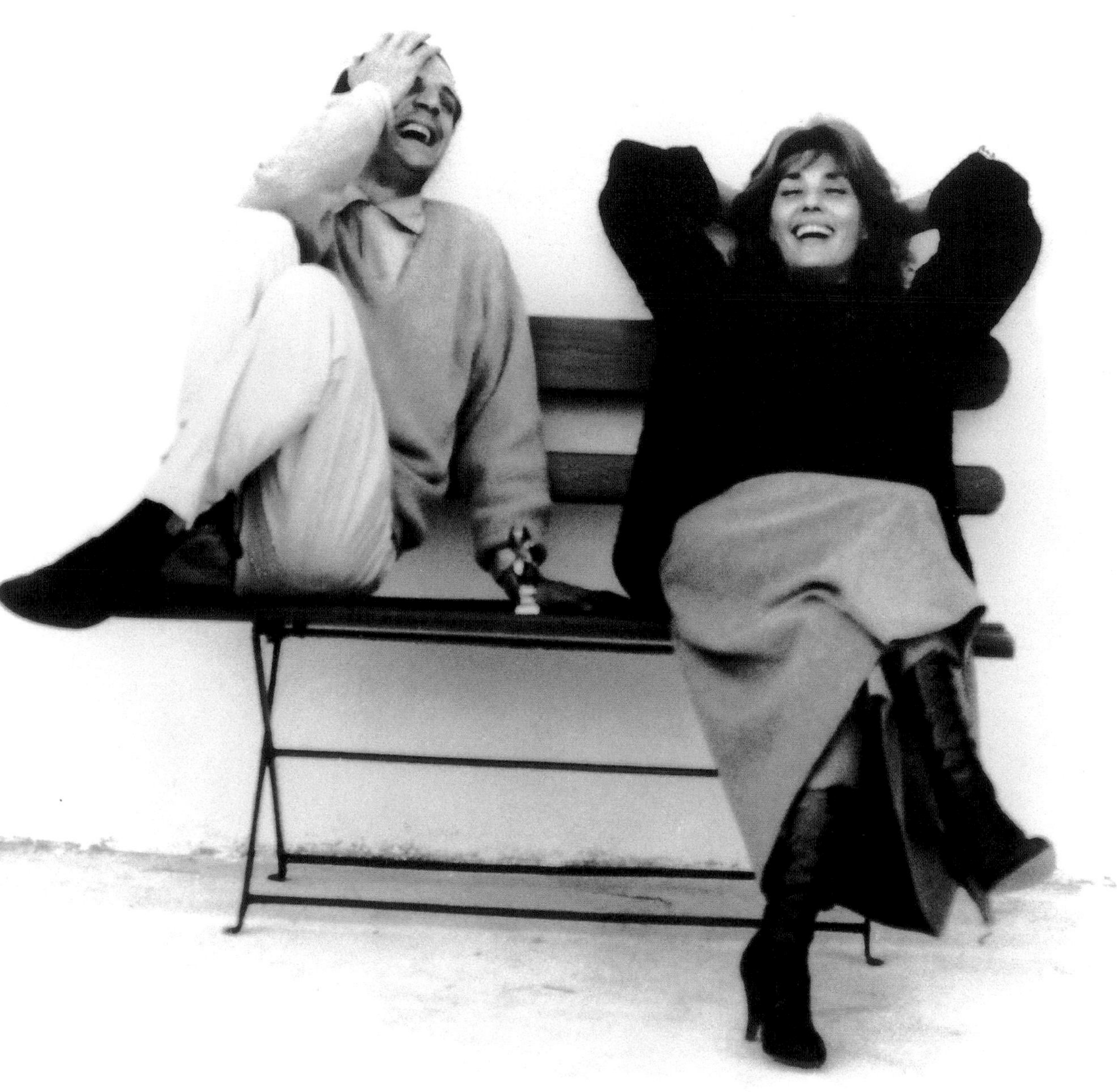

Born in 1932, the director had just completed his first short film. Drafting of the screenplay for *Jules et Jim*, however, proved difficult and Truffaut contacted Roché, then seventy-four years old, for help. Their first version hewed too closely to the novel and proved fruitless. Finally the film was made based on Truffaut's very personal take on the book. He concentrated the story on the trio, whereas the novel leaned more toward nymphomania and unspoken homosexuality. From a rather sordid romance and a novel in which the author loses himself in the maze of unfulfilled feelings, Truffaut collected, concentrated, and gave life to a love story full of magic and gaiety, as if he had wanted this story to be a little bit his own. And in a sense it was.

The Whirlwind of Life

In September 1960 Truffaut stayed at the Colombe d'or in Saint-Paul-de-Vence and reworked his adaptation of *Jules and Jim*, gathering inspiration from the notebooks of Henri-Pierre Roché and his own personal life. Married to Madeleine Morgenstern and father of two little girls but in love with Jeanne Moreau, who would act in his new film, he wrote to his collaborator Helen Scott: "*Jules et Jim* will be a hymn to life and death, a demonstration through joy and sadness of the impossibility of any love combination outside of a couple." Moreau, then separated from Louis Malle, was delighted to work on the film and welcomed Truffaut to her home in La Garde-Freinet in the Varois hinterland. There he met the painter and writer Serge Rezvani, who lived in the same village and who wrote songs under the pseudonym of Cyrus Bassiak. He would write the movie's theme song, "Le Tourbillon de la vie":

We met with a kiss
A hit, then a miss
It wasn't all bliss
And we parted
We went our own ways
In life's whirlpool of days . . .

They had a great time that summer in La Garde-Freinet. In the evenings Moreau would sing under the chestnut trees. Truffaut, by nature more reserved, launched into a duet with Jean-Louis Richard, Jeanne's former husband. *Jules et Jim* took shape in life before being incarnated on the screen. "Jeanne gave me courage each time I was overcome by doubt," said Truffaut. "Her qualities as an actress and as a woman rendered Catherine real in our eyes, plausible, crazy, abusive, but above all, passionate, adorable, that is to say, worthy of adoration." Truffaut's and Moreau's identification with the characters of *Jules et Jim* came to an end when the filming was over, not with drama or a grand scene but with an enduring friendship that would last until the filmmaker's death in 1984—a very different conclusion from both the novel and the film, in which Kathe/Catherine deliberately causes the drowning death of herself and of Jim. It was very different too from the dramas that marked the true history of Franz-Jules and Pierre-Jim. By dying only several days before meeting Moreau and several months before the release of the film, Roché never knew the fate that awaited his novel. But in that dark room on the evening of the premiere, Helen Hessel, the only survivor of the trio, attended the screening incognito. She saw the film several times, relieved at its truthfulness. She did not create the work, but she was the only one to have lived long enough to see her character become a modern myth, a symbol of a liberated life without restrictions.

Bibliography

Baecque, Antoine de, and Serge Toubiana. *François Truffaut: A Biography*. Berkeley: University of California Press, 2000.

Flügge, Manfred. *Le Tourbillon de la vie: La véritable histoire de Jules et Jim*. Paris: Albin Michel, 1994.

Hessel-Grund, Helen. *Journal d'Helen: Lettres à Henri-Pierre Roché, 1920–1921*. Marseilles: André Dimanche, 1991.

Roché, Henri-Pierre. *Carnets: Les années Jules et Jim, 1920–1921*. Marseilles: André Dimanche, 1990.

———. *Jules et Jim*. London: Marion Boyars Publishers, 1981.

Lolita McMurray
Charlie Chaplin
Vladimir Nabokov

Lolita, The Kid, and the Nymphet

The similarities are striking between the real Lolita McMurray, an actress in *The Kid* and the sixteen-year-old child-bride of Charlie Chaplin who gave birth to his first two sons, and the mythic Lolita created by Vladimir Nabokov, the twelve-year-old girl seduced by her stepfather. But if Nabokov could not ignore the history of the Chaplins, which ended in 1927 with a divorce that made the front page of newspapers around the world, the relationship between the two Lolitas remains hypothetical.

"Lolita, light of my life, fire of my loins. My sin, my soul. Lo-lee-ta: the tip of the tongue taking a trip of three steps down the palate to tap, at three, on the teeth. Lo. Lee. Ta." These were words of love and desire. Words that caused a scandal because they were spoken by an older man about a very young girl. These are the first words of *Lolita*, the novel published in France in 1955 by Vladimir Nabokov, a distinguished professor at several American universities and the faithful husband of Vera Evseievna Slonim since 1925. Similar words no doubt must have been spoken in 1924 by the thirty-five-year-old Charlie Chaplin shortly before his marriage to Lolita McMurray, then aged 16. But when Chaplin divorced her in 1927 the world press took up his defense, judging the young woman's financial claims to be excessive. For Nabokov, the Lolita affair took another turn and continued to get new impetus with Stanley Kubrick's 1962 film adaptation and the more recent one made in 1997 by Adrian Lyne, whose version could not find distribution for several years in the United States. Indifferent to the turmoil she aroused, the legend of Lolita has become common for the archetype of the nymphet.

"Don't trust nymphets!"

Writing in the June 16, 1959 issue of the scholarly magazine *Arts*, the journalist Pierre Déméron warned readers with the headline: "Don't trust nymphets!" which suggested a link between the real Lolita, an actress and Chaplin's wife in the 1920s, and Nabokov's later fictional one. What was the subtitle of the article? "Chaplin lived the real novel of Lolita, and she cost him a million dollars." What were the differences between the two nymphets? None at all. Chaplin had met Lolita in a Hollywood tea salon where, accompanied by her mother, she tried to catch sight of celebrities. Nabokov's Humbert met Lolita on a small staircase that led from his landlady's house to the garden. Chaplin married the girl and had to take care of her mother. Humbert married the mother in order to be near the daughter. Chaplin's Lolita, thanks to the courts, obtained a million dollars, while Nabokov's begged for three or four hundred dollars from her "daddy," Humbert. The conclusion? Reality always surpasses fiction. The final connection? The mystery of its origins. In his autobiography Chaplin almost skips over this affair that had occupied several years of his life and left him with two children. He summed up the entire story simply without even mentioning the name of the person whom he himself renamed: "During the filming of *The Gold Rush*, I married for a second time. Because we have two grown sons of whom I am very fond, I will not go into the details. For two years we were married and tried to make a go of it, but it was hopeless and ended in a great deal of bitterness." For his part, Nabokov never mentioned the existence of an inspirational Lolita and insisted on the purely fictional nature of his character. Without distorting the truth of the creative process, let us simply compare the two stories and let reality and fiction straighten it out between themselves.

Charlie Chaplin, the Originator of the Lolita Myth

"I first saw Charlie Chaplin on April 15, 1914. It was my sixth birthday, and to celebrate my mother took me to Hollywood, a short trip by trolley from our home in downtown Los Angeles. With luck, she said, we'd have a chance to see some movie stars." Chaplin was seated at a table and Mrs. McMurray asked the waiter, "Do you think that it would disturb Mr. Chaplin if my daughter were introduced to him?" Chaplin, who was lunching still dressed in his costume with his black mustache and his made-up face, agreed and asked, "Well now, what would your name be, young lady?" "Lillita McMurray," replied the little girl. End of act one. Six years go by and Chuck Riesner, Chaplin's assistant and the McMurrays' neighbor, was looking for a child to play an angel in *The Kid*. He spoke about it to Lillita's mother, who jumped for joy. The girl's second meeting with Chaplin took place at the studio and the director fell for her charms. "I'm pleased to know you," he said, nodding slightly to Mrs. McMurray. "You're an extremely pretty child, my dear," he said warmly. Turning toward his assistant, he confirmed, "She reminds me a bit of the child in the painting *The Age of Innocence*." To preserve this image, he soon asked her to pose for a portrait. Chaplin was thirty-five, Lillita twelve. He was preparing his sixty-eighth film and his renown was enormous—as a filmmaker, author, actor, producer, editor, and even as a seducer. In addition to his innumerable conquests, he had already been married in 1918 to Mildred Harris, a young girl of sixteen, and the affair had generated a scandal when Chaplin divorced two years later, accused of mental cruelty by Mildred who demanded part of the profits from his new film, *The Kid*. To prevent her from seizing the film, Chaplin fled with a copy across the deserts of Utah. The press carried on about the scandal, which ended up being resolved amicably in 1920. Miss Harris received a hundred thousand dollars and a part of Chaplin's wealth. Even though he had been burned by this romance, Chaplin set out the same year to seduce Lillita McMurray. In 1921 he had her act in *The Kid* and then in *The Idle Class*, in which she and her mother both played maids. The young girl fascinated him to the point that he decided to mold her as he thought best and gave her, first of all, a new name and a new history. Lillita McMurray became Lita Grey.

The Infanta of the Screen

No longer was she that poor little girl without a father, under the control of a possessive mother, who lived in a crummy house in a Los Angeles suburb. She entered into a legend fabricated in every aspect by Chaplin. A model of disinformation, the press release that announced her good fortune said: "Charlie Chaplin has chosen a true daughter of California, whose family goes back to the Spanish pioneer Antonio Navarro. A descendant of the Hidalgos, Miss Grey is a superb brunette with black eyes, ivory skin and red lips, all notable characteristics of the Spanish race. Born on the outskirts of Hollywood in Whitley Heights, having grown up since her childhood in the center of the screen world, one can justifiably say that she was born a movie star. Miss Grey is not yet nineteen [she was fifteen] and her beauty is such that this young Spanish beauty can be called an Infanta of the screen. From her most tender childhood, Lita has always been entrusted to the good care of her mother and her grandmother. She has been chaperoned, a custom still in use among the old Spanish families." To seduce her Chaplin invited her to all the soirees, sending a limousine for her, offering her gifts. But above all, he let her take screen tests and promised her a starring role in *The Gold Rush*. Over a period of several months, they became inseparable.

Chaplin's assistant was skeptical about the young girl's cinematic charms. Chaplin was wildly enthusiastic: "She has a gift and I hope to be able to develop her talent and to put to good use all the facets of her personality and her remarkable beauty. . . ." In March 1924 she signed a contract of seventy-five dollars a week. The chaperons, however, did not attend to their role with sufficient conviction because Lita soon discovered she was pregnant. Her family demanded marriage, to which Chaplin submitted, coerced and forced. On the pretext of filming in Mexico, he embarked on a trip with Lita and her family, followed by a horde of journalists. There, technicians received the order to rent a fishing boat and to stay out all day to make believe that they were filming at sea. Chaplin, Riesner, Lita, and her mother went to Empalme in the state of Sonora where, on November 24, 1924, Lita Grey became Mrs. Chaplin. After the ceremony, Chaplin left to go fishing. A press release soon after curtly announced that the starring role of *The Gold Rush* would now be played by Georgia Hale. Lita was sixteen, she was pregnant, and the Los Angeles school authorities compelled her to continue her studies. They hired tutors, and this mistress of a forty-room residence with an army of servants made desperate efforts to pass her exams.

A son, Charles Spencer Chaplin Jr., was born on June 28, 1925. Nine months and two days later, on March 30, 1926, a second boy was born, Sydney Earle Chaplin. The two y's in Sydney were the subject of a dispute between the parents. Lita found it more chic to put in two, while Chaplin wanted to remain faithful to the spelling of his brother's first name.

Chaplin often sought refuge with his friend Marion Davies, at her estate in Santa Monica. Returning late one night to his home, he found the house completely invaded by drunken guests. Voices were raised and Lita left with the children. On January 14, 1927, she filed for divorce, supported by a forty-two-page document in which she described the cruel and inhuman treatment Chaplin had inflicted on her. In the January 11, 1927 issue of the *New York Times*, Lita Grey detailed her accusations. "Chaplin pretended that the marriage was a forced marriage; he said that marriage seemed to him a useless institution." He kept a loaded revolver, suggesting to her that he would commit suicide. He treated her like a gold digger. He read obscene books to her. She accused him of abnormal, unnatural, and indecent acts, and of conduct that undermined, demoralized, and "ruin[ed] the character of the plaintiff by despicable practices." Copies of Miss Grey's divorce request sold by the thousands at the rate of twenty-five cents apiece. Chaplin countered by accusing his wife and her family of conspiring to extort money from him. In the guise of a defense, he pointed out his pleasure in being surrounded by young girls because of the paternal feelings they inspired in him. Women's groups were angry and called for a ban of Chaplin's films and succeeded in several states.

The first cinematic adaptation of Vladimir Nabokov's novel, directed by Stanley Kubrick, was created in a tragicomic style in collaboration with the writer. Starring James Mason, Shelley Winters, Peter Sellers, and Sue Lyon (below) in the title role, *Lolita* caused a scandal in 1962. In 1997, Adrian Lyne brought his version to the screen.

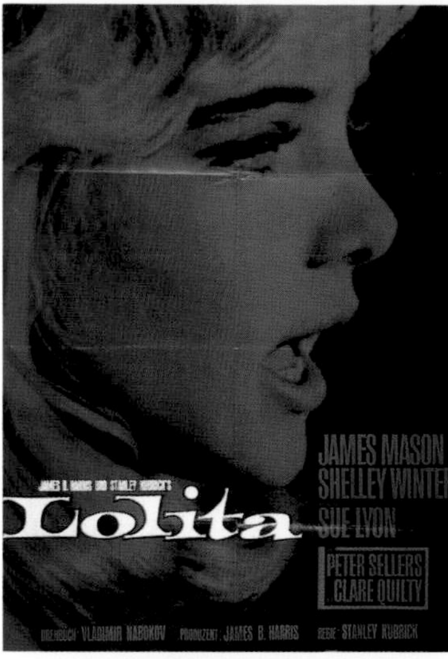

Left: **the movie's poster.** Opposite: **Vladimir Nabokov in Montreux, Switzerland, 1968. Photograph by Philippe Halsman.**

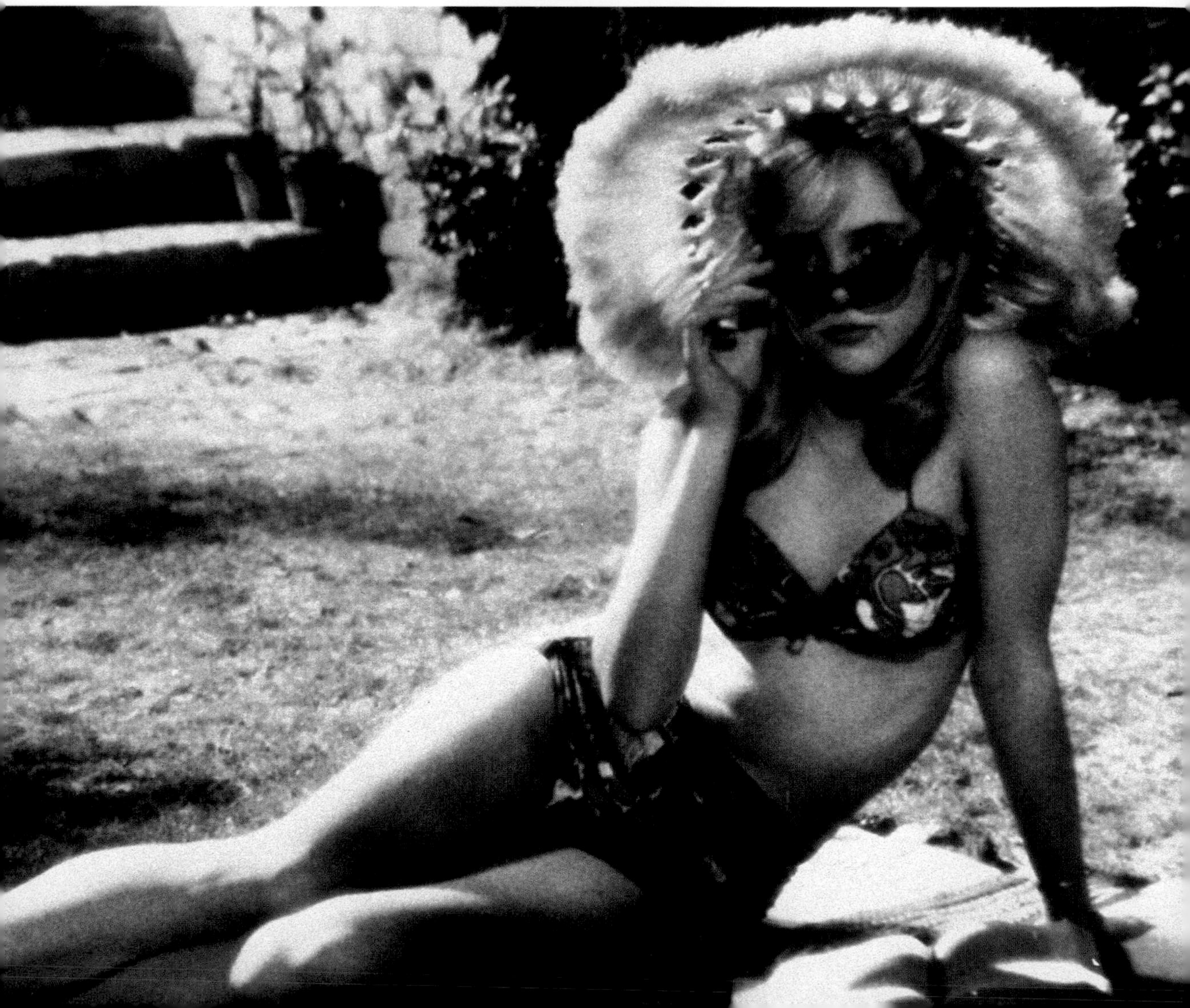

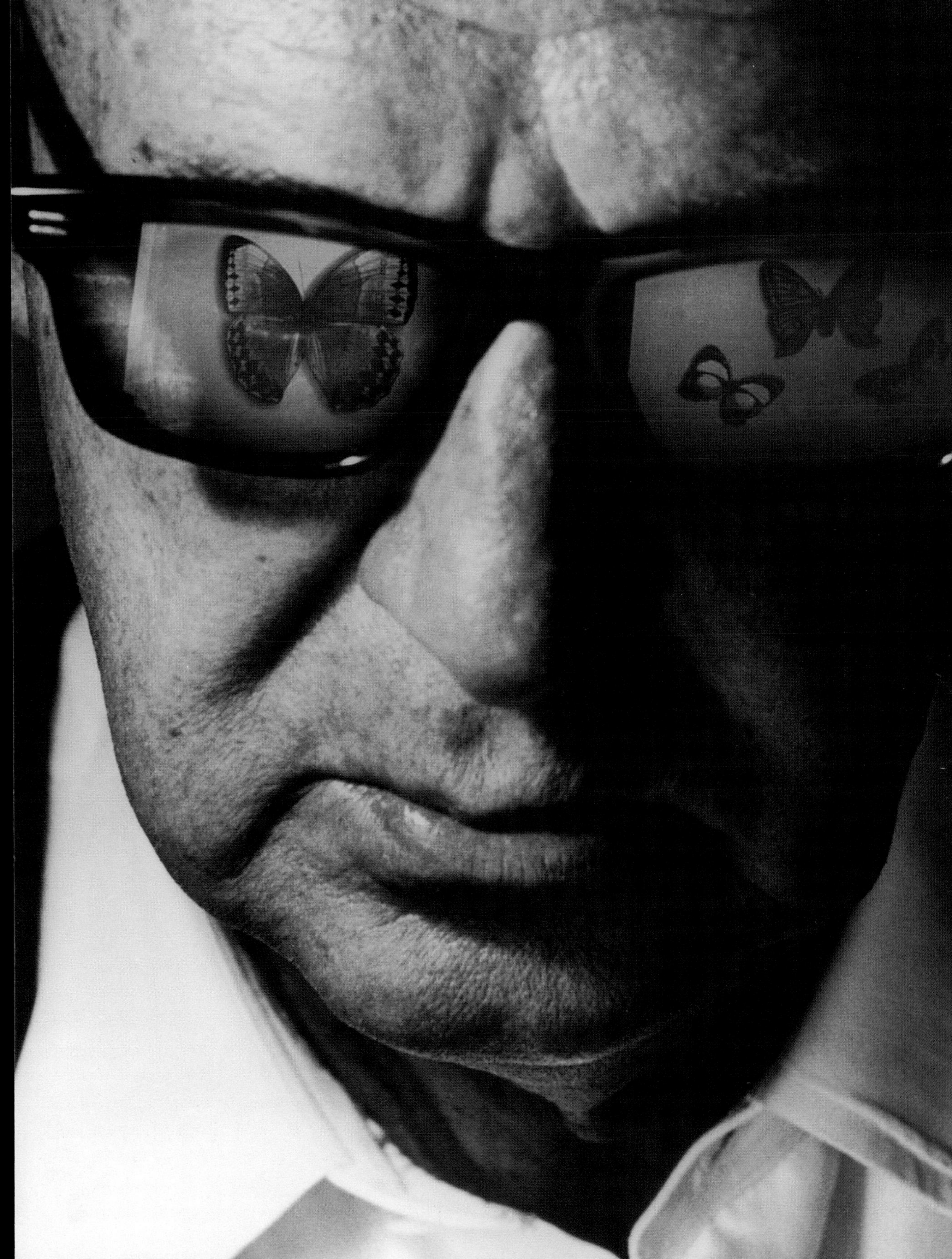

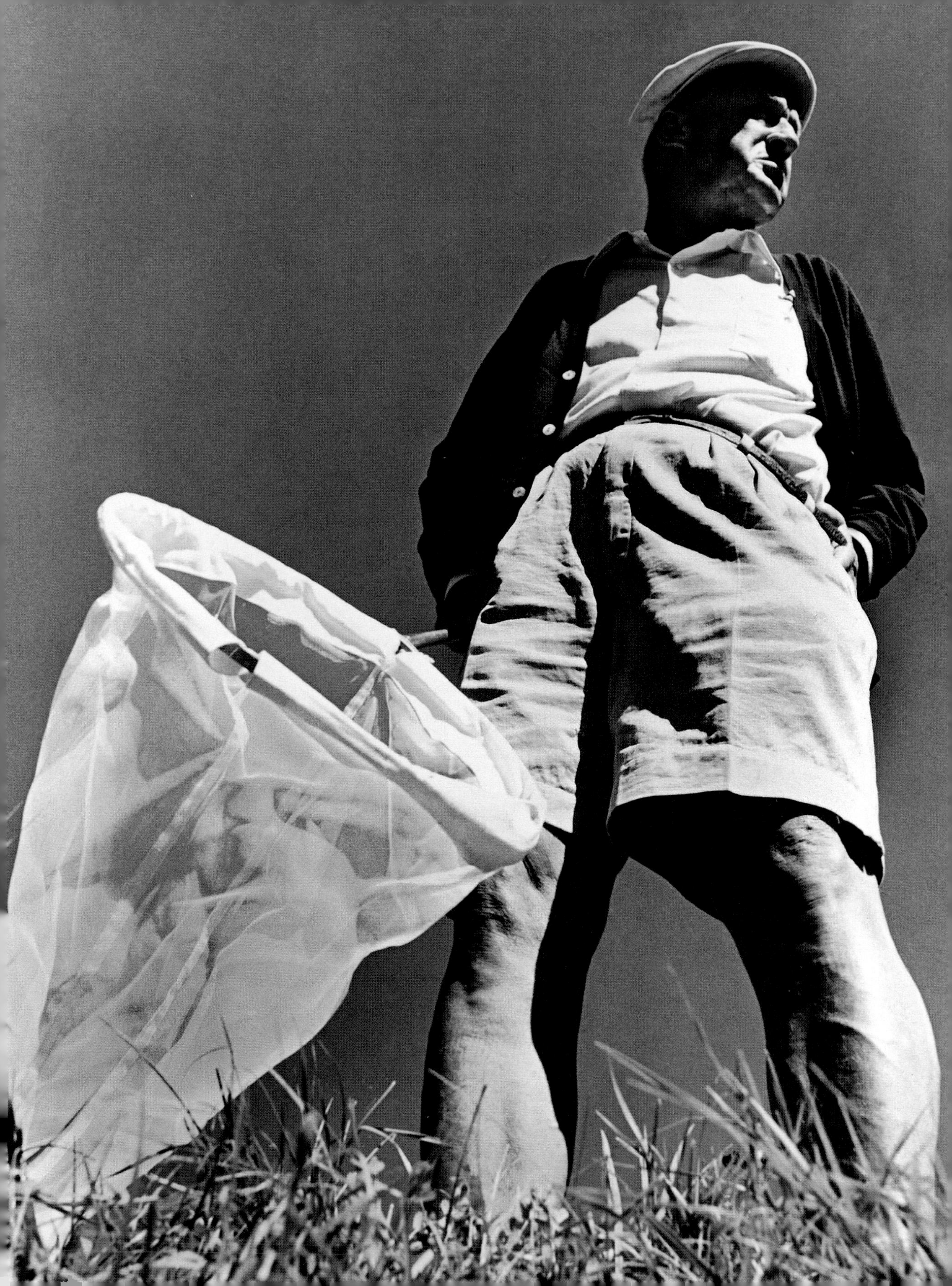

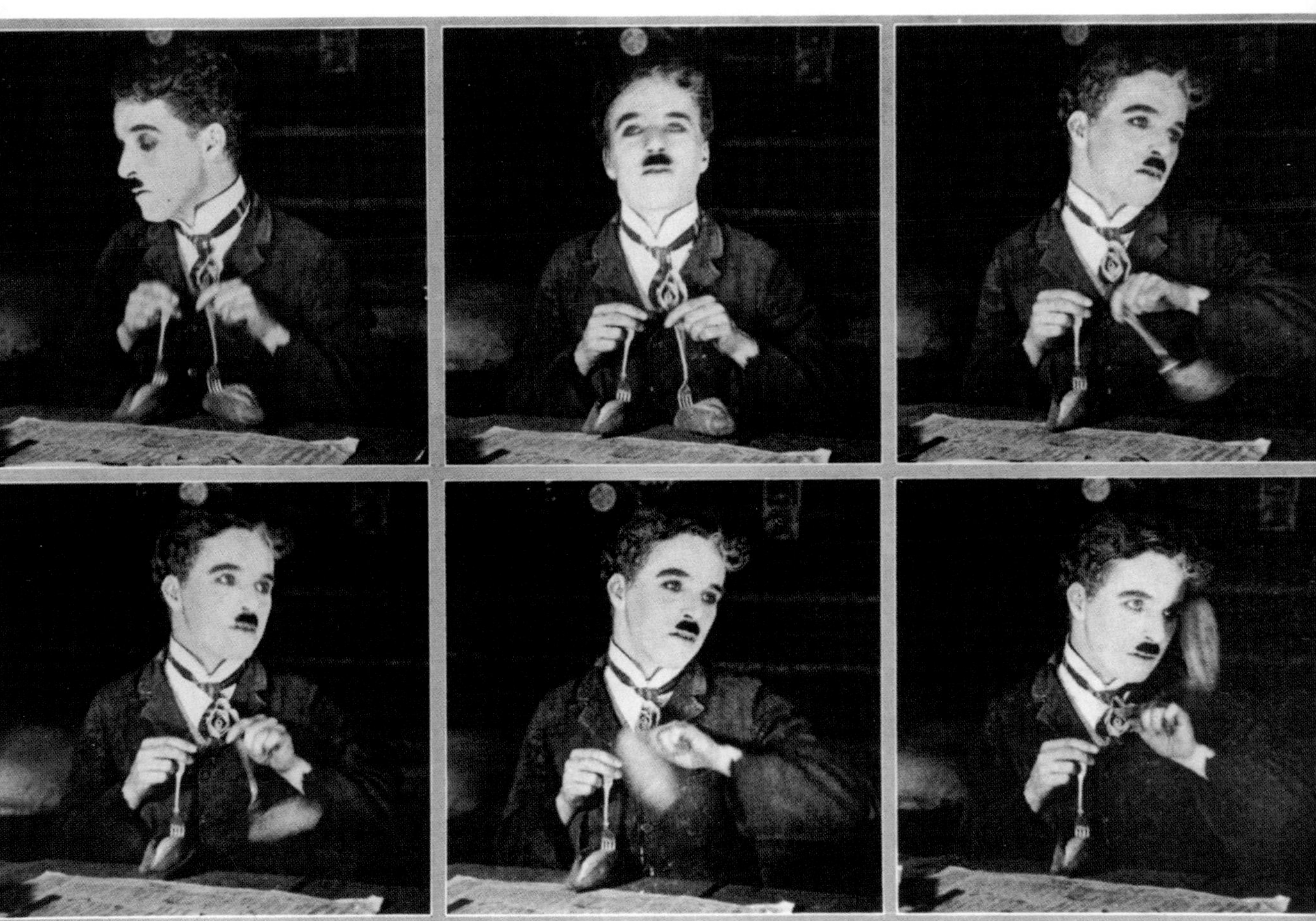

Opposite: **Vladimir Nabokov chasing butterflies, Montreux, Switzerland, 1968. Photograph by Philippe Halsman.**

Above: **A screenwriter and composer, Charlie Chaplin here plays the role of the Charlot, a lone prospector dying of hunger in *The Gold Rush*. The scene in which he eats the sole of his shoe and treats the shoelaces like spaghetti is one of the most famous in cinematic history.**

Right and opposite top: **March 1924. Under the gaze of her mother and Charlie Chaplin, Lillita McMurray signs the contract that would have made her the lead actress in *The Gold Rush*. When she became pregnant, she had to renounce the role but not Chaplin, marrying him in November that same year.**
Below: **Charlie Chaplin, Lillita McMurray, now Lita Grey, and their first child, Charles Spencer, born in June 1925. The following March, Sydney Earle was born.**

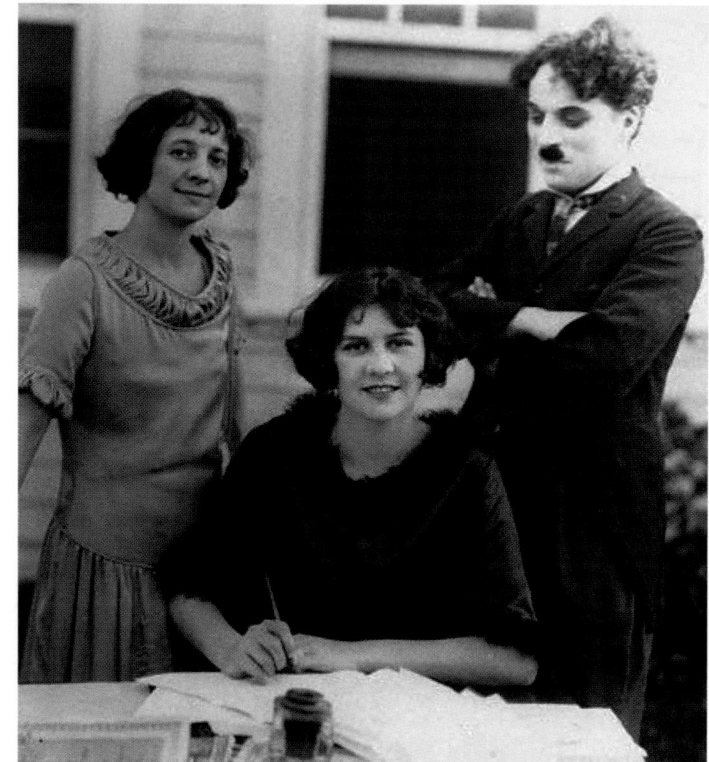

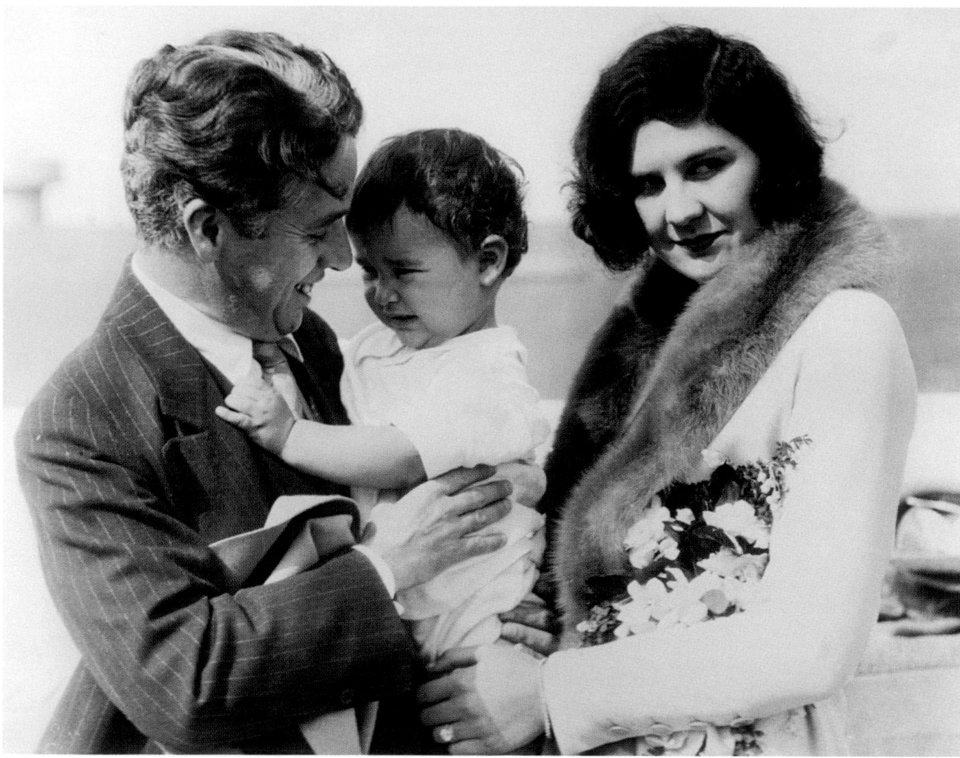

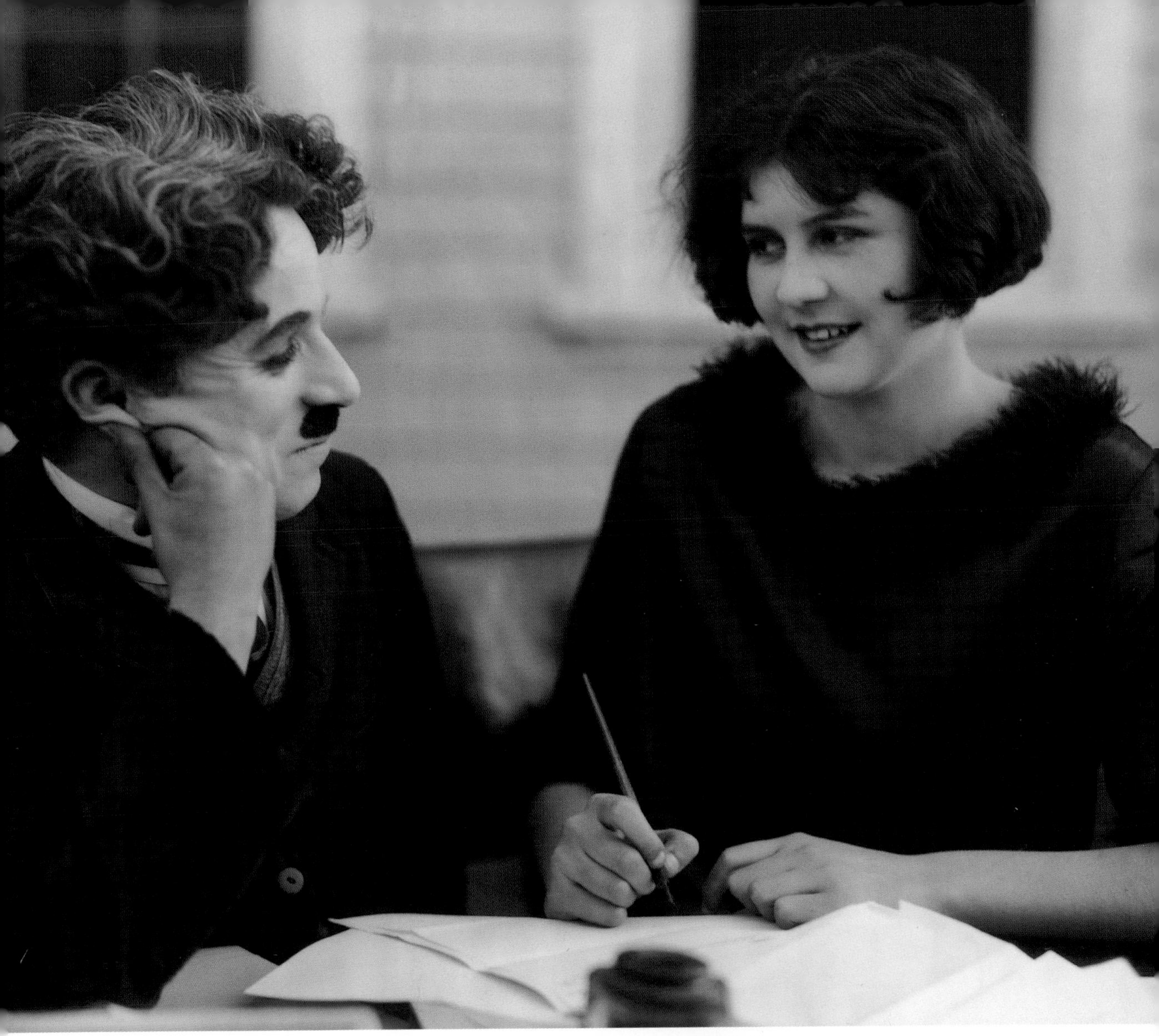

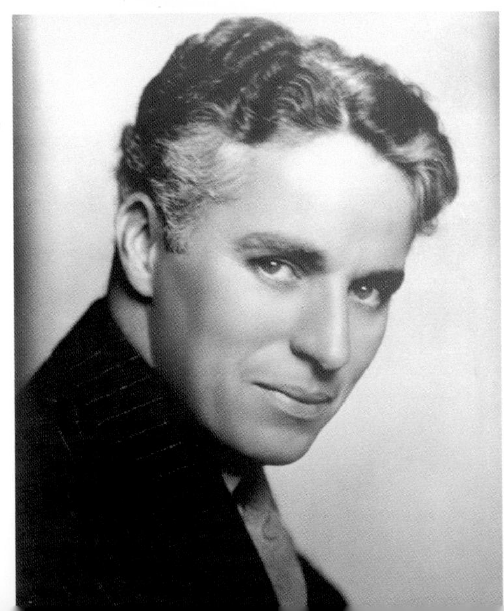

Right: **Crowned with the worldwide success of *The Gold Rush*, Charlie Chaplin found himself in 1927 at the heart of family and media turmoil. His divorce had a great impact just at the height of his acclaim. People everywhere scrambled for copies of the divorce request, and women's groups were angry and called for a ban on the director's films, which they judged immoral.**

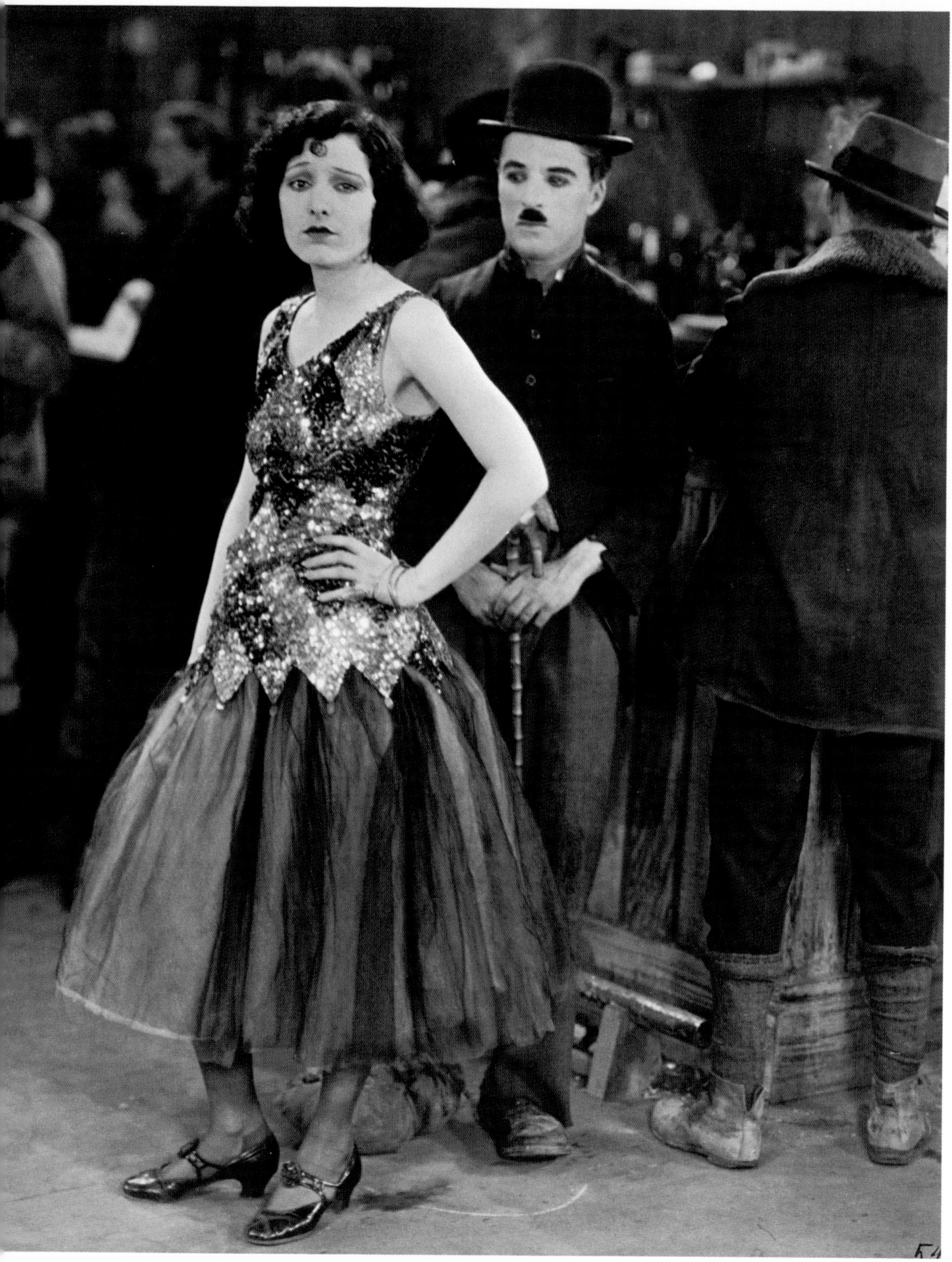

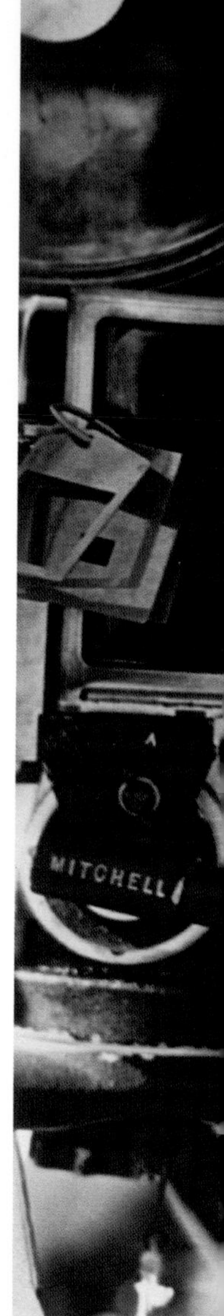
MITCHELL

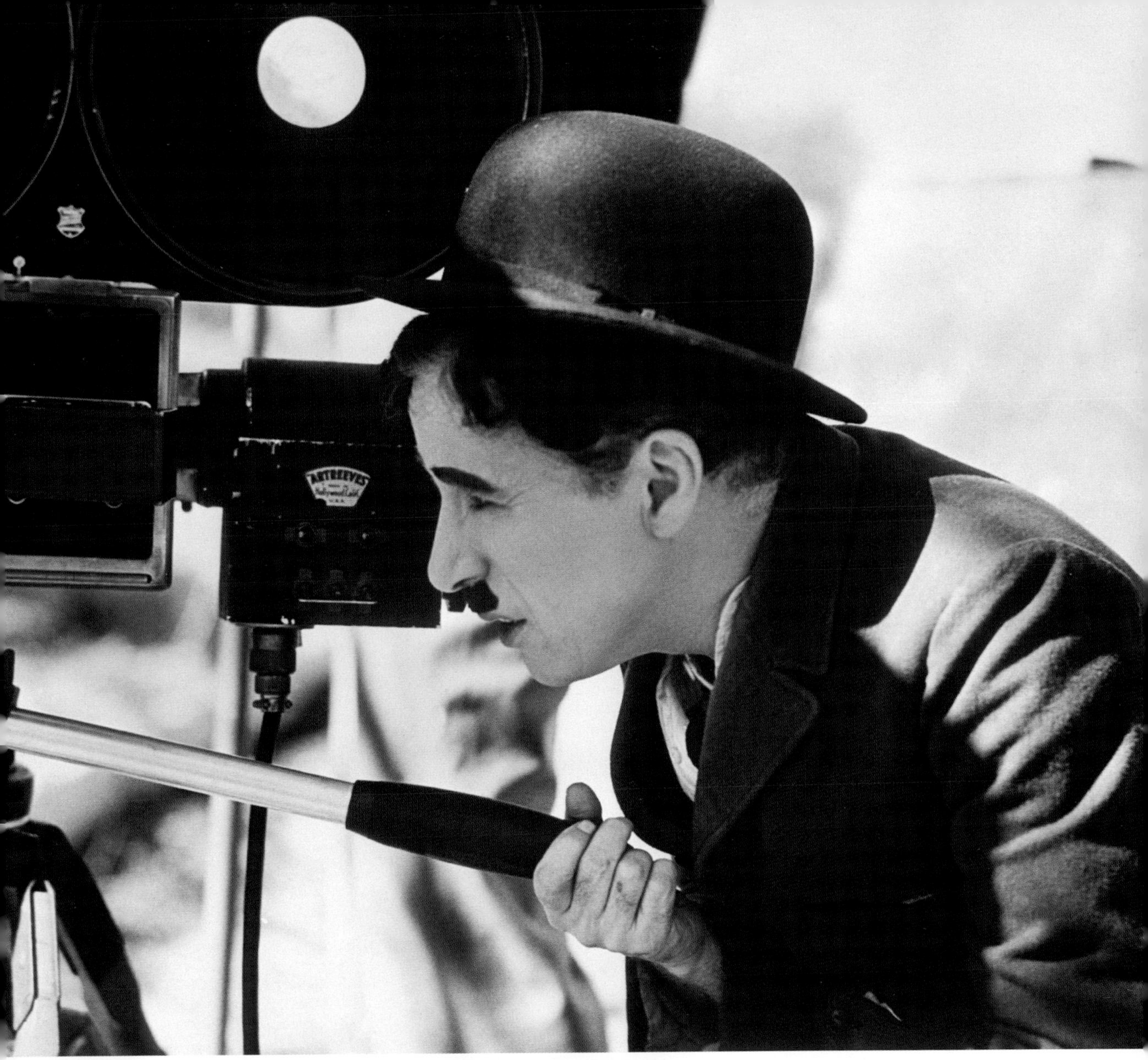

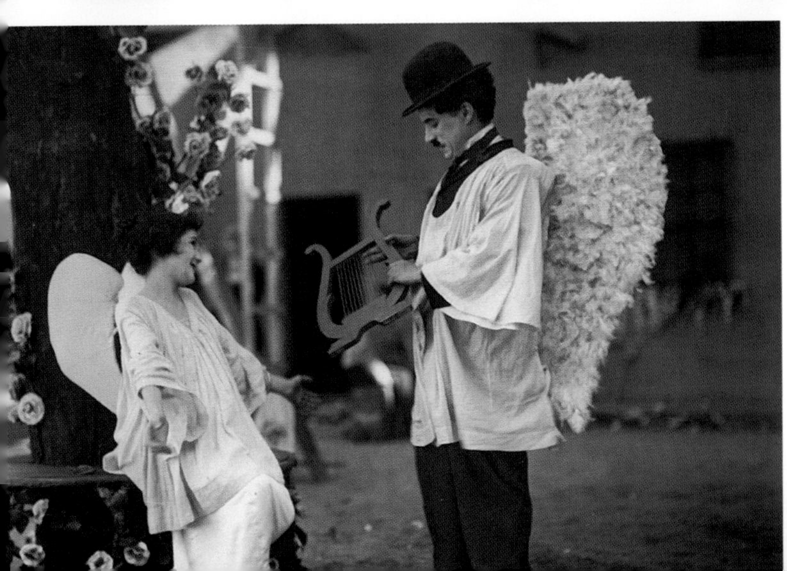

Left: **Charlie Chaplin first saw the young extra in *The Kid* as an angel, then later renamed her Lita Grey.**
Opposite: **To hide Lita Grey's pregnancy, Charlie Chaplin replaced her with Georgia Hale in *The Gold Rush*.**

Intellectuals and artists in France protested against the boycotting of Chaplin's movies. Among the first signatures were those of Germaine Dulac, Louis Aragon, Man Ray, Robert Desnos, and René Clair. The Surrealists, ever the last to play "moral judges" in dubious causes, mobilized themselves for this effort. Finally on June 1, 1927, Lita's lawyers decided to push matters along and threatened to reveal the names of five actresses with whom Chaplin had had affairs during their short conjugal life. An agreement was reached to avoid a scandal. Lita received one million dollars and the custody of the children. She traveled to Europe, performed in nightclubs under the name of Lita Grey Chaplin, and in 1966 wrote a rather tender book called *My Life with Chaplin*, which held her mother largely responsible for her unhappiness.

The Other Lolita

In 1927, the year of Chaplin's divorce, Vladimir Nabokov, the recently married young Russian aristocrat exiled himself from his native Russia and moved to Berlin. He adored Chaplin's films and in particular *The Gold Rush*, whose similarities to his own text *Despair*, published in 1937, he would later emphasize. With the rise of Nazism, Nabokov fled Berlin, first for Paris, then New York. Contrary to Chaplin, who kept his English nationality after settling in America, Nabokov took American citizenship on leaving Europe and began to write in English. The writing of *Lolita*, a novel he was certain would have no success, coincided with one of the couple's long journeys out West in 1951, where they met up with their son Dimitri. While his wife, Vera, drove the Oldsmobile, Nabokov took notes, and often settled into the car again at night to write in solitude. In Telluride, Colorado, he discovered the small mining town that would be the setting for the end of *Lolita*. On returning to Ithaca, he pursued his research and gathered information on prehistoric art for the last paragraph of the novel, in which Humbert hopes to keep Lolita alive: "I am thinking of aurochs and angels, the secret of durable pigments, prophetic sonnets, the refuge of art. And this is the only immortality you and I may share, my Lolita." (Hadn't Lita Grey also been an angel in her time for Chaplin?) In the buses that he took to teach his classes at Harvard, Nabokov conscientiously noted the fashionable expressions used by young girls. "She's quite a kid," "Listen, I met—," or "It's a sketch." He cut out brief articles from newspapers concerning sexual crimes involving young women. He picked up the song titles from jukeboxes and instructions given to motel clients;

he consulted a history of the Colt revolver and read articles such as "Sexual Maturation and the Physical Growth of Girls Age Six to Nineteen" and "Attitudes and Interests of Premenarchal and Postmenarchal Girls." This butterfly hunter's attention to detail should not surprise anyone. His great pride during the years of writing *Lolita* was to capture a rare butterfly specimen after hours of waiting in mud and cow dung. It was never about Charlie Chaplin. All that's left are the troubling coincidences like those revealed by Pierre Déméron and many others. Humbert, Nabokov's hero, is first married to Valeria, who was permanently "engrossed in *Paris-Soir*," one of the French tabloids that fed on Chaplin's divorce. Lolita was conceived in Mexico during her parents' honeymoon; Chaplin and Lillita were married there. Lolita was twelve when she met Humbert, the same age as Lillita when she met Chaplin. Always coincidences. Nabokov left America in 1961 and settled in Montreux, Switzerland, not far from Lausanne, where Chaplin, sickened by McCarthyism and money problems, had moved several years earlier in the company of Oona O'Neill, whom he married when she was seventeen years old. But the two men probably never met. On December 6, 1953, Nabokov noted in his agenda: "Finished *Lolita*, which was begun exactly five years ago." With or without Chaplin, Nabokov gave birth to a myth that would outlive them both.

Bibliography

Chaplin, Charlie. *My Autobiography*. New York: Simon & Schuster, 1978.

Chaplin, Lita Grey. *Wife of the Life of the Party*. Metuchen, N.J.: Scarecrow Press, 1998.

Milton, Joyce. *Tramp: The Life of Charlie Chaplin*. New York: HarperCollins, 1996.

Nabokov, Vladimir. *Lolita*. New York: Vintage reissue, 1989.

Robinson, David. *Charlie Chaplin: Comic Genius*. New York: Harry N. Abrams, Inc., 1996.

The Perfect Model

Sigmund Freud's work "Delusion and Dream in Wilhelm Jensen's *Gradiva*" immortalizes the image of a young girl spotted among the ruins of Pompeii in whom an archaeologist recognizes the female form from a bas-relief that had hung in his study for years. This seemingly predestined meeting between a creator and the model he has pursued all his life suggests a kind of miracle. This miracle, however, actually occurred when the sculptor Aristide Maillol discovered Dina Vierny, or when the artist Salvador

Dalí first encountered Gala, or writer Jean Cocteau met Jean Marais. Sometimes the model brings about the birth of a vocation, as in the case of Jean Renoir, who became a filmmaker for the sole aim of making his wife, Catherine Hessling, a star. The relationship between artist and muse can sometimes be quasi-exclusive—like the film work of actress Gena Rowlands with her actor-director husband John Cassavetes or Josephine Hopper and her husband, the painter Edward Hopper—leading to a strange back and forth between reality and fiction.

Dina Vierny
Aristide Maillol

A Living Maillol

Aristide Maillol's sole model during the last ten years of his life, Dina Vierny was for him the incarnation of the harmony he had searched for in his sculpture. Upon his death in 1944, the twenty-five-year-old Vierny went on to champion the work of one of the most important artists of the twentieth century in whose honor she created the Maillol museums in Paris and in Banyuls-sur-Mer.

"I have known three divine flowers: the rose, the carnation, and Dina." In dedicating a drawing to the young Dina Vierny, the sculptor Aristide Maillol unhesitatingly declared his fascination with her. He rarely sculpted using a model but rather worked from a certain idea of harmony that he had in his mind. He only posed women to verify this or that anatomical detail—the "information" as he called it—on the curve of a hip or the roundness of a stomach or the shape of a breast. This is how he had worked from the beginning of the century with his wife Clothilde. "She lifted up her blouse and I found marble," he recalled a long time after her thickened silhouette no longer provided the necessary information. And this is how he worked with Laure, a neighbor in Banyuls, the village of his birth, who had posed for his *Pomone* in 1910, which was an artistic triumph. Nearing eighty now, the artist decided to make an exception and sculpt directly from nature. Dina Vierny would become his sole model. At the start of 1940, he began a portrait of Dina that he called *La Rose*, which would become the offered drawing.

Maillol Discovers a Living Maillol

Maillol met Dina in the spring of 1934 through one of his friends, the architect Jean-Claude Dondel, who talked endlessly about the young girl's physique. The sculptor sent her this note: "Mademoiselle, they tell me that you resemble a Maillol or a Renoir. I would content myself with a Renoir." The daughter of immigrants of Russian descent, Dina Vierny was then fifteen. She was curious about everything from chemistry, which she wanted to study, to political science and economics. She read George Sand, loved poetry, and visited museums. Not impressed with the idea of meeting the man considered the greatest sculptor of his era, she more or less forgot about the letter, and it was only on Dondel's insistence that she decided to attend one of the famous Sunday gatherings in Marly-le-Roi where numerous artists and intellectuals flocked around Maillol.

Maillol was stupefied upon seeing Dina. She corresponded exactly to the description that the novelist Octave Mirbeau had given one of his sculptures at the beginning of the century: "Everything about her is strong, full, firm, and round . . . like an egg, like everything containing strength and a seed." The sculptor soon declared to her, "If you want to become a model all my painter friends will employ you, but none will be able to do it like I can because you are the exact image of the young girl that I have always had in my head." This image had come to him from the girls he had seen in his childhood walking along the beach in Banyuls "with the assurance of a Vénus de Milo. . . . One could only see their admirable legs! What must the rest be like!" he remembered with regret.

The idea of posing appealed to Dina. She had already acted as an extra in the films of Jean Renoir, the son of the Impressionist painter, but that work required total availability whereas she could continue her studies while posing. The sculptor invited her to the house he had constructed at the edge of the forest. He showed her paintings done by the friends of his youth: Pierre Bonnard, Édouard Vuillard, and Maurice Denis, the older illustrator whom he had received like a peer in their group. In front of his sculptures, Maillol spoke to her about his work: "Ah! Like I often said to Rodin, which made him laugh each time, 'art is complicated.'" Dina listened and looked at him. She was astonished by his youthful allure. Despite his seventy-three years, the sculptor comported himself like his name, which meant "young vine plant" in his native Catalan. Even famous he remained a mysterious character who, to put it bluntly, "stumbled into Paris from his small village without any stopovers."

A collaboration was born between the old sculptor and the young girl. However, Vierny often read while posing and her head moved to the rhythm of the reading. Furious, Maillol swore, "My next model will be illiterate!" But in the ten years of his life that remained he had no other model and, since she could not give up reading, he built a lectern for her. Despite his protestations, Maillol was delighted to have finally found a model with whom he could speak of Ovid and Cervantes. At the end of a year the schoolgirl decided to pose in the nude: "It was difficult for him to use me for the nudes; the modeling just wasn't working out," recounted Vierny. "Maillol was very reserved; he was more timid than I. I was already part of youth movements like the friends of nature or the nudists for whom nakedness didn't count; it was very fashionable. But he had no concept about all that, he was very nineteenth century. He came to me with the utmost respect, a respect that he always maintained. . . . By the time my father knew about all this it was too late, his daughter was already famous."

During a school vacation in 1938, Dina left to join Maillol in Banyuls in the Pyrénées-Orientales region of France, near the Spanish border. "Banyuls—a corner of Greece transported to the Spanish frontier," Maillol said after returning from a voyage to the land of Phidias where he had been taken by his first patron, Count Henry Keßler. When Dina disembarked in Banyuls, it was still a little fishing port. She quickly located the sculptor's house in the old village, a tall pink building dominating the old town. From the terrace you could see the surrounding hills covered in olive trees, grapevines, and cypresses. The studio was situated on the first floor of the house, on the same level as the garden, where Maillol had spread out his sculptures amid a crowd of trees. Not all of them had been created there. The artist possessed another studio just outside the village in Puig del Mas, which he shared with his only son, Lucien, a painter whose talent remained hidden by the illustrious name he bore. And then there was La Métairie, or "mé'trie" as Maillol pronounced it, a house out in the open countryside, reachable only by a steep path that cut across the vineyards. It was a large house nestled in the heart of the small valley where a small stream, the Roume, ran. Maillol normally worked there in January and February, but since his wife's personality had become more and more cantankerous, he often sought refuge there, far from a world that, for the third time since his birth, was sinking deeper in war.

La Rose

When Dina returned to Banyuls in February 1940, Maillol had the idea of creating his sculpture *La Rose.* "It will be my legacy," he said. They settled into the first floor of the pink house and Maillol began the project as though he were attacking his first sculpture. Work progressed slowly. The sculptor lived in fear that his indispensable model would fall sick or leave. One day he noticed that Dina was terribly exhausted. Finally she risked admitting to him that, since July, she had been helping refugees cross the border into Spain each night. Realizing that she was a member of the Resistance, Maillol exclaimed: "Poor girl! Do you know the mountain?" He pointed out a shorter path known by smugglers, which would be nicknamed the "Maillol-Dina" route after the war by those refugees who recognized Dina Vierny as the young girl in the red dress who led them wordlessly toward Spain and freedom. In admiration for her, as much as in concern, Maillol painted Dina in this red dress and offered up his studio in Puig del Mas so that the refugees could rest before crossing in the night.

In mid-August the American intellectual Varian Fry disembarked in Marseilles with a list of two hundred European artists and intellectuals to be ushered into Spain, and established contact with Dina. During the summer, thanks to Fry, close to two thousand people made it across the border. But Dina was arrested in October and accused of aiding these escapes. Thanks to her silence and, above all, to the intervention of the lawyer Pierre Camo, her 1941 trial in Céret was narrowly won. However, now in constant fear of losing his model, Maillol tried to distance her from the frontier by sending her to Le Cannet to pose for Bonnard, to Perpignan for Raoul Dufy—who always used to say to him, "I am the youngest of your old friends"—to Nice to see Matisse, where she was accompanied by this note: "I am sending you the object of my work. You will transform her into an outline." Which, in effect, is what Henri Matisse did over the period of several months. Vierny spoke to him of *La Rose*, the sculpture Maillol was creating. Matisse did not care for its name. Maillol, who generally did not title his works, would change it during a visit from the art historian John Rewald in February 1941. The author of the book *Les Ateliers de Maillol* had come to spend a week near the sculptor before his return to the United States and had remarked while contemplating *La Rose*: "She is complete harmony." Suddenly the old sculptor began to sing a tune by Berlioz: "Everything on earth is in harmony, nature and our life."

Harmonie, Maillol's Unfinished Symphony

And so it was *Harmonie* that Bonnard came to admire in 1943. But the sculpture was far from finished. Maillol multiplied the plaster casts, which he later broke or asked Dina to saw off parts, which led her to mistakenly cutting off the head of one of the versions. When the sculptor put it back on a new torso, *Harmonie* had lost about a half-inch in height. "Chance is a great artist," Auguste Rodin was in the habit of saying. Maillol, for once, shared his opinion. The sculpture continued to be off about a half-inch in the neck and, by an incredible coincidence, his model would suffer a similar loss in height some time later because of an accident. The arms of the piece also posed several problems for him. "Maillol," recounted Dina Vierny, "did not like to sculpt arms even though he

Page 72: **Although primarily a sculptor, Aristide Maillol did not abandon painting. His *Dina au foulard* (*Dina with a Scarf*; 1941) recalls the sessions in La Métairie, his countryside studio near his house in Banyuls where Maillol discovered Dina Vierny's body was too tanned for his taste.**

Page 73: **Aristide Maillol, *Dina à la natte* (*Dina with a Braid*; 1940). "Everything about her is strong, full, firm, and round . . . like an egg, like everything containing strength and a seed," wrote the novelist Octave Mirbeau at the beginning of the twentieth century on the subject of Maillol's sculpture. In Dina Vierny, the sculptor discovered the incarnation of the model he had always searched for.**

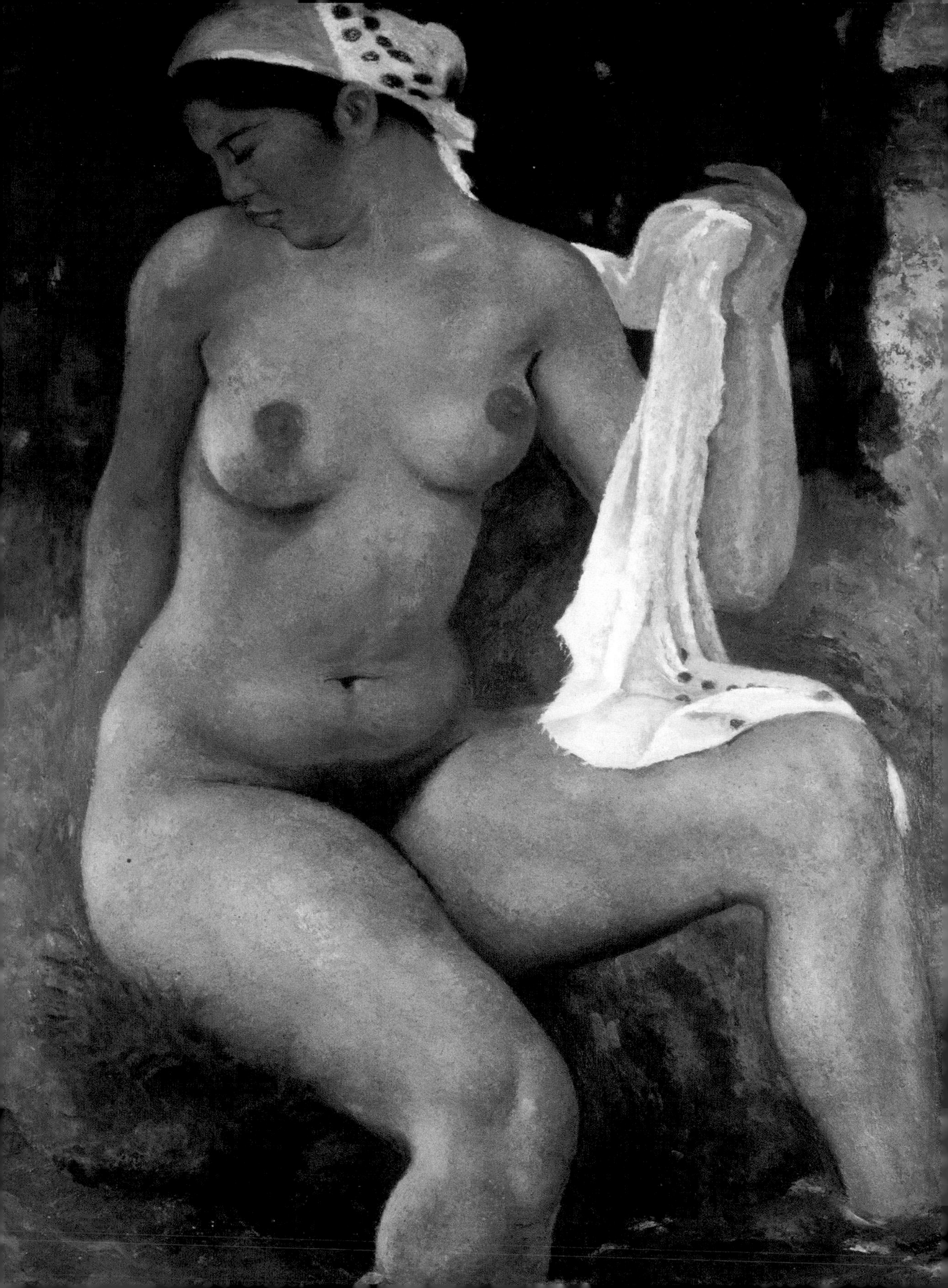

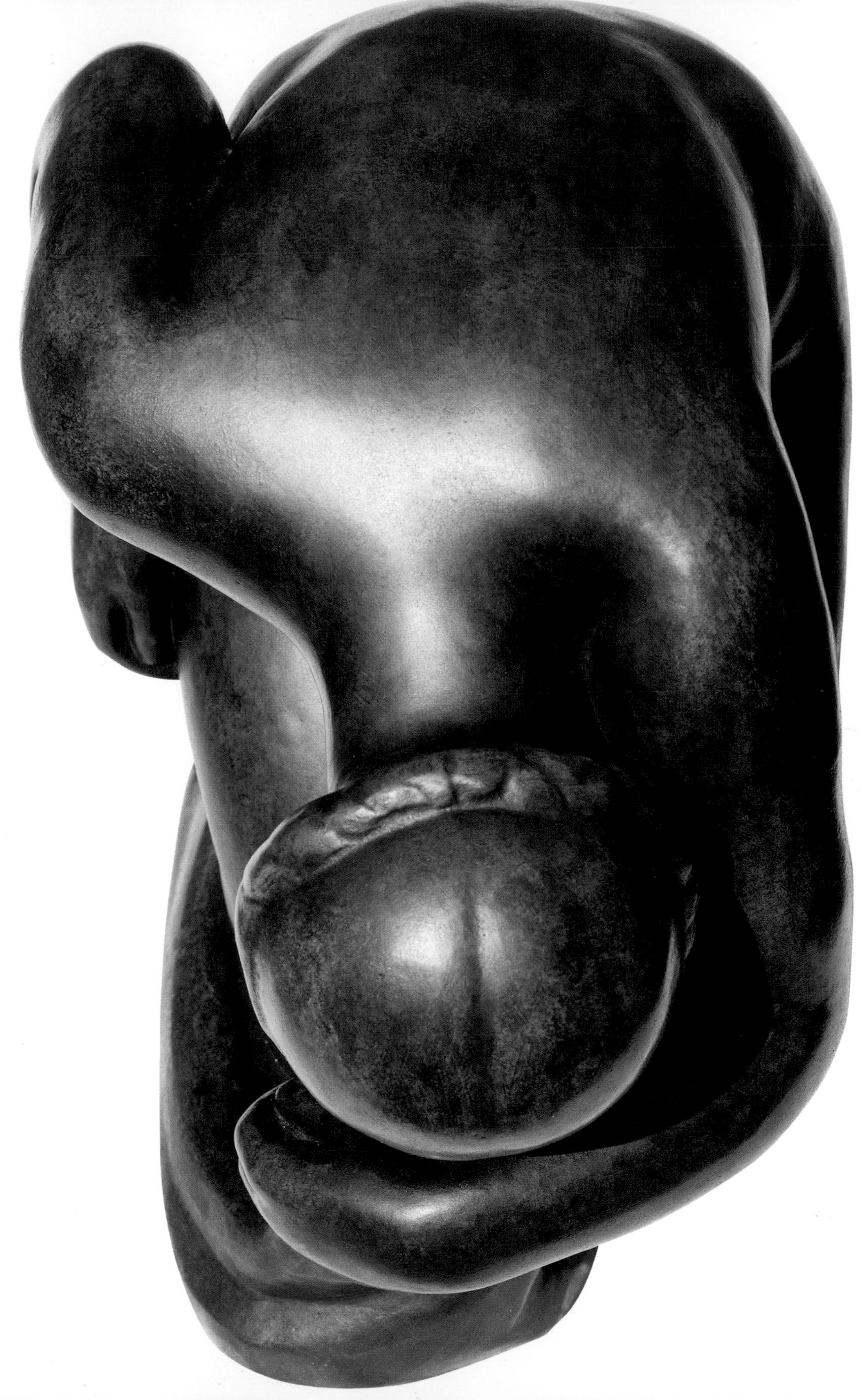

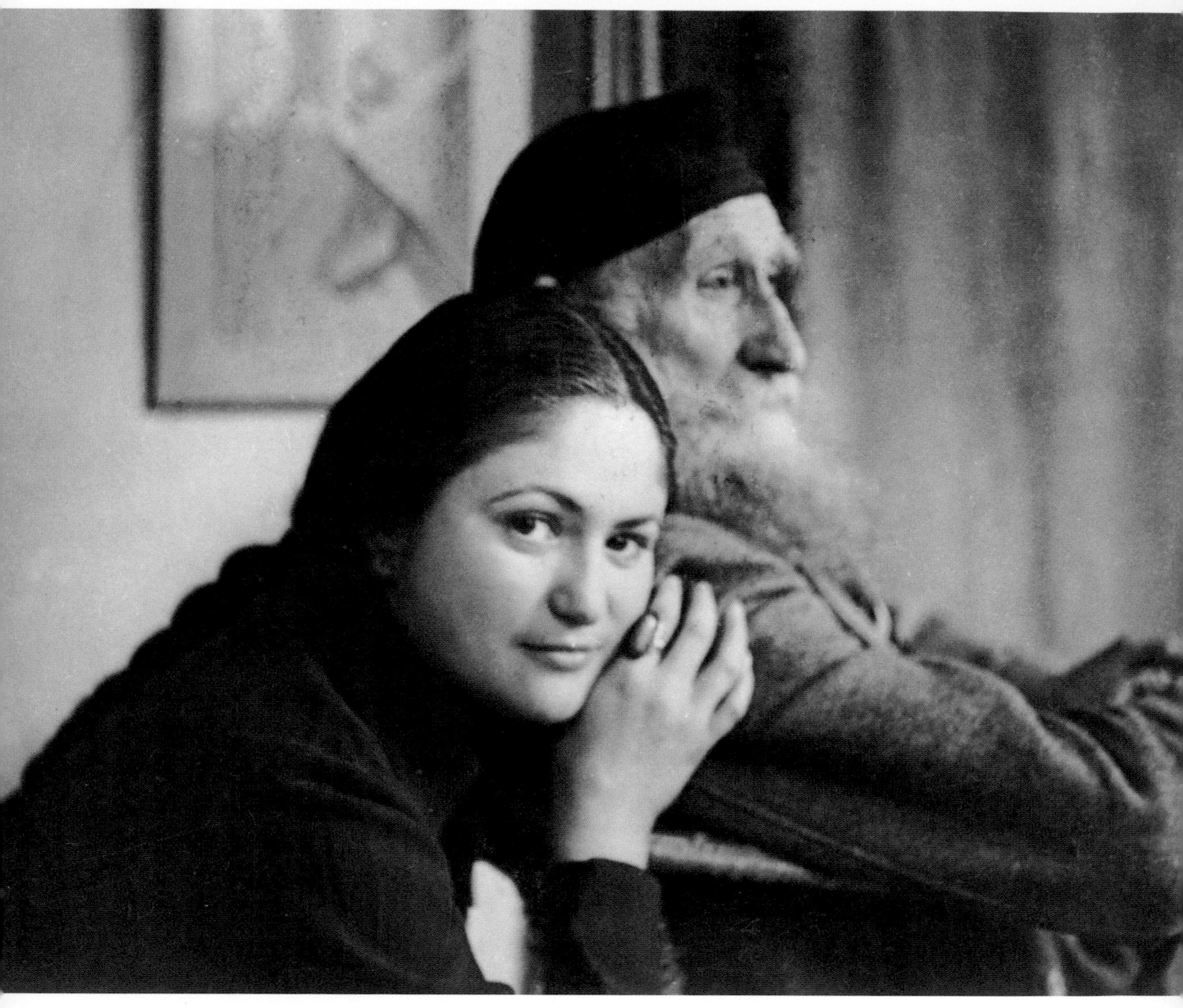

Above: **The famous merchant Louis Carré took this photo of Aristide Maillol and Dina Vierny in 1944, the same year of the sculptor's death. It speaks to the bond that existed between Maillol and his model.**

Opposite: **Aristide Maillol, *Dina à la robe rouge* (*Dina in a Red Dress*; 1940). Maillol painted Dina Vierny in her red dress, a color that allowed the refugees wanting to cross over to Spain to identify the young girl who guided them across the mountains on the path to freedom.**

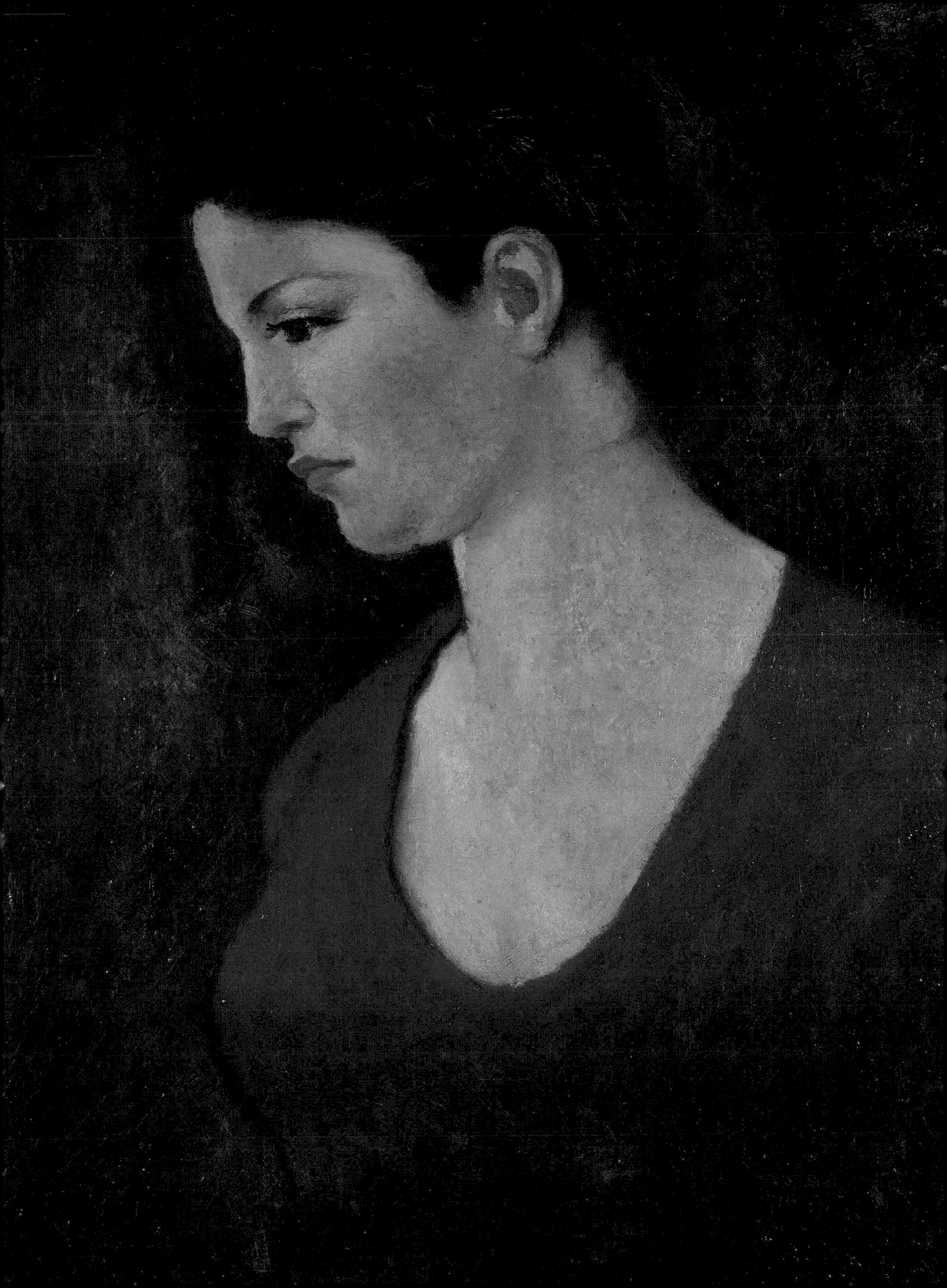

Below: **Anxious to distance Dina Vierny from the Resistance activities which he judged too dangerous, Artistide Maillol sent her to stay with Henri Matisse, accompanied by this note: "I am sending you the object of my work. You will transform her into an outline." Matisse did this even after Maillol's death, as we see in this magnificent drawing from 1949 that Matisse gave to Vierny.**

Right: **Pierre Bonnard, who was a close friend of Artistide Maillol's within the Nabis movement at the end of the nineteenth century, also became fascinated by Dina Vierny's figure. She sat for him during the war in his studio in Le Cannet. The title of his painting, *Le Nu sombre* (*The Dark Nude*; 1942–46), alludes, once again, to Dina's bronzed body.**

Opposite: **Photograph of Dina Vierny.**

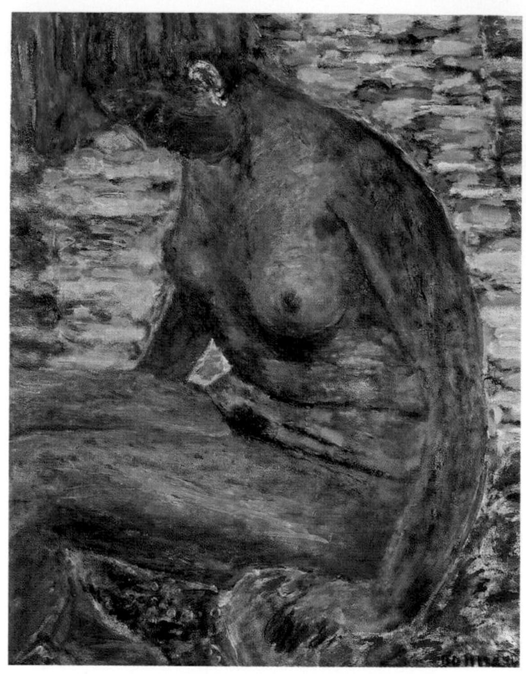

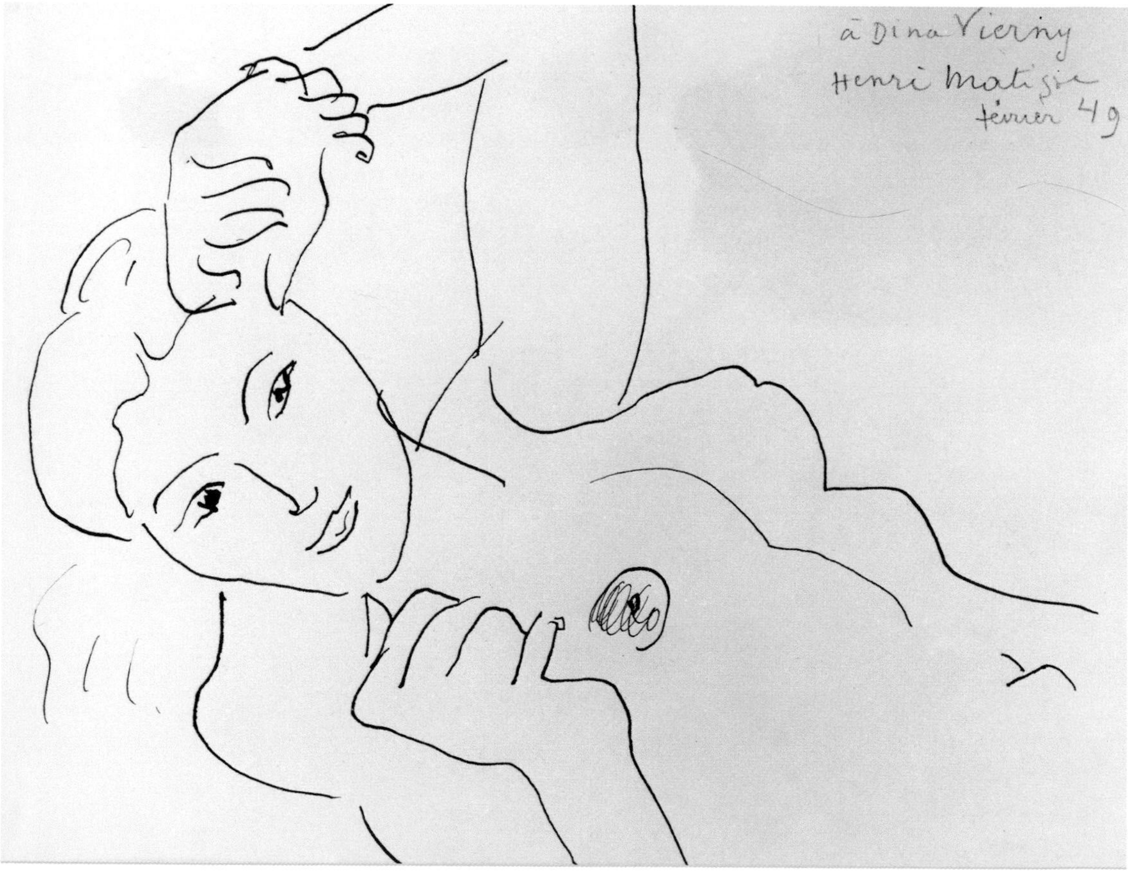

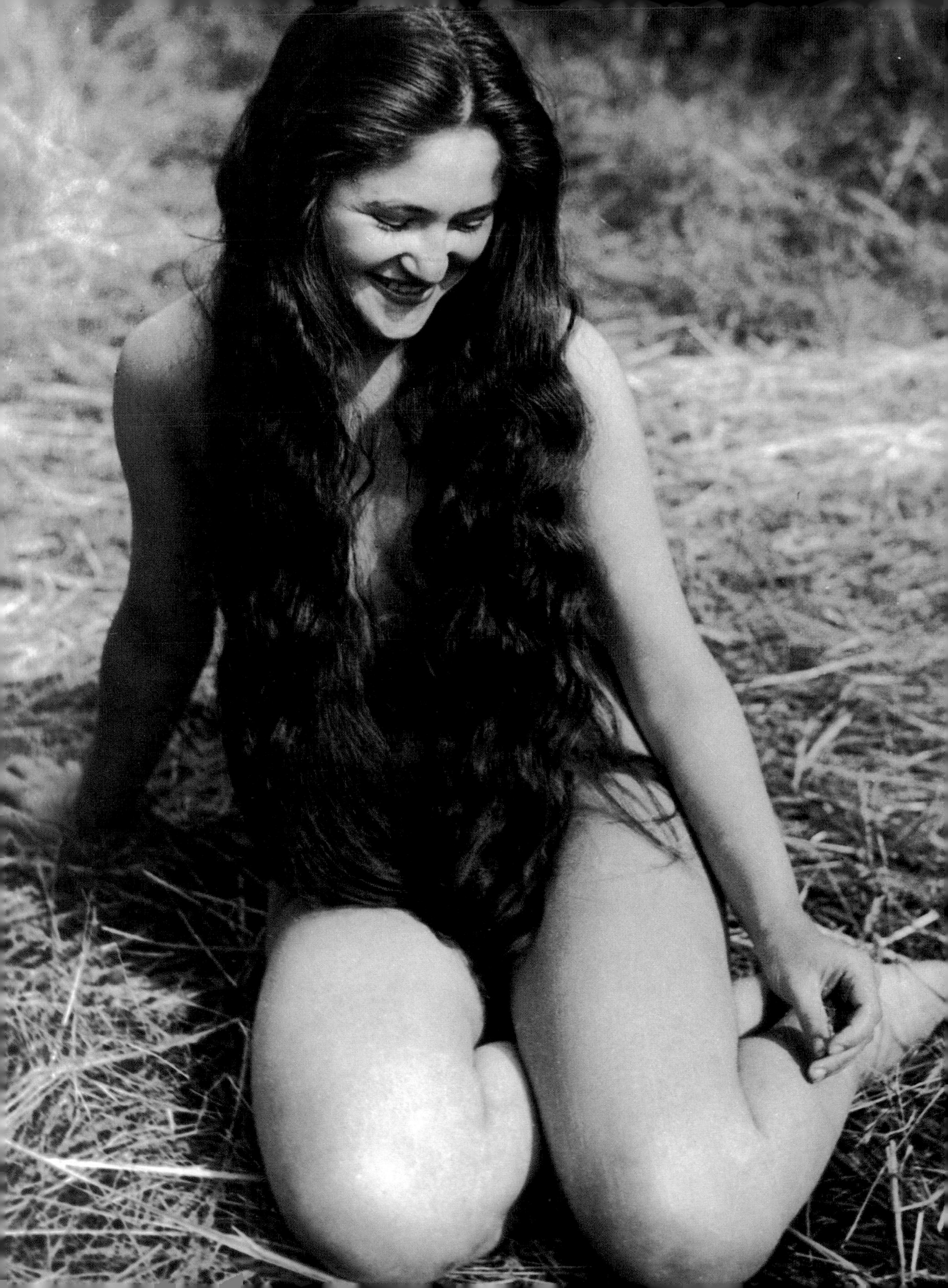

could do it very well. 'Arms bore me,' he would say to me. 'They get in the way of looking at the profile. Arms reach for the ground, whereas the torso is higher, further away. It disappears.'"

Constantly under suspicion by the Vichy authorities, Dina Vierny was put under house arrest at the beginning of 1942, but she did not stop working for the Resistance at the request of Max*, himself a painter. Dina agreed to send the escape network through the Pyrenees to the Free French Forces. But that was not the reason she was arrested in May 1943. Caught in a trap in Paris on a day when she was supposed to lunch with Pablo Picasso, she spent six months in a prison in nearby Fresnes, always at the point of being deported. She somehow managed, however, to keep Maillol current about her situation. The sculptor was distraught at having lost his model, whom he had come to consider over the years as his adopted daughter—"You have done little," he said to Dina's father. "But I have invented her!"—and he did everything he could to save her.

Among Maillol's numerous admirers was the German sculptor Arno Breker. "He was one of the Montparnasse artists," recalled Vierny. "Everyone knew him. Breker was very poor until his wife, an extremely ambitious model, convinced him to participate in the art competition for the 1936 Olympic Games in Berlin. He won and became Hitler's favorite artist. Maillol hated Breker's sculpture, which represented the exact opposite of what he was searching for. Breker nevertheless managed to make him come to his 1942 exhibition at the Orangerie in Paris. Maillol did not understand, despite my warnings, how damaging his presence was." Maillol, who was fundamentally a pacifist and humanist, had nothing to do with the ideology that the Nazi sculptor glorified, but he wished to see his house in Marly-le-Roi again and the sculptures he had abandoned in his hasty exodus. This contact with Breker, whose reputation would go on to suffer, nevertheless allowed him to get Dina out of Fresnes. In Paris for the funeral of his friend, the painter Maurice Denis, Maillol was surprised to find his model in a restaurant. "When I arrived," recounted Dina, "Maillol was crazy with joy because without me he could not finish *Harmonie*. For my first day of freedom, we worked until midnight correcting *La Rivière* (*The River*), which was being kept in the studio of his doctor in Paris, the sculptor Robert Couturier."

Harmonie, the sculpture that the artist considered as his final testament, would become the "unfinished symphony." He never had time to fashion the arms. Maillol died in September 1944 at the age of 83 following a car accident. Dina, who was involved in the Paris insurrection, could not return to Banyuls in time. Not being present at the moment of Maillol's death remained one of her deepest regrets. She was then twenty-five years old and decided to dedicate the rest of her life to championing his sculpture. Becoming Maillol's executor, she made a gift of a group of his sculptures which can be seen today in the Tuileries gardens in Paris, and spent her inexhaustible energy to open two Maillol museums—one in Banyuls in 1994, the other in Paris the following year. "I had the chance to participate in the creative process of one of the greatest artists of the century," she said. "You cannot put a price on that; that cannot be forgotten."

* Dina Vierny never knew Jean Moulin other than under the pseudonym of Max. It was only after the war that she learned he was the head of the Resistance, and a great admirer of Maillol's, whom he planned to visit the same week he was arrested and assassinated by his tormentors shortly thereafter.

Bibliography

Bormann, Béatrice von. *Maillol and Dina*. London: Marlborough Fine Art, 2001.

Cahn, Isabelle, et al. *L'Abcdaire de Maillol*. Paris: Flammarion, 1996.

Lorquin, Bertrand, and Dina Vierny. *Aristide Maillol.* Paris: Skira, 2002.

Vierny, Dina, et al. *Maillol*. Paris-Perpignan: Éditions Benteli, 2000.

Jean Marais
Jean Cocteau

Beauty and the Beast

Lovers, friends, poet and inspiration, artist and subject, Jean Cocteau and Jean Marais played all these roles for each other for over thirty-five years. This couple, one of the first to openly display their homosexuality, has continued to fascinate the public the world over, even after the death of the prince of poets in 1963.

"I love actors because they transform writing into a very strange painting. We need them because we are the room and they the stage, we are of the darkness and they are of the light. As far we are concerned, they are plants that attract insects with their perfumes and their colors; they help us to spread our seed far and perpetuate the species." This could be Cocteau speaking about Marais, but in fact it was Marais in 1983 performing his own work, *Cocteau-Marais*, on stage. Cocteau had been dead for twenty years when Marais offered up this homage. Beyond death, these magnificent lovers, the first to have openly displayed their homosexuality in France, attracted thousands of spectators across the world just on the basis of their names. Created for the Théâtre de l'Atelier in Paris, the production was restaged in Germany and across Europe in 1986, and even in Japan in 1988.

A Second Birth

Jean Marais was born twice: the first time on December 11, 1913, the second upon his encounter with Jean Cocteau in 1937. He had few memories of his early years spent in Cherbourg, in France, or of his father who had gone to war. He lived with his mother, a beautiful, lively, mischievous, unpredictable woman who liked to disguise herself and change her identity. Sometimes the woman he nicknamed Rosalie disappeared for several weeks at a time, and when Marais became an adult he discovered that her kleptomania had often led her to prison. When Marais's father returned from the war in 1919, she left him and went off to settle in Paris with her two children, her aunt, and her mother. Jean and his brother Henri were raised by three women and without a father. A poor student who specialized in doctored notes and forged excuse slips, he had always dreamed of "becoming an actor." At the entry exam for the conservatory, he judged his own work sublime, but the jury found him hysterical and made it clear to him. Marais got the message and decided to take acting classes with Charles Dullin. Then came the hour when everything would change: an audition one day in June 1937 in front of Cocteau, who was staging the play *Oedipus Rex* with a troupe of young actors. Jean Marais was twenty-four years old, Cocteau forty-eight. Cocteau, a friend of Marcel Proust and the dancer Sergei Diaghilev, of Raymond Radiguet and Pablo Picasso (who would have these nasty words to say about him: "I am the comet and Cocteau is the spark from my ass"), fell under the charm of the beautiful Adonis. "We saw Jean Marais, immobilized by the crisscrossed bandages, fight a mocking crowd and, despite his lack of movement, burn with such an intense anger against the uncultivated foolishness that fire shot out of him and, like a dragon guarding his treasures, he managed to vanquish the stupid laughter with only the intensity of his soul," wrote Cocteau. Marais was added to the chorus and soon obtained the principal role in *Les Chevaliers de la Table Ronde* (*The Knights of the Round Table*). "It is true that what interests me interests you and that our common soul is the theater," he wrote to Cocteau.

The Adored Angel

For twenty-five years he was Jeannot, the adored angel of the lines tenderly written by the poet. From the first love letters in 1938, addressed with deep feeling to the young Adonis, until the last notes scrawled by a frail hand to an eternal friend, there was not a page that did not convey their passion.

Friends and lovers, they were also because of their age difference, father and son. Without any illusions about the exclusivity of their relationship, Cocteau wrote in 1939 to Marais, then already in love with the handsome Paul Morion: "Think! If you meet someone of your age whom you hide from me or whom you hesitate to love for fear of making me despair, I will be upset with myself until my death. Without a doubt it's better. . . . Become brave enough so that you feel you are even more free than if you were with a father or a mother." Marais recounted his childhood among women to Cocteau, and when Cocteau began to write *Les Parents Terribles* (*The Holy Terrors*) in February 1938, he was inspired directly by the complex relationship between Marais (Jeannot) and his mother Rosalie. Naturally it was Marais who would play the role of Michel in this tragicomedy where the disorder of youth is in full swing. The twenty-three-year-old child opens up to the world in the middle of the family jumble organized around the intractable relationship between a mother and her son. Marais settled into Cocteau's home at 19, place de la Madeleine, and on the day of the premiere on November 14, the success of *Les Parents Terribles* at the Théâtre des Ambassadeurs was no longer in doubt. Marais was in seventh heaven: "This year my joy in life truly begins." Called up for military duty, he returned to Paris in June 1940 with his dog Moulouk,

Opposite: **Undated photograph of Jean Cocteau by Walter Limot.**

Page 86: **Jean Marais in *L'Éternel retour* by Jean Delannoy in 1942.**

Page 87: **Portrait of Jean Marais drawn by Jean Cocteau in 1943.**

whom he had found in a forest. During the war Cocteau and Marais remained in Paris, and their collaboration did not slow down. Whether visiting resisters and collaborators or writing an homage to Adolf Hitler's favorite sculptor, Arno Breker, Cocteau cultivated political ambiguity. As for Marais, he played Britannicus, designed the sets for *La Machine à Ecrire* (*The Infernal Machine*) and, on June 12, 1941, led his own sort of resistance by publicly thrashing Alain Laubreaux, the collaborationist theater critic of *Je Suis Partout*.

During their war, cinema and theater continued. In September 1941 Marais was admitted to the prestigious Comédie-Française, where he wanted to perform the main role in *Renaud et Armide*, written for him by Cocteau. But he left this project before it was finished to act in the movie *Juliette ou la Clé des songes*, which was eventually abandoned by its producers. In June 1943 he filmed *L'Éternel retour* by Jean Delannoy, a modern version of the myth of Tristan and Isolde with dialogue by Cocteau. He enlisted with the Second Armored Division at the end of August 1944 and, the following year, made *La Belle et La Bête* (*Beauty and the Beast*) with Cocteau, which was the director's paean to the beauty of his favorite actor, who was magnificently lit and filmed in the role of the unhappy lover. The climax of their personal and creative relationship, the movie also marked the end of their close collaboration. In 1950 Marais met the young American dancer George Reich, with whom he settled into a new home that he had built by parc de Saint-Cloud in Paris. The two would always write to each other, and Cocteau's paintings continued to feature the profile of Marais. From that point on, they made their relationship their common work. By 1951 Cocteau had already written the first biography of the actor, titled simply *Jean Marais*. Next was an album *Jean Marais chante et dit Cocteau* and Marais's theater piece *Cocteau-Marais*. Then there was the publication of *Lettres à Jean Marais* by Cocteau, and *L'Inconcevable Jean Cocteau* by Marais. Cocteau left Marais in 1963 with this shattering goodbye: "Jean, do not cry. I am going to sleep. I am going to fall asleep looking at you and die, so that from then on I can pretend to live."

Bibliography

Cocteau, Jean. *Lettres à Jean Marais*. Paris: Albin Michel, 1987.

Cocteau, Jean, and LePrince de Beaumont. *Beauty and the Beast: A Diary of a Film*. New York: Dover Publications, 1972.

Marais, Jean. *L'Inconcevable Jean Cocteau*. Monaco: Éditions du Rocher, 1993.

Steegmuller, Francis. *Cocteau: A Biography*. Boston: David R. Godine, 1992.

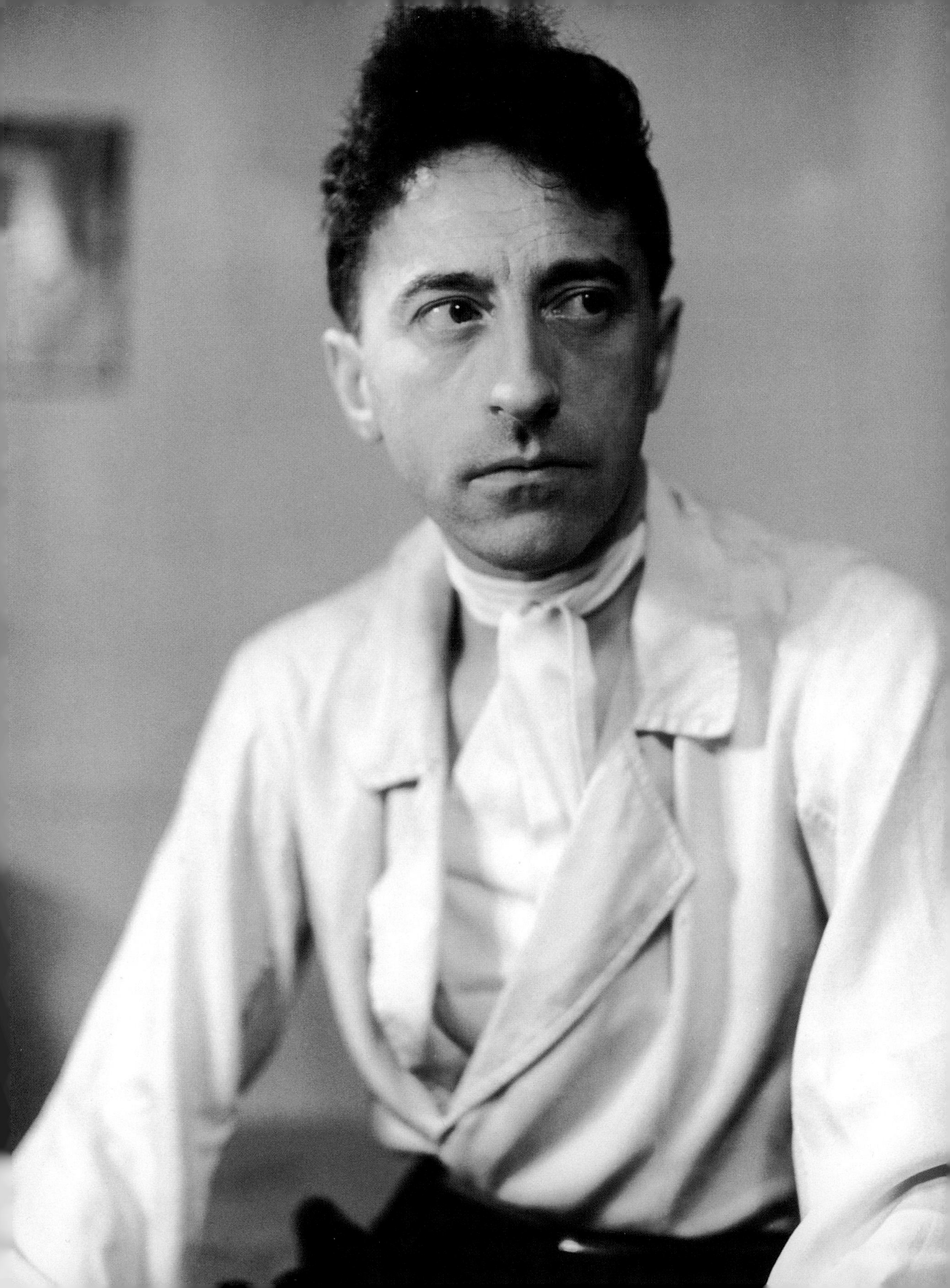

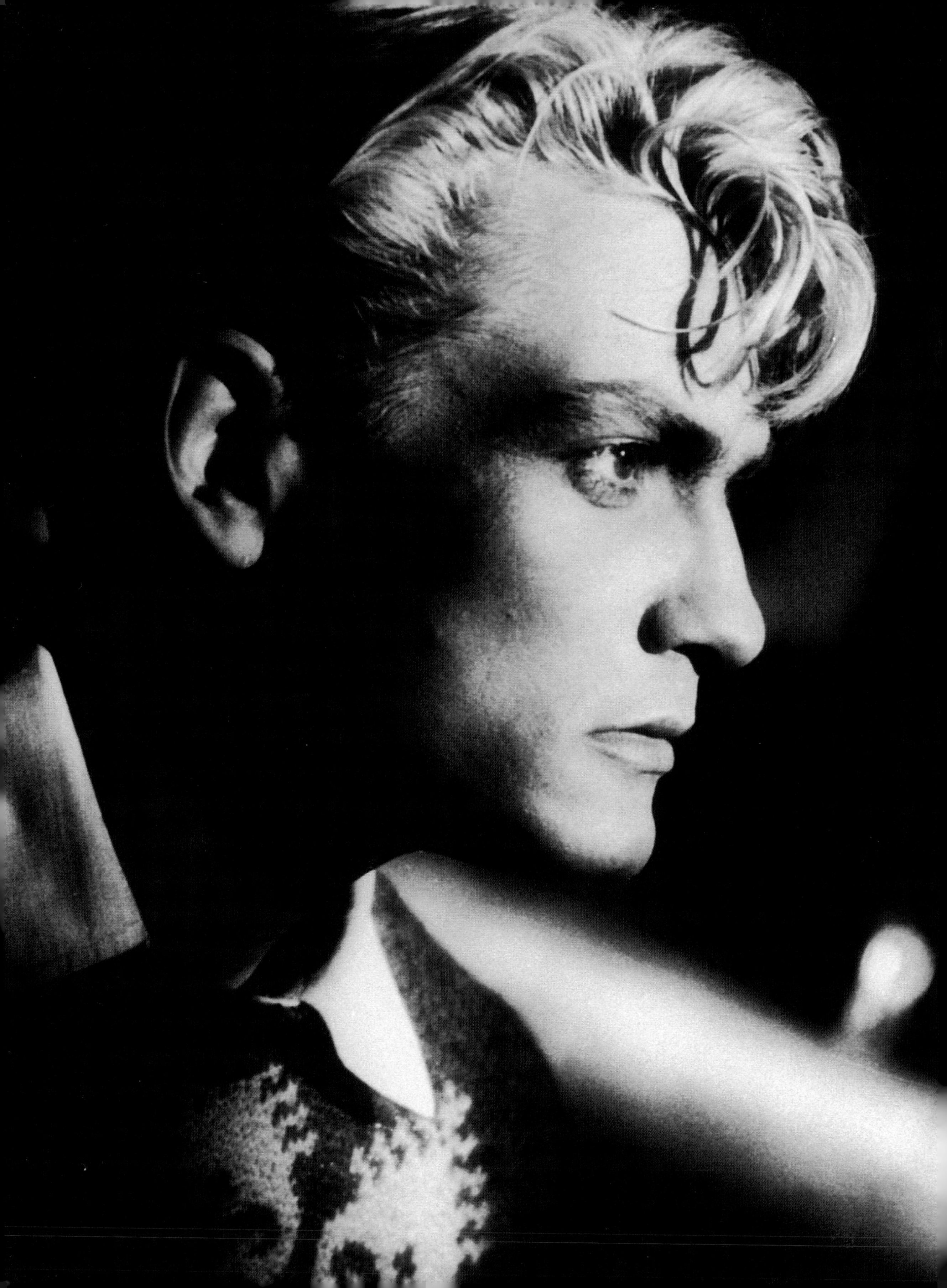

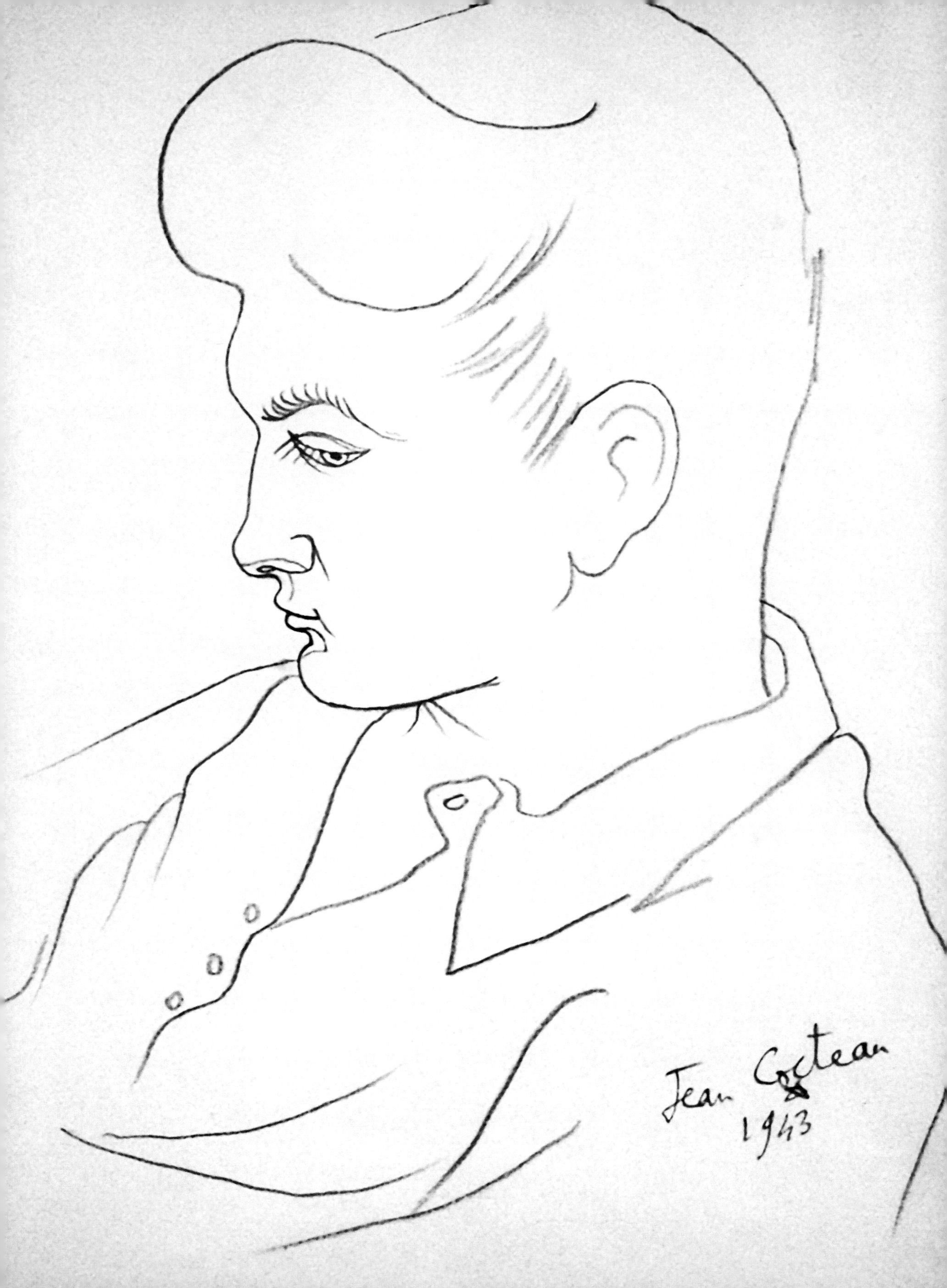
Jean Cocteau
1943

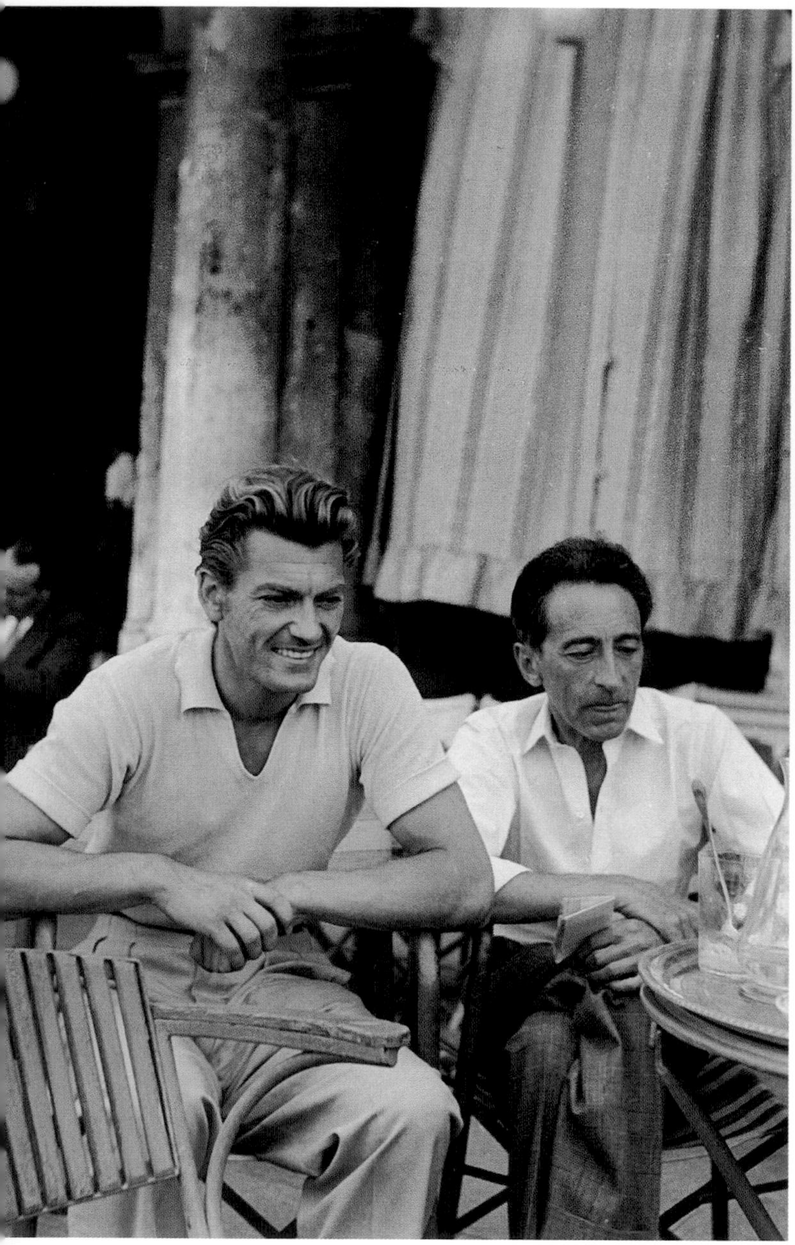

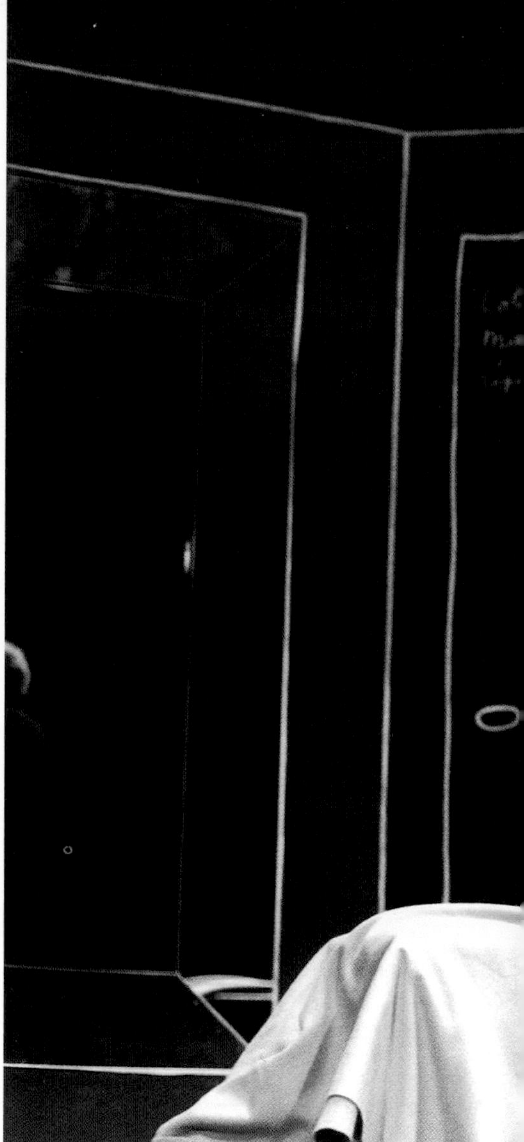

Above: **In 1983 Jean Marais performed in the Théâtre de l'Atelier production of *Cocteau-Marais* in front of Jean Cocteau–designed scenery.**
Left: **Jean Marais and Jean Cocteau on the terrace of the Café Florian in Piazza San Marco, Venice, in 1947.**

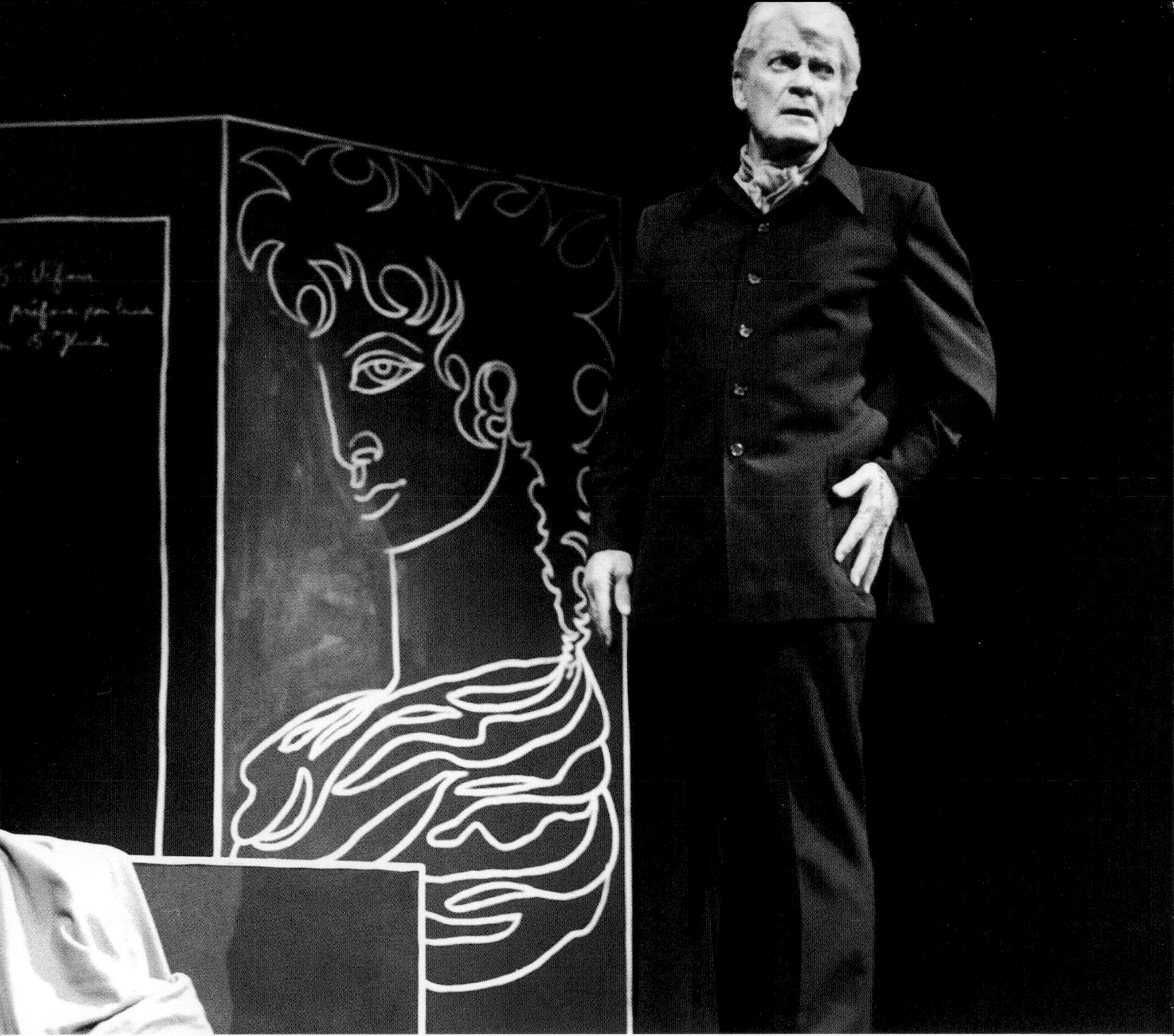

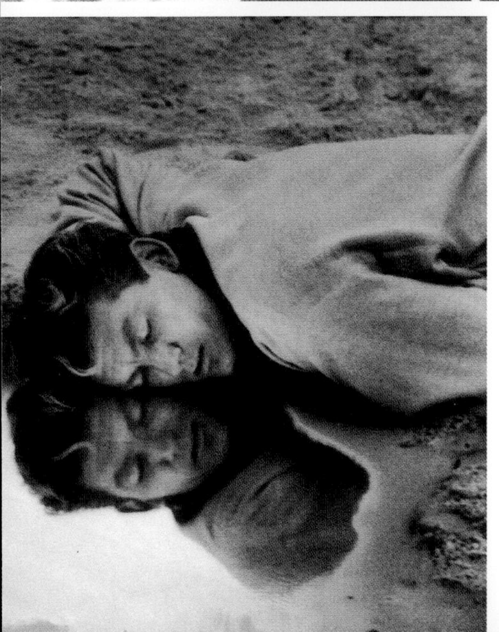

Left: **In *Orphée* (*Orpheus*), Jean Cocteau's magical cinematic poem directed by the author in 1949, Jean Marais is Orpheus, accompanied by Maria Casarès as the princess and François Périer as Heurtebise. The film was studded with audacious special effects and punctuated by realistic scenes set in 1950s Paris. Using the same fantastical approach to address the theme of the loneliness of the artist, Cocteau shot his last film, *Le Testament d'Orphée* (*Testament of Orpheus*) in 1959. Detail of photograph by Roger Corbeau.**

Catherine Hessling
Jean Renoir

Model and Light

Several months after World War I ended, a young woman from Nice turned up at the studio of the aged painter Pierre-Auguste Renoir. The artist's last model for his *Baigneuses* (*Bathers*) series, Catherine Hessling also became the wife and leading actress for Renoir's son Jean. She helped give birth to his vocation as a filmmaker before leaving him and the cinema forever.

Freeze frame. In Renoir's atelier near Nice, a young girl strikes a pose. She is sixteen, a redhead, plump, and very jolly. Her presence helped soothe the grief and the sadness of the painter who had lost his wife and suffered from growing paralysis. World War I had just ended and, several months before her death, Madame Renoir, in search of new models for her husband's series *Les Baigneuses* (*The Bathers*), found an ideal young woman in the art academy in Nice. "Her skin 'took the light' better than any model that Renoir had ever had in his life," recalled the director Jean Renoir, son of the painter. "She sang, slightly off key, the popular songs of the day; told stories about her girlfriends; was gay; and cast over my father the revivifying spell of her joyous youth. Along with the roses, which grew almost wild at Les Collettes, and the great olive trees with their silvery reflections, Andrée was one of the vital elements which helped Renoir to interpret on his canvas the tremendous cry of love he uttered at the end of his life."

She arrived each morning from Nice by streetcar and rushed into the studio where the painter awaited her. While preparing herself for the sitting, she would loudly sing popular songs, which delighted the old man. The artist passed away soon after in 1919, and his sons offered his final masterpiece *Les Baigneuses* (*The Bathers*) to the Louvre in Paris. The gift was refused the first time around, then finally accepted because of the interest manifested by American collectors. If the fate of the works by the master still retained several surprises, that of the two Renoir boys had been sealed a long time before: Claude would go into painting and Jean into ceramics.

Last Gift

Had Pierre-Auguste Renoir foreseen that his model, Dédée—"the last present given to my father by my mother before her death," according to Jean Renoir's charming expression—would be the last gift that he would give the son? It is impossible to say. "I met the future Catherine Hessling during a leave that I spent at Les Collettes, the property near Nice owned by my parents. Her name in those days was Dédée," recalled Jean Renoir. More exactly, it was Andrée Heuschling. Jean and Dédée married on January 24, 1920, and lived in Les Collettes, where their first child Alain was born. They both worked in ceramics and, when they could, they went to the cinema to see American films. Dédée adopted the walk, the manners, and the clothes of Gloria Swanson or Mary Pickford. Passersby would stop her in the street to ask in what American film they had seen her. "I must insist on the fact that I set foot in the world of cinema only in order to make my wife a star, intending, once this was done, to return to my pottery studio," confirmed Renoir in *My Life and My Films*. The inheritance left to him by his father allowed him to consider getting into film without too many worries. But after having decided to finance his wife's debut in the movies, he still had to find a subject. The absurdity of the stories that their friend Pierre Lestringuez proposed to them pushed Renoir into writing a small screenplay entitled *Catherine*, which was directed by Albert Dieudonné. The storyline was troubling—that of an innocent young girl pursued by an evil man—and the final film would be just as bad. But Renoir had caught the cinema bug and Dédée Heuschling became Catherine Hessling.

How the Cinema Came to Renoir

While relying on his actress's purposely jerky onscreen movements, Jean Renoir experimented over several years with a cinematic look that he wanted to be radically new, and he always involved his wife in his research. "*La Fille de l'eau* was born in 1924 of the strange juxtaposition of Catherine Hessling and the forest of Fountainbleau," he wrote. With this film, he could finally give free rein to his aesthetic experiments. Because the cinema was in black and white, he made up Catherine in those same colors and accentuated her natural penchant to behave like a puppet. To avoid all realism, he went so far as to forbid her to cry in one scene, preferring to replace the real tears with fake ones that were more obvious and stylized. Renoir dreamed of remaking cinematography, of playing with violent contrasts, and of finding "magical elements in the most commonplace circumstances and settings." Passionate about lizards and crocodiles, he spent hours in realizing a childhood fantasy of shooting a lizard in close-up so that the image filled the screen. *La Fille*'s plot was only a pretext for filming Catherine Hessling's beauty and for rendering palpable Renoir's dreams: Catherine riding on a horse galloping through the clouds, then later falling from the sky. The filmmaker

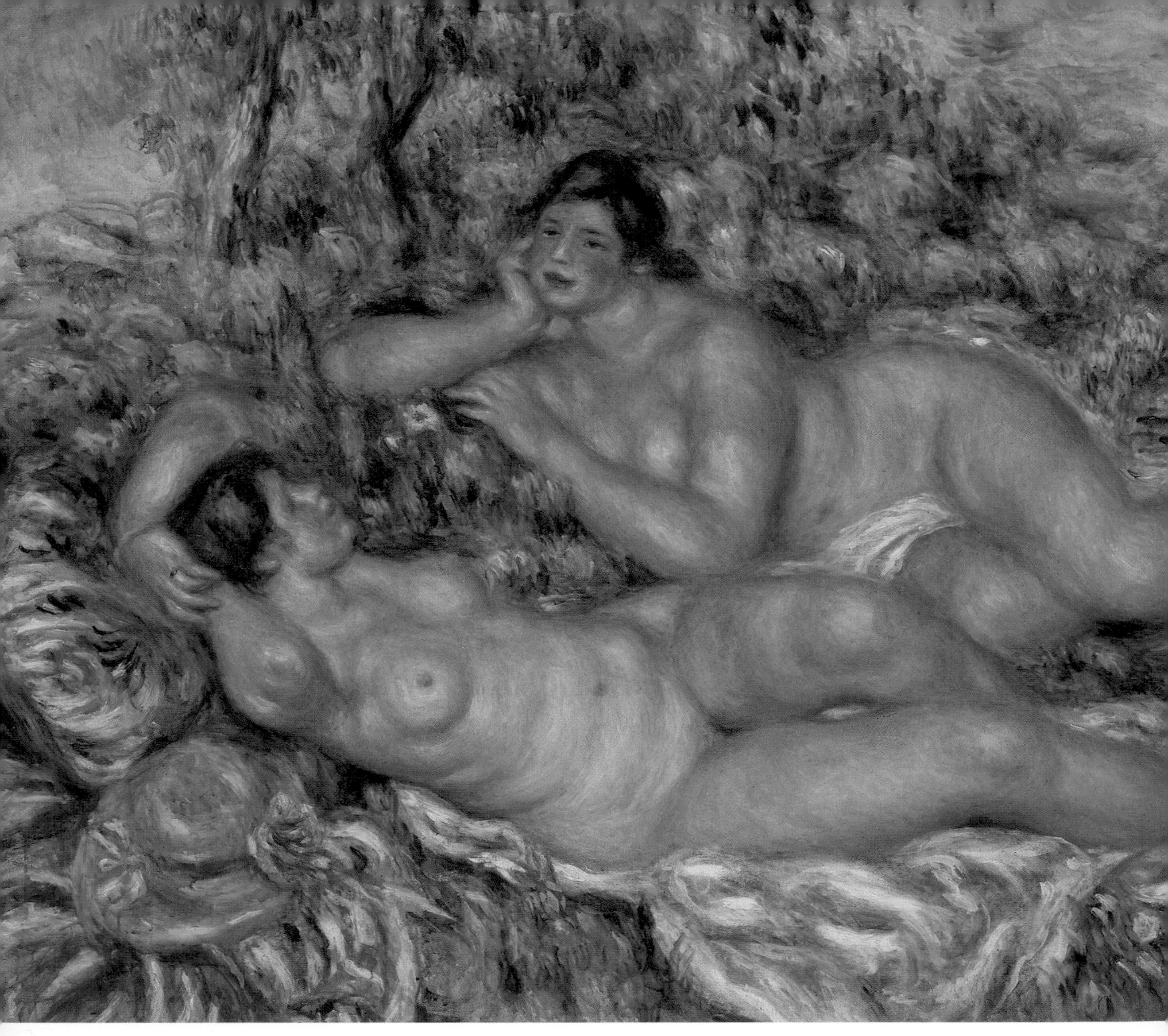

Above: **Pierre-Auguste Renoir, *Les Baigneuses* (*The Bathers*; 1918–19). Renoir considered this pictorial testament his culminating work. The painting shows the artist's pleasure in depicting Andrée Heuschling, the figure of the superb redhead at the bottom of the canvas whom Jean Renoir married and renamed Catherine Hessling. Given to the government of France by the painter's sons in 1923, this study of female nudes set outdoors echoes the theme of *Les Grandes Baigneuses* (*The Bathers*) of 1884–87 painted by Renoir thirty years earlier.**

Opposite: **Pierre-Auguste Renoir and Jean Renoir photographed in 1916 by Pierre Bonnard.**

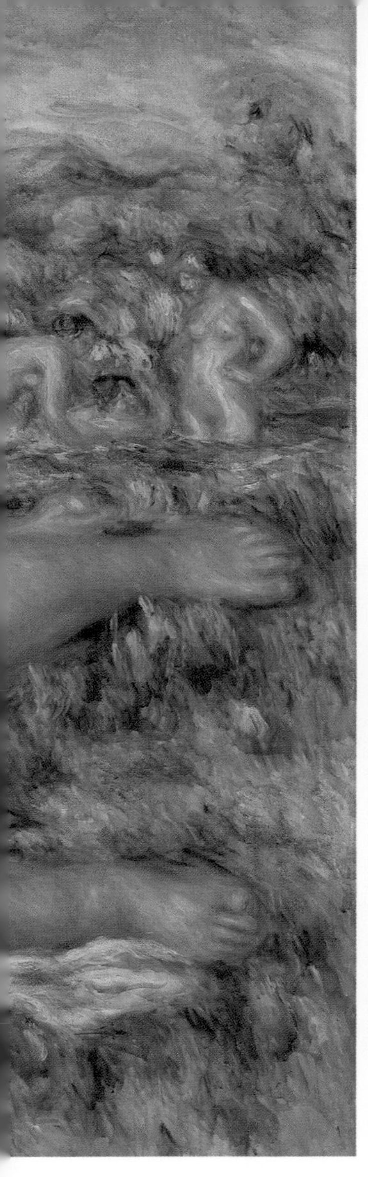

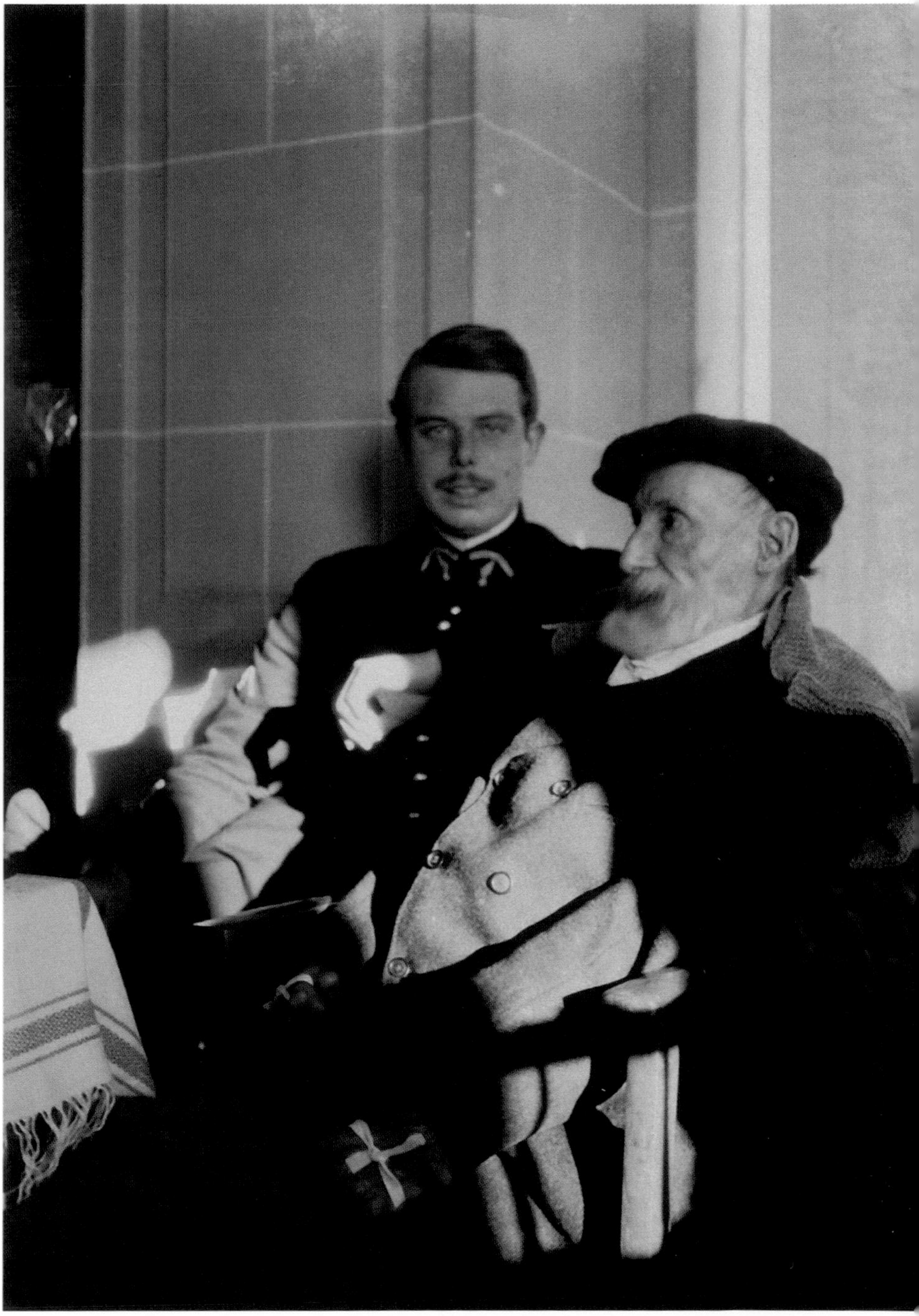

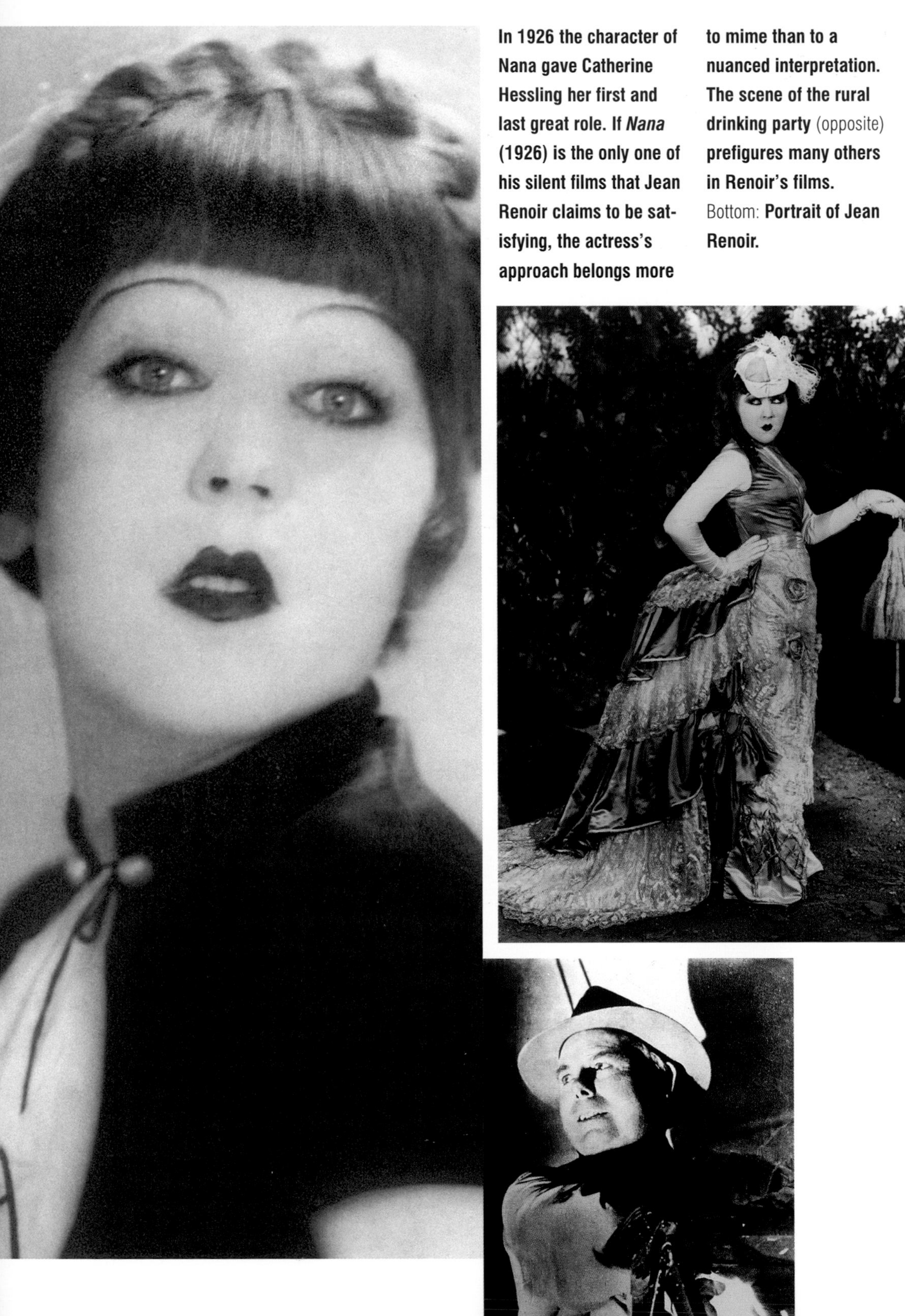

In 1926 the character of Nana gave Catherine Hessling her first and last great role. If *Nana* (1926) is the only one of his silent films that Jean Renoir claims to be satisfying, the actress's approach belongs more to mime than to a nuanced interpretation. The scene of the rural drinking party (opposite) prefigures many others in Renoir's films.
Bottom: Portrait of Jean Renoir.

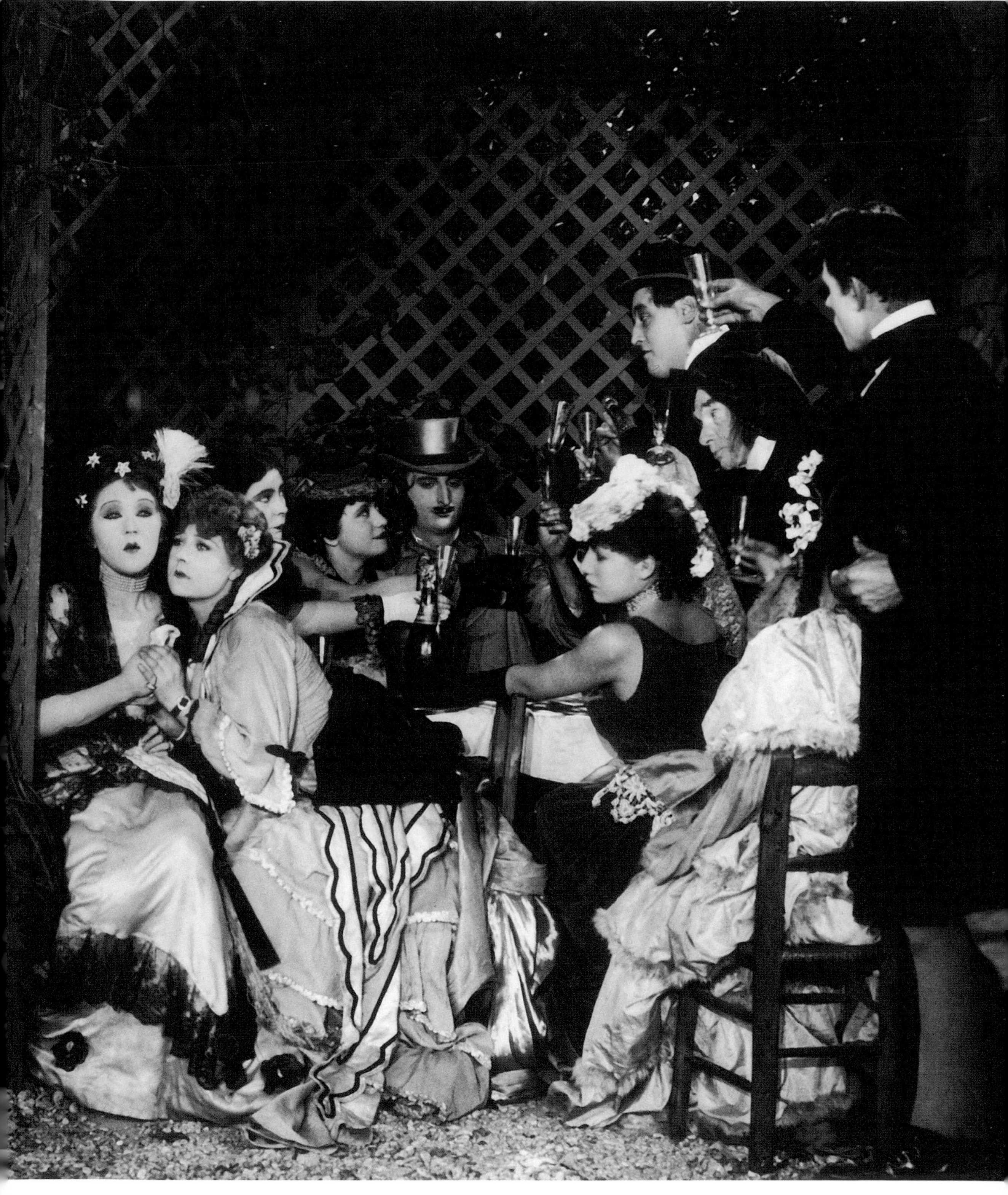

notes modestly in his memoirs that these two shots were "particularly successful." The reaction of the exhibitors, however, was not surprising. The film could not be booked into a cinema and Renoir, in desperation, decided to return to his pottery.

Renoir then threw himself into the adventure of *Nana* (1926), an adaptation of the powerful and popular Émile Zola novel that retraced the story of a woman who needed to have everything forsaken for her. The subject matter echoed the filmmaker's personal situation. In order to offer Dédée the great film of her dreams, Renoir sold almost all of the canvases he had inherited from his father, thereby accomplishing an act he judged sacrilegious in retrospect: the son sold the work of the father in order to create his own work, and thereby doubly disobeyed his father's advice to be a simple potter. To launch *Nana*, nothing was spared. There was enormous publicity, posters all over Paris, and a preview held with great pomp in the main hall of the Moulin Rouge. *Nana* was a flop, but Renoir was certain of his calling from then on. At his home in Marlotte, he could only contemplate the empty frames that had held his father's paintings, all sold to make the film, and he dwelled on his shame in having "discontinued the conversation" with his dead father. Renoir meanwhile had fallen in love with jazz and, to distract himself, made an intimate little film called *Charleston* (1927), a film closer to a "home movie" than to professional cinema, in which Catherine Hessling plays a dancer with a dress slit down to her waist, black gloves, and flowers strewn through her long locks. Renoir was on the brink of renouncing cinema entirely, but when an excerpt of the horse sequence from *La Fille de l'eau* was shown at the new avant-garde cinema in Paris, the Théâtre du Vieux-Colombier, it was enough for him to change his mind. It was acclaimed by the audience and he took hope. A new era was beginning.

Thanks to Her and Without Her

Now lacking sufficient funds, Renoir could no longer be his own producer. After experimenting with and questioning what cinema should be, now came the time to make some money. Renoir's first compromise was *Marquitta* (1927), a commercial banality, soon followed by *La Chienne* (1931), his first successful film—and the first made without Catherine. Was it possible to make a movie without betrayal? Renoir asked himself that question for some time. But by deciding to give up his leading actress, he had already found his answer. A separation and a divorce followed.

From then on the filmmaker could express his love of actors differently and claim responsibility for his prestigious achievements. "I tried to follow the teachings of Shakespeare and Molière, both of whom wrote for actors." He added, "The actor is a being who troubles me and worries me." Catherine Hessling made only a few more brief appearances in talkies, the last of which was *Crime and Punishment*, directed by Pierre Chenal in 1935. She died in 1979, the same year as Jean Renoir.

Bibliography

Durgnat, Raymond. *Jean Renoir*. Berkeley: University of California Press, 1974.

Renoir, Jean. *Renoir, My Father*. New York: New York Review Books, 2001.

———. *My Life and My Films*. New York: Atheneum Publishers, 1974.

Gala
Paul Éluard
Salvador Dalí

The Surrealist Gradiva

Helena Dimitrieva Diakonova is better known simply as Gala, a nickname invented by her first husband, the poet Paul Éluard, and which her second husband blended into his own at the bottom of some of his paintings: Gala Salvador Dalí. This Russian woman, who was born in Kazan around 1895 and died in 1982 in the house in Port Lligat, which she made the center of the Dalí myth, remained an enigma. This enigma also had another nickname: Gradiva, the heroine of the Pompeian fantasy created by nineteenth-century writer Wilhelm Jensen, whose novel tells the story of an archaeologist who falls in love with the image of a woman on a Roman bas-relief.

Gradiva, "a complete female figure in the act of walking; she was still young, but no longer in childhood and, on the other hand, apparently not a woman, but a Roman virgin about in her twentieth year." This is the description of the heroine in Jensen's eponymous tale, and this is how Gala must have appeared to the young poet still known as Paul-Eugène Grindel.

The scene moves in 1912 to a sanatorium in Clavadel, Switzerland. A young Russian woman and a seventeen-year-old future poet are receiving treatment. Both come from bourgeois backgrounds: Gala is the adopted daughter of a rich, cultured Muscovite; Paul-Eugène is the son of a wealthy merchant. For two years they find themselves attending the same readings and cultural events. Then Gala returns to her country and announces that she is going to marry a French poet, while the well-bred son writes to his father: "I am taking a wife whose virtues of simplicity, purity, gentleness, and love are not to be displayed in front of you who know them."

Simple, pure, gentle—and a little dominating—is how Gala appears in the 1913 photograph taken in Clavadel. She balances herself on the arm of a sofa while the poet closes his eyes to the sun.

For a long while I had a useless face,
But now
I have a face for being loved
I have a face for being happy.

Paul-Eugène Grindel is happy. It is now 1917 and for the first time he writes a collection of poetry, *Le Devoir et l'Inquiétude*, under the name of his maternal grandmother, Éluard. But it is Grindel the soldier who requests a three-day leave from the military authorities to marry Gala, back from Russia. A year later their daughter Cécile is born, and in 1919 demobilization comes. Life could now begin.

Paul Éluard, who worked in his father's flourishing business, entered into his career as a poet when the crazy Dada years began in Paris. The movement, launched from Zurich during the war by Tristan Tzara, had spread to and won over Germany and, under the aegis of the painter Francis Picabia and the young poet André Breton, Dada arrived in France. "Dada stirs up everything," said the young people. Since the world of yesterday had only led to the absurdity of the war, the thinking went, it was necessary to destroy all art from days gone by.

Éluard managed to integrate himself into the movement quickly, and his poems were published in the third issue of the Dadaist revue *Littérature*, an innocent-sounding name that masked the subversion of its contents. Gala participated in this artistic adventure as well and performed in *Le Poids public*, a stage piece created by Éluard for the tumultuous Dada festival. The couple changed subtly as the young pair became two figures taken over by Parisian intellectual life. Dada liberated Éluard's poetry and made it more audacious, and Gala was always the inspiration for it. It was Gala to whom he dedicated *Le Grand Jour*. But, in the middle of the big Dada festival, their mutual affair with Max Ernst began.

An exhibition of collages by Max Ernst opened at the Sans Pareil, a Dadaist bookstore, in May 1921. The German painter was far from an unknown, since his Dadaist provocations had earned him several run-ins with his country's government. Éluard, who had begun to collect artworks, was enthusiastic about Ernst's collages and decided to pay him a visit in Germany. October 1921 marked what Éluard ironically called the reunion—"Max and I were together in Verdun. We did well together." There was an immediate understanding between the young French couple and the German painter. Ernst and Éluard considered themselves like brothers and Gala was their common sister. In the year that followed they went on to produce three works together, including *Répétitions*, which opens with a poem entitled "Max Ernst":

In the corner agile incest
Hovers over the virginity of a little dress.

Incest and virginity were clearly illusions to the affair conducted by Ernst and Gala. According to Éluard, Gala the *Gravida revivida* brought back to life the painter who described himself as having "died in 1914."

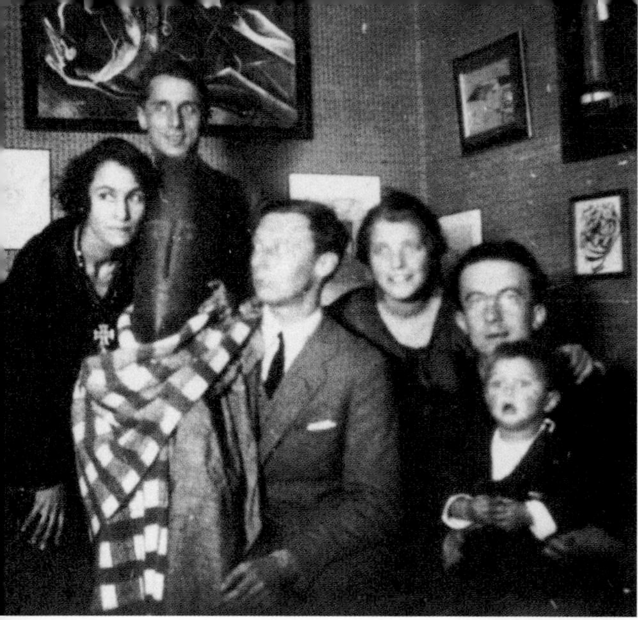

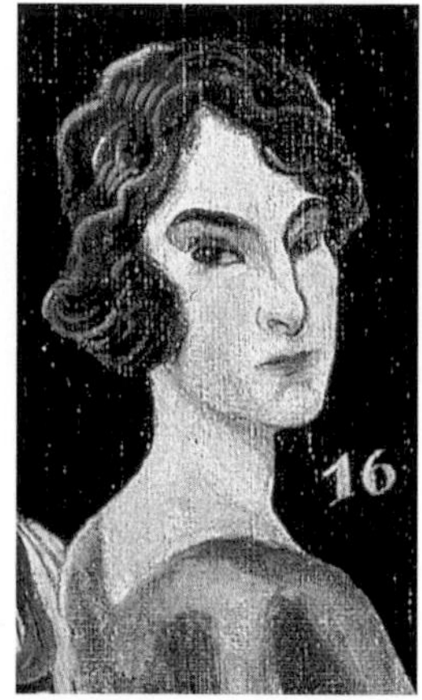

Opposite, bottom: **Max Ernst, *Au rendez-vous des amis* (*The Meeting of Friends*; 1922). Gala (#16) is at far right. The only woman in the bosom of the future Surrealist group, Gala was already the mysterious Gradiva who always seems to distance herself.**

Above and right: **At Max Ernst's home during his first encounter with the Éluards in 1921. In the photo above from left to right, Gala, Max Ernst, the Dadaist Johannes Baargeld from Cologne, Max's wife, Lou, and Paul Éluard holding Jimmy Ernst on his knees.**

Opposite, top: **Gala, Paul Éluard, Salvador Dalí, Valentine Hugo (the poet's favorite illustrator), and René Crevel posing in a fake cart at the Montmartre Fair in Paris in 1931.**

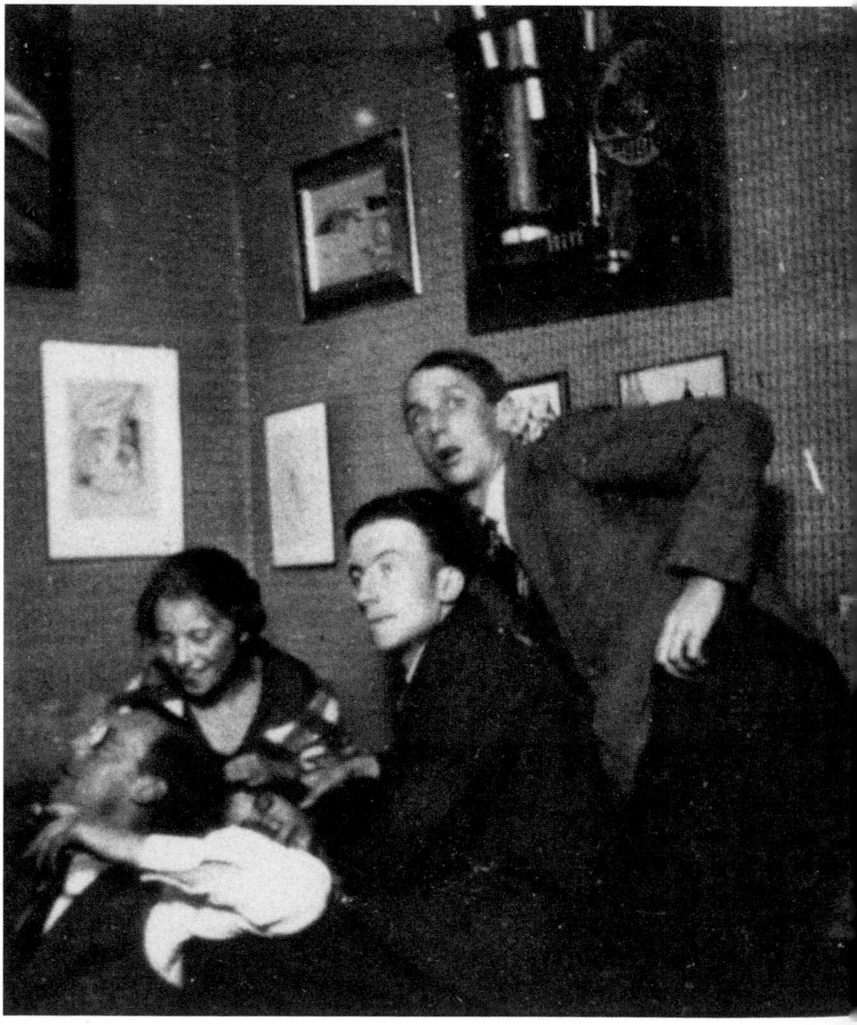

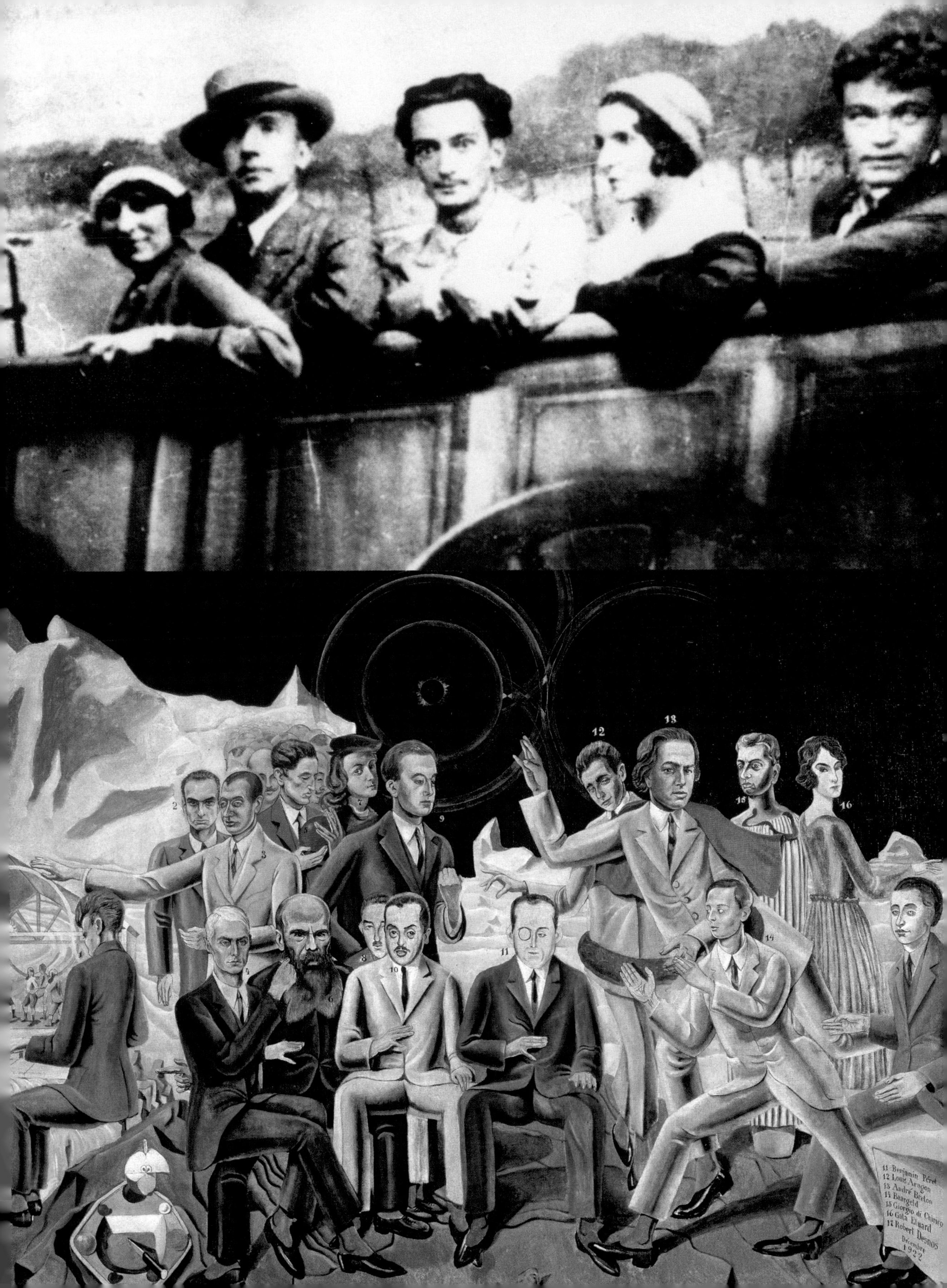
11 Benjamin Péret
12 Louis Aragon
13 André Breton
14 Baargeld
15 Giorgio di Chirico
16 Gala Eluard
17 Robert Desnos
Décembre
1922

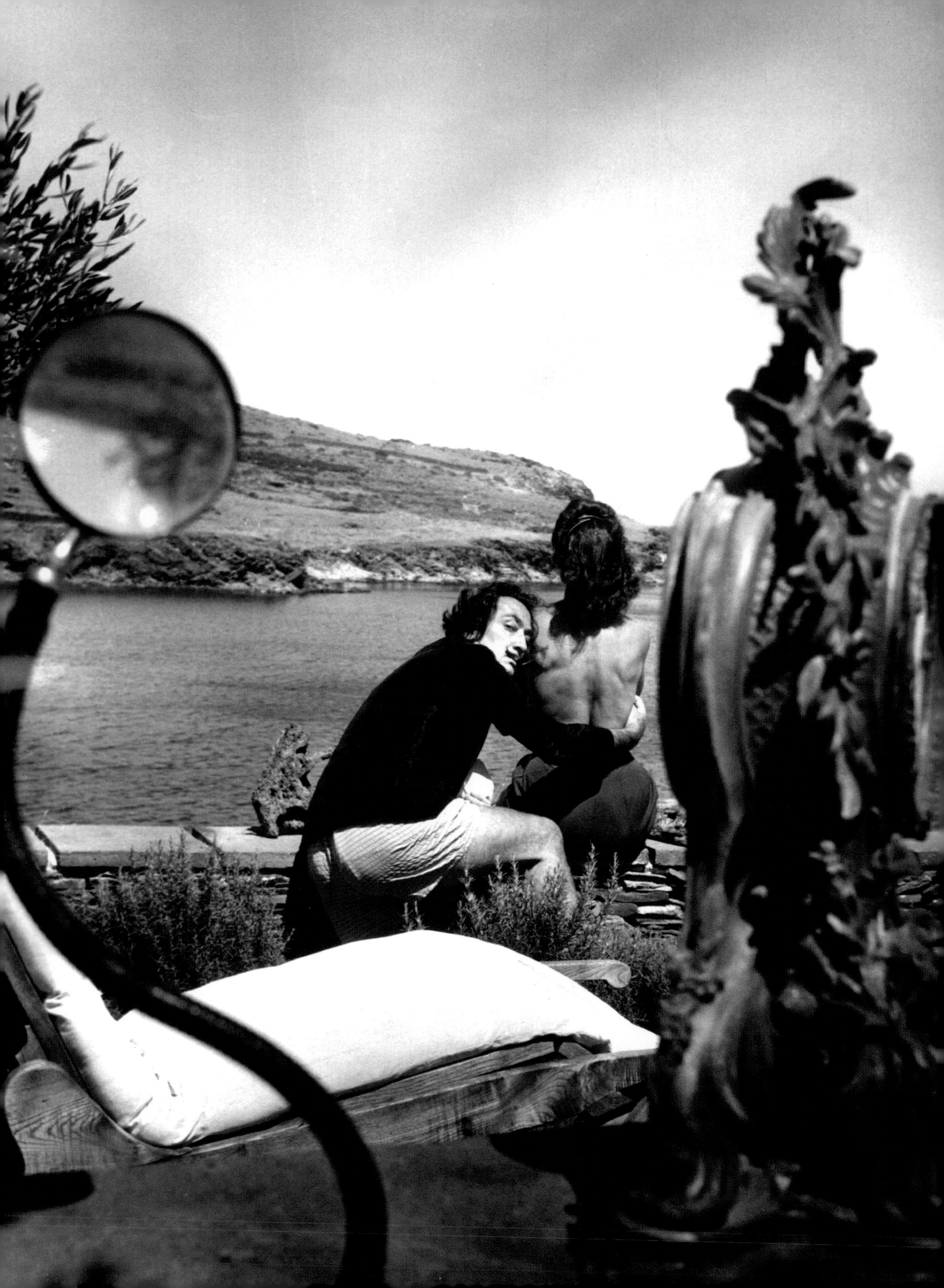

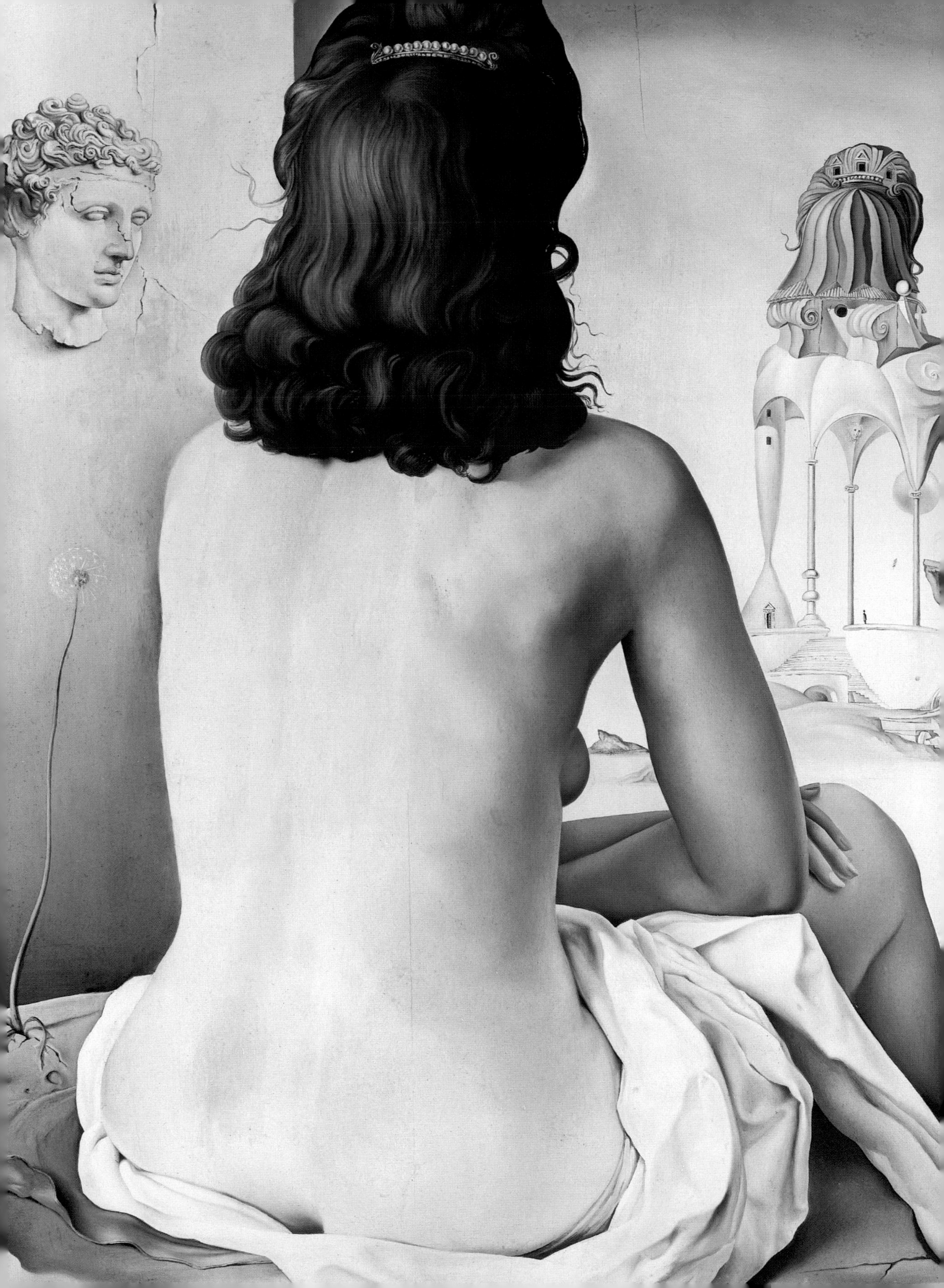

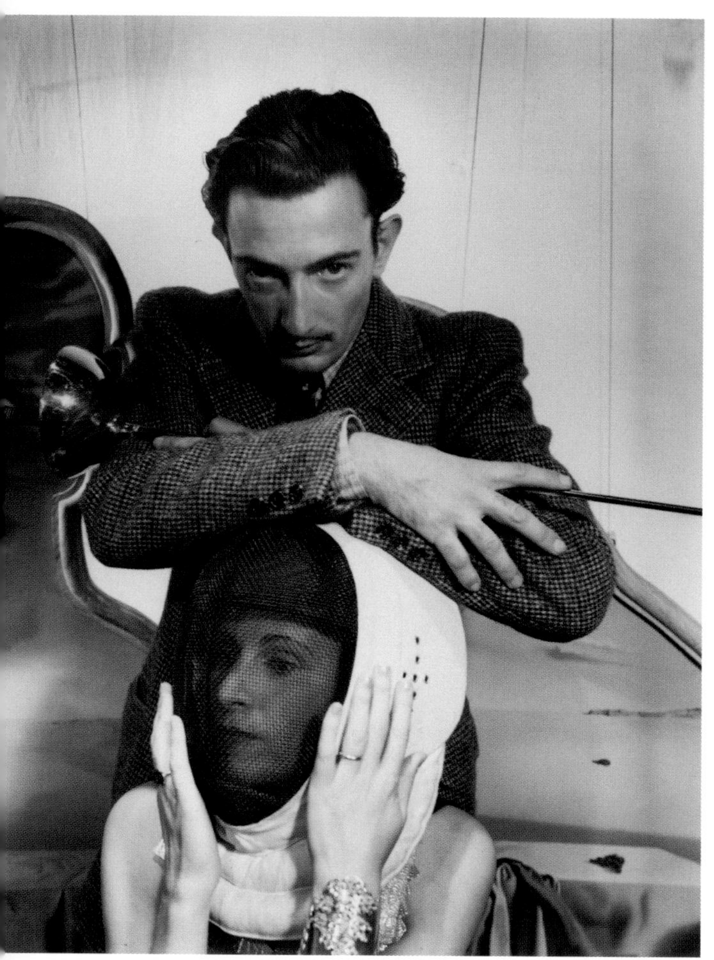

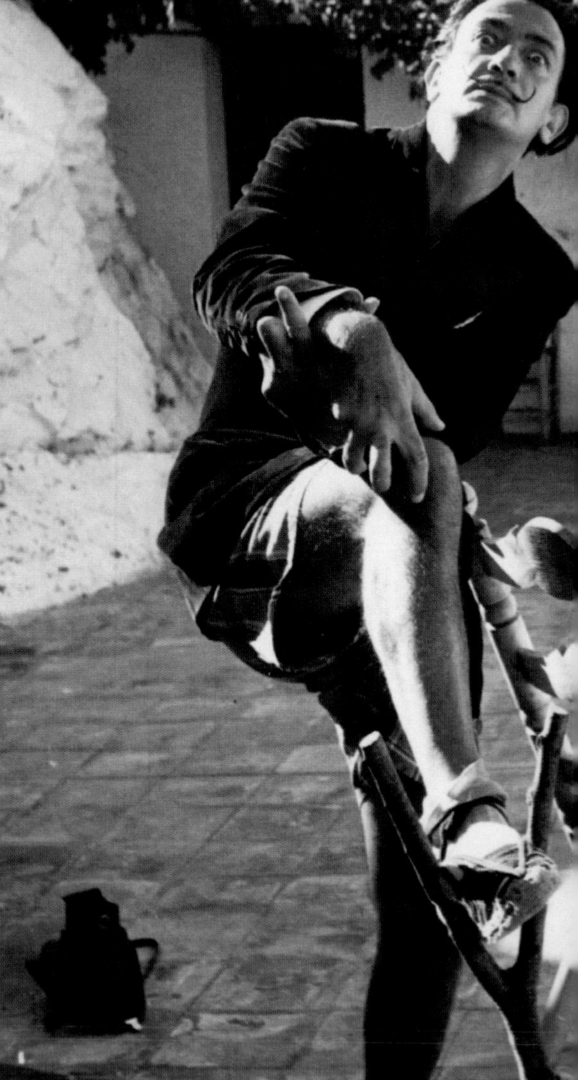

Above: **Salvador Dalí and Gala, her face covered by a fencing mask, sitting in front of *Un couple aux têtes pleine de nuages* (*Couple with Their Heads Full of Clouds*), the diptych painted by Dalí in 1936. Photograph taken by Cecil Beaton in the 1940s.**

Top and right: **Salvador Dalí and Gala on the terrace of their Port Lligat home in November 1951. After returning from their long stay in the United States, the couple began to construct the Dalí myth.**

Right: **1970: Salvador Dalí painting Gala, who had become his "Immaculate Intuition."** Below: **A detail from Salvador Dalí's *Le rêve de Christophe Colomb* (*The Discovery of America by Christopher Columbus*; 1959) with Gala as the "Madonna of Port Lligat."**

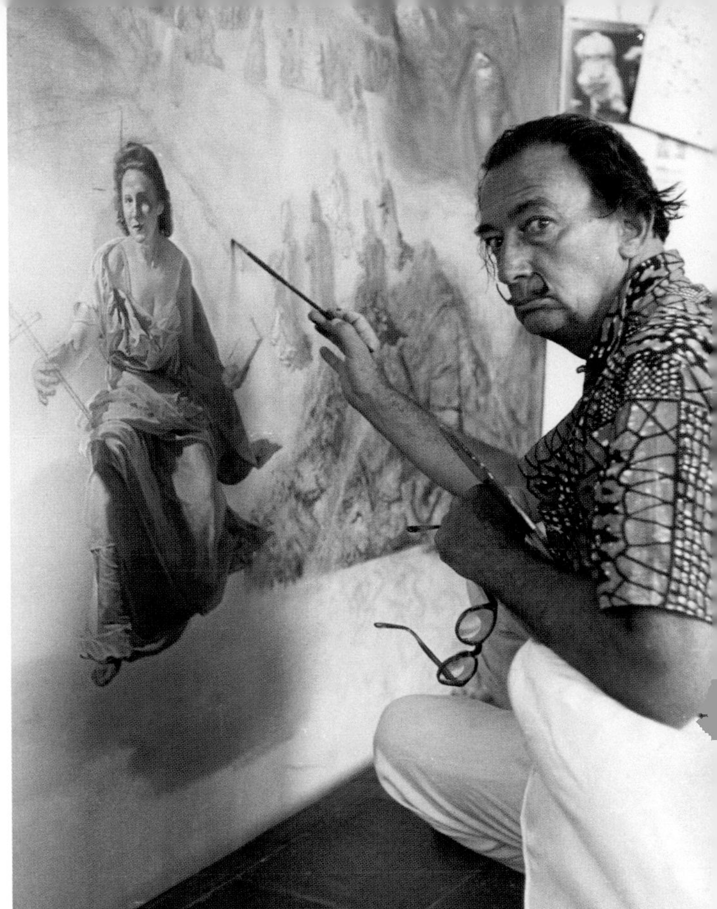

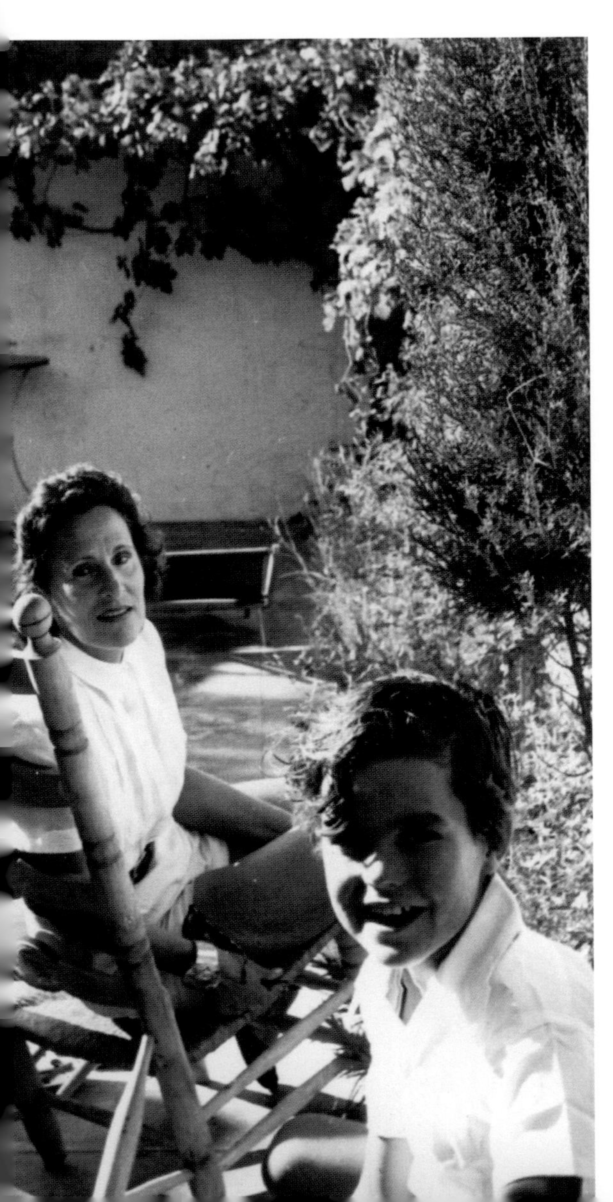

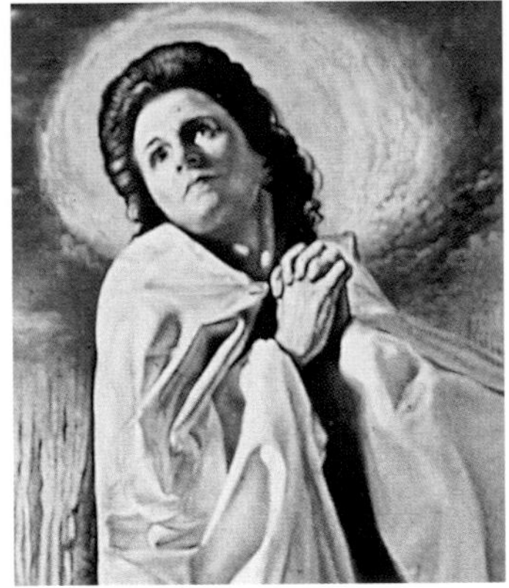

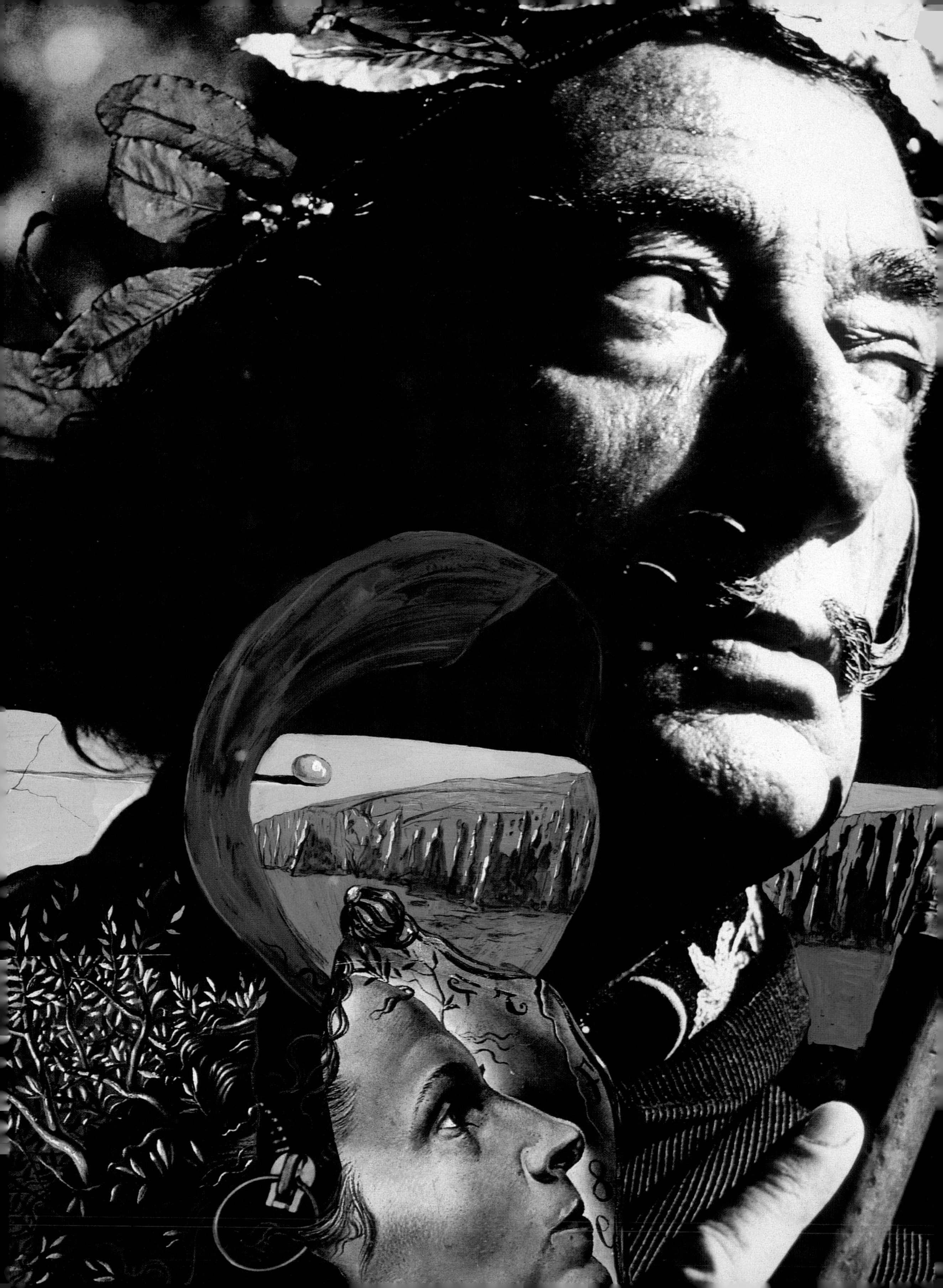

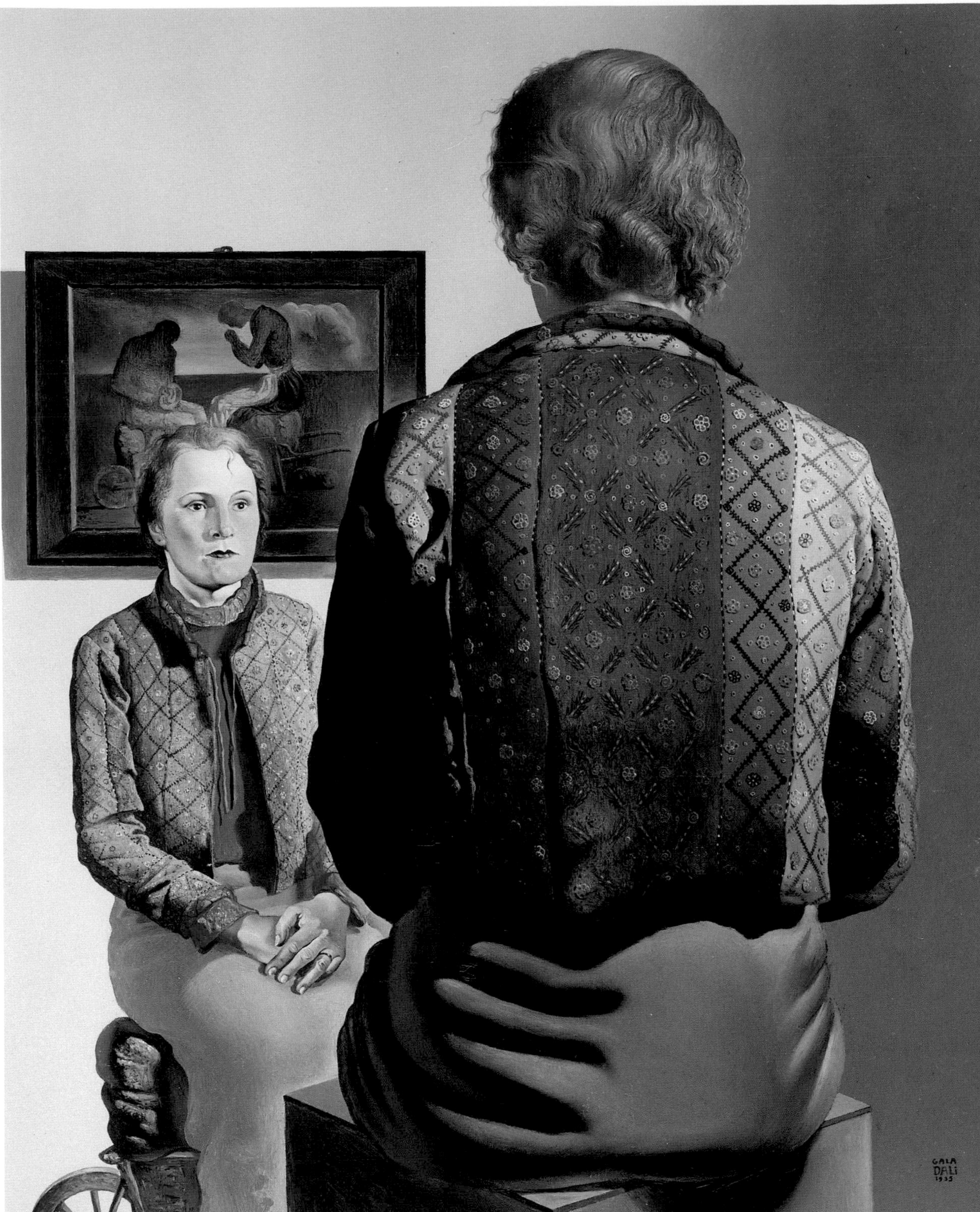
GALA
DALi
1935

Page 106: **Gala and Salvador Dalí on January 8, 1955. This landscape and Gala's back were part of the recurring obsessions in the life and art of Dalí.**

Page 107: **Salvador Dalí, *Ma femme nue regardant son propre corps devenir marches, trois vertèbres d'une colonne, ciel et architecture* (*My Wife Naked, Looking at Her Own Body Transformed into Steps, Three Vertebrae of a Column, Sky, and Architecture*; 1945). This is one of the numerous visions of Dalí's paranoiac-critical method inspired by Gala.**

After Éluard succeeded in smuggling Max Ernst into France by lending him his own passport, all three lived together in the house that Paul's father had bought for him in Eaubonne near Paris. From September 1922 to March 1924, the romance continued between the two artists and their muse, who inspired Ernst to say: "Men will never know anything." And then one morning, Éluard was gone.

"My dear father, I've had enough. I'm leaving on a trip." Like the archaeologist in *Gradiva,* "He had to recognize that he was running without end and without reason." For six months he sailed from the Antilles to Oceania, from Java to Ceylon. In August Gala joined him in Saigon where they met up with Ernst. The painter continued his voyage and the couple returned to Marseilles at the end of September. We have never known the reasons that prompted Éluard to want, like Rimbaud, "to disappear forever." But Gala, if not Éluard, must have come out of it transformed. She had been the inspiration for his first poems, the muse of two great Surrealist artists, and, by giving her power of attorney over his extensive collection of contemporary art, Éluard allowed Gala to emerge as a formidable businesswoman. The correspondence they exchanged between 1924 and 1948 bears witness to their descriptions of unbridled sensuality, and at the same time to the rise of a Gala domineering in love, in business, and even in poetry.

She was for Éluard the "little shadow that overtook him, an enchanted shadow." But she was only a shadow, and Gala could not content herself with that role. Gradiva was the one who battled for love, but she was also *Gradiva revivida*, the one who gave life. Gala would go on to fulfill this role with Salvador Dalí.

Gala's Cosmopolitan Charm

According to the Surrealist Philippe Soupault, Salvador Dalí, the future genius, had been "an insignificant enough young man with a pale face, an upper lip shadowed by a very small moustache . . . the profile of a mouse," and he had the irresistible propensity to be overcome by wild laughter that prevented him from speaking. Everything changed one evening in March 1929, beginning with his meeting with Éluard at the Tabarin ball in Paris. Realizing immediately that this "legendary character"—who was also a collector—would be a great catch, Dalí invited him to Spain. Paul, Gala, and their daughter Cécile went to Cadaqués in August, where they found other Surrealists like René Magritte and Luis

Buñuel, for whom Dalí had just written the screenplay for the 1928 *Un Chien andalou*.

The meeting of Dalí and Gala, this couple who for half a century would dazzle and excite the whole world, was improbable. "I was actually snubbed by Gala's cosmopolitan charm," wrote the painter in *The Secret Life of Salvador Dalí.* "I had in the reach of my hand, in the reach of my mouth, a Parisian, the wife of the celebrated Surrealist poet." He identified in her his Gradiva—his "Galotchka revivida whom I recognized from her naked back," he wrote. And, like Jensen's hero, he had the feeling that his eyes "sought to discover the means of entering into her spirit in order to explore it like a drill in shining steel." Dalí decided to seduce Gala. He perfumed himself with goat dung, stuck a geranium behind his ear, and flayed his armpits—scattering blood all over—"out of coquetry." And Gala "knew [that he was not] the frivolous Argentine tango dancer he appeared to be but a brilliant little boy lost in the world." It seemed that Gala, accustomed to Surrealist provocations, had been intrigued by his painting *Le Jeu lugubre* (*The Lugubrious Game*; 1929), which blended castration fantasies with the presence of excrement. She summoned him to explain his apparent coprophilia. They walked for a long time along the rocks of Cap Creus, and Gala discovered a new power in herself: she would no longer be the poet's "little enchanted shadow," but the one who would reveal a genius to himself. At the end of the month Éluard departed with his daughter, leaving Dalí and Gala alone.

"Gala liberated me from my madness"

Gala "taught me the reality of everything. She taught me how to dress, how to go down a stairway without falling thirty-six times, how not to be continually losing the money we had," wrote Dalí in his autobiography *The Secret Life*. In *Diary of a Genius*, he recognized that "Gala will always be right with regard to my future." And with good reason: that future was totally fashioned by Gala.

Gala intervened directly in his painting; she bought him his brushes and his colors and got into the habit of visiting his studio each morning to critique the painting made the day before. She created an association of collectors that included the writer Julien Green, Prince Faucigny-Lucinge, the Vicomte de Noailles, and the woman who would become their patron in the United States, Caresse Crosby. Gala constructed the Dalí legend piece by piece. At the center of the myth was Port Lligat. Thanks to the help

Page 110: ***Autoportrait avec Gala* (*Self-Portrait with Gala*), a photocollage by Salvador Dalí. Crowned by a laurel wreath, the painter presents himself behind his unfinished *Commencement automatique d'un portrait de Gala* (*Automatic Beginning of a Portrait of Gala*; 1932) and one of his soft watches.**

Page 111: **Salvador Dalí, *Portrait de Gala ou l'Angélus de Gala* (*Portrait of Gala or the Angelus of Gala*; 1935). In 1963 Dalí dedicated an entire piece of work to the painting by Jean-François Millet, the center of numerous obsessions in which Gala played a role.**

of the Vicomte de Noailles, the Dalís were able to buy homes of nearby fishermen where the Surrealists, as well as French high society, could meet each other to commune.

The couple's first trip to the United States came in 1934. Dalí seduced the Americans by explaining to them that "the sole difference between me and a madman is the fact that I'm not mad," while Gala busied herself with contracts and sales. "She does nothing, she relaxes, she poses . . . she creates silences." Such were Gala's magic secrets. On returning to Paris, she increased Dalí's notoriety by arranging for him to collaborate with the two great couturiers of the era between the wars, Coco Chanel and Elsa Schiaparelli, for whom he created a shoe hat. André Breton nicknamed him with the anagram Avidadollars (I need dollars). Gala was becoming more than ever the female cash register that Dalí would literally represent in some of his paintings and sculptures, like the one of the Venus de Milo with her body covered in drawers. But even more than the money, Dalí was excited by the celebrity, particularly the kind you could achieve in Hollywood through the movies. During their long stay in the United States during World War II, Dalí attempted to collaborate on a film with Walt Disney and succeeded in convincing Alfred Hitchcock to entrust him with the set decoration for *Spellbound* (1945).

A *Continuum* with Four Buttocks

The organizer of his life, Gala was equally omnipresent in his work, which was completely focused on his various obsessions, including painting women's backs. Here too Gala was like Jensen's Gradiva: "Suddenly an unexpected impression went through him like a shock . . . below in the street, turning her back on him walked a woman." This is how Dalí painted Gala in *La Harpe invisible* (*The Invisible Harp*; 1934), slender and average, walking away among the cabanas of Port Lligat. Is the Gradiva a cast of a relief representing a walking woman? Dalí seems to echo a response: "They have finally delivered the plaster cast of my emotion and I decide to take a photograph of this four-buttock continuum . . . and suddenly I have an insight: the person who is now before me, turning her back to me, has exactly two of the buttocks of my continuum." Later he would paint *Ma femme nue regardant son propre corps devenir marches, trois vertèbres d'une colonne, ciel et architecture* (*My Wife Naked, Looking at Her Own Body Transformed into Steps, Three Vertebrae of a Column, Sky, and Architecture*; 1945). The image of Gala from the back is transformed into architecture, as if the painter had found in her the childhood memory of an insect eaten by ants and of which nothing remains but the exoskeleton. Gala made Dalí view the world through his paranoid, critical lens, the delirium of interpretation with which he had seduced Breton at the beginning of the 1930s, before his fascination for "Hitler's plump back" led the father of Surrealism to excommunicate the Spaniard.

With paintings like *Le Grand Paranoïaque* (*The Great Paranoiac*; 1936), Gala was no longer just a model but "the soft engine that made [his] paranoic critical method work." Her face continued to reappear in the landscape of his Spain. "Thanks to the fear of touching Gala's face, I have ended up learning to paint," wrote Dalí in his *Diary of a Genius*. Soon after she also took on the traits of the Virgin Mary to become *La Madone de Port Lligat* (*The Madonna of Port Lligat*; 1950).

One prefers not to tell the story of the end of this ageless muse. The multiplicity of young lovers; the sessions of Dalí's sexual investigations where Gala was the only woman admitted; the sordid confrontations; Gala surrounded by swindlers who made her sign anything to Dalí. Gradivas must not be allowed to age. One prefers not to describe Gala agonizing in her round room in Port Lligat. Gala dressed and coiffed, making believe she was still vivacious, and Dalí asking endlessly, "Is she going to die?" One prefers to imagine the painter, for one last time like Jensen's archaeologist, looking at an eternally young Gradiva moving away from him:

> *Please cross here!*
> *A happy and complicit smile slid across the lips of his companion and, lifting up her dress a little with her left hand, Gradiva revivida, while he gazed longingly with a dreamy and insistent look, reached the other side.*

Bibliography

Dalí, Salvador. *The Secret Life of Salvador Dalí*. New York: Dover Publishers, 1993 reprint.

———. *Diary of a Genius*. New York: Prentice Hall, 1986.

Descharnes, Robert. *Dalí: The Work, The Man*. New York: Abradale Press, 1997.

Éluard, Paul. *Letters to Gala 1924-1948*. New York: Paragon House, 1989.

Jensen, Wilhelm, and Sigmund Freud. *Gradiva/Delusion and Dream in Wilhelm Jensen's Gradiva*. Los Angeles: Sun & Moon Press, 1992.

Josephine Hopper
Edward Hopper

Pierrette and Pierrot

By putting her own art second and demanding to be her husband's only model, Josephine Hopper played many roles on canvas. In painting after painting by Edward Hopper, she appeared young or old, blonde or redhead, sexy or indifferent, presenting herself as such diverse characters as a secretary, prostitute, detective, and stripper until Hopper's last work, *Two Comedians* (1965), in which the painter represented himself standing beside his model for the last time.

"E. Hopper House, founded in 1882. Objects of art and utility. Oil paintings, engravings, etching, courses in painting, drawing and literature, repair of electric lamps and windows, removal and transportation of trunks, guide in the countryside, carpenter, launderer, hairdresser, fireman, transportation of trees and flowers, wedding and banquet halls, readings, encyclopedia of art and science, mechanic, rapid cure for illnesses of the spirit such as flightiness, frivolity, and pride. Reduced prices for widows and orphans. Samples upon request. Demand the registered trademark. E. Hopper House, 3 Washington Square."

This advertising sales pitch, created on the eve of World War I by a tall young man born in 1882 with blue eyes and a sensual mouth, was not lacking in humor. Nevertheless it hinted at the despair of a painter who had not succeeded in selling any of the canvases inspired by his recent voyages to Europe. With no buyers, the artist resolved to try his luck as a commercial illustrator.

In fact he had not yet found his style. In several years he would become the champion of American realism, painting for the first time landscapes that no other artist until then had found worthy of interest. We see in the long enumeration of the specialties of "E. Hopper House" that almost all the subjects of his painting were already in place. The one exception: Josephine Nivison, the woman who would become his wife and his only model starting in 1924.

They met at the beginning of the twentieth century in the studio of realist painter and teacher Robert Henri at the New York School of Art. Nothing about them suggested that they would be more than just friends. A little later, a still timid and prudish young man headed off for a voyage to Europe in the direction of Paris, as was typical for many young American students at the time. He landed in the French capital in October 1906 and stayed there until August of the following year, returning again in 1909 and 1910. Hopper fell in love with the city and the language forever—and perhaps also with the demimondaines he drew and the beautiful women he passed in the street.

When he returned to the United States in July 1910 for a last time (he would never cross the Atlantic again), he was still completely dazzled by the "City of Light." In America everything seemed ugly and coarse to him. "It took me ten years to get over Europe," he would later say. As a way of prolonging the effects of his time abroad, he tirelessly painted subjects with French titles: *Les Poilus*, *La Barrière*, *Les Deux Pigeons, Aux fortifications*. But the art dealers and the public remained unmoved. Only Josephine Nivison, his old comrade from school, seemed to share his passion for a country she had never visited but whose language she knew a little and whose literature she knew quite well. One day when Edward was reciting Verlaine and suddenly stopped, to his great surprise Josephine recited the end of the poem. They began the habit of speaking to each other in French and, at Christmas 1923, Hopper offered her a drawing showing both of them, seated on a French window ledge with a full moon and the towers of Notre-Dame in the background. In the guise of a dedication, he inscribed six lines from "La Lune blanche" ("O'er the Wood's Brow") by Paul Verlaine, a poem dedicated by the poet to his fiancée:

A huge and gentle
Peacefulness
Seems to come
From the heaven
That the moon illumines:
It is the exquisite hour.

Soon after he asked her to marry him. "Why me?" she asked, after accepting. Hopper replied because "you have curly hair. You know some French. And you're an orphan." The marriage took place on July 9, 1924, in the Huguenot church on West 16th Street in New York, not far from their respective studios. And as if the magic spell of France came undone with the new marriage, Hopper's nostalgia for France slowly faded and he turned himself toward American subjects. But the French influence remained perceptible even in the late paintings, as if the dreamy worker in *New York Movie* (1939) were simply the American cousin of the raped woman in *Intérieur* (1869) by Edgar Degas, and his last painting, *Two Comedians,* after Honoré Daumier's *Rappel de la chanteuse.*

The Sole Model

Few things are known about Josephine Nivison as an artist except that she exerted a decisive influence on the beginning of

Page 121, top: **Edward Hopper, *Office at Night* (1940). In one of his most famous paintings, Josephine Hopper wears a skintight dress and opens the file drawer without managing to disturb the apparent indifference of her boss. The cinematic composition intensified the erotic atmosphere of the scene.**

Page 121, bottom: ***Jo in Wyoming*, watercolor by Edward Hopper in 1946. Edward and Josephine Hopper crossed the United States by car several times in the 1940s. This impression of being in the middle of nowhere can be found in numerous paintings by Edward, with scenes of hotels and service stations. Here, Josephine painting a landscape from the side of the road.**

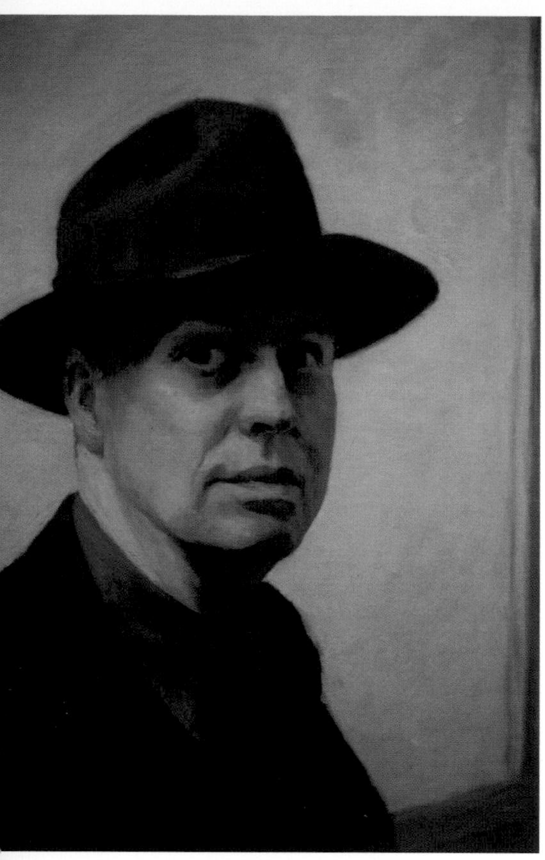

Below: ***Jo Seated*, drawing by Edward Hopper around 1925. The two had met at the New York School of Art and Josephine Nivison shared Edward's fascination for France and knew how to impress him by reciting Paul Verlaine. After their marriage on July 9, 1924, she insisted on being his one and only model.**

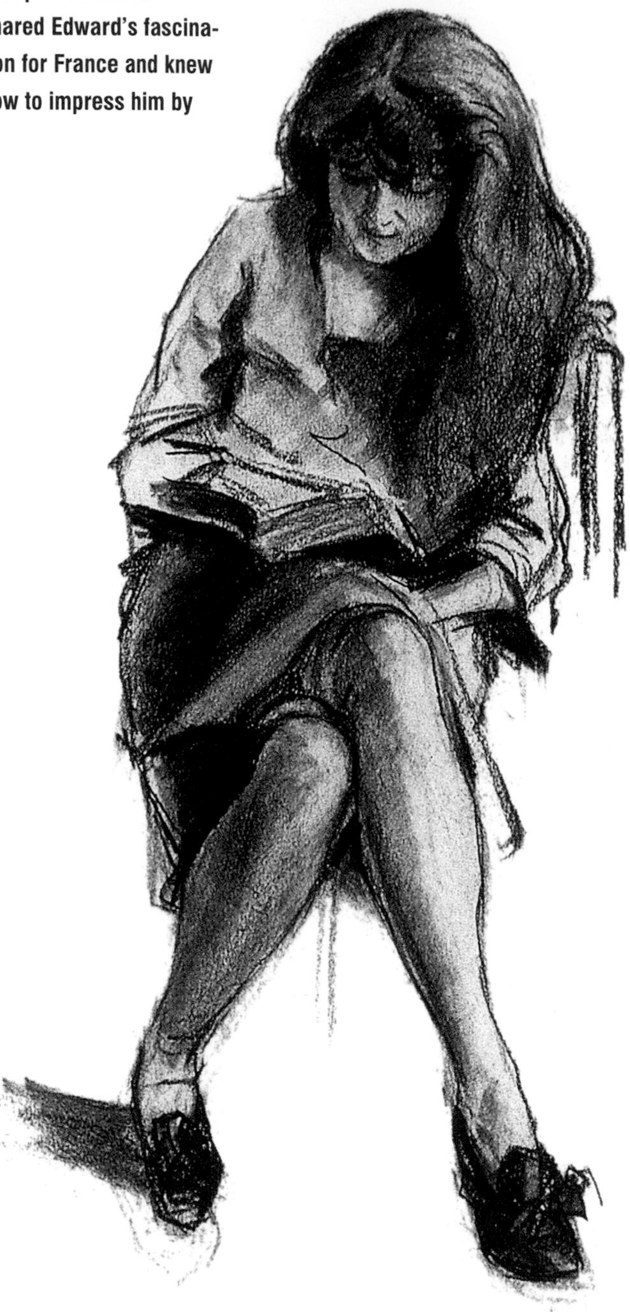

Above: **Detail of Edward Hopper, *Self-Portrait* (1925–30). "All art is an exploration of the subconscious." And so this self-portrait depicts Hopper as a mature man and artist. He had just married Josephine Nivison and had begun to achieve some success with subjects portraying American life.**

Edward Hopper

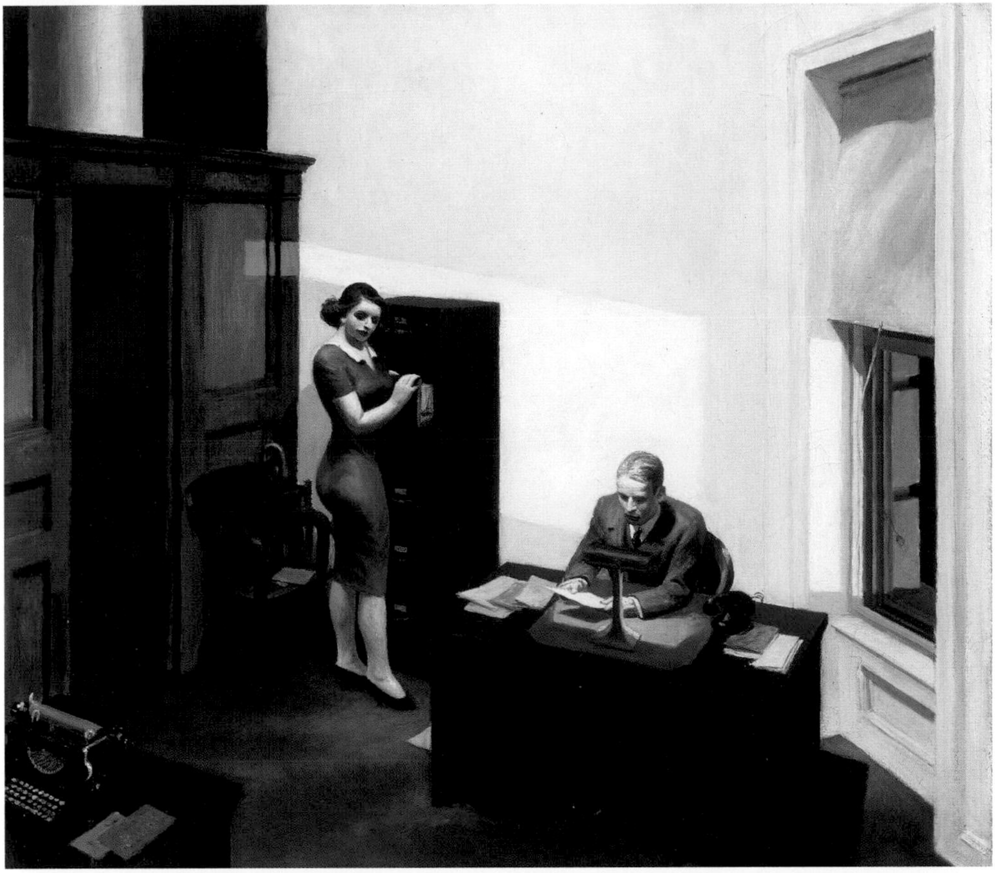

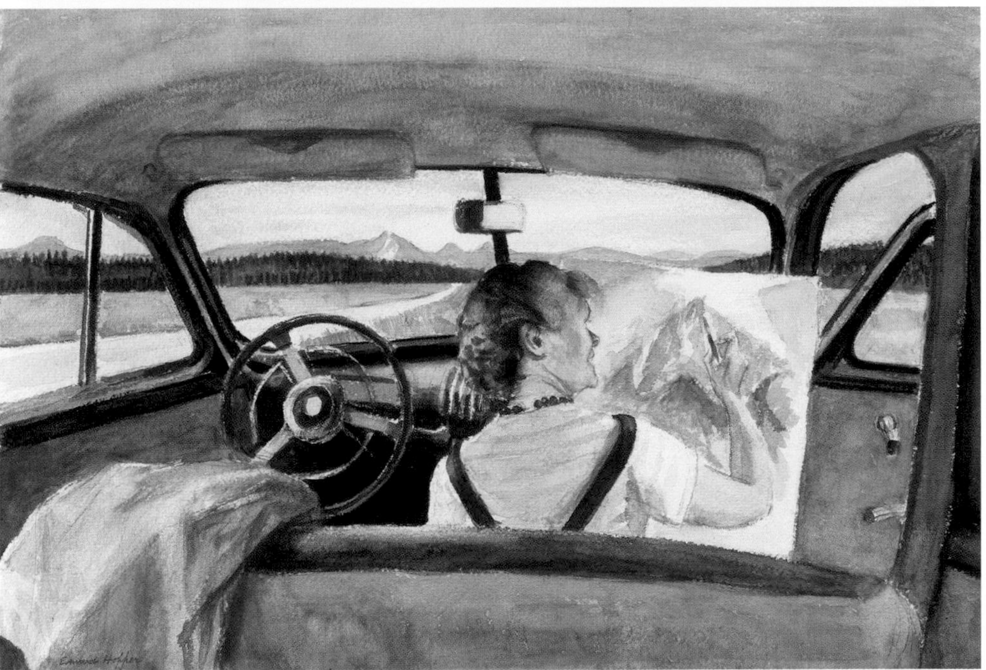

Above: **Edward Hopper, *Two Comedians* (1965). As the ultimate depiction of the couple, this last canvas by Hopper shows both the travesty of their lives and his nostalgia for French painting, the touchstone of his early years. This work recalls *Le Rappel de la chanteuse* by Honoré Daumier.**

Below: **Edward Hopper, *Jo Painting* (1936). Edward had married Josephine Nivison because, as he said to her: "You have curly hair. You know some French. And you're an orphan." She was also a painter, as shown by this canvas, but she put her own work second to that of her husband.**

Opposite: **Edward and Josephine Hopper photographed on Cape Cod by Arnold Newman in 1960. It was in South Truro, Massachusetts, that the famous and successful Hopper built a house.**

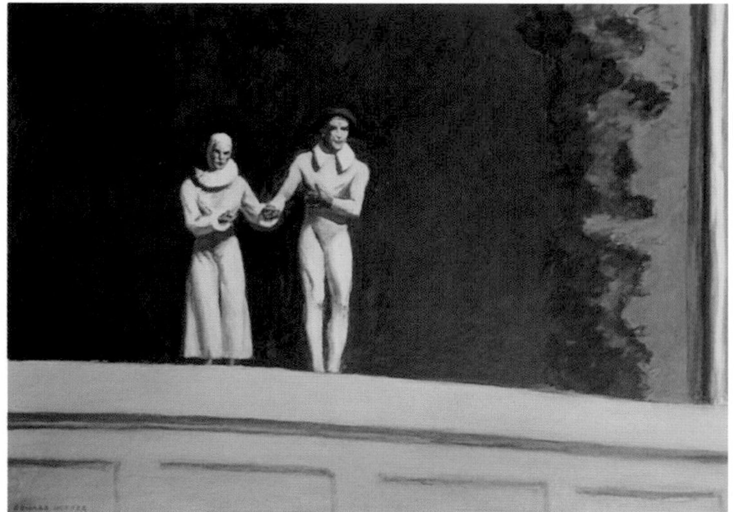

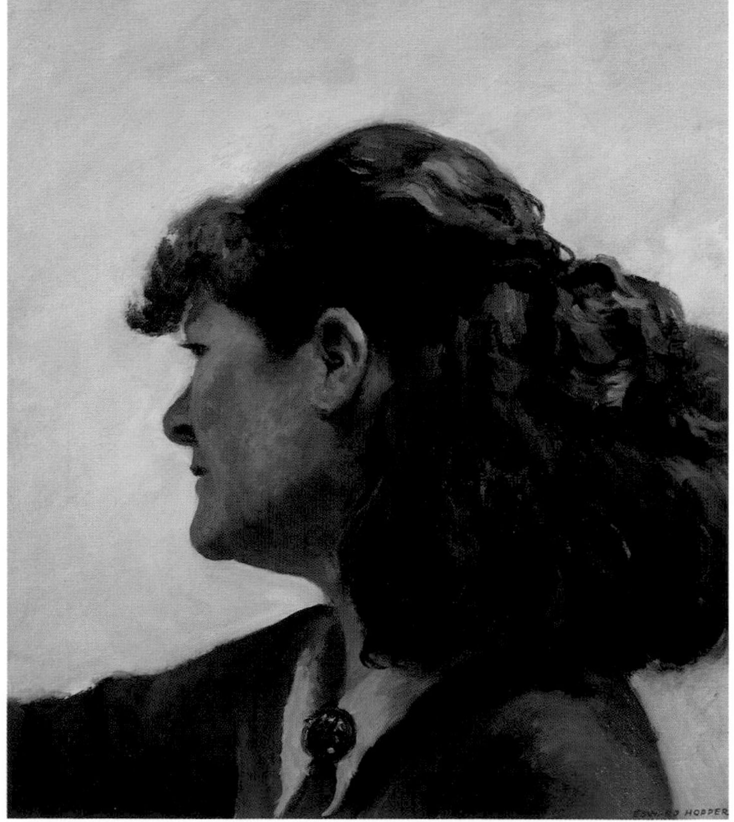

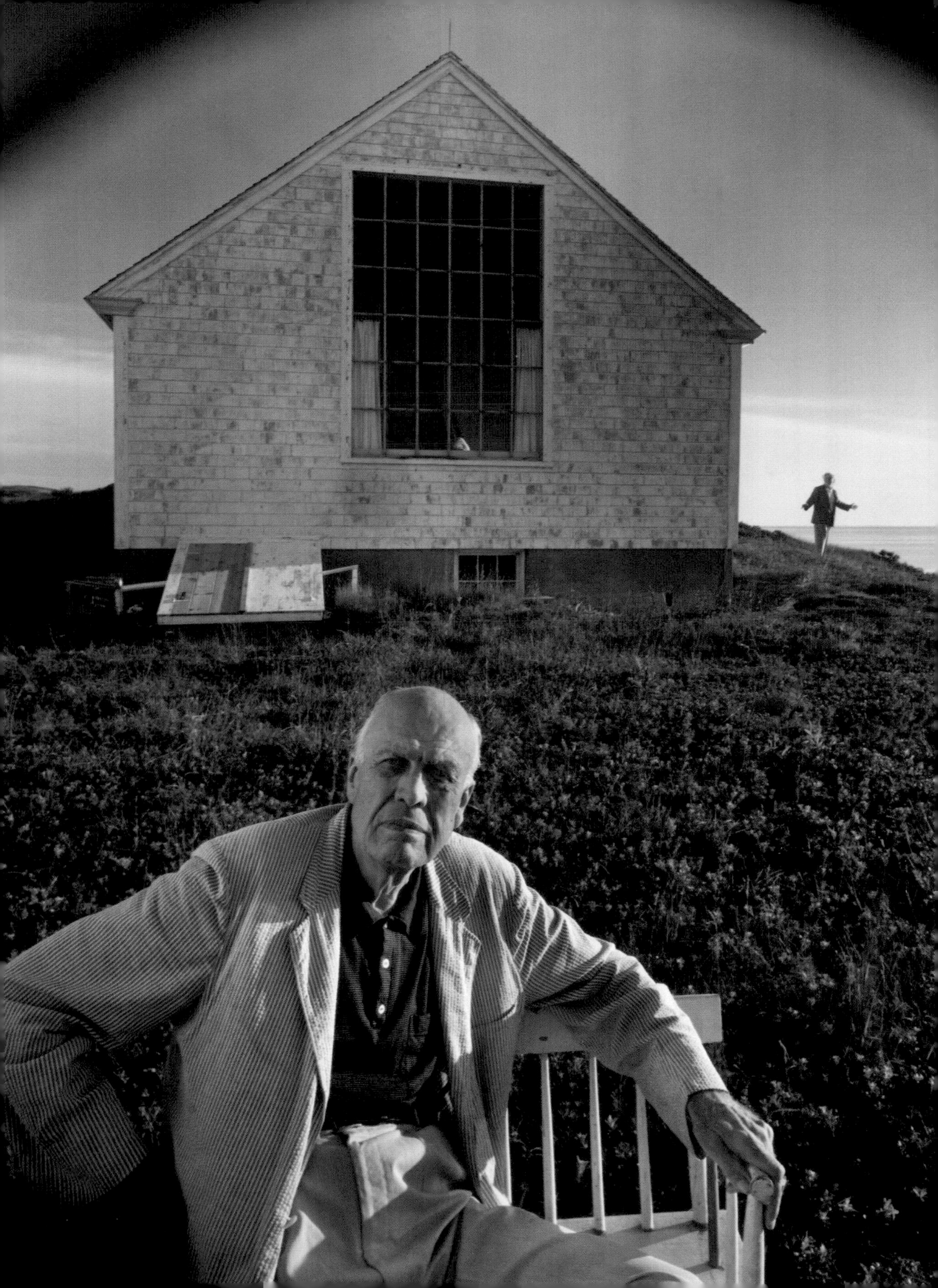

Edward Hopper's success. Invited in 1923 to participate in a collective exhibition at the Brooklyn Museum, she introduced her future husband to the institution. She had recently convinced him to begin doing watercolors and, shortly after, the museum bought *The Mansard Roof* for one hundred dollars. It was his first work acquired by a museum, and the first he had sold in more than ten years. Hopper became the portraitist of America as it revealed itself through its architecture. His first successes, after so many years of setbacks, allowed him to abandon illustration, which had never really interested him. He went back to working with live models, but a short time after their marriage, Josephine insisted on being his only one.

In Hopper's mature work, Josephine, who had had some small experience as an actress, assumed all sorts of roles. She seized the idea, inventing names and lives for the characters Hopper asked her to interpret. Sometimes she disguised herself as a femme fatale, sometimes an antique hunter looking for incredible objects. She was young or old, sexy or indifferent, depending on the painter's will. In *Girlie Show* (1941), she enticed her audience by waving a blue skirt around her naked body. Hopper imperceptibly transformed her feminine silhouette in the preparatory sketches into the body of a tall voluptuous redhead. In *Tables for Ladies* (1930), she became a pretty blonde waitress and, to add an erotic touch, she selected fruit, classic symbols of pleasure and beauty, as well as chops echoing an expression Hopper particularly enjoyed: to lick one's chops. In the troubling *Office at Night* of 1940, we see her again, an attractive brunette secretary in a skin-tight dress and high heels who does not manage to attract her boss's attention. The following year the Hoppers took to the road, crossing the United States. Josephine, whom we had already discovered reading on the edge of a bed in *Hotel Room* (1931), could now be found nude in a bedroom of an unknown town in *Morning in a City* (1944).

Did the couple transfer those fantasies that they dared not achieve in real life to the canvas? The question may be asked since many of their contemporaries have all emphasized the frequent quarrels between the pair, as well as their silences. Like in *Hotel by a Railroad*, painted in 1952, where the woman shuts herself away in her reading—perhaps the Gideon Bible—indifferent to her companion who smokes at the window with his back turned to her. To those observers who remarked on the absence of communication between the characters in his canvases, Hopper replied: "Without a doubt it's a reflection of my own solitude, if I can say it. I don't know. It could just be the human condition." For her part, Josephine confided: "Sometimes talking with Eddie is just like dropping a stone in a well except that it doesn't thump when it hits bottom." Edward was sometimes concerned by the misunderstanding Josephine could have of his work. She described *Cape Cod Morning* as depicting a woman looking through a window to see if it's nice enough to hang her laundry outside. "Did I say that?" replied Edward. "For me, she is just looking out the window." And he reproached her for turning his painting into something by Norman Rockwell, who represented the paragon of American virtues—just the opposite of the ambiguous Hopper.

A childless couple, the Hoppers maintained a rather austere and frugal life despite the recognition and the success that made Edward one of the most celebrated American painters. They alternated their winter trips to New York, to the same Washington Square studio that the artist had mentioned in his early self-promotion, with long periods in their country house in South Truro, Massachusetts, which they had constructed on Cape Cod in 1930. When Hopper died at eighty-five years of age, Josephine only survived him by a few months, bringing up the rear, just as Hopper had painted her in his last work.

Bibliography

Edward Hopper. Exhibition catalogue. Musée Cantini, Marseilles. Paris: Adam Biro, 1989.

Goodrich, Lloyd. *Edward Hopper.* New York: Abradale Press, 1993.

Levin, Gail. *Edward Hopper: An Intimate Biography.* Berkeley: University of California Press, 1995.

Gena Rowlands
John Cassavetes

The Astronaut and the Moon

A victim in *A Woman Under the Influence*, a fighter in *Gloria*, both one and the other in *Opening Night*, Gena Rowlands nourished and inhabited the cinema of her husband John Cassavetes more than that of any other director, thereby giving a positive response to the question posed by the hero in *Love Streams*: "Would love be considered an art?"

What do Gena Rowlands and John Cassavetes talk about in the half-dozen films that they made together, usually with a glass of whiskey in one hand and a cigarette at their lips? Love, always and forever. Not the joy of love. But " . . . *love*. And the lack of it. When it stops. And the pain that's caused by loss or things taken away from us that we really need," Cassavetes confided one day. Echoing him, Gena Rowlands's character in *Love Streams*, one of Cassavetes's last films, asks Robert (played by Cassavetes), "Would love be considered an art?"

The Art of Love

This image of love as a work of art that haunts Cassavetes's films has as its counterpoint their life as an ordinary couple. Married for thirty-five years, the parents of three children, they were together until John's death in 1989. An ordinary life punctuated, however, by fights and reconciliations. "At the beginning of our marriage, we made a deal: Gena fought me till the end, and I fought her till the end, but the deal was always respected. We have led a magnificent and dislocated life together, moving and undisciplined. You fight, you tell each other off, and you kill each other every day."

When she met Cassavetes—the legend goes that it was in a cinema at a screening of *The Blue Angel*—Rowlands was a novice actress who had left her native Wisconsin to work in the theater in New York. Gena (Virginia) Cathryn Rowlands was born into a family of Welsh origin in Cambria, Wisconsin, on June 19. Of what year? Like the alcoholic and aging theater actress of *Opening Night*, she never told her age and different biographies contradict each other on the subject. For his part, John Cassavetes (born in 1929 in New York) was already a known actor who competed with Marlon Brando and James Dean for certain Hollywood roles. He almost starred in *Rebel Without a Cause* and, at the wheel of his convertible, this son of Greek immigrants embodied the myth of the successful immigrant on which America had been built. Gena the magnificent blonde and John the Greek lover had everything they needed to seduce Hollywood and Broadway and to create classic acting careers. Rowlands recalls: "At the beginning of our life together I imagined both of us as theater actors in New York for the rest of our lives. I never would have believed that he would be crazy enough to embark on making films." But the meeting with Gena radically altered the course of Cassavetes's career, just as Maurice (John Cassavetes) admits in addressing Myrtle (Gena Rowlands) in *Opening Night*: "You are my inspiration. Before I met you, I was like a Dean Martin without charm, W.C. Fields without a nose. You're just a girl with two legs, but I love you."

Love led them from the beginning of their marriage to make *A Child Is Waiting* (1963) together. It was a traumatizing experience for Cassavetes, who saw the producer use his right of final cut to transform "his" film into a melodrama set against a background of violins. It was also a beneficial experience in that he realized that he did not want to repeat the usual Hollywood clichés. "We simply wanted to make another kind of film. Films closer to the way people live in daily life," remembers Rowlands. *Exit* Hollywood and the beginning of Système D (Low-Budget), the brand name of Cassavetes and Co. Wife, children, mother-in-law (listed on the credits under the name of Lady Rowlands, a nickname given to her by her grandson Nick), brother-in-law, mother, and friends—in particular Seymour Cassel, Peter Falk, and Ben Gazzara—all were enlisted to act, for free at the beginning and preferably at night so that they could go to their jobs during the day. The movies were filmed in lofts or even at the Cassavetes home, and the children—Alexandra, Nick, and Zoe—were surprised to see their mother going through terrible crises. The most memorable was for *Gloria*.

The Culture of Misunderstanding

In 1958, while the New Wave of directors in France discovered the lightweight camera and real surroundings, Cassavetes had a parallel experience with an Arriflex camera. He shot everyday stories in which people loved each other, argued, cried, drank, made music, or collapsed in laughter. *Shadows* (1959), the only film that Cassavetes made without a screenplay, launched the myth of improvisational cinema. Afterward all the screenplays of his films were carefully written. A special *Shadows* screening was organized for two nights at a New York auditorium that attracted five thousand spectators. If New York journalists remained unconvinced, the movie won critical acclaim at the 1960 Venice Film Festival. Moving on to Paris, Cassavetes entered into the pantheon

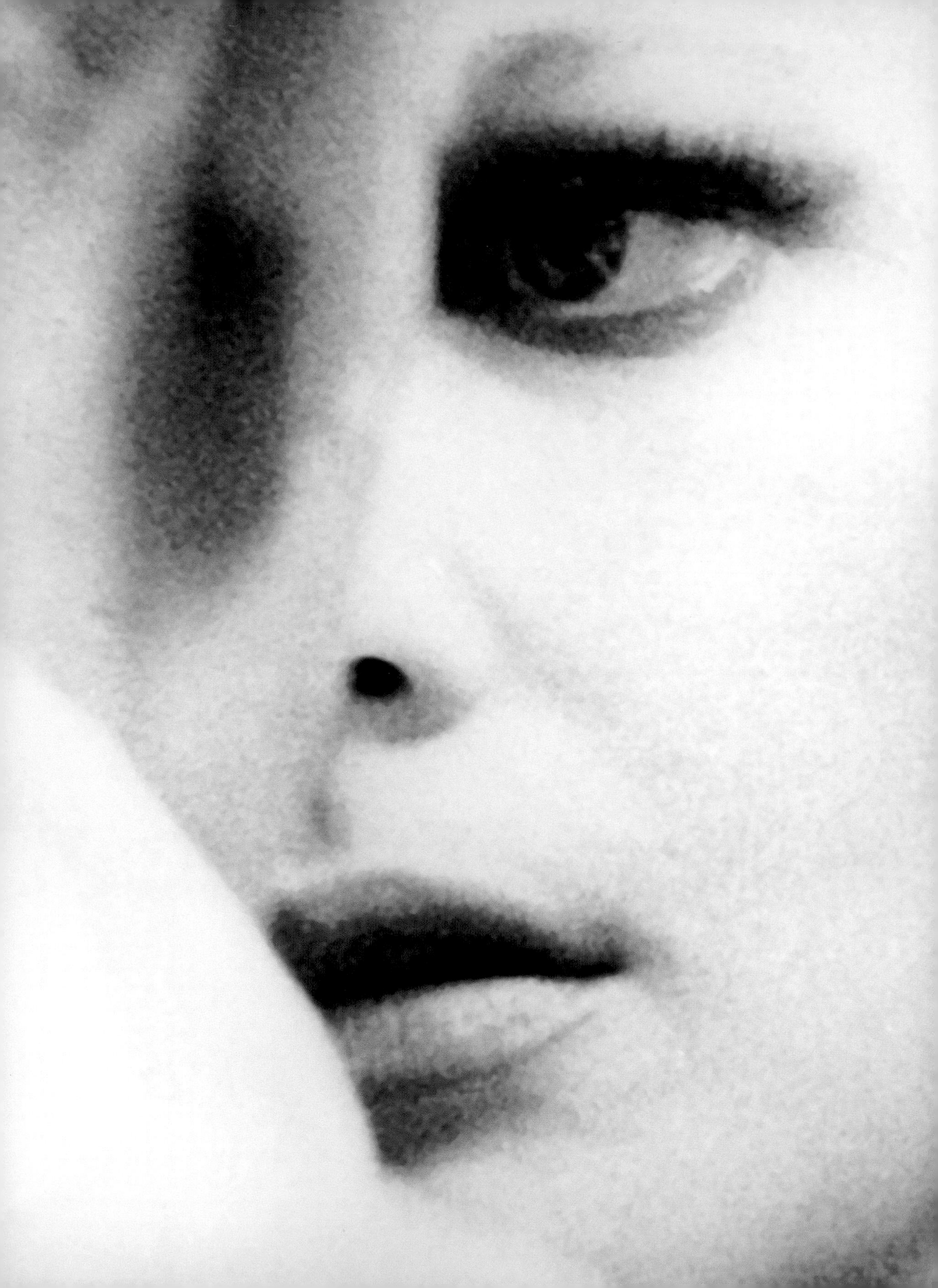

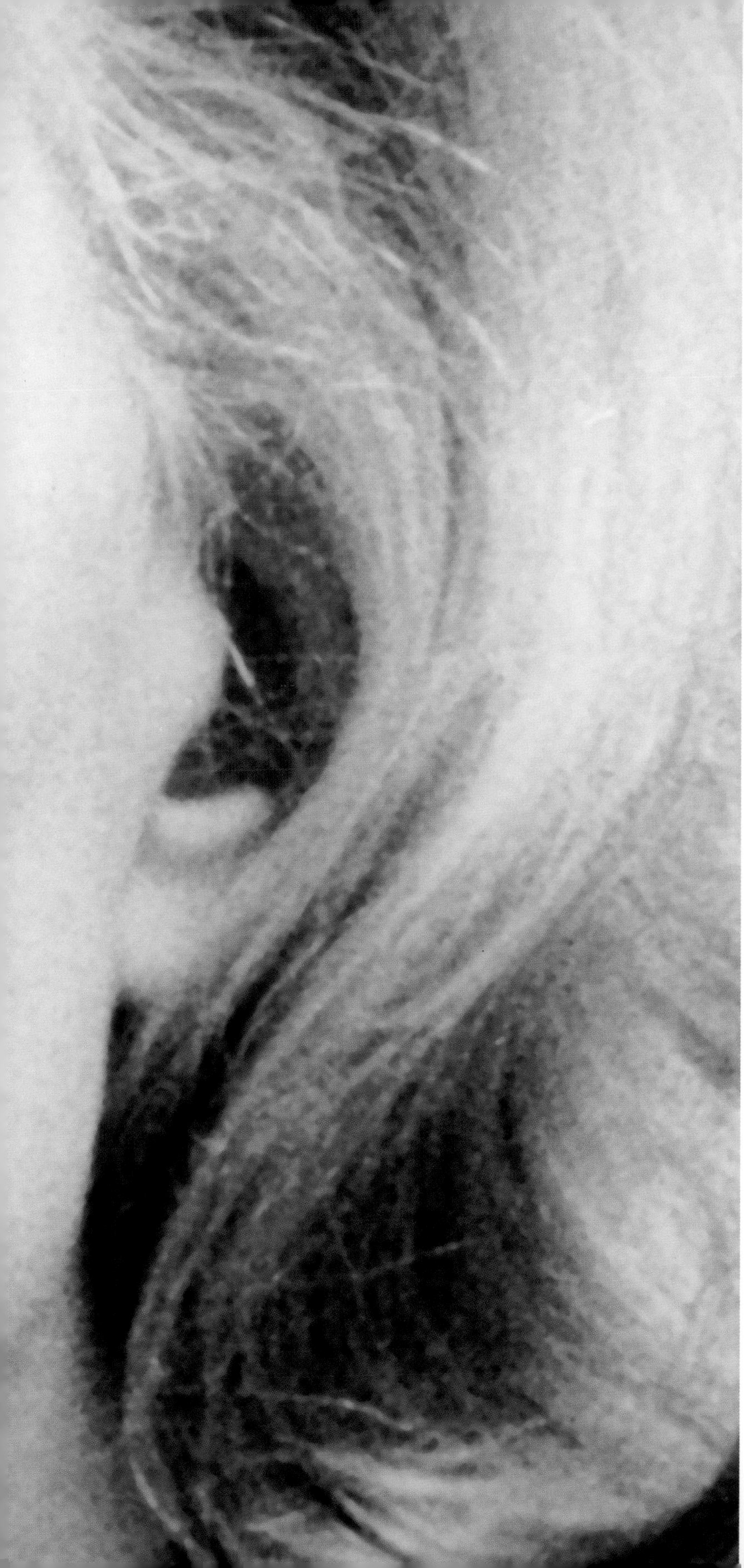

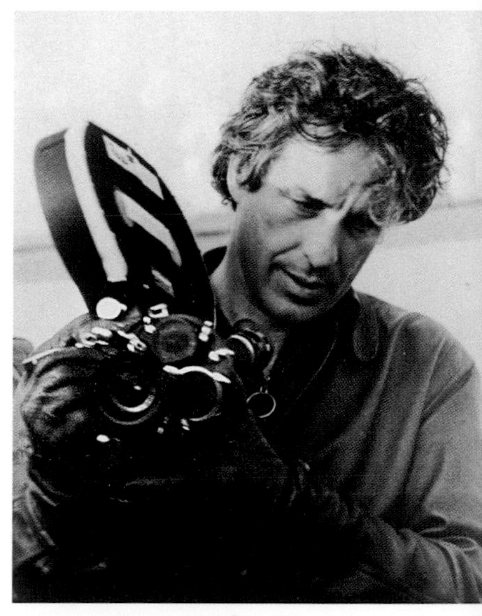

Above: **Liberated from the heavy machinery of the Hollywood studios, John Cassavetes wanted a mobile camera that would track the truth of his actors and their sometimes abrupt and unexpected movements.**
Left: **Accepting the usual harsh treatment of actors by John Cassavetes, Gena Rowlands hid none of her grimaces or her tears in this close-up shot from a scene in *Faces* (1968).**

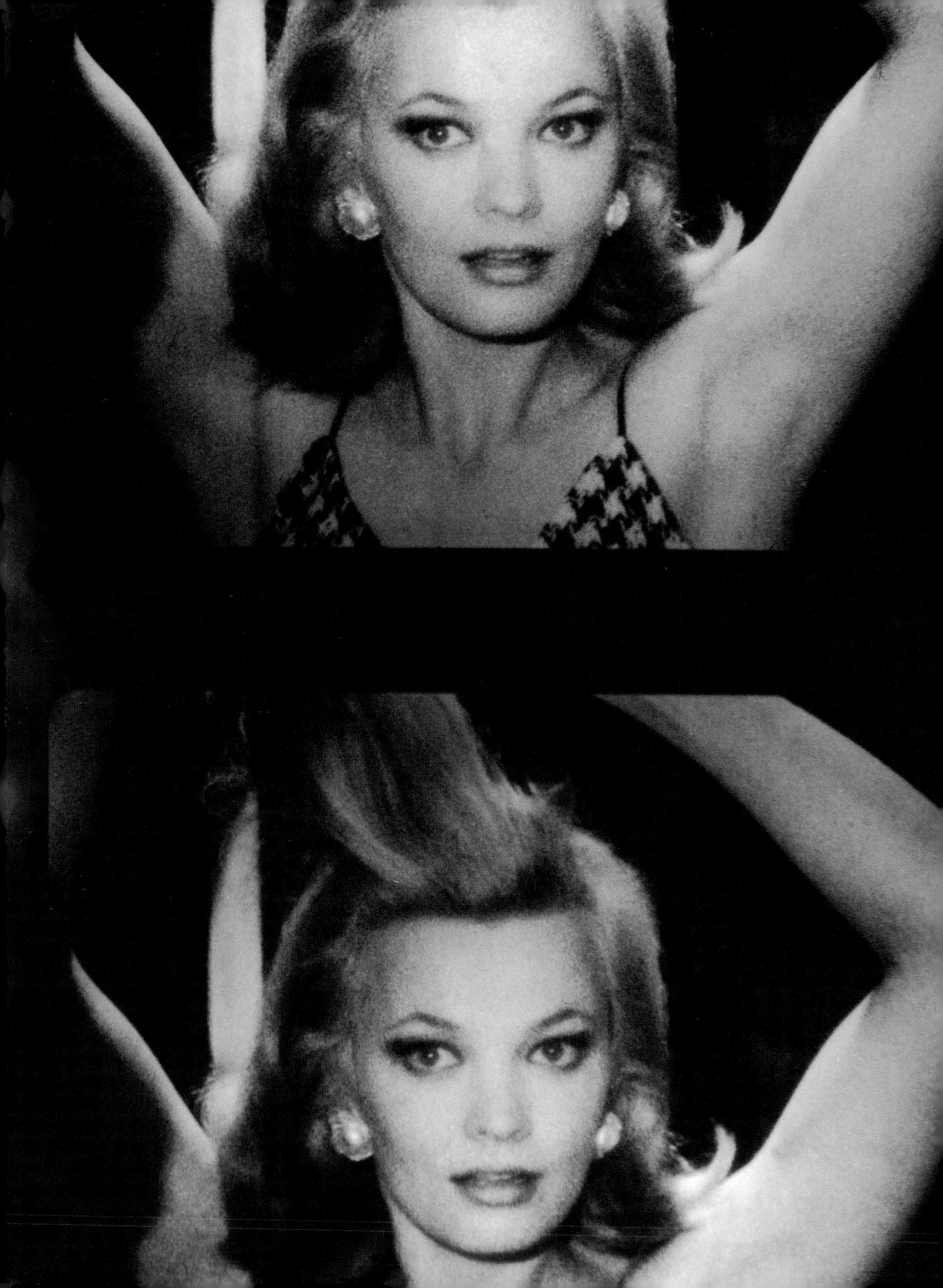

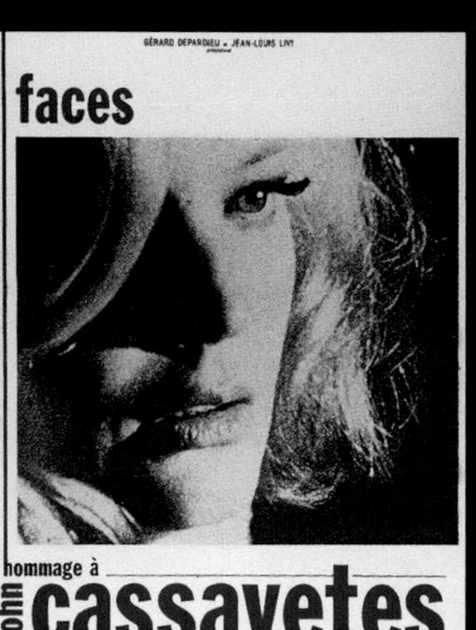

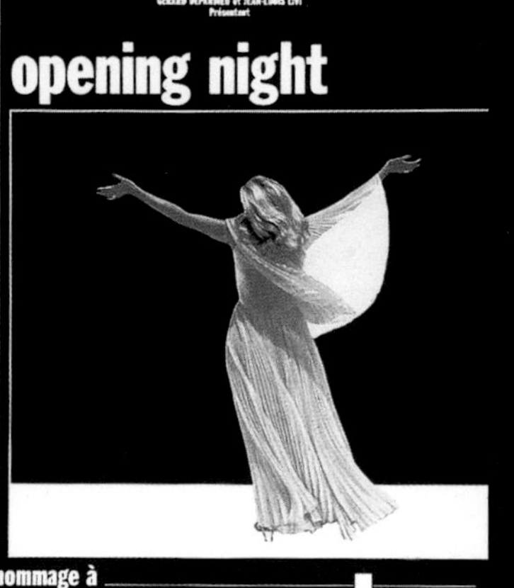

Opposite: **After the disappointing experience of making a movie in Hollywood, John Cassavetes created *Faces*. Shooting seventeen hours of 16mm film over five months in a totally homemade production, he dissected an impossible marriage, all while creating a paean to the beauty of Gena Rowlands.**

Left: **Gena Rowlands won the prize for Best Actress at the Berlin Film Festival in 1978 for her role as the aging and alcoholic actress in *Opening Night* (1977).**

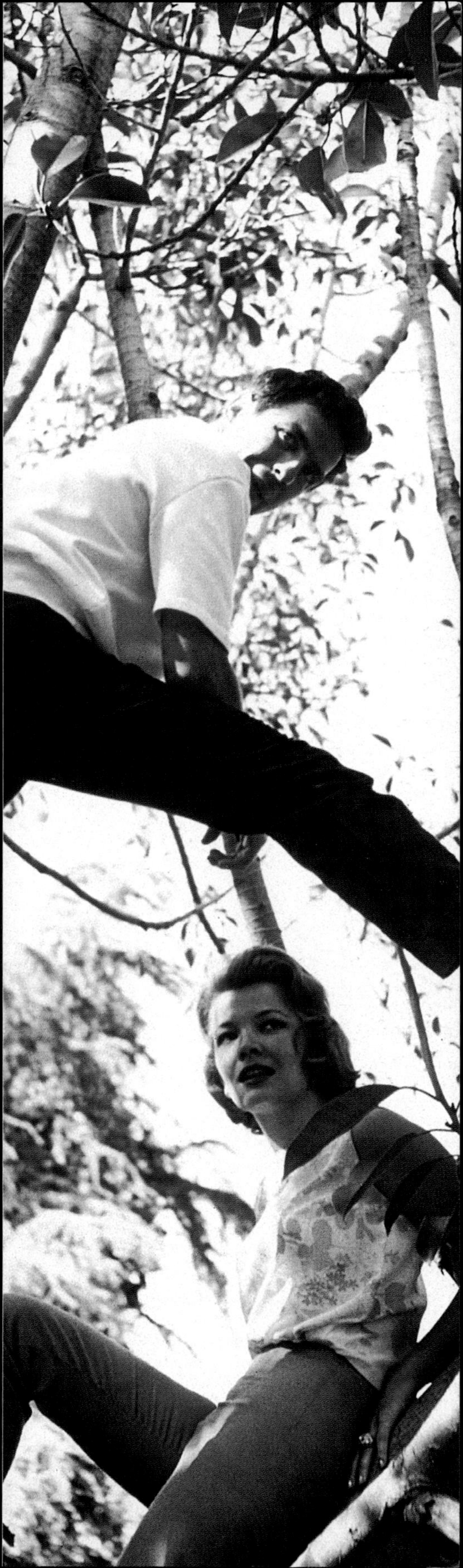

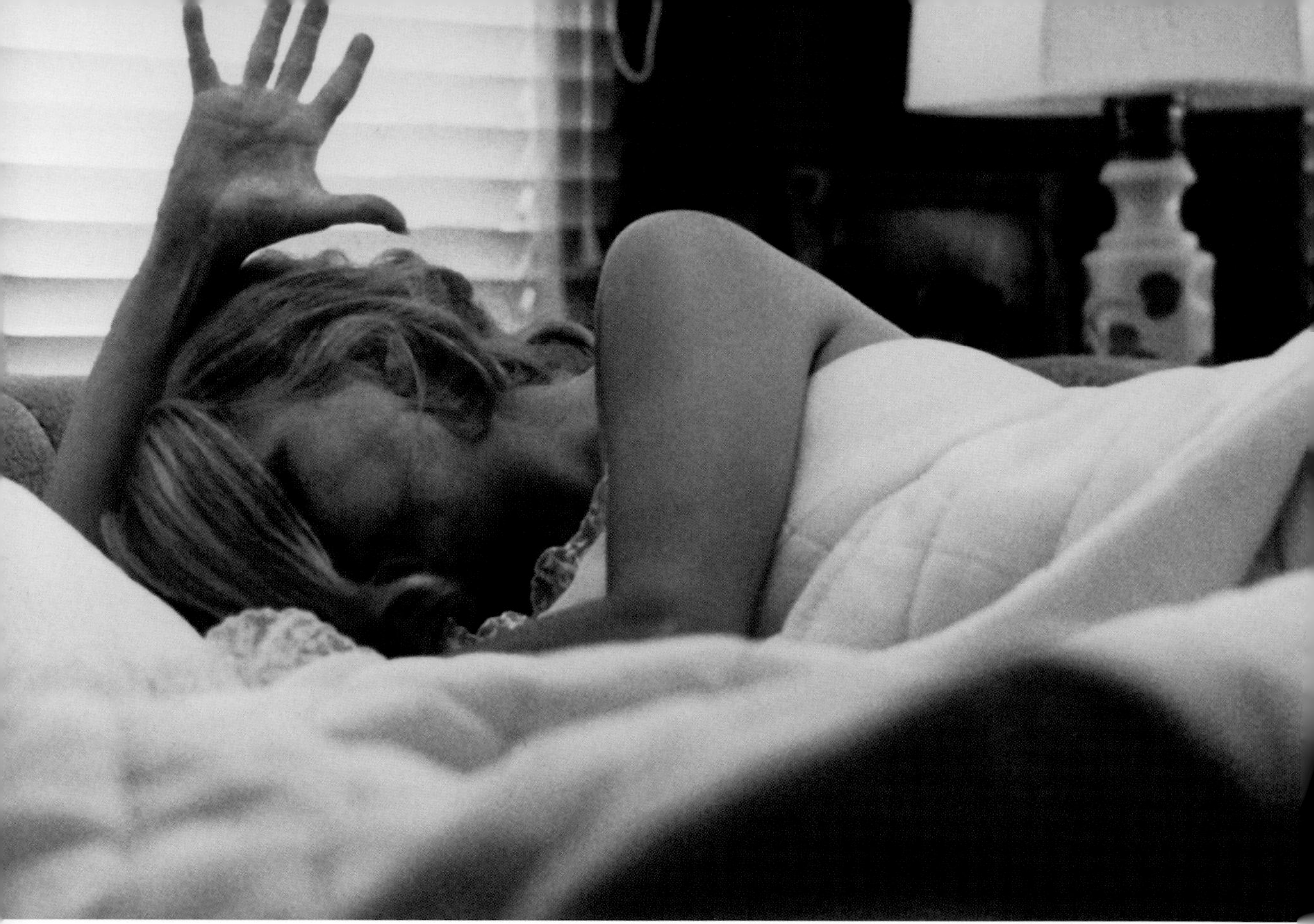

Above: **The role of Mabel, the housewife in *A Woman Under the Influence* (1974), whose world consists of cleaning, cooking, and sewing, earned Gena Rowlands an Oscar nomination, the first official recognition of an independent production by the American film world.**

Opposite: **In *Love Streams* (1984), the couple's last film together, John Cassavetes is the seductive dandy and brother of a lost and abandoned Gena Rowlands.**

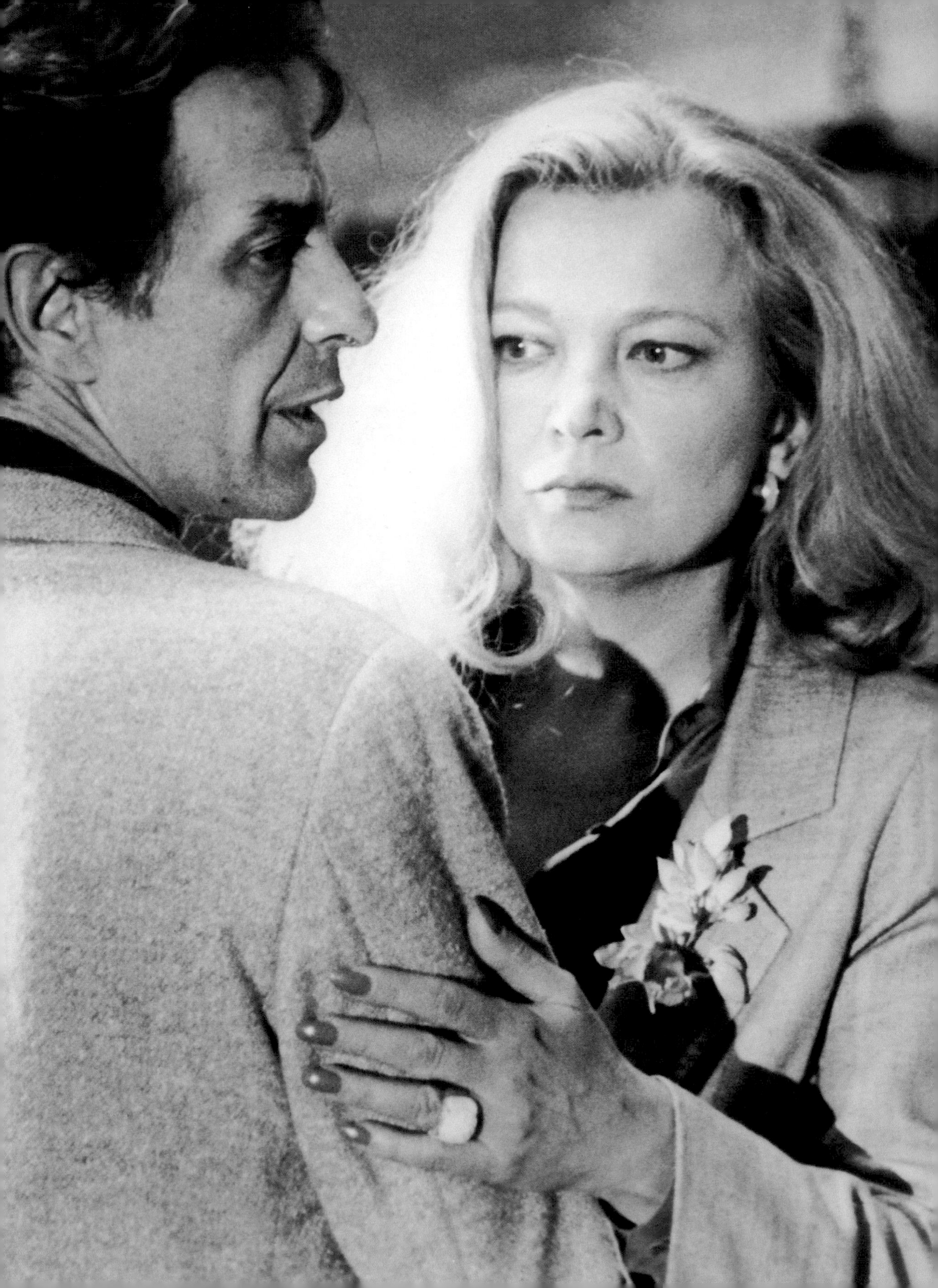

of cinema enthusiasts from the outset by giving a copy of his film to Henri Langlois's Cinémathèque Française. It was an unusual fate for a director usually classified by critics and the public as an "intellectual," but who once said that he did not want to see a Bergman film because he was not in the mood to be depressed.

If the legend of his improvisational cinema style remains tenacious, it is because Cassavetes allowed his actors, and especially Gena Rowlands, the task of enriching their own roles. "He told me, 'I wrote this role for you. It's yours. No one knows more about it than you. . . . Right now I know less than you do about this character, fill it up, fill it up, fill it up,'" recalled Gena.

It was in *A Woman Under the Influence* that Rowlands showed her true worth for the first time. "John's screenplays gave me a sense of discovery. I was like an astronaut who reached the moon for the first time. The air there was very thin, and you needed to put on heavy boots so as not to fly away and you were forced to get about this terrifying territory very quickly." Cassavetes expressed himself more precisely: "Gena and I were speaking about the pictures we were going to make, how the roles are so thin. . . . We were talking about how difficult love was and how tough it would be to make a love story about two people who were totally different culturally. . . . A story like this is not newsworthy really. . . . It's a man and woman relationship, which is always interesting to me. It's an optimistic film. The situation is simple: a couple has nothing in common if it's not love."

Love and Dreams

Even more than love, Cassavetes's films speak about dreams. The dreams that women and men have and that cinema so often forgets. "They ignore women's dreams and the woman as the object of a dream," said Cassavetes. *Faces* (1968), *Minnie and Moskowitz* (1971), *A Woman Under the Influence* (1974), *Opening Night* (1977), *Gloria* (1980), and *Love Streams* (1984) are all portrayals of women lost in middle-class America and beset by unhappiness, filmed by Cassavetes and performed by Gena Rowlands. They were women who dreamed. In *Faces* Jeannie is a big-hearted whore who consoles husbands with nothing left to say to their wives. Mabel, in *A Woman Under the Influence*, is a housewife married to Nick, the head of construction at a masonry company, a wife and a mother who breaks into hysterical laughter and funny faces. Myrtle, in *Opening Night*, is an aging alcoholic stage actress, rejected by her old lover, who is played by

Cassavetes. In *Love Streams*, their last film together, if Robert (Cassavetes) swears always to love Sarah (Rowlands), it is because they are brother and sister, and so they do not love each other like the others—"It's not what you think," says Robert to his son. Meanwhile Sarah dreams of a reconciliation with her daughter and her former husband against the backdrop of a musical comedy.

Even in dream sequences, humor plays the role of relaxing the atmosphere in often very dark situations. A great lover of humor, Cassavetes did not hesitate to punctuate his screenplays with terrible jokes: "Why should you throw your alarm clock out the window? To see time fly." Or even: "What does Dracula do every day at midnight? He has a little glass of red."

The bard of misunderstanding, Cassavetes reached a summit in April 1976 when he made his first appearance on French television with Rowlands on a popular Sunday night program during the release of *A Woman Under the Influence*, co-starring Peter Falk. There, to the cries of "Columbo! Columbo!" the entire cast was applauded by a public brought to a frenzy by the presence of the celebrated detective. Peter Falk tried desperately to say that the star was Cassavetes. His words were wasted.

Gena Rowlands said one day regarding their common cinematic adventure: "It should be like writing. You stick to the things you've noticed, things that make you think. People in a restaurant, some detail you've chosen from over here, something from over there. . . . Over time, it forms a whole."

Even death did not seem able to break apart all that made up their life and their films: in *Unhook the Stars* (1996), the first film by the young filmmaker, Gena is still the woman loved and dreamed about by a Cassavetes, but this time it was her son Nick who took his father's place behind the camera.

Bibliography

Björkman, Stig. *Gena Rowlands, Mable, Myrtle, Gloria...et les autres.* Paris: Cahiers du cinéma, 2001.

Carney, Ray. *Cassavetes on Cassavetes*. London: Faber and Faber, 2001.

Charity, Tom. *John Cassavetes: Lifeworks*. London: Omnibus Press, 2001.

The Eternal Return

The myth of Dionysos—"his eternal fertility and his eternal return"—does not belong to the philosophy and life of Friedrich Nietzsche alone. Always the same but always different, the muse of the eternal return accompanies the creator throughout his life without real interruption. Alfred Hitchcock's blondes, for example, brought the fantasies of a director platonically in love with all his actresses to life on the big screen, while Jane Birkin's name continues to remain associated with Serge Gainsbourg's, long after their separation and his death. But some muses also experience long eclipses, witness Giulietta Masina, absent from the credits of Federico Fellini's films for eight years but who reemerged in his last works, like the common destiny that the director could not escape.

The Blondes
Alfred Hitchcock

Golden Locks

More than just a physical detail, the blondeness of the actresses in Alfred Hitchcock's films was a driving force in his cinema. Always the same but always different, the blonde brought to life on the big screen the fantasies of a director platonically in love with all his actresses. A director who, nonetheless, remained the faithful husband of his brunette wife Alma for nearly sixty years.

Close-up on the nape of Eva Marie Saint. Light on her blonde hair. The camera pulls away slowly and frames a wide shot of her flawless figure and her impeccably coiffed blonde hair. A typical scene from *North by Northwest*, as there are many such shots in Hitchcock's films. Nothing unusual in that: "Me. . . . I have a passion for blonde hair," he says to the detective in *The Lodger*, one of his very early films made in 1926. The movie is known in France by the even more evocative title of *Les Cheveux d'or* (*Golden Hair*). Hitchcock, who was not yet thirty, put a blonde wig on the naturally brunette hair of his actress June Tripp, just as he had done to Virginia Valli, the heroine of his first film, *The Pleasure Garden*, the year before. But this time he enhanced her blondeness with lighting effects, particularly during the scene where, in her role as a model, she descends a staircase as part of a fashion show at a couture salon.

Fascination

Throughout his more than fifty films, there are countless close-ups on the hair that distinguished the director's view of his actresses. As a filmmaker in love with convention, Hitchcock very often made the blondeness of his heroines a central element of the story, sometimes even letting it become the key to the mystery, as in *Vertigo* (with Jimmy Stewart) where Kim Novak's passage from blonde to redhead signifies her crime.

> *NOVAK—Couldn't you like me—just the way I am?*
> *STEWART* [gazing at her red hair but obviously thinking of the blonde he had adored]—*The color of your hair!*
> *NOVAK—Oh, no!*
> *STEWART—Please, it can't matter to you.*
> *NOVAK—If I let you change me, will that do it? If I do what you tell me, will you love me?*
> *STEWART—Yes . . . yes.*
> *NOVAK—All right then, I'll do it. I don't care anymore about me.*

Hitchcock explained the explicitly sexual nature of this scene: "I was very intrigued by the basic situation of *Vertigo*—of changing the woman's hair color—because it contained so much analogy to sex. This man changed and dressed up his wife, which seems the reverse of stripping her naked. But it amounts to the same thing. I really made the film in order to get through to this subtle quality of a man's dreamlike nature." A man who is no other, of course, than Hitchcock himself. In another interview the director specified even more exactly what kind of blonde corresponded with his fantasy. "The conventional big-bosomed blonde is not mysterious. The perfect 'woman of mystery' is one who is blonde, subtle and Nordic. . . ." It is impossible not to recognize in this description the four blonde actresses who have become icons of Hitchcockian cinema: Grace Kelly in *Dial 'M' for Murder* (1954), *To Catch a Thief* (1955), and *Rear Window* (1954); Kim Novak in *Vertigo* (1958); Eva Marie Saint in *North by Northwest* (1959); Tippi Hedren in *The Birds* (1963) and *Marnie* (1964).

Hair, the classic erotic fixation, also played a major role in the films in which Ingrid Bergman appeared, although she was not really blonde. When the color was not a sufficient symbol of the character's detached aloofness, the hairstyle spoke—knotted or flowing, set into a twisted bun or let free. In *Vertigo* again, Madeleine's (Novak) chignon closely followed the vertiginous turns taken by the screenplay. The director's legendary meticulousness precluded all interventions of chance. Edith Head, his frequent costume designer, recalled in regard to *Dial 'M' for Murder* that Hitchcock specified the colors of each item of Kelly's clothing in the screenplay: "There was a reason for every color, every style, and he was absolutely certain about everything he settled on. For one scene, he saw her in pale green, for another in white chiffon, for another in gold. He was really putting a dream together in the studio." Sometimes this dream made room for brunettes, such as Teresa Wright in *Shadow of a Doubt* (1943), Margaret Lockwood in *The Lady Vanishes* (1938), and Laraine Day in *Foreign Correspondent* (1940). But these were also strong women who, without arousing the desire of the director and the audience, put their power into action. Here precisely is what Hitchcock did not want for his women: "It is a blessing from heaven that women do not exercise their power more often because we could not resist it. We congratulate ourselves if these pleasant creatures are like the birds of the sky and do not know their power; otherwise they would keep/maintain us completely at their discretion." Should we reexamine *The Birds* in the light of this admission? A blonde witch in the country of black birds?

Therefore it is not enough to be blonde to be Hitchcockian. In an article entitled "How I choose my heroines," Hitchcock further specified his requirements: "I must know if my potential heroine . . . is the kind of girl that I can shape according to the heroine I have created in my imagination." These were women sufficiently docile to accept being molded—or even slightly reinvented—like Tippi Hedren. Hitchcock asked her to make her name more "Nordic" with the help of mysterious apostrophes, as in 'Tippi' Hedren. They were women with enough resources to keep surprises always in store. As he admitted in regard to Grace Kelly during his interviews with François Truffaut: "We're after the drawing-room type, the real ladies, who become whores once they're in the bedroom." Or still the women who "get into a cab with you, to your surprise, [and] probably pull a man's pants open."

Much has been written about the form of "cinematic perversion" that allowed the director to satisfy his attraction-repulsion for those wicked and false untouchable blondes on the screen. The best-known example is the actress Kim Novak in *Vertigo*, whom it amused him to terrorize on the set. His biographer Donald Spoto has emphasized the Victorian puritanism of his childhood, his quasi-confinement with his mother until the age of twenty-seven, and finally his fifty-four-year-long marriage to Alma. He has also pointed out the obesity behind which Hitchcock hid himself, as if to protect himself from all attempts at physical seduction. The fact remains that his fantasies about blondeness came to life, thanks to the flesh and blood actresses. "Suspense is like a woman. The more left to the imagination, the more the excitement." And for that, there's nothing like a close-up on the hair of a cool blonde.

Opposite: **Tippi Hedren and Alfred Hitchcock during the filming of *The Birds* (1963).**

Pages 146–47: **Alfred Hitchcock, master of the photogenic. Tippi Hedren photographed in 1962 by Philippe Halsman.**

Bibliography

Hitchcock et l'Art: Coincidence fatales. Exhibition catalogue. Paris: Éditions du Centre Pompidou/Mazotti, 2001.

Spoto, Donald. *The Dark Side of Genius: The Life of Alfred Hitchcock*. Boston: Little, Brown & Co., 1983.

Truffaut, François, and Helen Scott. *Hitchcock, Revised Edition*. New York: Simon & Schuster, 1983.

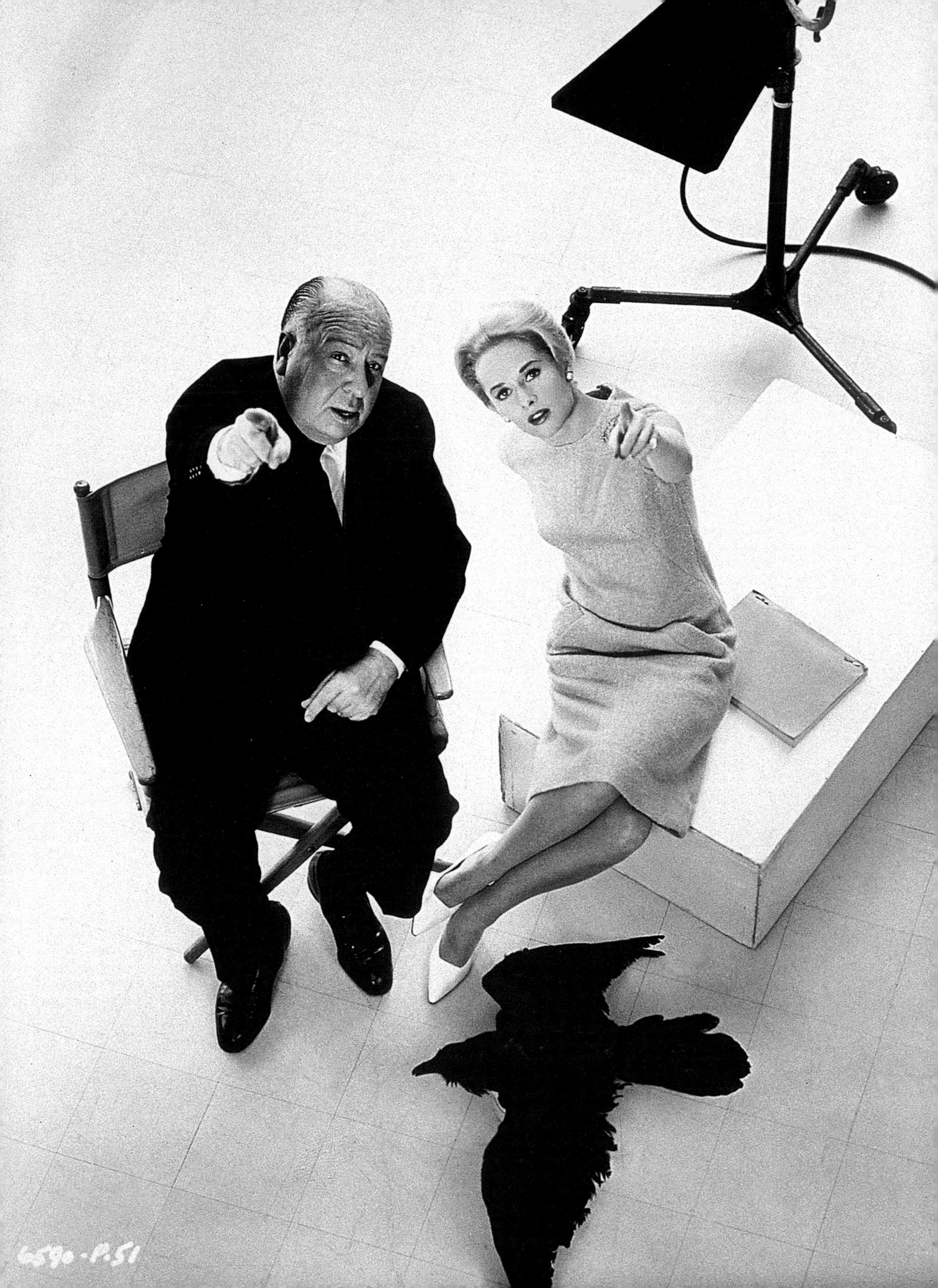
6590-P.51

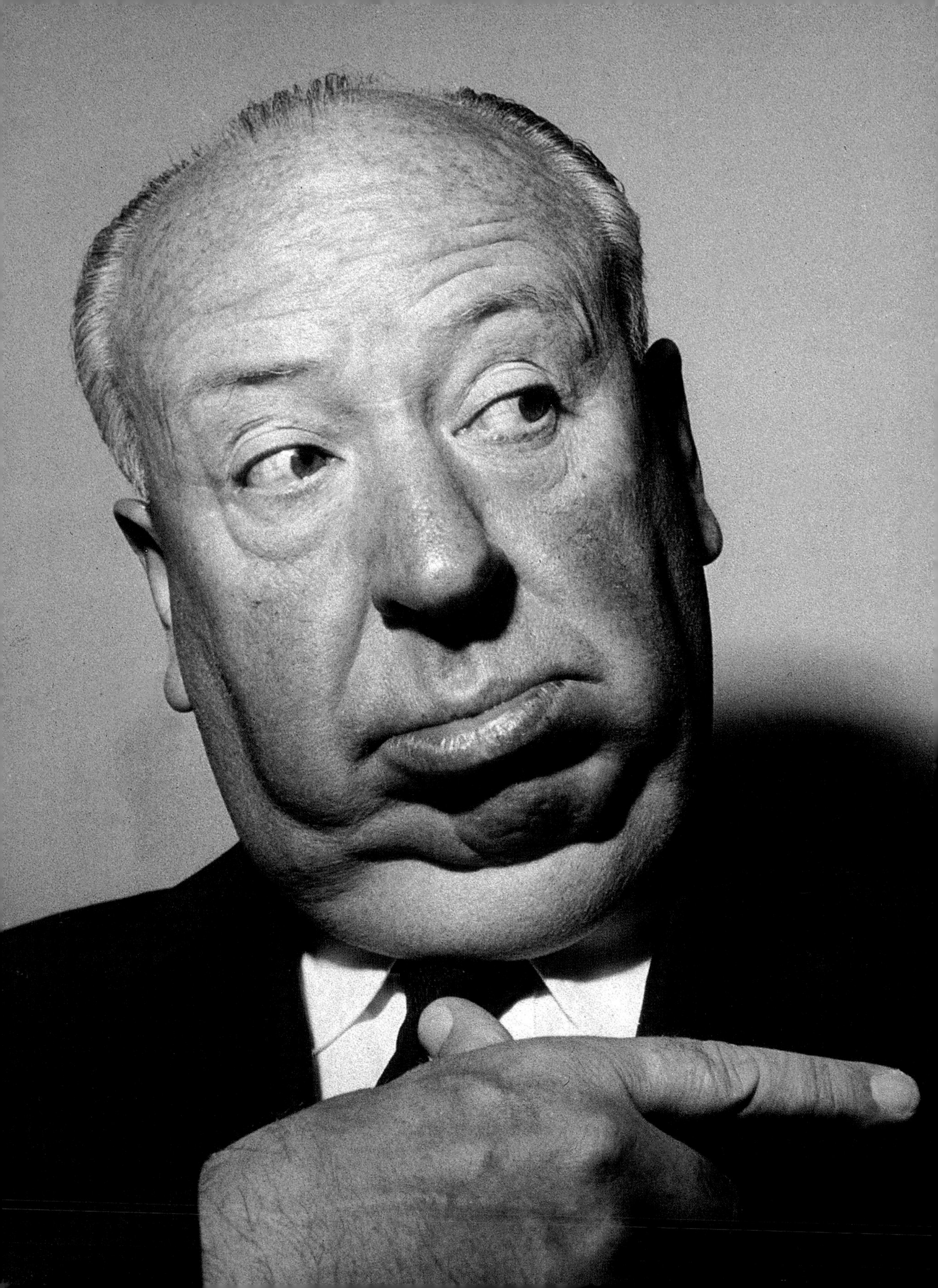

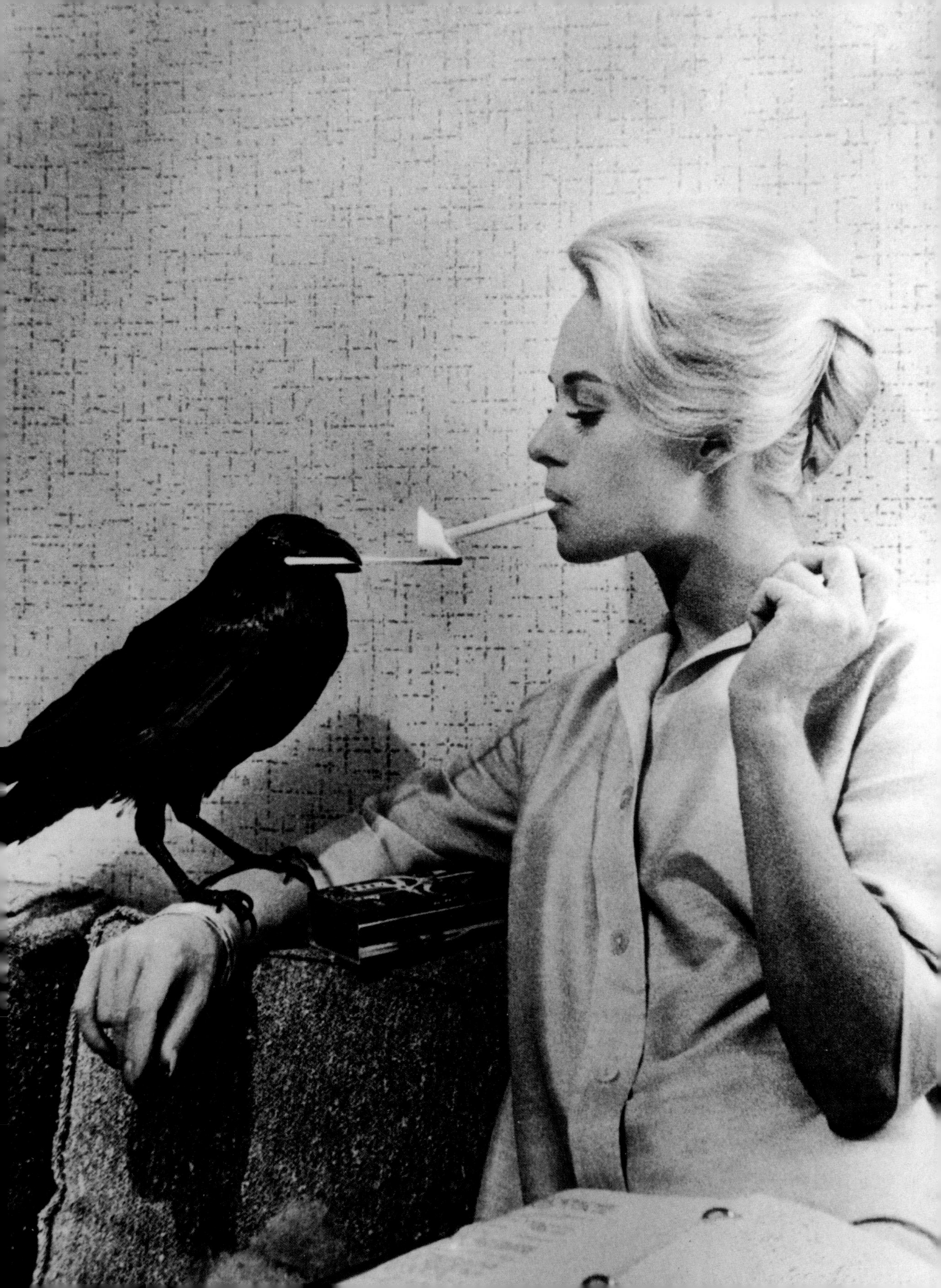

Below: **Close-up on the hair of a cool blonde. Alfred Hitchcock remained faithful to his credo, especially in this scene from *Vertigo* (1958) in which Scottie (James Stewart) grapples with Madeleine/Judy, the blonde and wicked Kim Novak.**

Opposite: **In a bun, shoulder length, or curly, the blonde hair of Alfred Hitchcock's iconic actresses in film after film embodied his fantasy. From top to bottom and left to right: Janet Leigh in *Psycho* (1960), Tippi Hedren in *Marnie* (1964), Kim Novak in *Vertigo.* (1958), Eva Marie Saint in *North by Northwest* (1959), Grace Kelly in *Dial 'M' for Murder* (1954), and Tippi Hedren in *The Birds* (1963).**

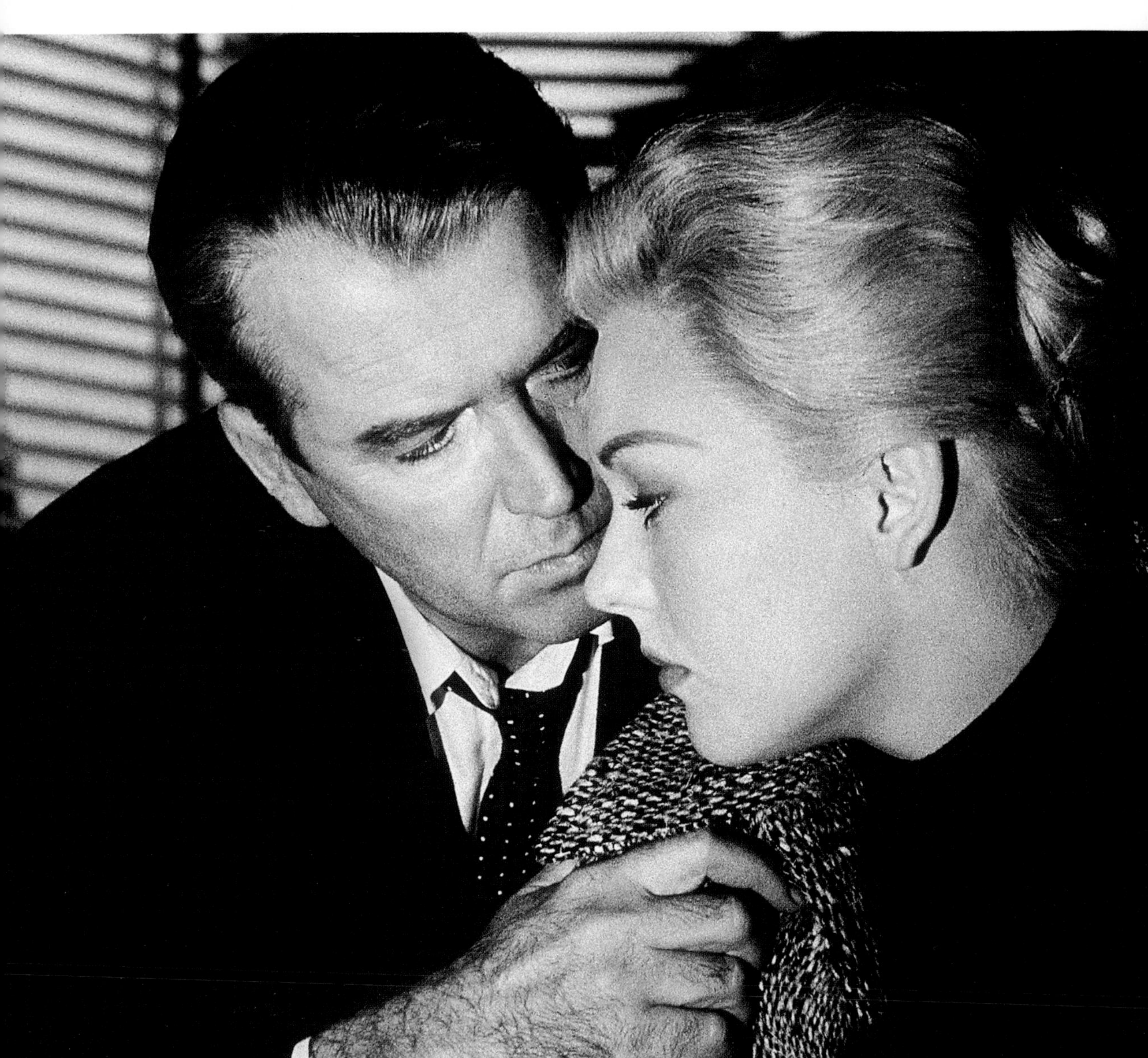

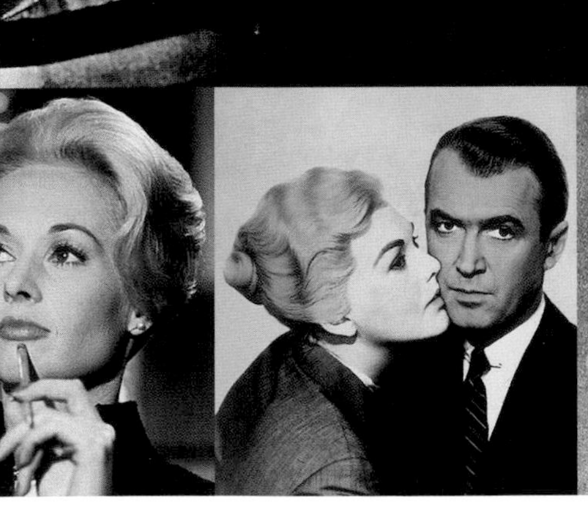

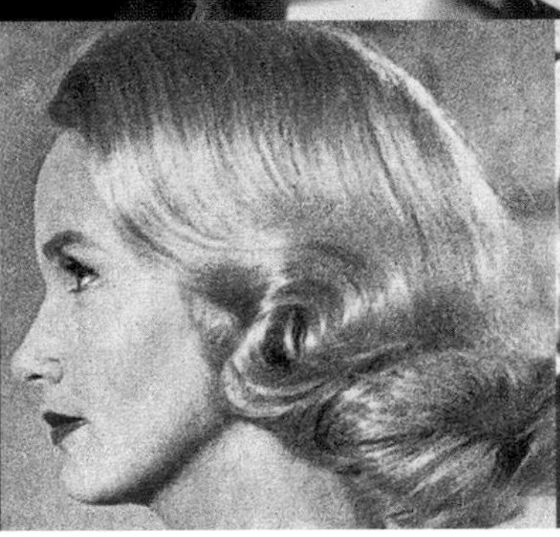

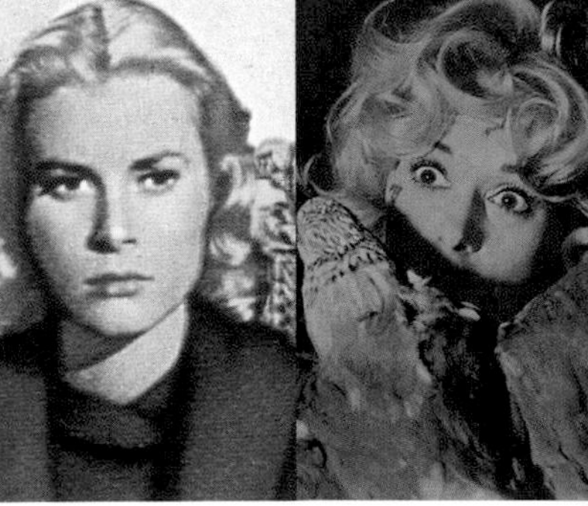

Youki
Foujita
Robert Desnos

The Snow and the Siren

Lucie Badoud was nineteen years old when she met the Japanese painter Tsuguharu Foujita in Montparnasse in Paris. But more than her youth, it was her milky skin, as white as snow—or *youki* in Japanese—that seduced the artist before his escapades separated them. Foujita transferred his passion in due form to the poet Robert Desnos.

"Who here knows an Asian with glasses and bangs on his forehead?" It was with this missing person's description directed at no one in particular on the terrace of La Rotonde, at that time the new café in Montparnasse, that nineteen-year-old Lucie Badoud made her entry into the world of painting and Surrealism. The year was 1921 and the young girl, who was not yet nicknamed Youki, was a melancholy beauty with an opulent body, chestnut hair, and huge bright eyes. She had recently become an orphan—her mother had died of liver cancer and her father was killed falling down a hidden staircase fleeing from his mistress's husband—and she had a sad, lost look that few men could resist. Several annuities gave her the financial freedom to ride out the inevitably difficult beginnings in the theater and cinema calmly, and while she waited for her big break, she passionately read everything she could get her hands on. In *La Femme assise*, by Guillaume Apollinaire, she discovered the existence of a neighborhood of artists in Montparnasse and soon took the subway there to sit on the terrace of one of those famous cafés where everything happened. At La Rotonde she noticed an odd character with bangs, a tiny moustache in the shape of an M, and a red and black shirt. He looked around for someone but remained alone. The following day Lucie's question quickly found a response. "Yes, I know him," soon replied another Asian man. "He's called Foujita and I was even a witness at his wedding." Upon further investigation, it appeared to her as if the marriage between the Japanese man and the brooding Fernande Barrey was struggling. Fernande was the queen of Montparnasse and a painter in her own right. At the beginning of their idyll together, she did not hesitate to go around to the galleries and present the work of her "little Japanese man." Her initiative was a success and, thanks to her, the dealer George Chéron took Foujita under contract and exhibited him beginning in 1917. But time passed and Foujita's ascetism became a burden to her. "I love to laugh," she said to Jean-Paul Crespelle. "I have ten flirtations a day. I'm bored with Foujita." Tired of watching him painting cats, Fernande became involved with his cousin. Foujita, who had been indifferent to her affairs with Westerners, considered her liaison with another Japanese man as an affront, and began to distance himself from her.

Foujita was in his full glory at that time. The prices of his paintings had risen—to eight thousand francs for a nude in 1922—and his gouaches were such a success that one of his collectors, Doctor Seeholzer, took him to the Vatican to paint the portrait of Pope Benedict XV. From the moment she saw Foujita, Lucie fell in love with him immediately. He didn't even notice her. It was only with the encouragement of her medical school friends that she decided to force her way through his door several days after their first meeting.

Fire and Snow

In the small paved courtyard at 5, rue Delambre in Montparnasse, an old stable had been converted into a studio. Opening the door, Lucie discovered a huge canvas with five nude women who wore early-morning expressions. Amused to see her, Foujita offered her a fan and set up a rendezvous that same night at La Rotonde. The beginnings of the conversation were difficult. Finally Foujita launched into things. "You are not Russian?" Lucie, stunned, explained that she was Belgian. Foujita's face lightened up: "I hate the Russians; they're all troublemakers." The two became inseparable and spent three days together in a hotel in Montparnasse. As a souvenir, Foujita sketched a drawing of her dancing on their bed.

The meeting with Lucie marked a turning point in Foujita's career. On his arrival in France from Japan, he had tried several styles and was influenced by the naïve paintings of Henri Rousseau ("Le Douanier") and then by Cubism. But it was while working with a celebrated model, the famous Kiki of Montparnasse, that he adopted a new approach—a more fluid painting combining off-white tones and very precise drawing—that was a synthesis of Japanese traditions and Western art. He was fascinated by the discovery of Lucie's body and her milky skin. This whiteness of flesh was the same as the white surface of the canvases he had been trying to refine for such a long time. He had found his ideal, and he called her Youki, which means "snow" in Japanese.

Fernande was now playing the role of the abandoned woman, so the couple settled into a furnished room in Passy to distance themselves from her jealous fits. Lucie, now Youki, sat for Foujita. At the 1924 Salon d'automne, *Youki, déesse de la neige* (*Youki,*

Goddess of the Snow) was a triumph. When Pablo Picasso met her, he said to Foujita: "This is Youki? She's even more beautiful than in your painting." Almost every night their friends, like Marie Vassilieff and Nicole Groult, the sister of the couturier Paul Poiret, stopped by to raise a glass at Foujita's bar, the nickname of their small apartment in Passy. They dressed up as *Alice in Wonderland* characters and Foujita painted *Avant le bal*. By 1925 they were at the center of Parisian society, and associated with Princess Murat, Jean Cocteau, the poet Raymond Radiguet, and painters Jules Pascin, André Derain, and Chaim Soutine. The summers found them on holiday in Deauville, Cannes, Douarnenez, or Bréhat. In the winter, joyous banquets were organized at cafés like La Rotonde or Select. Foujita moved closer to Montparnasse in 1927, next to Derain and Georges Braque. At night they would take walks in the private parc Montsouris, to which they had obtained a key, and when they felt like it, they would go on a trip in the huge yellow convertible that Foujita had given Youki, with its bronze miniature casting of Auguste Rodin's *L'Homme au nez cassé* (*Man with a Broken Nose*) on the hood.

Ever the avid reader, Youki moved into the first floor of Foujita's house and bought books and magazines for him. One day he discovered an issue of *La Révolution surrealiste* and asked her to get information about the group. On Man Ray's advice she drove down to the Surrealist Gallery on rue Jacques-Callot and walked into a room covered with works by Giorgio De Chirico, Max Ernst, Man Ray, and Yves Tanguy. At the back of the gallery, some very serious young people were discussing very important things. Youki was impressed, bought the collection of *La Révolution surrealiste*, and departed in her car, leaving the gang of boys on the street dumbfounded by such luxury. A few days later she bought all the books by André Breton, Louis Aragon, Tristan Tzara, and René Crevel. Soon she was admitted into the holy of holies, the Café Radio in Montmartre, where Breton, leading his entourage, was singing the praises of one of the best poets of the group, Robert Desnos, who was on a trip to Cuba at the time.

One evening at the OK Bar on the rue Bréa, some friends introduced her to Robert Desnos, a thin young man with a clean face blocked by a stray lock that fell over his eyes. He was wearing a tuxedo and Youki found him unbearable. She did not change her mind when he launched into one of his Surrealist games. "You have the eyes of an oyster," he said to her, while taking off his glasses. Desnos took hold of three paper containers on the

Opposite: **Portrait of Youki Desnos.**

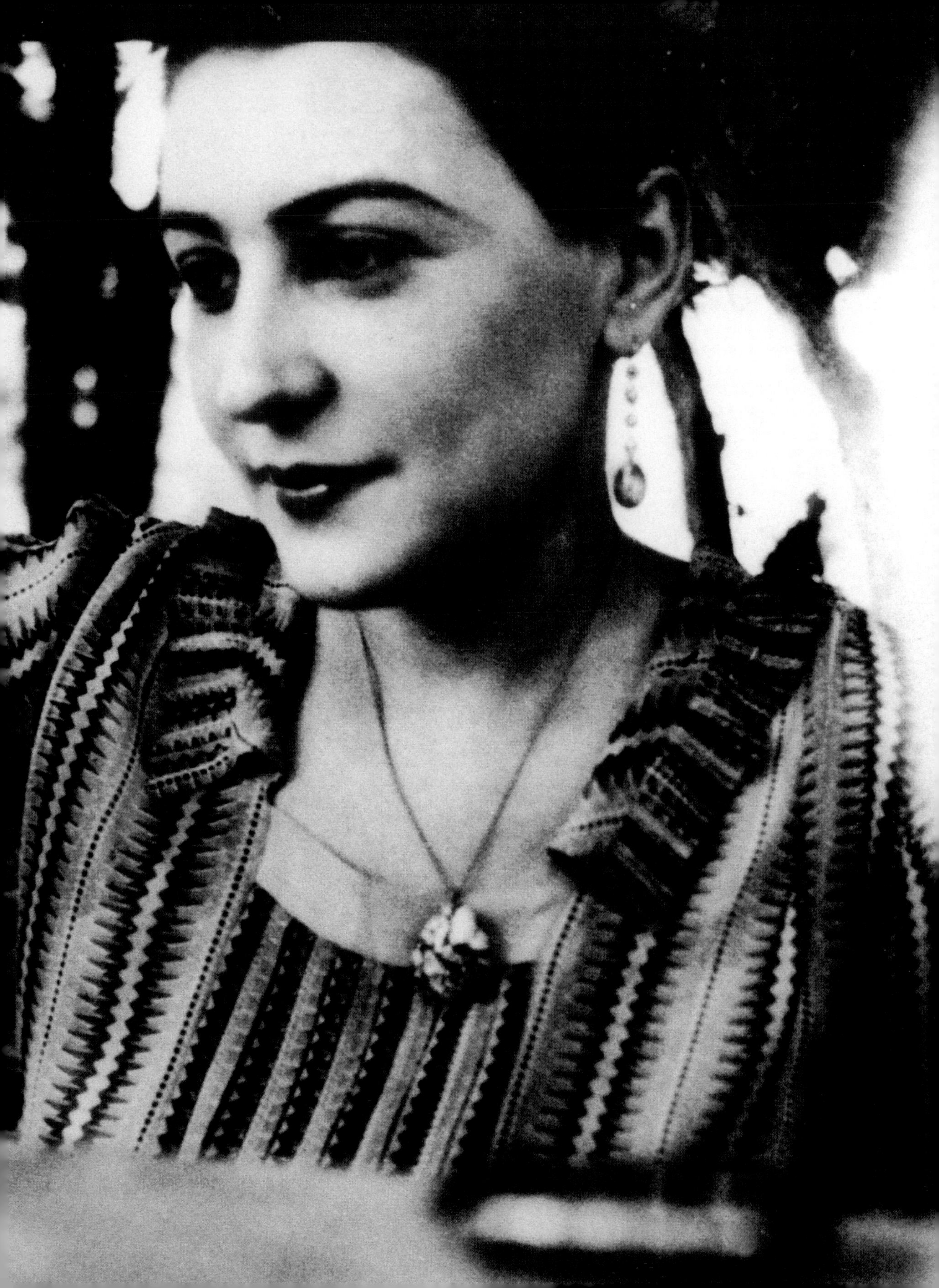

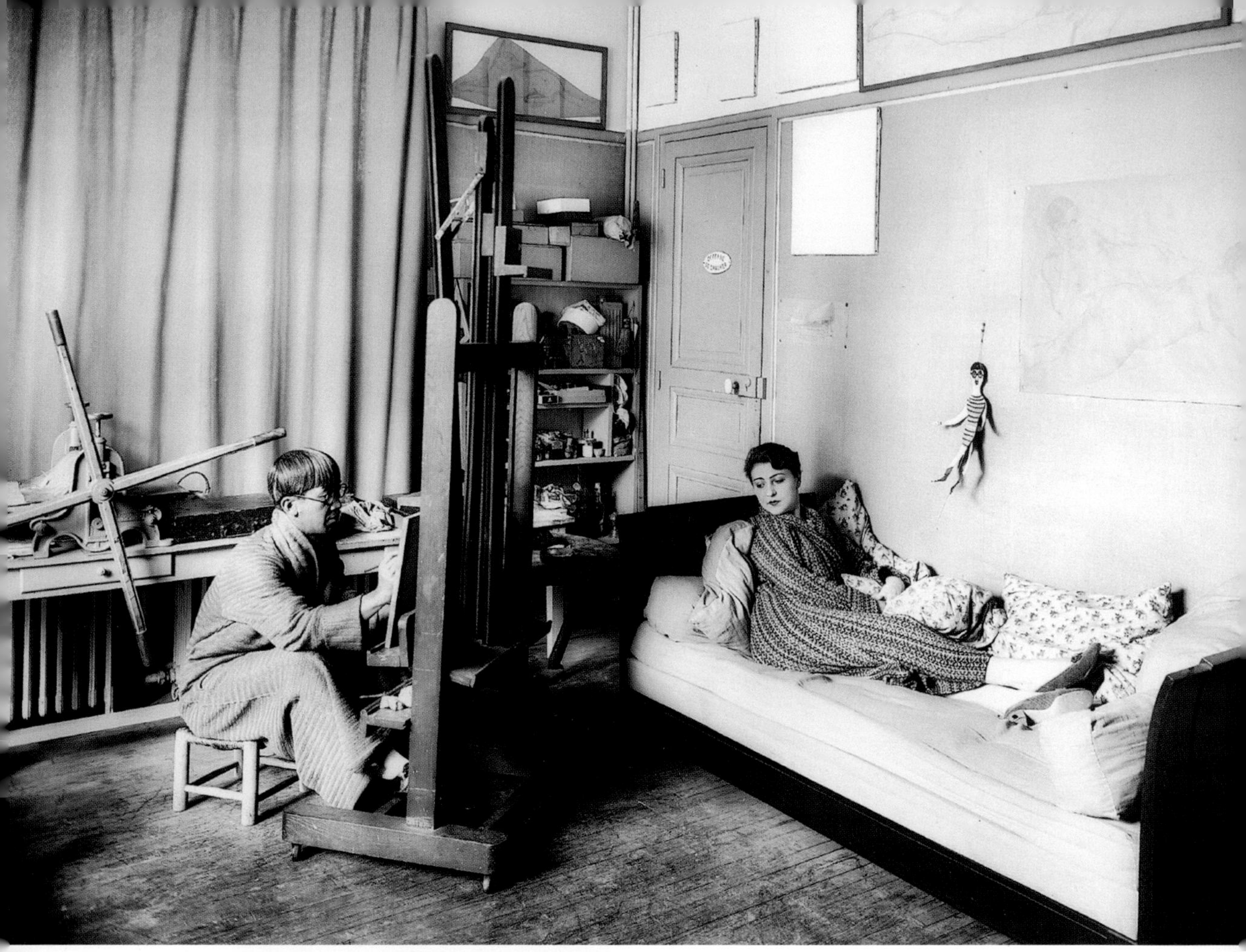

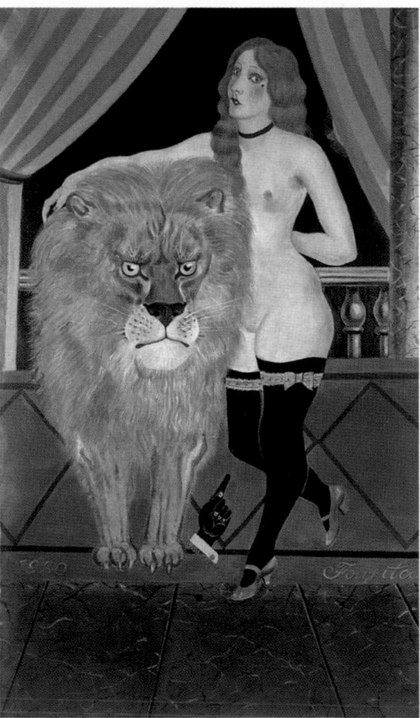

Above: **In 1920 in a former stable on the rue Delambre in Montparnasse that had been converted into a studio, Foujita never wearied of painting Youki. On the wall a puppet representing the painter surveys the scene.**
Left: **Foujita, *La Dompteuse et le Lion* (*The Lion Tamer*; 1930).**

Opposite, top: **Foujita, *Youki, déesse de la neige* (*Youki, Goddess of the Snow*; 1924).**
Opposite, bottom: **The couple at home in their library. When they separated, Foujita said to Youki: "For you, it's laughter. For me, silence."**

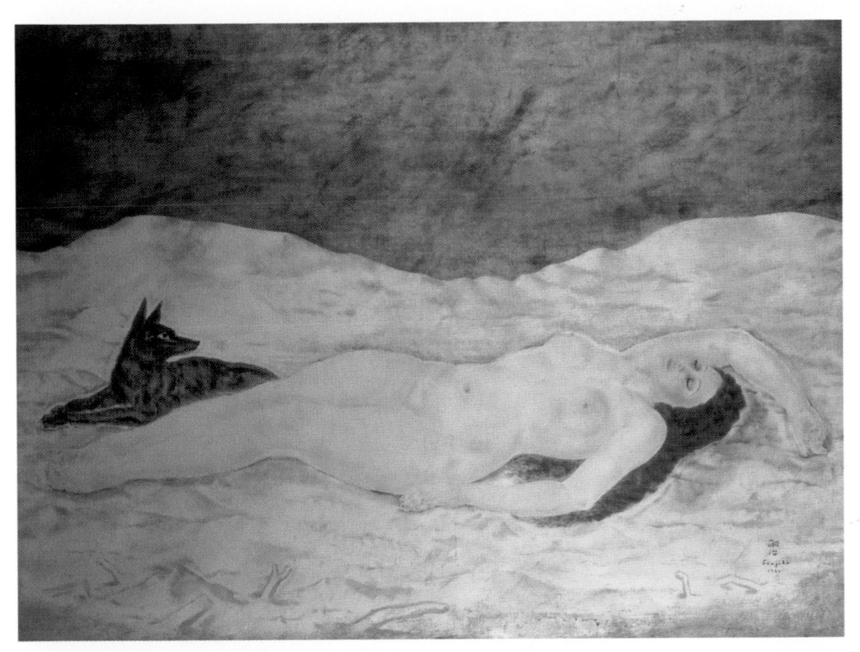

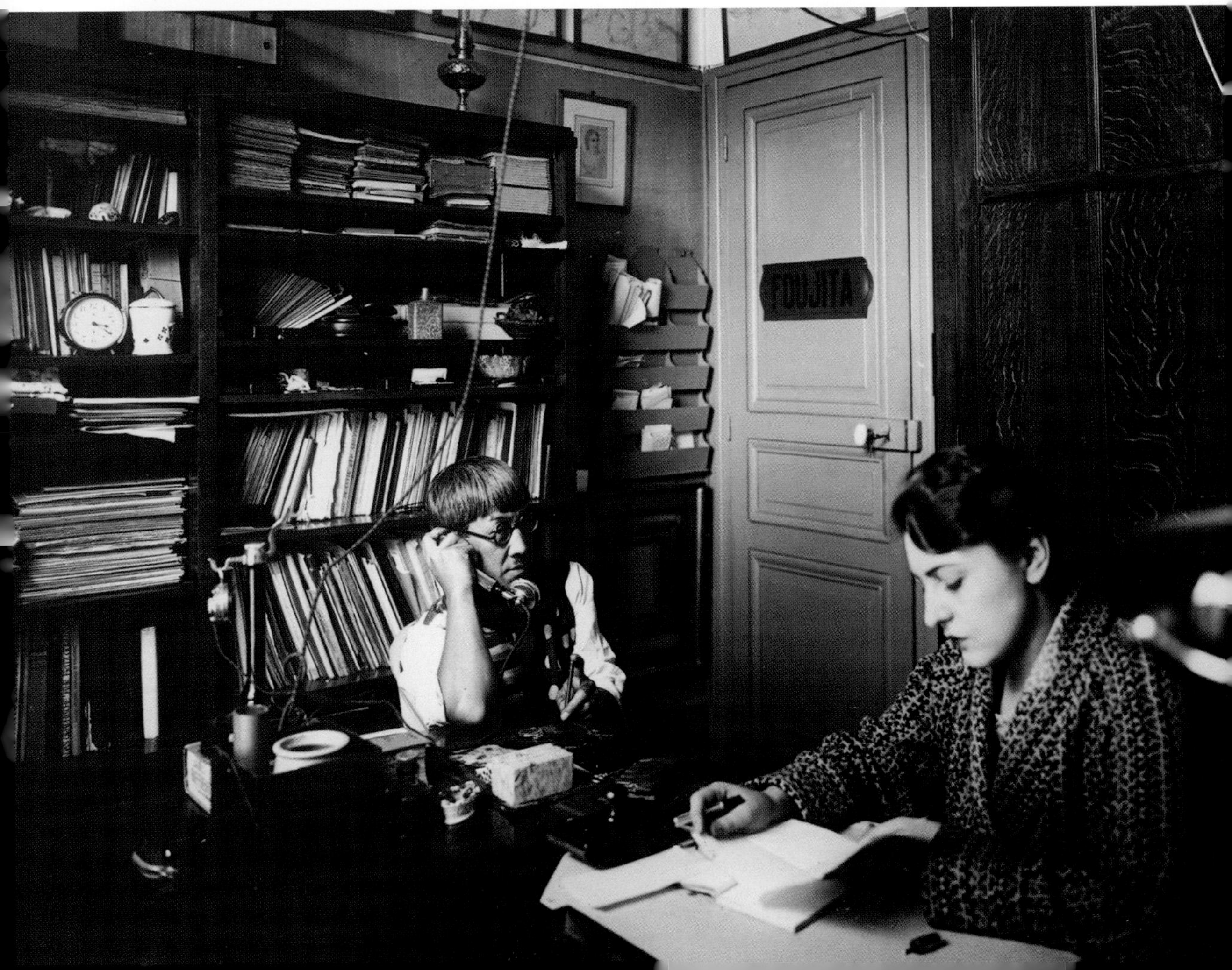

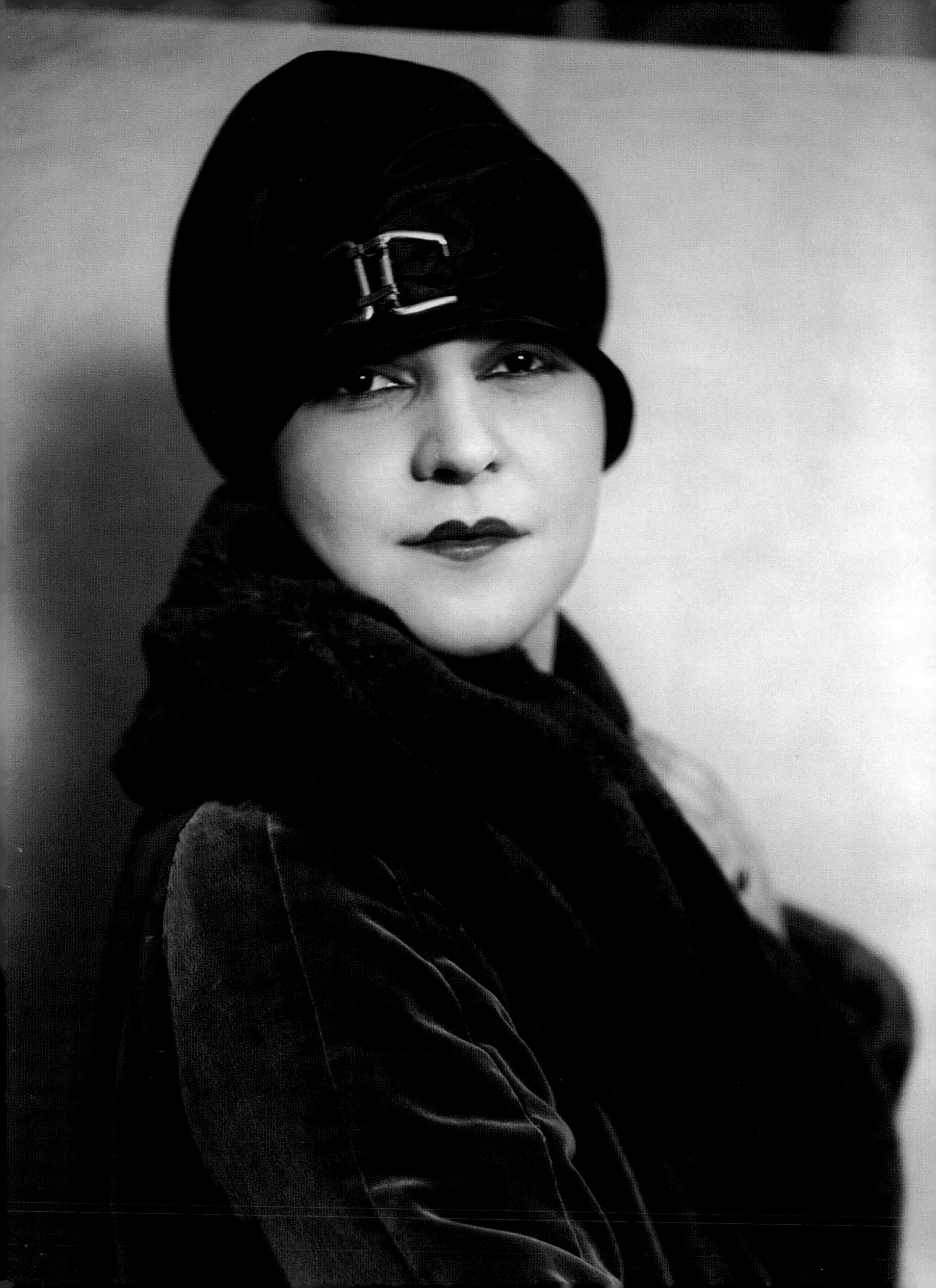

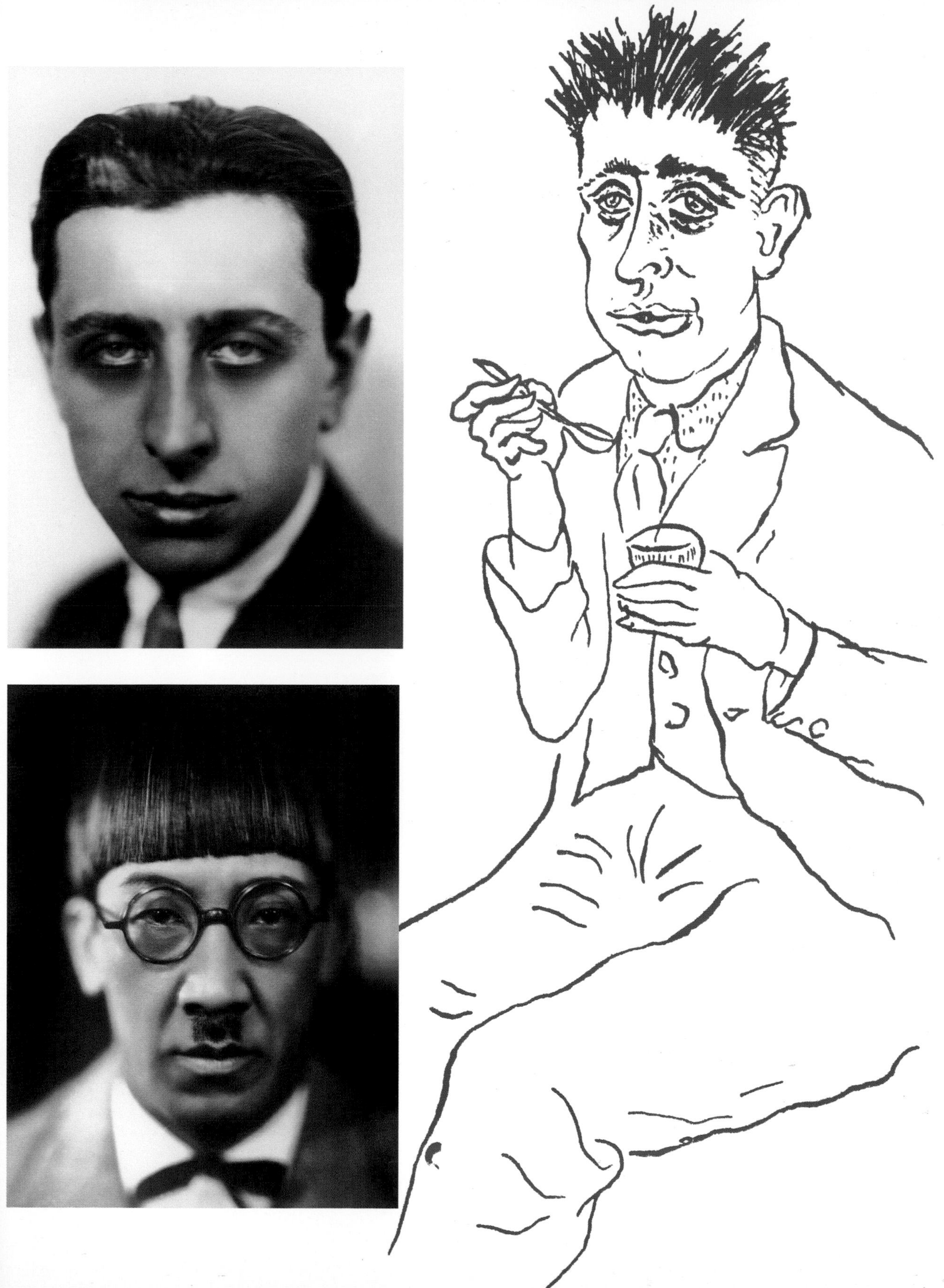

Page 158: **Portrait of Youki Desnos.**
Page 159: **(Top, left) Robert Desnos in 1927; (Bottom, left) Foujita; (Top, right) Desnos drawn by Foujita.**

counter, twisted them and made a spider. Then he gently let fall several drops of liquid into the center of the spider while agitating its legs. He explained that the wet moving paper was the man's sexual organ depositing his semen on the woman's. Youki was a little annoyed. When she recounted her meeting to Breton, who was quite puritanical despite his liberal airs, he was also shocked and swore to send a very blunt letter to Desnos. Several days later Youki met Desnos again and apologized for having spoken to Breton. Since his return from Cuba, the poet was no longer drawn to the pope of Surrealism and wouldn't tolerate his ukases, his mental rigidity, and his hypocrisy. Besides, Desnos was charmed by the story.

The Siren and the Sea Horse

Youki, Foujita's snow, became Desnos's siren. Until the poet's death, this bewitching woman and dangerous wisp would be at the heart of his creativity, like in the key poem "Siramour," which celebrates the union of Youki the siren and Desnos the sea horse. "O nothing can separate the Siren from the Sea Horse; Nothing can undo this union."

As if he had already given up the fight, Foujita tattoed a siren on Youki's thigh and a she-bear with stars on Robert's arm. He yearned for calm: "Youki, I am old. Youki I do not love alcohol. No noise. Not music all the time. For you, it's laughter. For me, silence." Foujita left alone on a trip to New York, and Youki moved in with Desnos. The three-sided relationship became four-sided when Foujita fell in love with Madeleine, a model with long red hair. Foujita and Desnos were friends, and jealousy does not seem to have taken hold of them. When, overwhelmed by financial problems, Foujita left France for good, he left these words for Youki: "You now have a faithful friend, Robert, he is very gentle and what admiration he has for you. He will no longer leave with you [*sic*]. He has taken my place, you basically live with him and for him you are the dearest thing in the world. . . . Youki, I am leaving, be healthy. Have pity for me. I am leaving forever. Adieu." A lamp decorated by Foujita lit up Robert and Youki's living room in their apartment on rue Mazarine. In the black-and-white tiled dining room, guests gathered around a big table dotted with bottles of red wine. On Saturdays Robert would prepare lobster à l'américaine, and when the meal was over, still more guests arrived who did not always know the master of the house. Youki often lingered dreamily in front of the painting *La Dompteuse et le Lion* (*The Lion*

Tamer; 1930), which hung on the wall. Youki was looking at Youki. There was also *Nature Morte au chat* (*Still Life with Cat*), which reminded them that thousands of miles away, the man with the glasses and the bangs on his forehead still watched over them. It was a fragile happiness, especially when Youki disappeared for whole days. Desnos wrote: "Youki, who often torments me, who is neither gentle nor tender and without whom I cannot do as easily as she can do without me." And it was a short-lived happiness as well. In the summer of 1939 they found themselves in Belle-Île on the Atlantic coast where they dreamed of taking a ninety-nine-year lease on a fort that was for rent. But the war arrived. Desnos, a journalist and a resistance fighter, was arrested in 1944 and sent to Buchenwald. In one of his last letters to Youki, dated July 1944 (he died of typhus on June 8, 1945), he wrote: "I would have liked to give you 100,000 American cigarettes, a dozen dresses from the great couturiers, an apartment on the rue Seine, a car, a cottage in the Compiègne forest, the one on Belle-Île and a little four-penny bouquet. While I'm gone, keep flowers around constantly. I'll pay you back for them. . . . But above everything, drink a bottle of good wine and think of me." By staying Youki Desnos, Lucie Badoud remained the snow and the siren forever, celebrating with her name the memory of the two great men in her life.

Bibliography

Desnos, Robert, *The Voice: Selected Poems of Robert Desnos*. New York: Grossman Publishers, 1972.

Desnos, Foujita et Youki: Un amour surréaliste. Exhibition catalogue. Paris: Musée de Montparnasse/Éd. des Cendres, 2001.

Klüver, Billy, and Julie Martin. *Kiki's Paris: Artists and Lovers 1900-1930*. Reissue. New York: Harry N. Abrams, Inc., 2002.

Selz, Jean. *Foujita*. New York: Crown Publishers, Inc., 1981.

Giulietta Masina
Federico Fellini

The Two Clowns

The diminutive Giulietta Masina played an extended role at the side of the towering Federico Fellini, and even disappeared from his cinema for some time before making a triumphant return. The woman who, by her own admission, was not at all her husband's type—he being a well-known lover of well-endowed beauties—remained his partner for fifty years and participated in seven of his most beautiful films.

> *—Guilietta is my ideal actress, the one who inspires me, a magical presence in my work.*
> *—You're lying. I was never allowed to set foot on the set of films I wasn't in because you found my presence unwelcome.*
> *—Giulietta is my Beatrice.*
> *—The truth is we have divided duties between ourselves. Federico rules supreme on the set; I in the home. But he has always made me pay for the sovereignty I exercise indoors. I have never loved myself: I am a dwarf with a little round face and bristly hair. Ever since he was preparing* La Strada *I have dreamed that Federico would give me the face of Garbo or Katharine Hepburn; instead he has made my face even rounder and my hair ever more bristly and has shrunk me even more. He turned me into a punk ante litteram.*
> *—I made you more seductive than Jean Harlow or Marilyn Monroe.*
> *—As you all know, Federico loves women who are monumental, curvaceous, sumptuous, but I, just because I am so little and skinny, managed to sneak in between those living statues, disguised in the clothes of Gelsomina, Cabiria, Juliet of the Spirits, Ginger, and thus enjoy my revenge on him.*

Having gone to Tokyo in 1990 to screen *The Voice of the Moon*, the director's twenty-fourth and final film, Federico Fellini and Giulietta Masina good-naturedly improvised this domestic scene in front of an enraptured audience. At the end the crowd broke into wild applause.

A Story of Love Letters

It is difficult to believe that Giulietta Masina was not Federico Fellini's "type" after forty-seven years and seven films together, including some of the director's most beautiful works inspired and performed by the actress. However, more than her physique, it was Giulietta's voice that first seduced Fellini. Their meeting was like one of those romances evoked in his second film, *Lo sceicco bianco* (*The White Sheik*; 1952). In 1942 a nice young girl of twenty-one, who had just graduated from the Ursuline school of Sant'Angela

Merici, was hired on the radio. She had already tried her hand at a little bit of theater at the university of La Sapienza in Rome, and dreamed of being an actress. Each morning she would leave her aunt Giulia's comfortable apartment—with its little lace mats and landscapes of languorous cows on the walls—to return to the radio studio. Every day she would read to listeners the new adventures of Cico and Pallina, a young married couple beset by all sorts of hard times. During the war young Romans were fascinated by episodes entitled "First Love," "Bridal Night," and "Honeymoon," but the program shocked her aged aunt, and she forbade her niece from reading the satirical newspaper, *Marc'Aurelio*, which published the stories. Federico Fellini, the author of these sentimental but satiric pieces, had quickly become a star of the radio waves, and accompanied the printed versions with his risqué caricatures. Giulietta would not, for anything in the world, miss an issue of the paper that she read on the sly. And so it was with a certain pride that she received a telephone call from Fellini one day complimenting her on her voice and asking her to send him her photo for the filmed version of the adventures of Cico and Pallina.

When they met in the offices of the radio station for the first time, Giulietta was struck at once by Fellini's very long and thick black hair and by his very short gray flannel suit. They spoke about the film, and the apprentice director invited the future actress to lunch the next day at Castaldi, the grand restaurant on piazza Poli. Giulietta was dressed like a well-bred girl, with a tartan skirt and a cardigan buttoned to the chin. With her short height and her ninety-two pounds (forty-two kilograms), she felt minuscule in comparison to Fellini, whose thinness and deep and inquiring anxious eyes struck her. He was only a year older but seemed much more mature. He was still wearing the same short pants he had on the day before, and Giulietta hesitated before selecting a dish for fear of spoiling things. Appetizers, main course, dessert, the meal went on and on, and Giulietta proposed to share the bill "in the Roman manner." Offended, Fellini pulled out a wad of bills and left an enormous tip "worthy of an Indian prince, a Rothschild, a Hollywood star," recalled the guest.

They saw each other again and Giulietta invited him to her home. Fellini courted her diligently. "An hour before his arrival a little boy brought us baskets of flowers, one for me, one for my aunt," recalled Giulietta. In the young woman's basket, there was an illustration of two little birds who were making tender love, and in aunt Giulia's, a little cocker spaniel who jumped in the air when you pulled on a cord. Giulia was won over. And Fellini no less so: "The day I was allowed to visit Giulietta's home, I was quite stunned to discover a world that I did not even dream existed. A world of serenity, harmony, gaiety. Outside on the street, it was a huge mess. Italy was already defeated, the Germans were thirsty for the final killings. There was the insane disorder of war. I adored Giulietta's home. A very turn-of-the-century atmosphere prevailed there. It smelled of wax polish, verbena, and starched curtains." Fellini got into the habit of visiting them. "For the first time in my life," he recalled, "I was completely comfortable with another person." The feeling was even stranger since he had the impression of knowing Giulietta before having met her: "Giulietta Masina was the woman of my destiny. I've come to believe that our relationship really existed before the day we met each other for the first time."

Gentleness and serenity. The contrast with his own family was striking, and Fellini would only remember sad and violent episodes. "I invented a youth, a family, relationships with women and with life," he repeated to would-be biographers. Childhood was the sun and sea of Rimini, half-naked bodies running toward the water, and the cadaver of an enormous sunfish stranded on the beach. There were the women with voluptuous breasts who descended on the Grand Hotel for the summer and the out-of-work gigolos—the *vitelloni*, or callow youths—who made love to them and who always found themselves alone and without a dime at the end of the season. Childhood was also a body that was still so thin that his friends called him Gandhi. He was ashamed of putting on a bathing suit, never learned to swim, and stayed in the sun fully dressed. To amuse himself, he collected everything that had fallen on the ground—plane tree leaves, dust, dung—and made cigarettes out of them using newspaper, then hid himself in the cabanas on the edge of the sea to smoke.

Although a brat, a little rascal, an unruly child in his memories, Fellini had actually been a nice and gentle little boy. He claimed to be a bad student, barely good in drawing and sketching, but his schoolbooks show excellent notes. He went to a college in Fano, a little town in the Marches region of Italy, which would be the inspiration for the traumatic memories in his film *Otto e Mezzo* (*8½*; 1963). Too bad it was his brother who frequented it. Giulietta didn't care whether he was a rascal or a brilliant student. Nor did she mind about her fiancé's position as a military draft dodger, which forced him to live in a certain secrecy. Unable to make the film of *The Adventures of Cico and Pallina*, the voice and the pen behind the soap opera decided to marry each other. All that remained was to win over her parents, who remained in Vicenza: Gaetano, the violinist father and now a cashier in Montecatini, and Flavia Pasqualin, a teacher. A group outing was organized and "Federico seduced everyone, without exception."

A Clandestine Marriage

The marriage took place October 30, 1943, but secrecy compelled them not to publish the nuptials. Their next-door neighbor, a priest from the basilica of Santa Maria Maggiore, married them. He received permission from the pope to celebrate mass at home due to his advanced age. The young couple entered through the front door, received the benediction in the living room in front of a chest transformed into an altar, and exited through another door. Riccardo, Fellini's younger brother, sang Franz Schubert's *Ave Maria*, as he would do later in *I Vitelloni* (1953). The scene was already Felliniesque.

To make a living, Fellini wrote for newspapers like *Marc'Aurelio* and for the cinema. When they had a few pennies, they frequented the most expensive restaurants. But most of the time their finances were very low. Fellini conscientiously noted receipts in a journal: ten lire in January 1944 and in February, "even less than the month before." Until the arrival of the Allies, the young couple lived primarily on the sale of furniture from Fellini's studio apartment and on private lessons given by Giulietta. Each time Fellini went out, he risked being arrested. One evening he was captured in a roundup but miraculously escaped. When he was late in returning, a worried Giulietta, four months pregnant, left to look for him but fell down the stairs and had a miscarriage. She became pregnant again the next year, and gave birth to a little boy christened Federichino who died two weeks later. "After that, neither Federico nor I thought any longer about children. It was a closed chapter," said Giulietta who would forever be the childless woman-child in life as in Fellini's cinema.

Acting parts for Giulietta poured in at the end of the war. In *Paisà* (*Paisan*; 1946) by Roberto Rossellini, she appeared in a checked dress on the staircase of their home where the director filmed several scenes of the liberation of Florence. More important roles soon followed, alternating between the theater and the cinema. In 1948 she played on stage with Marcello Mastroianni in *Angelica* by Leo Ferrero. She spoke to him again ten years later when Fellini was looking for an actor to play the role of the journalist in *La Dolce Vita*. Did Fellini really say to him: "I thought of

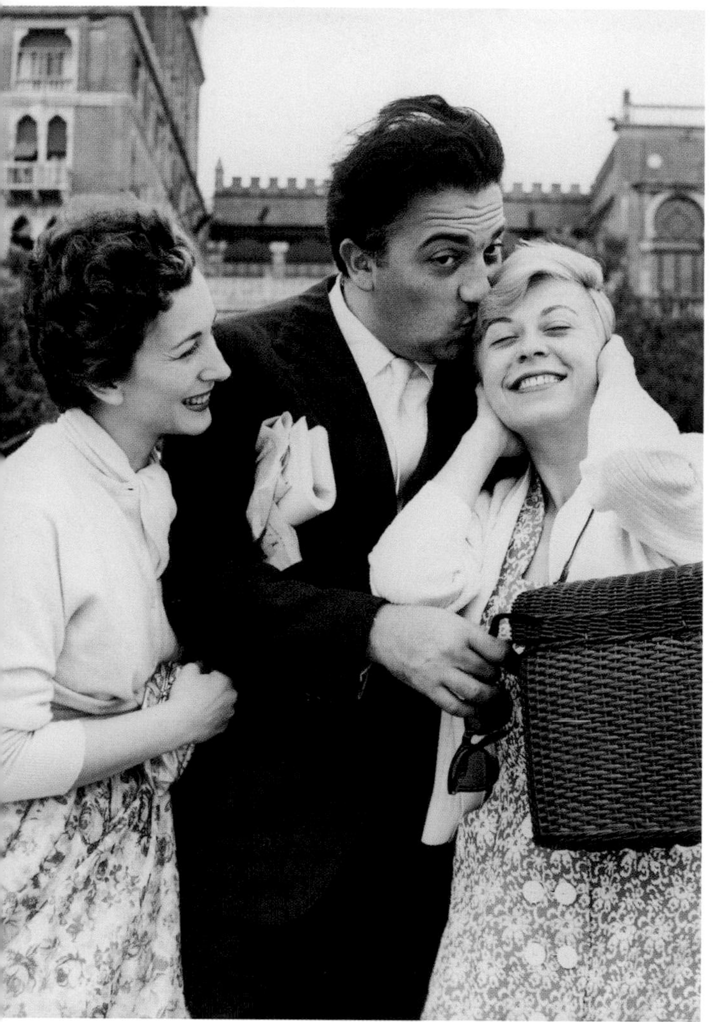

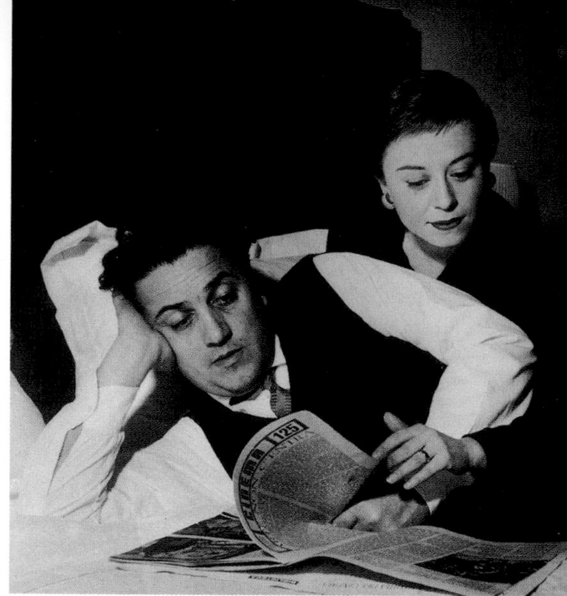

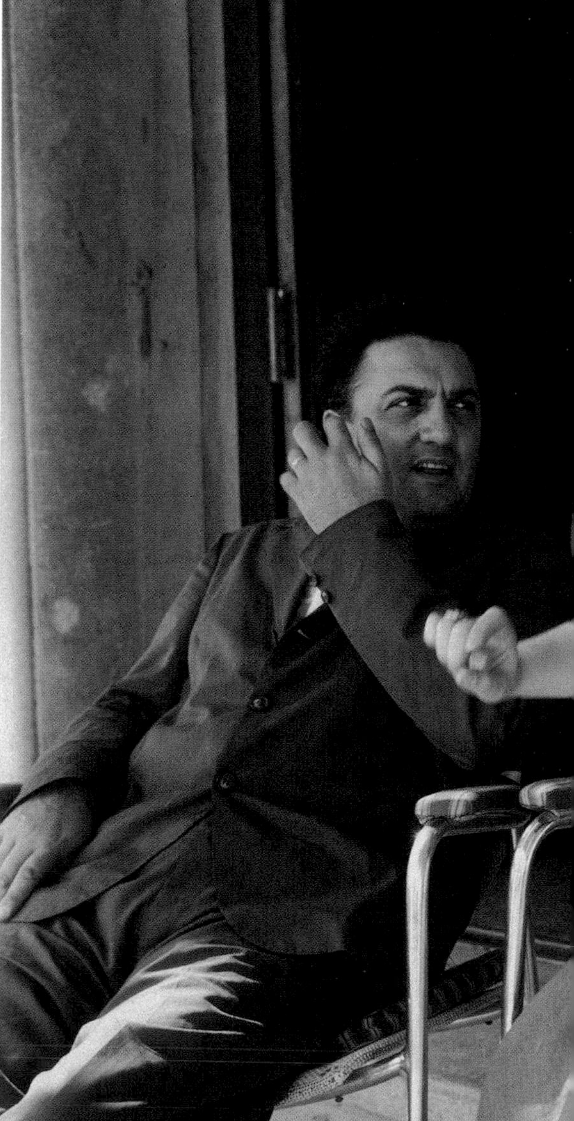

Above: **Valentina Cortese, Federico Fellini, and Giulietta Masina around 1955.**

Right, top and bottom: **For the Masina/Fellini couple, 1954 was the year of *La Strada*, with a role custom-made for Giulietta. The film's international success would turn their lives upside down. Paris and London celebrated them, and for better or worse, Giulietta became Gelsomina.**

Right: **Whether in the privacy of a hotel room or on a café terrace, paparazzi chased this couple who were so physically different from each other and who had given birth to an equally surprising film.**

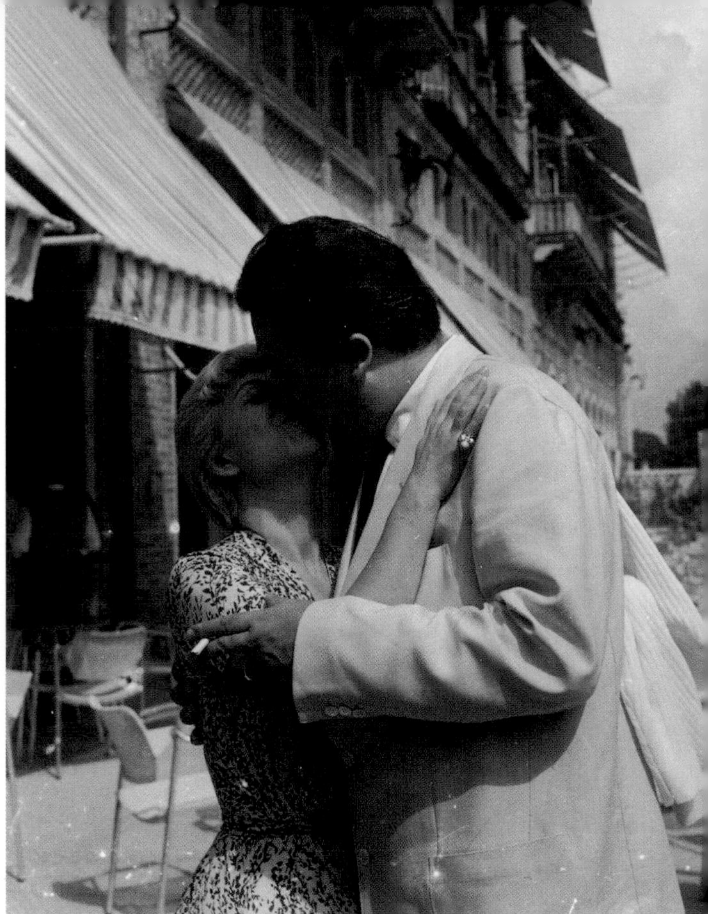

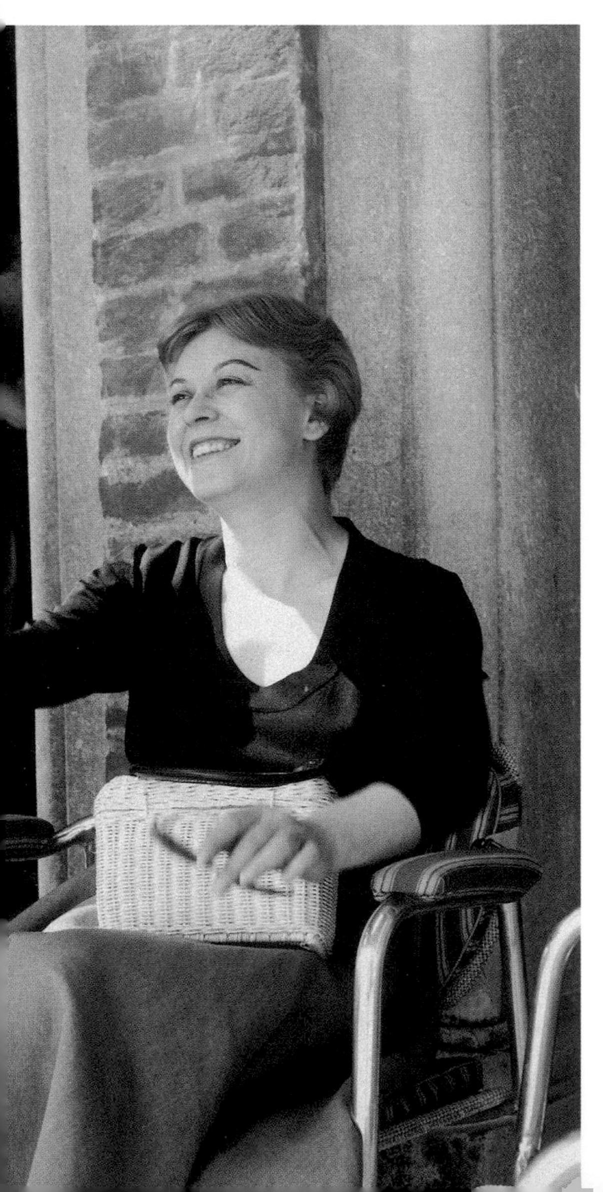

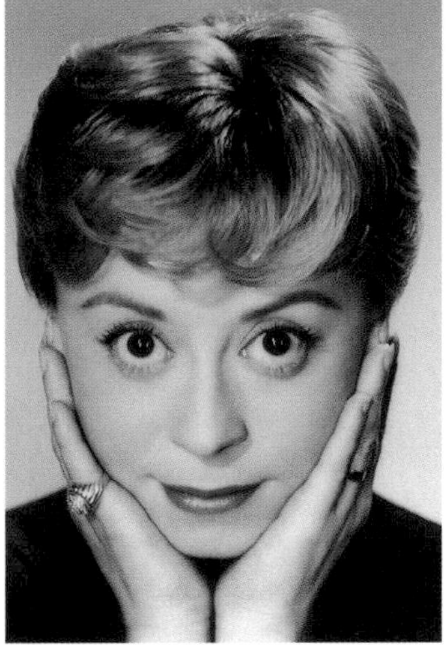

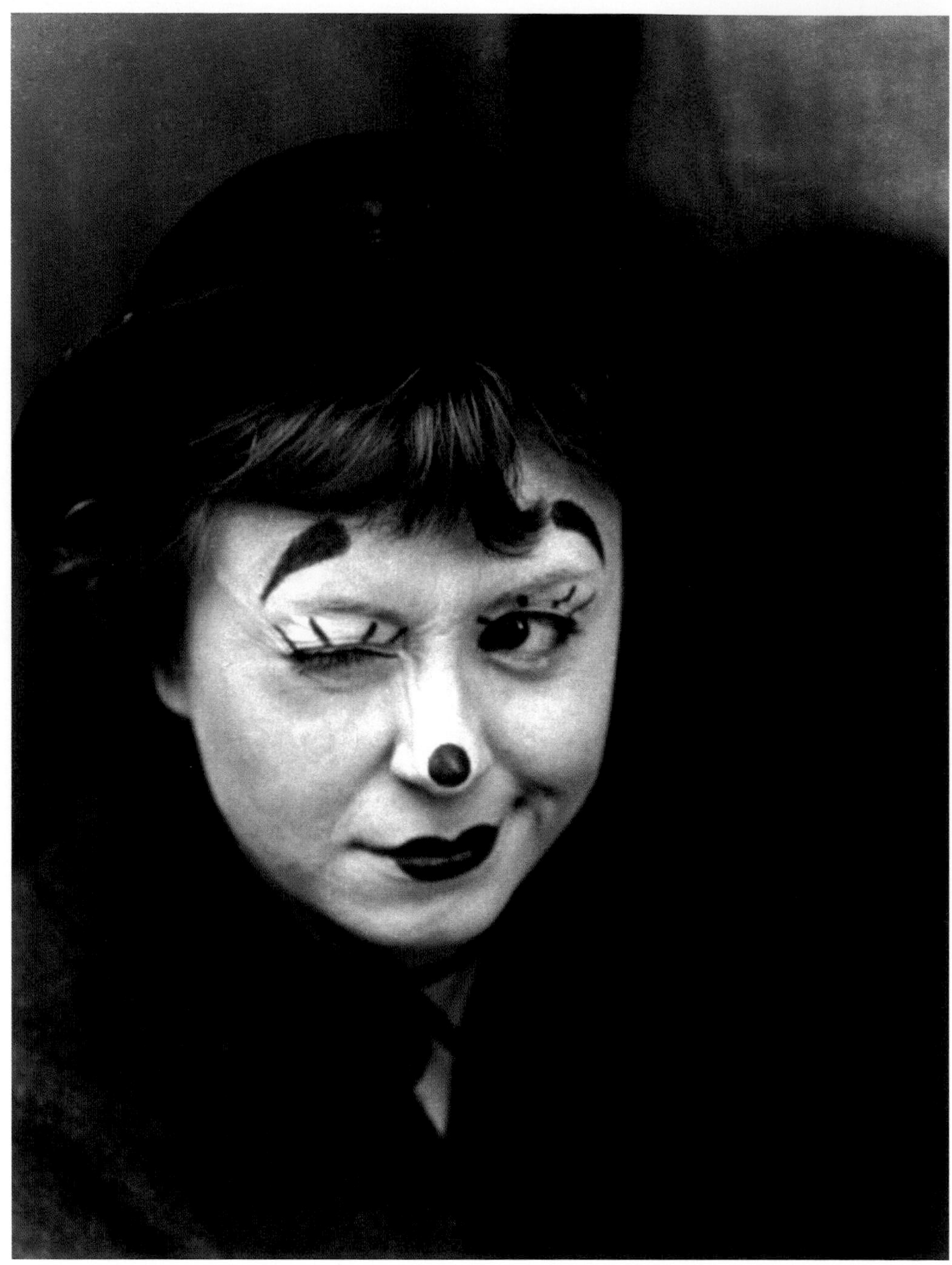

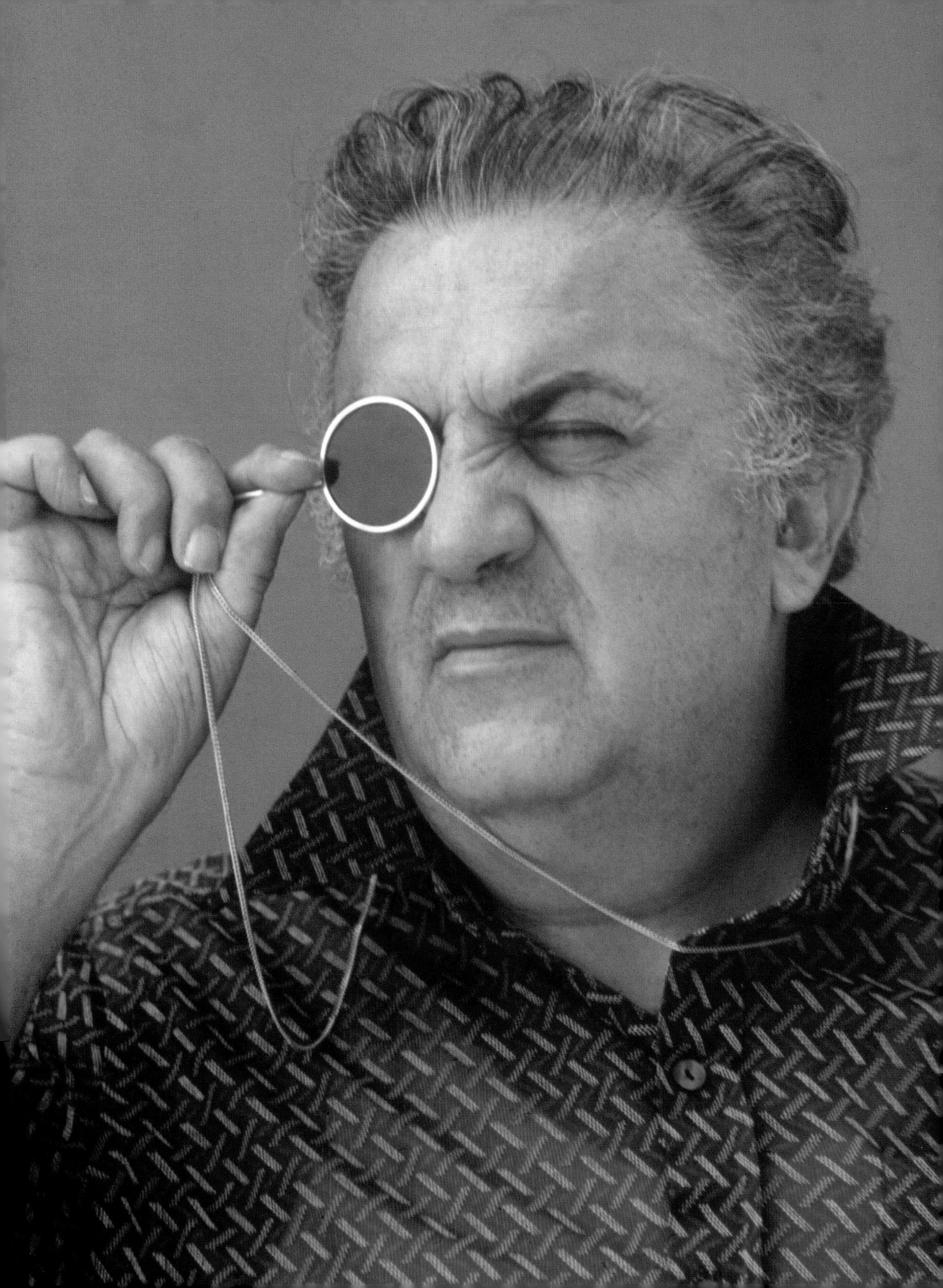

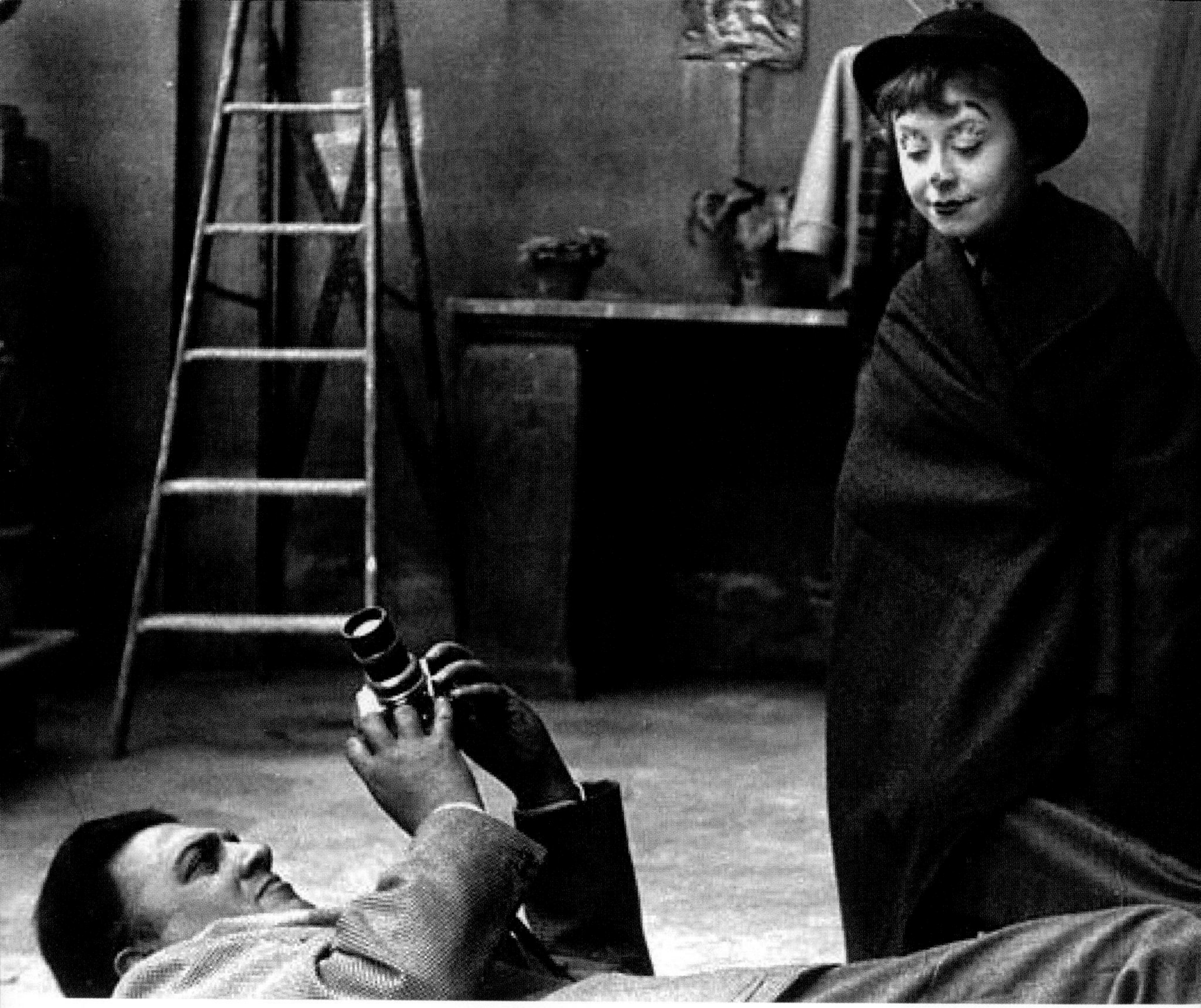

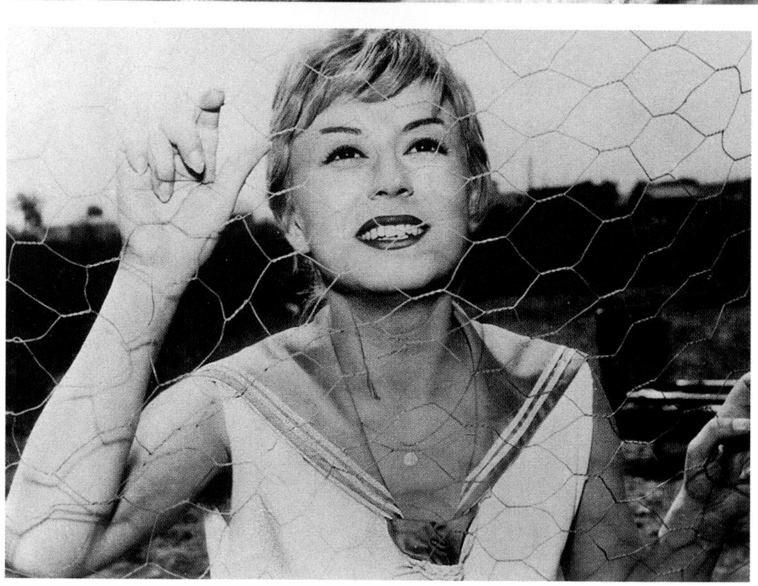

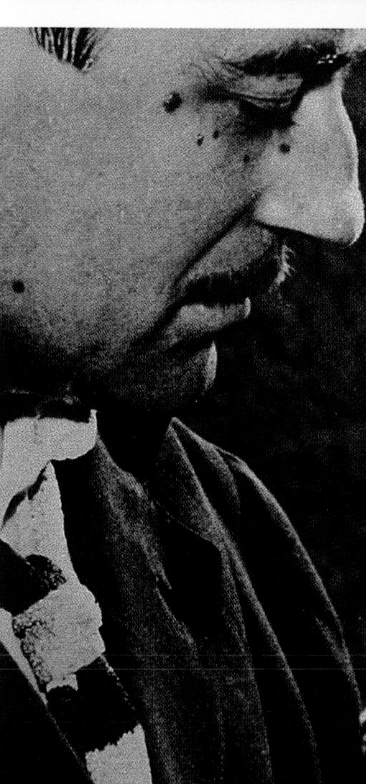

Page 170: **Giulietta Masina during the filming of *La Strada*.**
Page 171: **Federico Fellini on the set of *Il Casanova di Federico Fellini* (*Fellini's Casanova*) in 1975.**
Right and opposite: **Neither a man nor a woman, Gelsomina in *La Strada* was a badly coiffed and badly made-up androgynous clown whose pallor and sad eyes evoke Charlie Chaplin.**

Below: **In *Le Notti di Cabiria* (*Nights of Cabiria*; 1957), Cabiria (Giulietta Masina), a Roman prostitute, is thrown into the Tiber River by one of her clients and endures all kinds of humiliations, her innocent heart mistreated by the perfidy of men.**

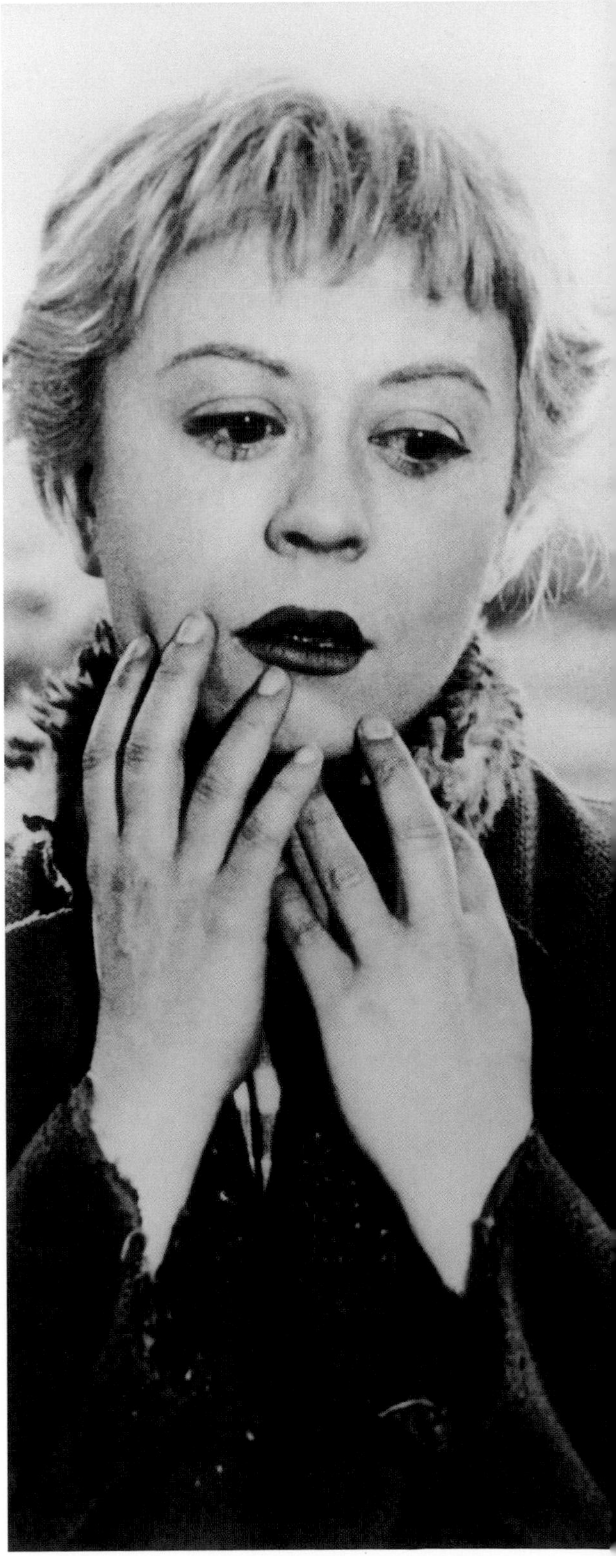

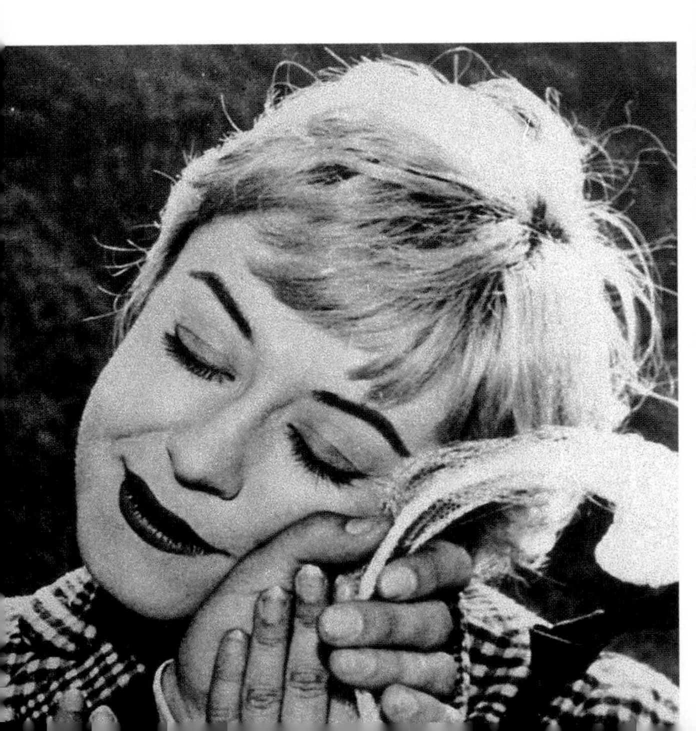

you for the part of the protagonist because you have such an ordinary face?" The legend persists.

Things were also not slow in changing for Fellini after the end of the war. In 1950 he succeeded in making his first film, *Luci del Varieta* (*Variety Lights*), followed in 1952 by *Lo sceicco bianco*. The screenplays were written for Giulietta, who transformed herself first into Melina Amour then into Cabiria, who lived in the world of the picture books, in which the woman looked for the hero on paper, the White Sheik, with whom she maintains an epistolary love affair, signing her letters the Passionate Doll.

But the great year for Giulietta was 1954 with *La Strada*—a custom-made part whose international success ended up by masking the harshness of the role. "Zampano buys a simple young girl named Gelsomina for ten thousand lire and leaves with her by night." So the script began. Neither a woman nor a man, Gelsomina is an androgynous clown, badly coiffed and badly made up, whose pallor and sad eyes evoke Chaplin. The victim of a brute, she manages by her goodness and her death to lead him to love, and a devastated Zampano weeps on the beach touched forever by his remorse. When the producers of *La Strada*—Dino de Laurentiis and Carlo Ponti—suggested hiring a pin-up girl for the role of Gelsomina, Fellini became angry and instead imposed the actress who had inspired his character, giving Giulietta the first major success of her career. In Paris photographs of Giulietta made the front page of newspapers; in London the film was shown for the royal family and all the major figures in Italian cinema, who congregated at the Italian embassy: Rossellini, of course, but also directors Luchino Visconti and Michelangelo Antonioni, and actresses Sophia Loren and Gina Lollobrigida.

The Legend of a Dream

Sitting next to Queen Elizabeth, who wore a dress of pink flowers and a crown on her head, Giulietta had on a dress of white tulle, embroidered in silver, that she had earlier worn in Venice. The only damper on this special evening was that Federico and Giulietta were not invited to the gala dinner that followed. They were still not well known enough. Amused, Fellini noted the affront. But the success of his actress, for whom he was full of praise, was much more important in his opinion: "Giulietta has the lightness of a phantom, a dream, an idea. She possesses the movements, the mimicry, and the cadences of a clown. She has the looks of amazement and of dismay, unexpected moments of joy and just as startling descents into the sadness." Indeed, Giulietta was compared to Harry Langdon and to Charlie Chaplin.

Like a slowly maturing fruit, the role of Gelsomina had been conceived jointly by Masina and Fellini over time: "We spoke about the creation of the role for months," explained Giulietta. "It was a sort of long childbirth by two people. When the character was finally born—the fruit of these interminable conversations that had taken place at home, in the street, in the car, and even at our friends' houses—I already knew all her facets. I love her. Violently. I became that character." Was she it already? In Fellini's mind, without a doubt. Even if Giulietta would have preferred a stronger Gelsomina. "I wanted her to rebel occasionally against Zampano. I said to Fellini: 'But, my God, why do I have to be so stupid?' And at the same time, I wanted to take her in my arms and carry her home, put her in a beautiful dress, warm her up, and give her food to eat." Fellini went even further, declaring: "The truth is that as an actress, she wanted to be the opposite of the characters which she played in my films." A pure woman-child in the first Fellini films, Giulietta soon played a Roman prostitute in *Le Notti di Cabiria* (*Nights of Cabiria*; 1957). The roles were linked in the eyes of many, and Giulietta found herself being considered as the character in *La Strada* far beyond what she had imagined. Though she kept saying regarding Gelsomina, "She is she and I am me," she refused the role Antonioni offered her as Lidia in *La Notte*, judging that, after *La Strada*, the public would not accept her playing a fickle woman who had taken a lover and "didn't mind being courted by another man." Cineastes believed for a long time that Giulietta had come from a family of performers. Some journalists, persuaded that the Fellinis lived against the backdrop of a circus, could not hide their disappointment upon visiting them. "Fellini lived in Parioli in an apartment with a terrace, like almost all the apartments in Rome. It was a middle-class apartment, colorless and without personality. Well-polished, well-maintained. His wife Giulietta Masina is clearly a good homemaker."

The confusion between life and cinema was even easier since Giulietta was often present on the set. When she acted in one of his films, their relationship sometimes became less serene. "I made more demands on her because, given our relationship, I expected her to pick everything up at once, without my having to give her a lot of instructions. . . . She never forgot and never forgets that she is my wife. On the set she behaves both like an actress and like my wife. In fact, she would persistently come on the set to find out if I felt cold, or had damp shoes, or wanted a cappuccino." It was a slight annoyance, but one that made it even more obvious that the couple did not live an eternal happily ever after. For Fellini loved women, these "monumental women, opulent, sumptuous" women of whom Giulietta spoke, and he found the petty demands of marriage ridiculous and outdated. With his wife's consent, he did not hide his affairs but placed their relationship on another plane. "I've succeeded in reaching a mutual understanding with Giulietta. I don't feel oppressed, mutilated, crushed. I have no need of a divorce."

While she inspired Fellini, Giulietta quickly understood that she would not be her husband's only actress. For eight years, between *Nights of Cabiria* and *Giulietta degli Spiriti* (*Juliet of the Spirits*), she did not make a film with him—eight years that were punctuated by Fellini's enormous success with *La Dolce Vita*, which revealed Anita Ekberg splashing around the Trevi Fountain, and *Otto e Mezzo* for which he underwent an unprecedented artistic crisis. Giulietta Masina made films with other directors until her last one in 1991, *Aujourd'hui peut-être* (*A Day to Remember*), by Jean-Louis Bertucelli. When she wasn't making films, she drew and organized daily life.

The Spirit of Juliet

Giulietta never asked for a role. When star Anna Magnani, with whom she made *Nella Città Inferno* (*Hell in the City*) by Renato Castellani in 1958, asked why she did not make Fellini write a new role for her, Giulietta responded simply: "You ask him that, Anna. If I ask him, he'll surely say no." Seven years later Fellini decided to get back in touch with his inspiration with *Juliet of the Spirits*. The film was conceived for Giulietta and based on Giulietta. "I wanted to make a character different from the Gelsomina and Cabiria she inspired in me. She is exactly the kind of human being and actress who stimulates and encourages the genesis and the development of my imagination. I felt it would be interesting to invent a character named Giulietta, and that the confrontation between her innocent and practical nature and hard and uncompromising reality could produce a series of fantastic mental projections, which would destabilize her for some time but which she would finally be capable of mastering." But the public still remembered the Giulietta of *La Strada* and was reticent about the character of this straight-laced middle-class woman who was plunged into her fantasies and her past. Even more reticent, since they had the impression of witnessing a sad episode in the conjugal life of the couple. In *Juliet of the Spirits*, Giulietta gets ready to celebrate the couple's wedding anniversary. She fixes her hair, tries on dresses, flits about with the servants, and waits for her husband. When he arrives, she turns off the light, but her husband has forgotten the anniversary, and the surprise is the guests who suddenly appear and burst Giulietta's dream. Forever sad, she refuses to be seduced by a man or initiated into new pleasures by her neighbor, Suzy, played by the luscious Sandra Milo. Several years later, Milo would reveal her romantic liaison with Fellini in her book *Caro Federico*. The film, made in Fregene, finishes with an open ending in which a liberated Giulietta opens the white gate of her villa and, carried by the wind, takes part in a grand parade in the skies.

Twenty years later, Fellini felt the need to see Giulietta Masina in a film again. It would be in *Ginger e Fred* (1985) where she performed with Marcello Mastroianni for the first time on the screen. The movie picks up the thread of the universe created in Fellini's first work, *Luci del Varietà*, but more than just nostalgia for a lost world, it is a formal attack against the Berlusconization of television and the impertinence of a system capable of cutting up films shown on television by innumerable commercial breaks. To show that Giulietta was forever inseparable from his cinema, Fellini demanded from then on that she participate in all his interviews. In front of thousands of people, he received an Oscar in 1993 for his life's work. Without seeing her but sensing her emotion, Federico spoke directly to Giulietta, seated near the stage, saying, "Stop crying!" The cameras of the world turned toward her and immortalized Gelsomina's tears. On June 16 that same year, Fellini was operated on for an aneurysm of the abdominal aorta. On his bedside table was the script he was working on that would reunite Giulietta and Mastroianni. But Fellini died in Rome on October 19, 1993. Dressed again in his Oscar-night tuxedo, Fellini's body was on view on November 1 in studio #5 at Cinecittà, where he had made so many of his films. The casket was topped by a crown of red flowers and guarded by carabinieri in full dress uniform. The next day he was buried in Rimini. Giulietta murmured, "I want to go with him." She would join him on March 23 of the following year.

Bibliography

Chandler, Charlotte. *I Fellini*. New York: Cooper Square Press, 2001.

Constantini, Costanzo, ed. *Conversations with Fellini*. Orlando: Harvest Books, 1995.

Fellini, Federico. *Je suis un grand menteur* (interview with Damien Pettigrew). Paris: L'Arche, 1994.

Mejean, Jean-Max. *Fellini: Un rêve, une vie*. Paris: Éditions du Cerf, 1997.

Jane Birkin
Serge Gainsbourg

Jane B. & Mister Hyde

The inventor of the erotic ingenue Jane B., Serge Gainsbourg saw his creation get away, but without abandoning her creator, she revealed an infinitely more complex Jane Birkin. From an insouciant Lolita to a politically active singer and fervent militant of humanitarian causes and human rights, Jane Birkin distanced herself from Jane B. without ever losing sight of her.

Description: blue eyes
Hair
Chestnut
Jane B., Female Englishwoman
Age between twenty and twenty-one

Jane B. as seen by Serge Gainsbourg. It was almost an anthropometric description, quite unerotic, and nothing less than exact. When Gainsbourg recorded the song in 1969, Jane B. was not between twenty and twenty-one, she was twenty-two and still a child. The misunderstanding was due to an arrangement between the registry office and the director Jacques Deray for the publicity needs of his film *La Piscine* (*The Swimming Pool*), which had come out the year before. Her true age would be established several years later, but the image would persist of an eternally young Jane B., an innocent androgynous Lolita and a seductress on whom good fortune seemed to smile naturally. Forever the "spoiled boy, portrait of my despised father, also dull as a boy. . . . Difficult for me to imagine that one of these four would happen to me," as she sang in 1973 in *Di Doo Dah*, with lyrics by Gainsbourg.

Jane was born in London on December 14, 1946, to a noted theater actress mother, Judy Campbell, who had become the army's mascot for recording "A Nightingale Sang in Berkeley Square," which provided a glimmer of hope during the war, and to a father, David Birkin, a marine commander, war hero and his daughter's idol. Jane's love was to be the cinema. It was enough that her cousin, the director Carol Reed, did not discourage her ("It depends on if the camera falls in love with you," he told her) for her to imagine doing this kind of work. Not that she found herself particularly pretty. "I have never really liked myself very much, not to say not at all, and if I find myself pretty at some point, or even beautiful, it will always be because of the expression of others, rather than by those who are in love with me or even those who are simply looking at me. Without a doubt, that's why you become an actress," she admitted to Gérard Lenne, one of her very first biographers. A part as an extra in *The Knack* (1965) by

Richard Lester, the cult film about "swinging London" in the 1960s, led to a sexy scene in *Blow Up* by Michelangelo Antonioni, winner of the Palme d'or in Cannes in 1967. Several months later she became a celebrity tainted by scandal for allegedly appearing fully nude in a scene that, in fact, did not show anything at all. Her brief marriage to the composer John Barry suffered when she was chosen by director Pierre Grimblat for his film *Slogan* (1969). Why would she act in a movie being made in Paris if she did not speak French? That is what Serge Gainsbourg, her co-star on the film, asked her between rehearsals. The son of Russian Jewish immigrants, Serge was born in Paris as Lucien Ginzburg on April 2, 1928. He originally wanted to become a painter but gave up on the idea. Then at thirty he became a jazz guitarist and pianist and a singer at the Milord l'Arsouille, a cabaret near the Palais-Royal where he enthralled and disgusted people with his image as a blasé alcoholic, inveterate smoker, and unrelenting misogynist.

From his first record in 1958, which included *Le Poinçonneur des Lilas*, he wrote under the name of Serge Gainsbourg and met with varied success. *La Javanaise* in 1962 and *Couleur café* in 1964 received good critical responses, and many top performers of the day—like Juliette Greco, Regine, Petula Clark, Michèle Torr, and Dalida—asked him to write lyrics for them. But the larger public continued to ignore him, all while humming generic songs from *Vidocq*, the most popular French television series of the decade. Gainsbourg enjoyed a semi-secret celebrity. According to the very French title of one of his first records, he was the "stunning Serge Gainsbourg." His short hair, which made his ears stick out like cabbage leaves, his tie, his muffled voice, and his sophisticated lyrics contrasted with the look of pop singers, who wore leather jackets and twisted knots; they were the "idols" of *Salut les copains* who shouted insipid lyrics. He became a point of reference for the intellectuals of Paris's Left Bank, just as his great model, Boris Vian, had been before him. In a song from his album *Confidentiel Gainsbourg*, he did not hesitate in asserting:

I have a machete with a switchblade
No nothing will get the better of me
I will go and look for you, my Lolita,
At the pop singers'.

Which is what he did by writing for France Gall, one of the young girls from the radio show *Salut les copains* whom he used marvelously to play against type. When she innocently sang "Les Sucettes à l'anis," he performed alongside her, emphasizing the song's erotic innuendos. Then came "Poupée de cire, poupée de son," which won the people's grand prize at the Eurovision festival in 1965. The hidden Gainsbourg had suddenly become the most sought-after composer-lyricist in France.

When Jane met her *Slogan* co-star, however, she ignored all of his French fame. With her bangs and her miniskirt, Jane was the perfect example of "swinging London," as perhaps Gainsbourg was of Parisian intellectualism. But what struck her was the "active hostility"of this personality. Gainsbourg had come out of a difficult romance with the star of French cinema, Brigitte Bardot. The brilliant singer confessed, "Perhaps it is my physical ugliness which in some way made me search for unbridled beauty," and increased his appearances next to the most beautiful woman in French film. He wrote *Bonnie and Clyde* for her, which was very successful, and the "biographical" *Initials BB*. On December 31, 1967, television featured the Bardot-Gainsbourg New Year's Eve party. Early in 1968, however, Bardot left Gainsbourg and he seemed to hold it against the entire world. To help the mood between the two principal actors, the director of *Slogan* reserved a table for three at Maxim's restaurant, and then at the last moment left them alone for a private conversation. "By Monday morning they were completely in love," he recounted to Gérard Lenne. Ever romantic, Gainsbourg described the scene in his manner: "It was not love at first sight, no, it was more precious, more insidious. Love at first sight is nothing, it doesn't stay the course."

"Je t'aime moi non plus"

The ice was broken for Jane when Gainsbourg made her listen to the music of "Je t'aime moi non plus" ("I don't love you anymore"), recorded secretly with Brigitte Bardot and banned from distribution at her request. Afterward they went to "a night club. . . . He didn't know how to dance at all, he was clumsy. But maybe it was this awkwardness that charmed me so," said Jane. Inspired by the true story of Pierre Grimblat's experience with a young girl, *Slogan* left its mark more on the history of music than of cinema by giving birth to the Birkin-Gainsbourg duo, who were chosen as couple of the year. Between the making and the release of the film, "Je t'aime moi non plus" exploded onto the scene.

Opposite: **Jane Birkin and Serge Gainsbourg photographed by Jean-Louis Rancurel in 1969.**

When Gainsbourg suggested recording the song to Jane, she

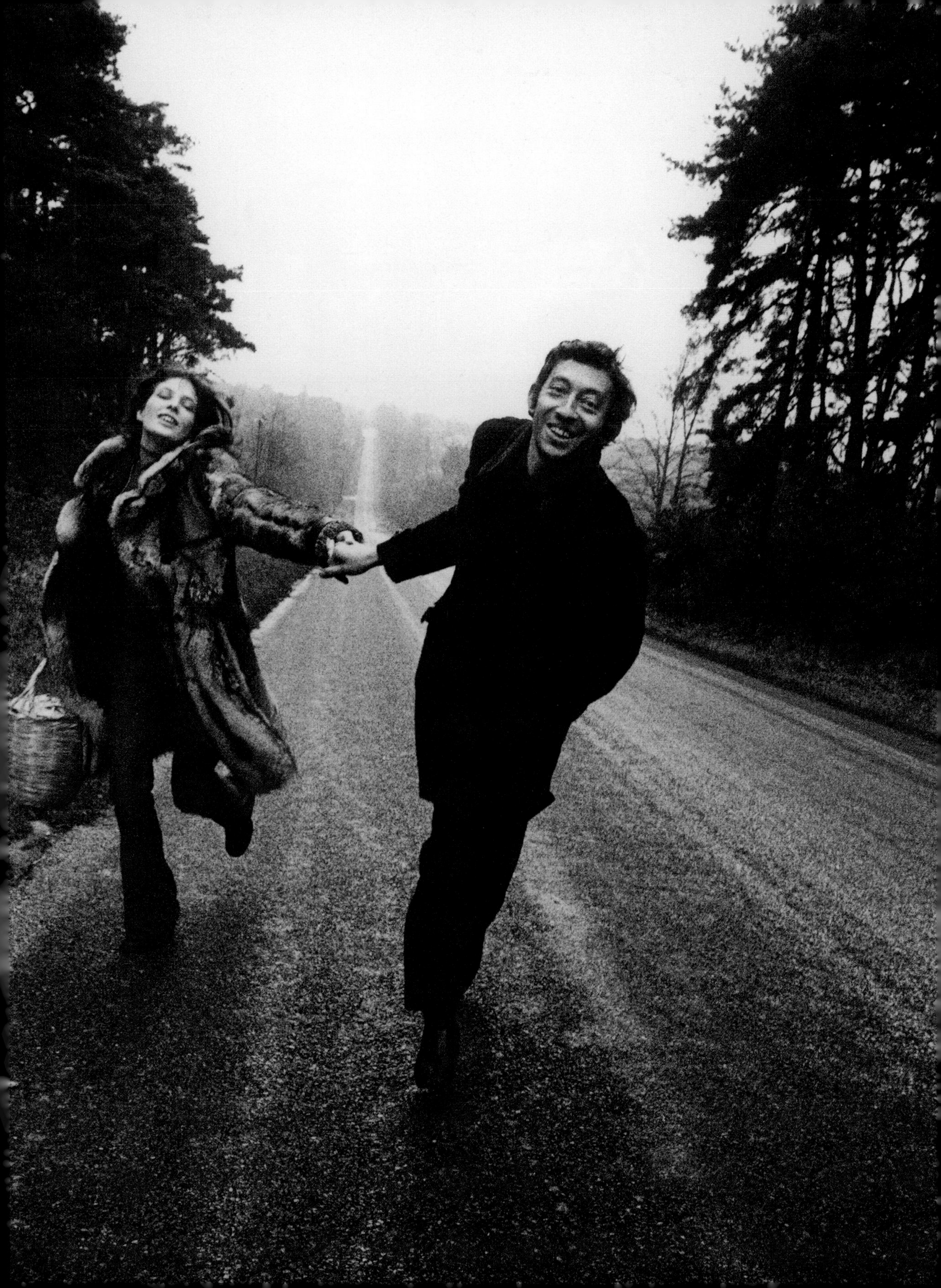

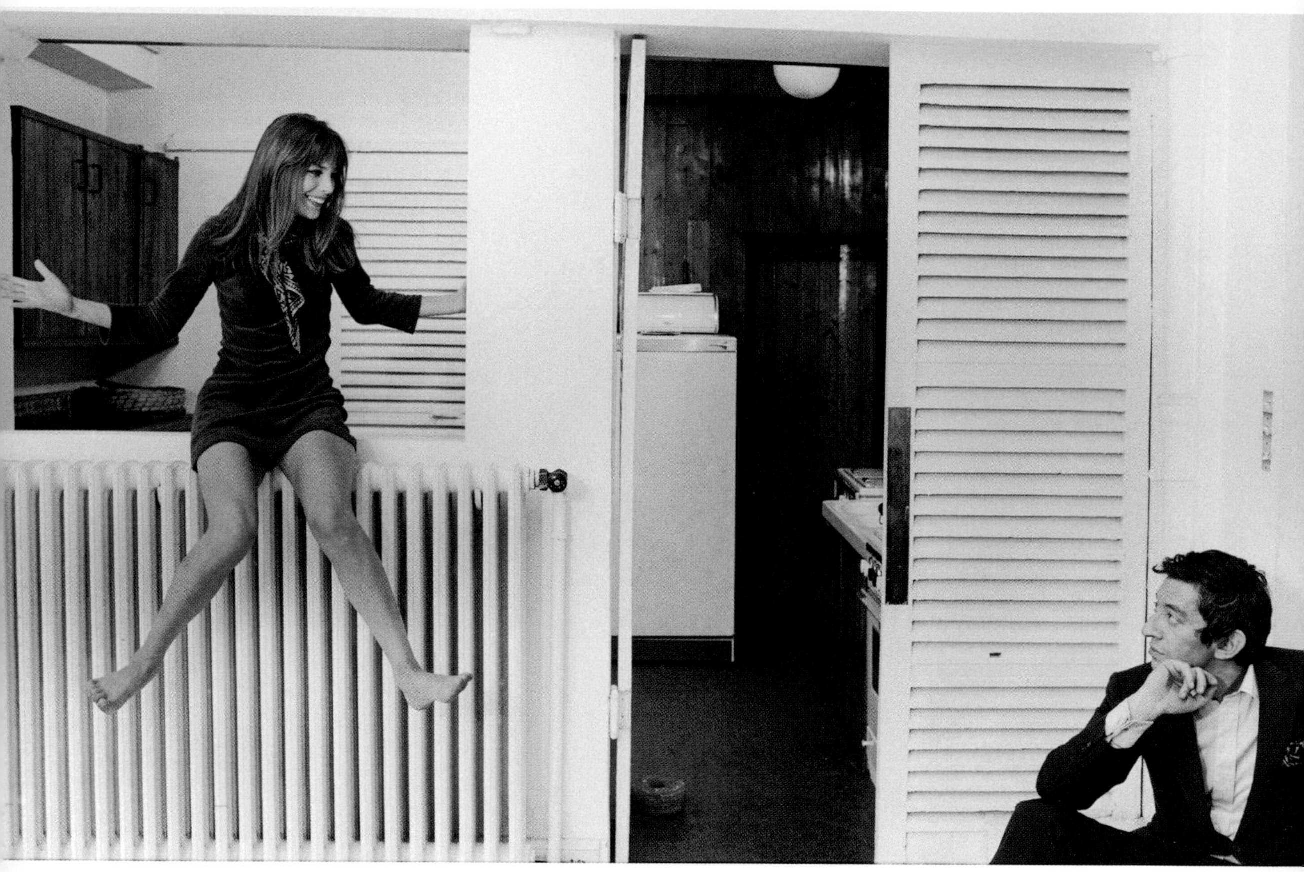

Opposite: **They met in 1968 during the filming of the Pierre Grimblat film *Slogan*. "It was not love at first sight," said Serge Gainsbourg, but the electricity was palpable between the still unknown young Londoner and one of the most famous French songwriters. That same year they acted together in Pierre Koralnik's provocatively entitled film, *Cannabis*. Photographs by Gilles Caron.**

Pages 184–87: **Serge Gainsbourg and Jane Birkin in their home on rue de Verneuil, Paris, in the 1970s.**

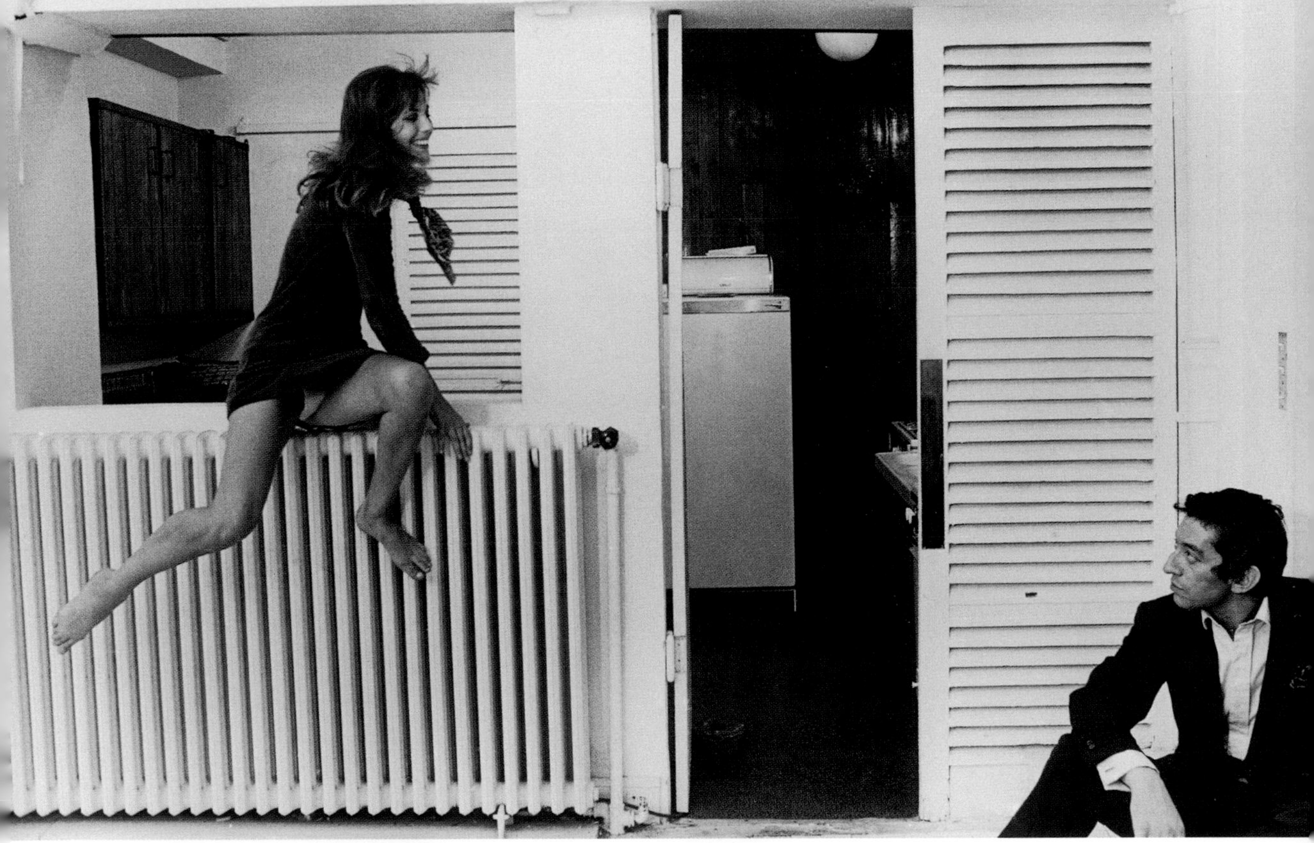

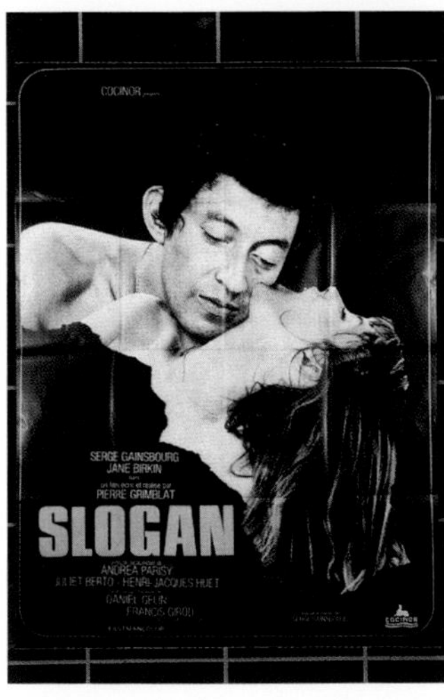

COCINOR
SERGE GAINSBOURG
JANE BIRKIN
PIERRE GRIMBLAT
SLOGAN
ANDREA PARISY
DANIEL GELIN
FRANCIS GIROD

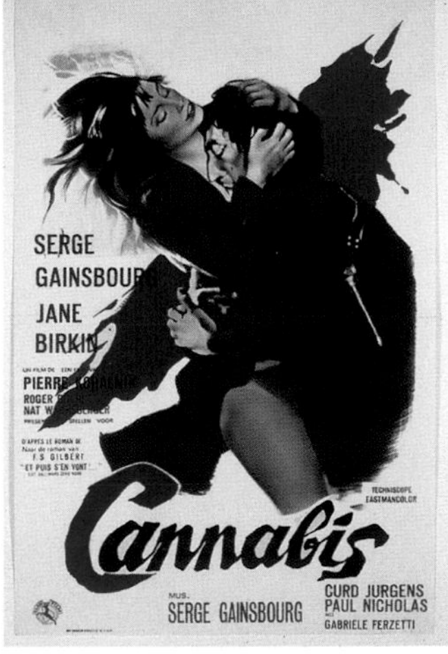

SERGE
GAINSBOU
JANE
BIRKIN
PIERR
ROGER
NAT W
F.S GILBERT
"ET PUIS S'EN VONT"
TECHNISCOPE
EASTMANCOLOR
Cannabis
MUS.
SERGE GAINSBOURG
CURD JURGENS
PAUL NICHOLAS
GABRIELE FERZETTI

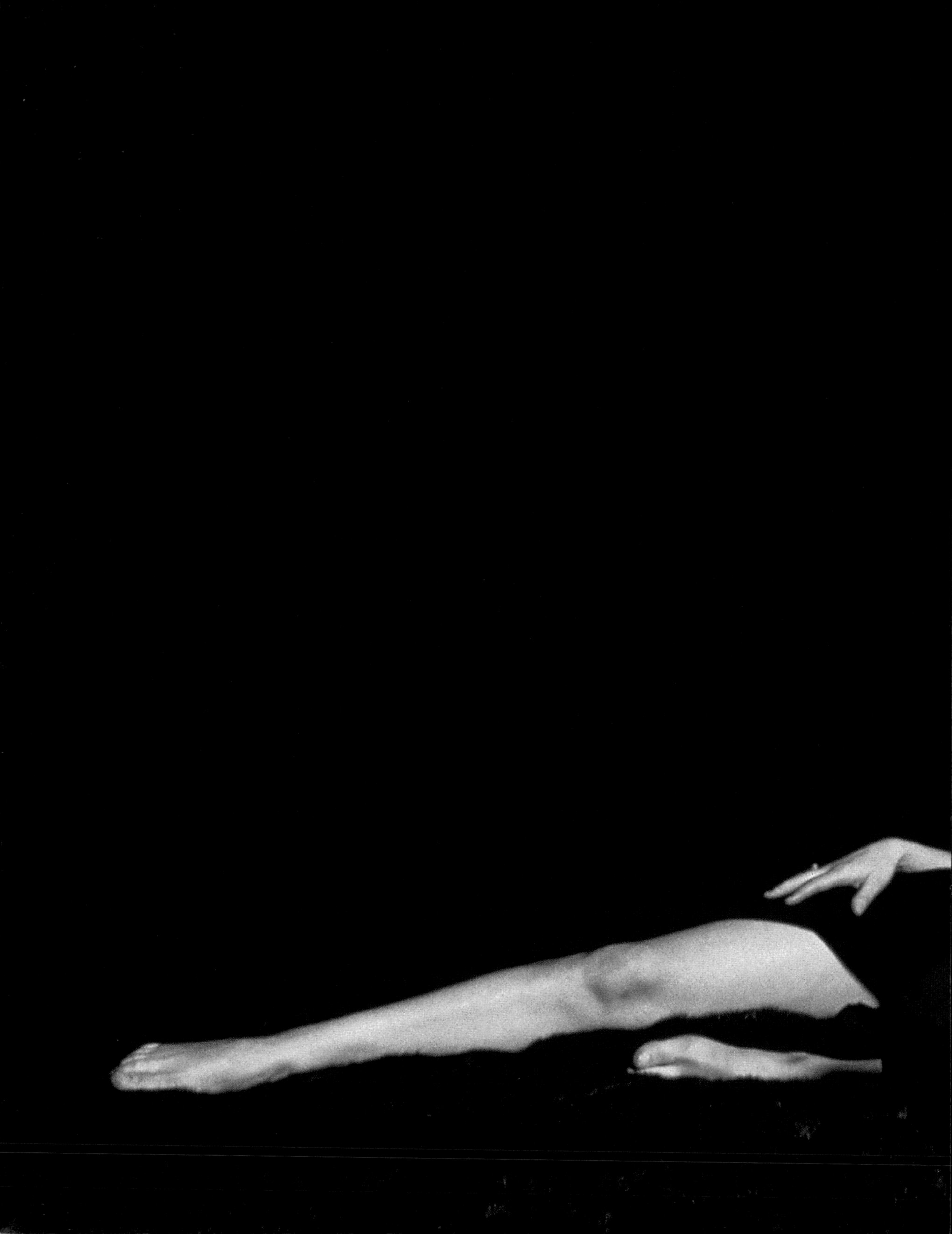

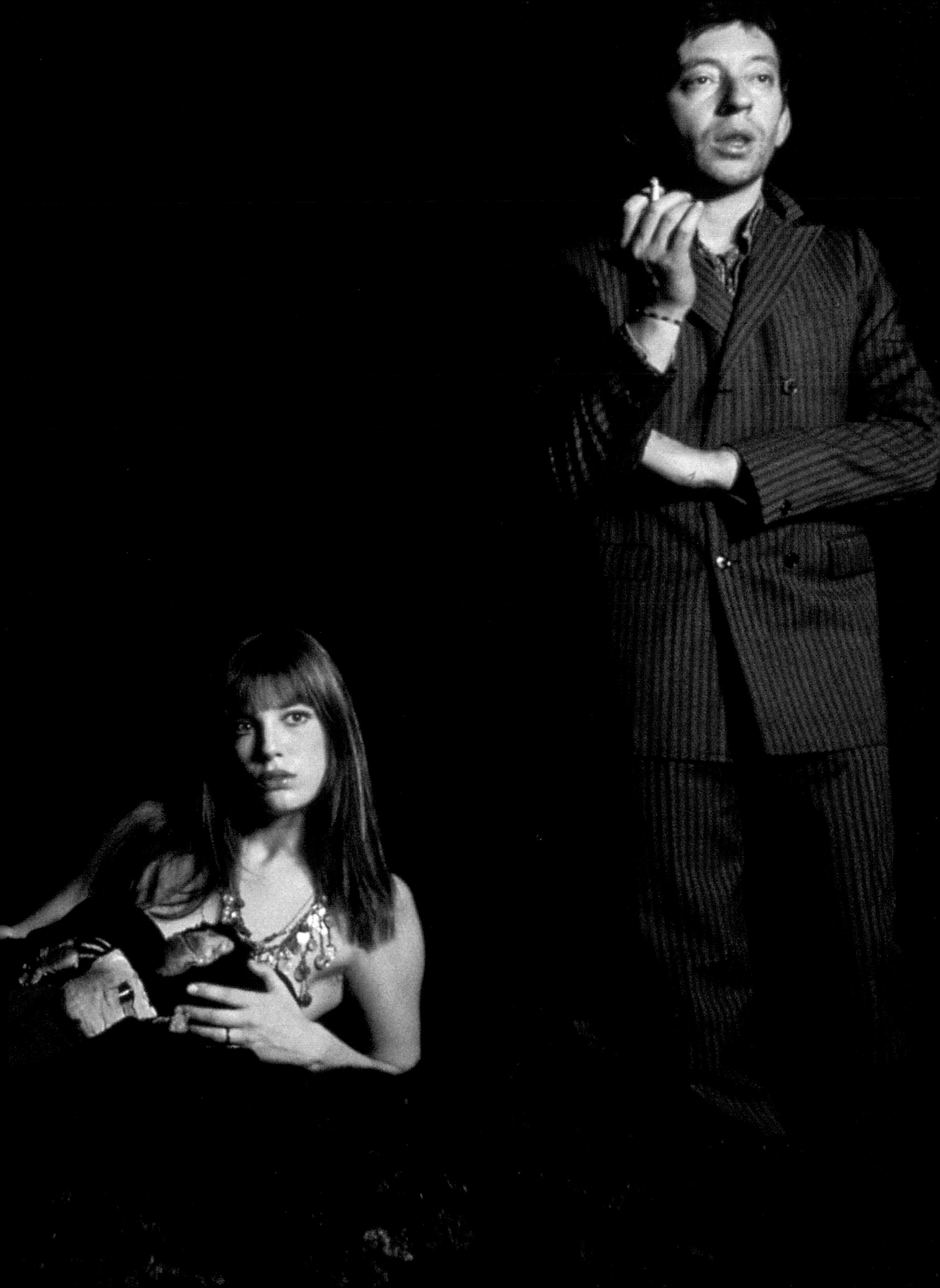

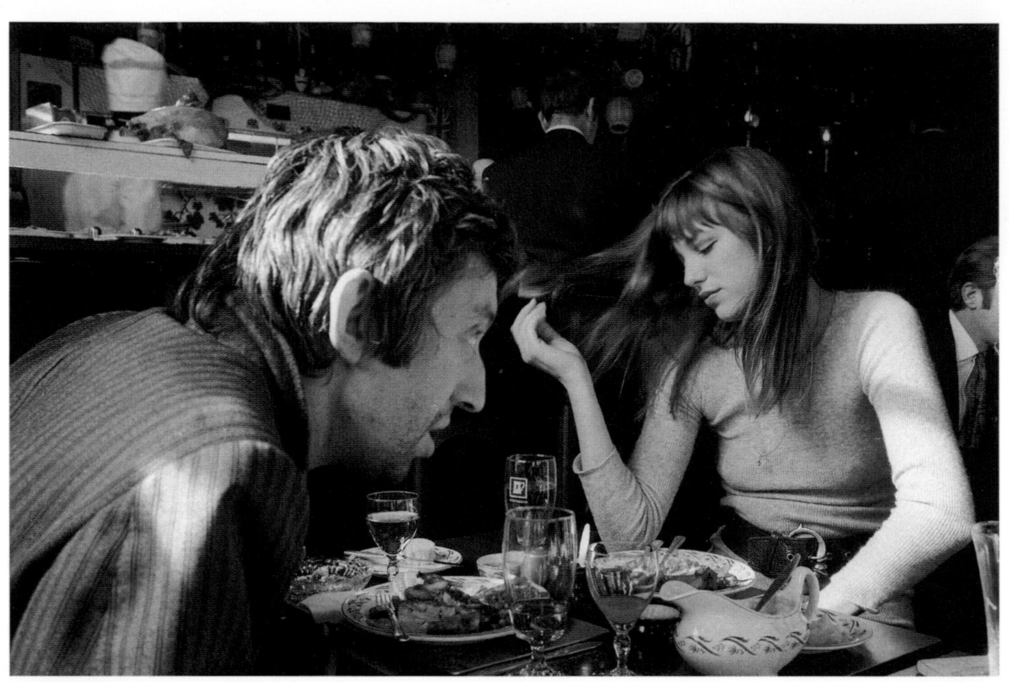

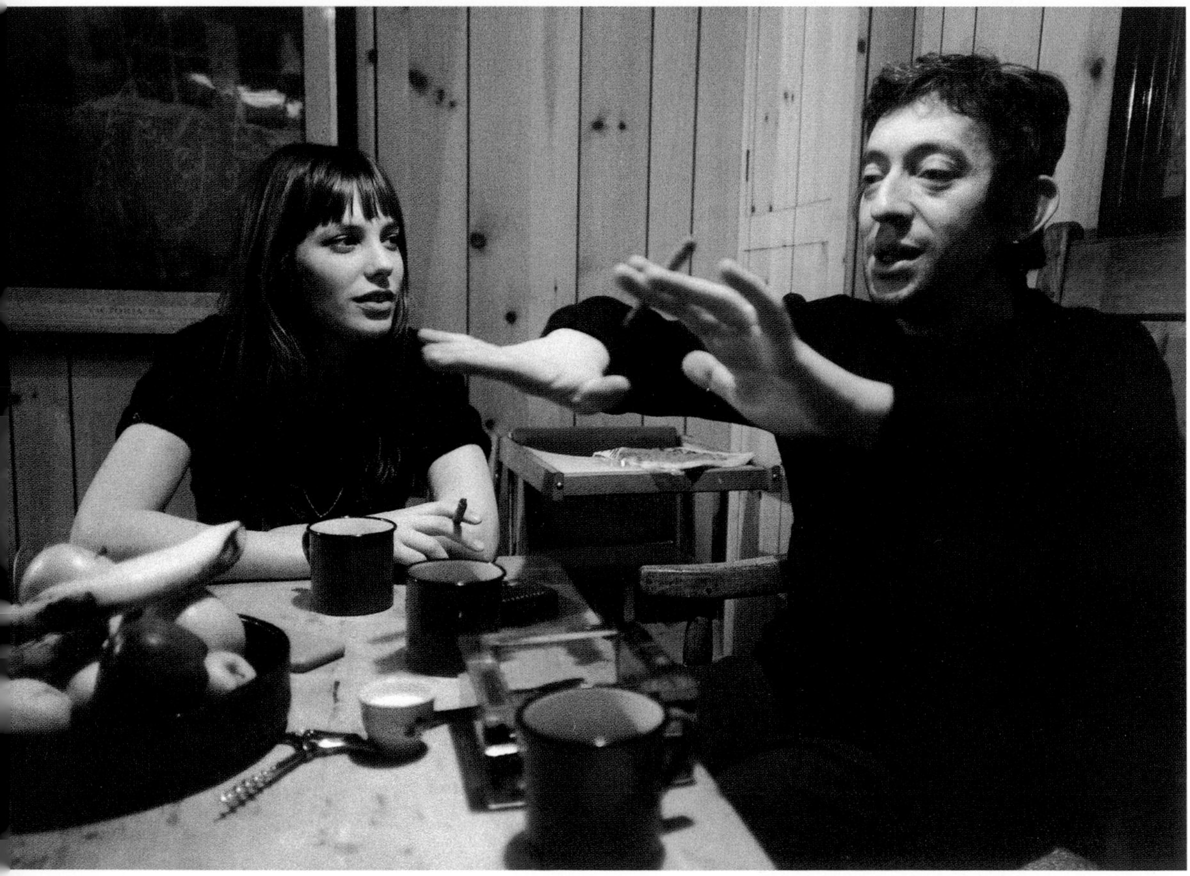

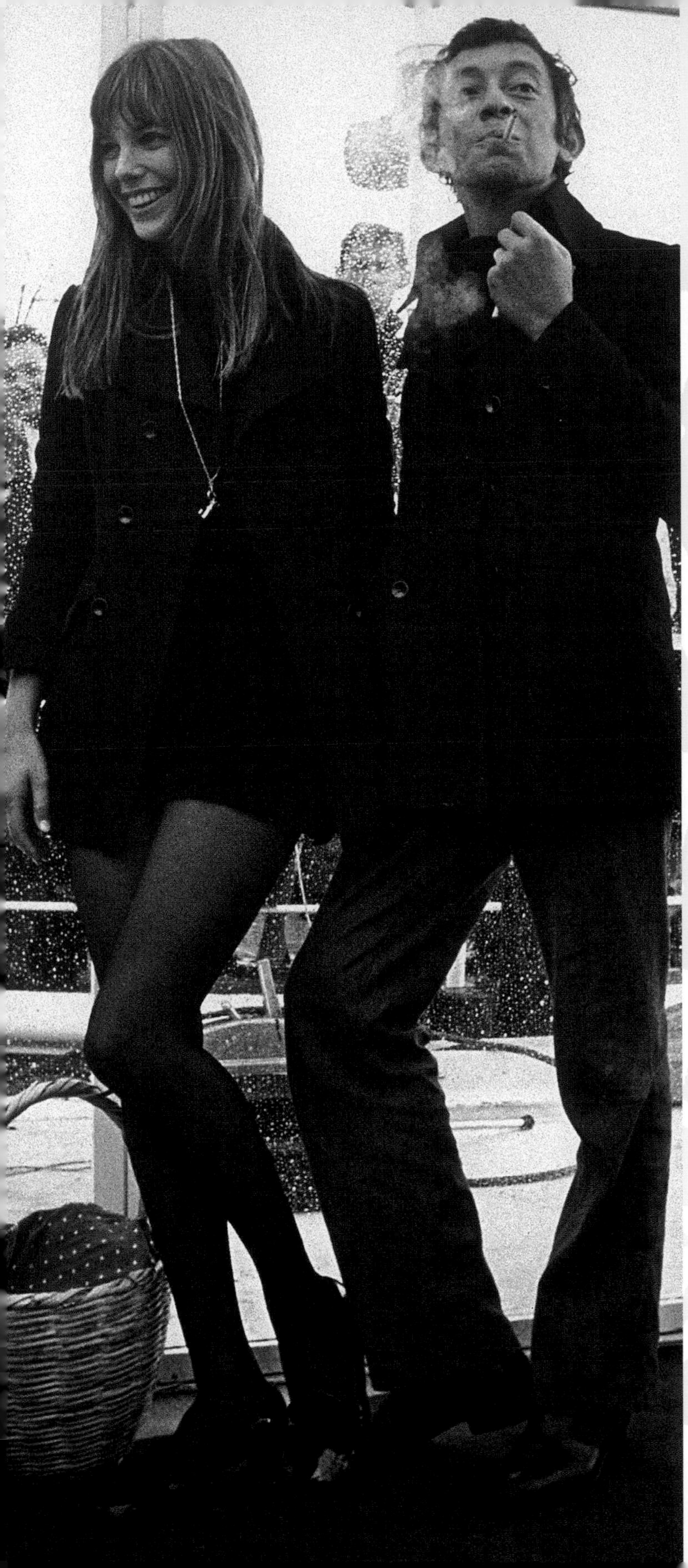

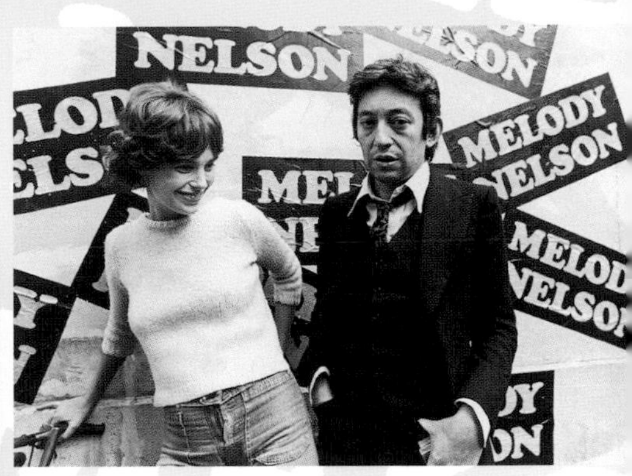

Above: **With *Melody Nelson*, Serge Gainsbourg's first concept album in 1971, Jane Birkin was the Lolita in flares, "the adorable tomboy . . . the lovely little bitch. . . ."**
Left: **Photograph from April 1969 during the recording on the radio program "RTL non stop."**
Opposite: **In 1970, the wild couple of *69, année érotique* was also an ordinary pair whose daily life began to thrill the media. The birth of their daughter Charlotte the following year increased the public's curiosity. Photographs by Ian Berry.**

was a little surprised. She had never sung before, except for a burlesque show in England and she still remembered the silly lyrics: "I must, I must increase my bust." She was the comic relief who sang stupid songs meant to make the audience laugh. Gainsbourg, however, was sure that she had potential: "I discovered her superb voice was very Lolita-ish." For in the world of Gainsbourg, no one needed a "beautiful" voice in the classic sense of the word, but rather almost a spoken tone, and he played around with the microphone and with her sensuality reinforced by her English accent. Jane's Englishness suited Serge, for he cultivated the blending of French and English in his song titles, such as "Qui est in qui est out" and "Docteur Jekyll et Mister Hyde." And it was on the banks of the Thames that he developed the habit of recording his albums with the greatest musicians in pop music. At the beginning of January, the couple flew to London and recorded a single with "Je t'aime" on one side, a blend of innocence and wickedness punctuated by sighs and moans, and *Jane B.* on the other. Upon their return the enthusiastic record company suggested they make a whole album together. An inspired Gainsbourg quickly wrote *69, année érotique*, which ended up giving the couple a wild image. But the news remained "Je t'aime moi non plus." Paradoxically what was originally a song inspired by the famous phrase by Surrealist artist Salvador Dalí, "Picasso is a genius, me too. Picasso is a Communist, me no longer," and sung as a duet with Bardot, became the hallmark of the Gainsbourg/Birkin duo. In singing "Je t'aime moi non plus," they made their intimate relationship a public event.

With the release of the album, a wave of censure assured its promotion even more effectively than the publicity campaign. The Vatican seized the albums followed by bans in England, Sweden, Spain, and Brazil. Millions of copies were sold, and the song was recorded in eight languages, even Japanese. The expression became common, picked up by advertisers and by newspaper headlines. The Gainsbourgian genius of self-promotion took its full measure for the first time. Soon five-hundred-franc bank notes were being burned up on television and the French national anthem of "La Marseillaise" was revisited in reggae. Every appearance by Gainsbourg on television was like an incitement to riot and helped construct his myth as a "destroyed" genius.

Gainsbourg rejoiced in his celebrity and posed for all photos and magazine covers with pleasure. Without questioning, Jane followed his actions. The Gainsbourg years had begun for her, twelve years during which she made thirty films, released four albums, and gave birth to a little girl, Charlotte, in July 1971. The public's curiosity redoubled and the popularity of the couple was at its height. "Serge found it great fun to be in the newspaper, to have a spread in the magazine *Jour de France* with the children. . . . There is a fine line between the singer and his public. Serge had always had a childlike side that I liked a great deal and it brought him pleasure if he was mentioned in the magazines." A happy family and a musical duo, their life was picture-perfect. Gainsbourg then wrote his first "concept album"—the running history of *Melody Nelson*, a very Birkin-like Lolita. He developed the lyrics over the period of a year, then recorded the rhythm section in London before working out the orchestration with the composer Jean-Claude Vannier. Fifty string instruments and seventy chorus members from the Jeunesses musicales de France joined in later, and French pop-opera was born.

My Melody Nelson
Lovely little bitch
You are the
Essence
of my senses

Jane lent her voice to *Melody* and appeared on the record sleeve dressed in flared jeans and a red wig, with an old stuffed monkey pressed against her stomach to hide the fact that she was pregnant.

For her part, Jane recorded several albums: *La Décadanse,* with music by Gainsbourg and (disappointing) lyrics by Philippe Labro, *Lolita Go Home,* and above all, *Di Doo Dah,* her first solo album. The latter was relatively successful but on a different scale from Gainsbourg's own projects, such as *L'Homme à la tête de chou* or *Sea, Sex and Sun.* She had to wait for *Ex-fan des Sixties* in January 1978 for Jane Birkin the singer to establish herself.

Already associated in music, their names were also found together on movie posters when Gainsbourg spent 1975 behind the camera inventing the film follow-up to the song "Je t'aime moi non plus," which had since become a cult classic. "When you're an actor, there's something irresistible about being seen by someone who has left his mark on you," Jane said. Breaking away from a series of light roles in French comedies made by directors Michel Deville, Claude Zidi, and Michel Audiard, she played the role of an androgyne caught between two homosexual truck drivers in Gainsbourg's directorial debut. The film, obviously conceived for her, marked the culminating point in their history.

If *Melody Nelson* gave the impression of absolute happiness, a song on the 1973 album, "Je suis venu te dire que je m'en vais" ("I've come to tell you that I'm going"), written and sung by Gainsbourg, announced the end of their romance.

> *You remember the days gone by, and you cry. . . .*
> *You choke, you pale now that the hour is here*
> *Of goodbyes forever*
> *Yes, I regret*
> *To tell you that I'm going*
> *Yes, I loved you, yes, but*

Soon it was Jane Birkin's turn to sing. But she modified the words slightly, and *"Yes, I loved you, yes, but"* became *"For you did too much to me."*

Fleeing the Happiness of Fear Which He Can't Escape

The couple announced their separation in 1980. Seized by a creative frenzy, Gainsbourg wrote for Bashung and Julien Clerc, recorded *Souviens-toi de m'oublier* with Catherine Deneuve, and composed *Pull marine* for Isabelle Adjani. "I wrote this album at the same time as Jane's. Twenty-two songs in three weeks. I like to work under anguish and stress," he confided. For far from putting an end to their musical collaboration, their separation seemed to inspire them more than ever. One day Jane was watching Michael Curtiz's film *Casablanca* on television. She imagined Gainsbourg writing a song on this theme and rushed to his home to ask him to do it. He had had exactly the same idea, and so *As Time Goes By* was born. In 1983 Gainsbourg composed *Baby Alone in Babylone* for Jane, an unprecedented commercial and critical success, her first gold record with more than one hundred thousand copies sold, and the winner of the grand prize from the Charles Cros Academy. With her refined voice Jane sang "Les Dessous chics" and "Fuir le bonheur," which became classics. She always sang Gainsbourg, but starting in 1980 her film career took a new turn. For Jacques Doillon, Jacques Rivette, and Agnès Varda, she was no longer the delightful idiot of her early work but a wounded beauty whose English accent accentuated her strangeness. In *La*

Fille prodigue (*The Prodigal Daughter*), a film that he wrote for her, Jacques Doillon offered her an unpretentious role of a hypersensitive person. Jane identified with the character during the filming. "I did not want anyone to touch my hair to the point that I had knots," she recalled. "I didn't even brush it any longer myself. . . . I didn't wear makeup, I was thrilled. I began to look like myself." Did Jane Birkin finally distance herself from Jane B. in order to become herself, or to be Jane B. and Jane Birkin at the same time, the insouciant Lolita of yesterday and the generous and enthusiastic supporter of humanitarian causes of today? Just after Gainsbourg's death in 1991, she went on stage at the Casino de Paris as if to exorcise her grief and triumphed while performing those songs that all seemed to lead directly back to their romance, like "Quoi":

> *Cruel love*
> *Like in a duel*
> *Back to back and without mercy*
> *You have a choice of weapons*
> *Think about it, Think about it*

Bibliography

Coelho, Alain, Franck Lhomeau, and Serge Gainsbourg. *Gainsbourg*. Paris: Denoel, 1992.

Lenne, Gérard. *Jane Birkin*. Paris: Éditions Henri Veyrier, 1985.

Simmons, Sylvie. *Serge Gainsbourg: A Fistful of Gitanes*. New York: Da Capo Press, 2002.

The Patroness

Marcel Proust gave the nickname of "the patroness" to Madame Verdurin, the great socialite who loved to live surrounded by artists and dreamed of being the inspiration for their creativity. Neither a wife nor a mistress, the "patroness muse" is more like the guardian figure who creates a working environment for the painter or the musician. And so it was for Misia Sert, married to the founder of *La Revue blanche*, who fascinated her weepy unrequited lover, the painter Édouard Vuillard, and for Peggy Guggenheim, who revealed the genius of the painter Jackson Pollock to himself. A reciprocal fascination with her protégés and the exercise of her power are not the only assets of the patroness. By offering him a home and by serving as a chauffeur, Pannonica de Koenigswarter was the most marvelous of inspirations for the jazz pianist Thelonious Monk.

Peggy Guggenheim
Jackson Pollock

The Collector and the Hero

Peggy Guggenheim—nicknamed the "dollar princess," deprived of a father who drowned on the *Titanic*, a collector of men almost as much as of paintings, and an unpredictable woman—was one of the essential figures in the international triumph of American art. Guided by the abilities of her talent-spotter, artist Marcel Duchamp, she launched the career of the hero of action painting, Jackson Pollock.

The photo dates from 1946. Under the attentive gaze of Jackson Pollock, Peggy Guggenheim holds two of her darling pet dogs in her arms in her New York gallery, Art of This Century. Their shadows merge on the immense painting in front of which they have chosen to pose like two heroes of American painting. They stand in the gallery where his triumph began and before his masterpiece that, three years earlier, almost did not see the light of day.

At the end of their first meeting in July 1943, Peggy Guggenheim, who was known above all as the American muse of the Surrealists, had had the curious idea of commissioning a painting for the entry hall of her new apartment from this young American artist who found the project as "exciting as all hell." Pollock had already purchased a very large canvas over seven by nineteen feet (two by six meters), and it was necessary to destroy a wall of his small studio in order just to set it up. But he remained hypnotized for months by the enormous white canvas. The painting had to be delivered at the time of his first exhibition in November, but by that date he had not even begun it. The painter shut himself up in his studio for whole days, and when he would emerge, his wife Lee Krasner could see through the open door that the canvas was still untouched. The patroness granted him an extension until the January evening when she had organized a grand reception in honor of a journalist and friends. Christmas approached and still the canvas remained pristine. Pollock and Krasner nevertheless left for the end-of-the-year holidays. Lee moved into her parents' home at the beginning of January to let Jackson work. When she returned on the eve of the new deadline to hand over the painting, he had still not begun. And then at the end of the day, Jackson said, "I had a vision." Fifteen hours later he had achieved the first great masterpiece of Abstract Expressionism. Pollock took it to Peggy Guggenheim's and undertook to install it in the prearranged spot, but the painting proved to be too long. Pollock now became hysterical and began to drink all the bottles of alcohol that Peggy Guggenheim had carefully hidden. Called to the rescue, Marcel Duchamp finally found the solution and proposed that trimming the canvas by several inches would not damage the work. At this point, its creator was too drunk to oppose the idea. His *Mural* finally painted and hung, Pollock crossed unsteadily through the crowd of guests and urinated in the marble chimney before leaving. Peggy did not take offense. She had just given birth to the hero of American painting who would, thanks to her, go on to triumph around the whole world.

The Orphan of the *Titanic*

With a childhood spent on the edge of Central Park in mansions filled with bear skins with snarling mouths and tapestries celebrating the triumph of Alexander, nothing would have predisposed the little girl painted in an eighteenth-century dress by Franz von Lenbach to become a collector of contemporary art. Nothing, perhaps, except her father's pronounced taste for art history. At the dawn of the twentieth century—she, Marguerite (Peggy), was born in 1898 into an important bourgeois Jewish family whose tastes were classic. Every summer when her father swept the family off to Paris where he met up with his mistress of the moment, he took care to engage the services of an art history professor who initiated the children into the treasures of the Louvre Museum, the Musée Carnavalet, and the châteaus of the Loire Valley. It was an unhappy childhood, she recalled, punctuated by her father's marital infidelities, and he ended up leaving the family to settle in Paris. But harm overtook him: he embarked in 1912 on the *Titanic* on a return visit to the United States. According to some witnesses, he drowned on board the ship with great panache, after pausing to put on his evening clothes again and helping women and children escape in the lifeboats. The heiress of a double family fortune in 1919 when she came of age, Peggy did not launch herself into collecting and patronage immediately. It was men who interested her more.

She married Laurence Vail, with whom she had two children known as Sindbad and Pegeen, but then left him to have innumerable affairs with, among others, an English dandy, the painter Yves Tanguy, and even with the writer Samuel Beckett, whose poetry however she found "puerile." In 1938 she opened a gallery on Cork Street in London named "Guggenheim Jeune" by her secretary, to distinguish her from the patronage activities of her uncle Solomon, future creator of the Solomon R. Guggenheim Museum in New York. He collected more classic artists and was offended by his niece's escapades. Ignorant of all contemporary art, she entrusted her friend Marcel Duchamp with the responsibility of counseling her. Constantin Brancusi, Wassily Kandinsky, Tanguy, Alexander Calder, Joan Miró, Jean Arp, Joseph Cornell—Duchamp's choices were eclectic and striking. But, as Peggy Guggenheim recalled, "The gallery was too expensive for its results. At the end of a year and a half, I decided to close it and to create a museum of modern art in London." The art historian Herbert Read made a list of paintings for her to borrow. She soon renounced the project, moved back again to France on the eve of the war, and decided to buy the works on Herbert Read's list for herself, as revised by the ever present Duchamp. "I put myself on a diet of acquiring a work a day. Nothing was easier then. The Parisians, waiting for a German invasion, only desired one thing—to sell everything and flee," she wrote in good conscience. When she finally decided to flee, she thought first of putting her collection in shelter and requested the aid of the Louvre, which refused on the grounds that Kandinsky, Paul Klee, Pablo Picasso, Brancusi, and so many others in her collection were not sufficiently important. Finally she found a way to take them with her.

A Laboratory of New Ideas

Peggy moved to New York in July 1941, and opened the Art of This Century gallery on October 20 the following year, as "a laboratory for new ideas," she proclaimed. The painter Max Ernst, whom she had married shortly before her departure from France, and André Breton were the real artistic forces of the gallery, and Jimmy, Max's son, was the secretary. This team stirred up the enthusiasm of the Americans who saw the finest of the European artists in exile and, above all, the Surrealists, who represented the avant-garde, arrive in New York. At the opening of the Art of This Century gallery, no American artist, with the exception of Calder, had made a career in France. While even she did not challenge this European—principally French—hegemony, Peggy was perplexed by it. Perhaps that was why she wore an earring by the Franco-American Tanguy and another by the American-French Calder on the evening of the opening. The press did not remark on it. To them, the Peggy Guggenheim gallery was only a "Surrealist circus."

Art of This Century would have been the only New York outlet of Parisian Surrealism, except for Breton's stinginess when he demanded she pay for an ad for the gallery which appeared in the magazine *VVV*, and for the affair between Max Ernst and the woman who would become his last spouse, Dorothea Tanning. As a consequence, these events pushed Peggy provisionally into the arms of Duchamp and launched her on the quest for someone or something new. "Art, an artist, or a lover, perhaps all three. Peggy did not make a distinction between them," remarked Stephen Naifeh and

Gregory White Smith, the biographers of the man who would go on to become the great pioneer of American art, but who, despite all of Peggy's efforts, never became her lover: Jackson Pollock.

Born in 1912 in Cody, Wyoming, the painter who found himself in New York in the 1940s was completely adrift. After difficult art studies—the publication of an anti-establishment newspaper led him to be thrown out of school—he was equally at odds with the WPA program of the 1930s, the federal art project aimed at employing American artists throughout the Great Depression. An excerpt from a letter exchanged between two of his brothers, Sandford (Sande) and Charles, gives an idea of Jackson Pollock's situation in 1941: "I must talk to you about the grave problem that preoccupies us at this moment but has lasted in fact for five years. It's about Jack. . . . The stating of certain symptoms will give you an idea of the nature of the problem: irresponsibility, depressive, mania (Dad), overintensity, and alcohol are among the most evident. Self-destruction, too. For the positive, we are sure that if he is able to hold himself together his work will become of real significance." The art to which his brother was alluding was a kind of automatic writing in paint that Pollock had begun to invent while fiercely refusing to be assimilated into the Surrealist style. Although isolated, he nevertheless had the absolute support of Peggy Guggenheim's close friend Howard Putzel. This penniless art lover, himself a former art dealer, would not stop talking on and on to Peggy about Pollock's genius, but with no more success than James Johnson Sweeney, director of The Museum of Modern Art in New York, who, from the beginning of 1942, spoke to her about this "very important artist." For Peggy Guggenheim, he had the irremediable fault of being American.

In the spring of 1943, her wrangles with the Surrealists gave Peggy the revolutionary idea of creating a painting salon solely reserved for Americans. One announcement was placed in the newspapers and soon all the artists flocked to drop off their works. Peggy made the first choice. Putzel managed to send her *Stenographic Figure*, a large canvas by Pollock done up in garish colors. Peggy thought it a horror. But the judgment of Piet Mondrian, one of the members of the jury, changed everything. Having also sought refuge in New York, the pioneering Dutch painter of abstract art with a severe and honest personality was one of the great reference points in matters of the avant-garde. Peggy was most astonished to find him planted in front of a canvas by Pollock. Approving of it with a nod of the head, he considered it "the most exciting painting that

Right: **Peggy Guggenheim in 1964 in front of her palazzo on the Grand Canal in Venice.**

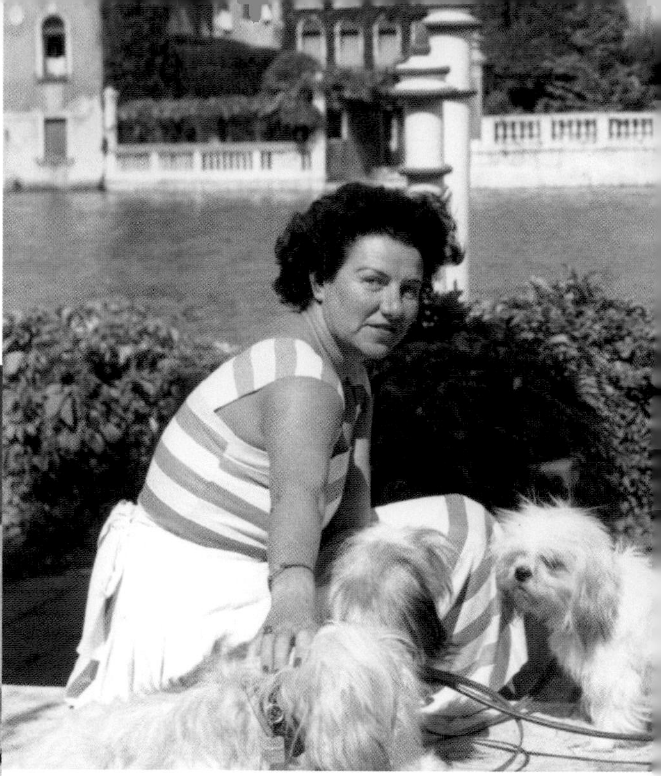

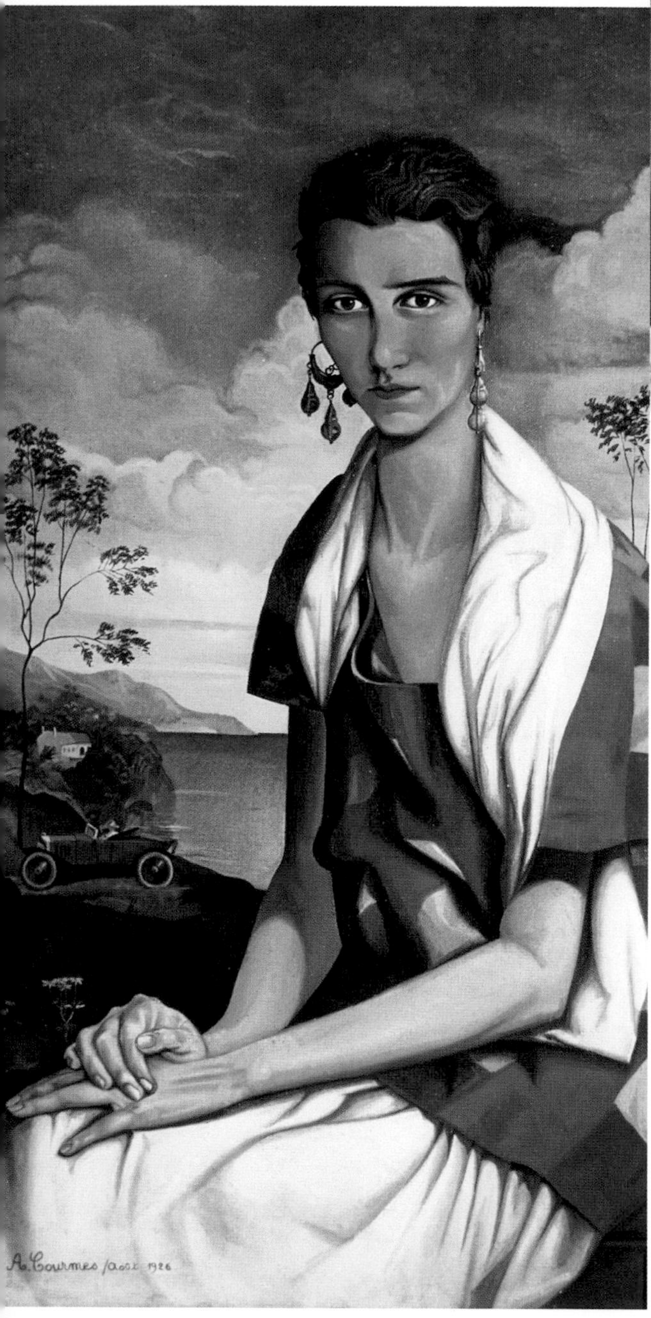

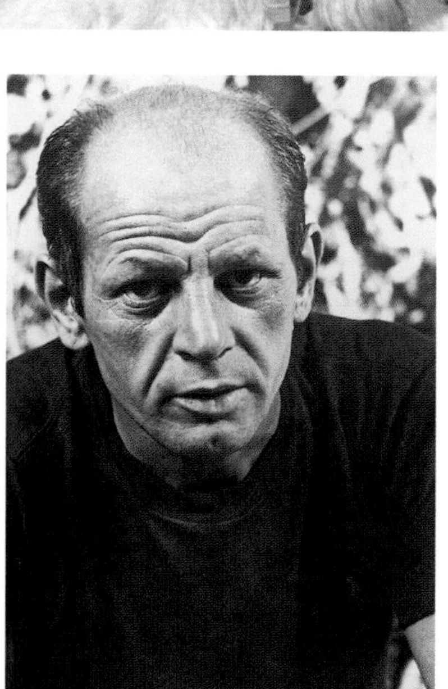

Left: **Alfred Courmes painted this portrait of Peggy Guggenheim (August 1926) at a time when she was only an eccentric American heiress. She poses in front of a landscape in the south of France, while in the background are glimpses of her home and her car.**

Above: **Jackson Pollock in 1949. Photograph by Hans Namuth.**

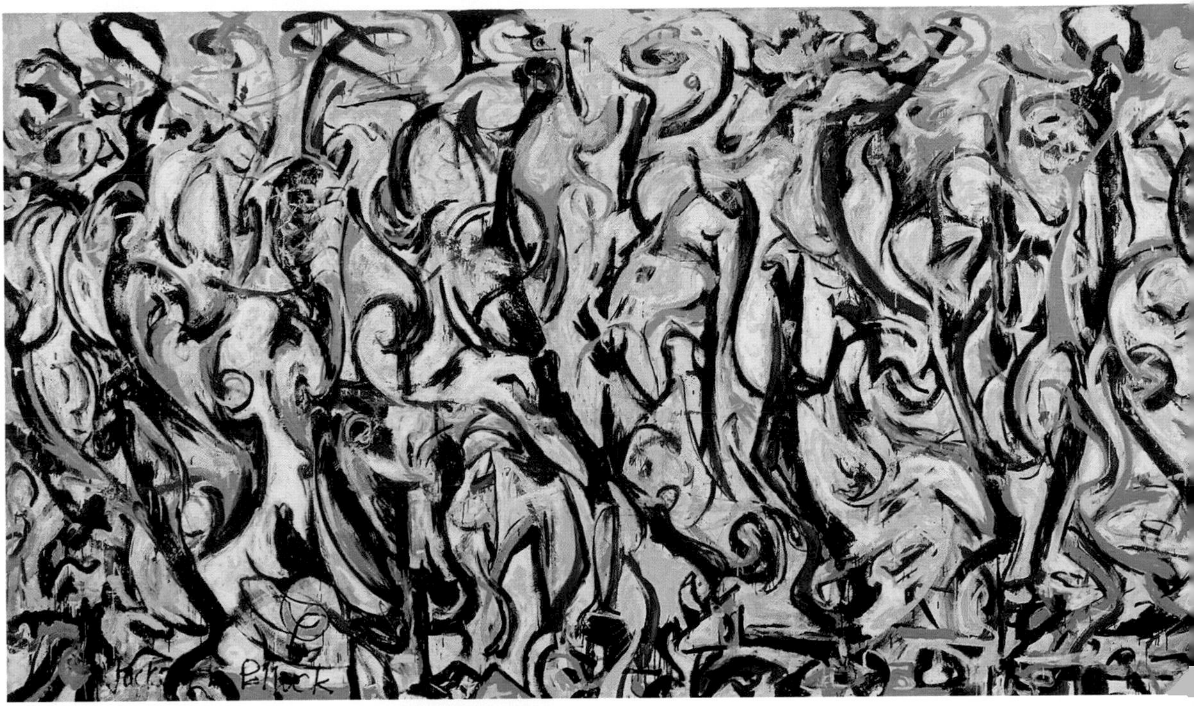

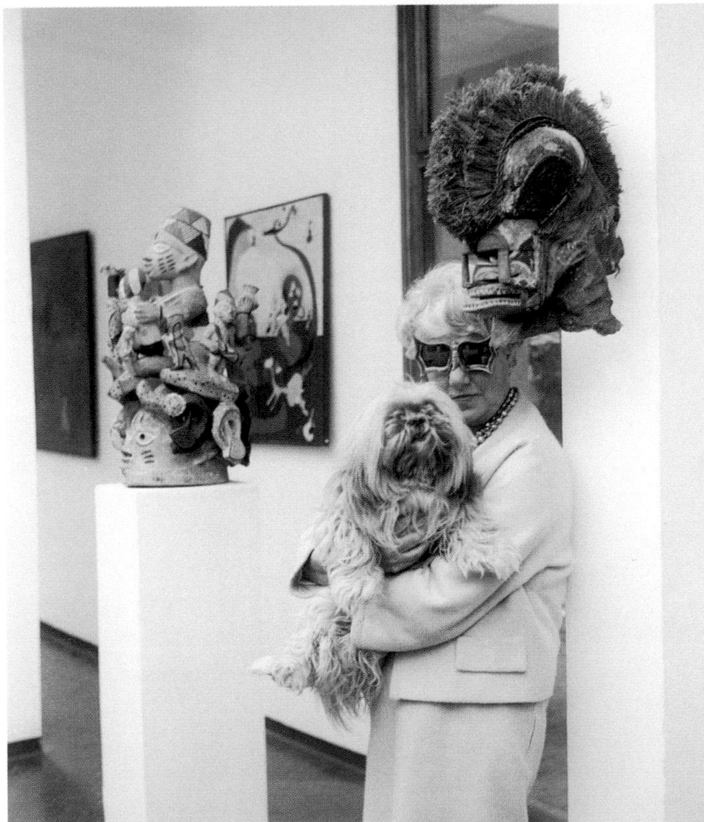

Above: **Jackson Pollock, *Mural* (1943). This commission, which for Pollock was "exciting as all hell," was for the foyer of Peggy Guggenheim's apartment. Pollock sat depressed for weeks in front of a blank canvas before painting this masterpiece in a few hours.**
Left: **Peggy Guggenheim in her museum in Venice in the 1960s.**

Right: **Exiled to the United States in 1942 where he had enjoyed a great prestige over the years, Marcel Duchamp advised Peggy Guggenheim in her choices as a collector and an art dealer. By declaring a canvas that Jackson Pollock had given her as "not bad," Duchamp helped her decide about exhibiting his work and launching his career.**

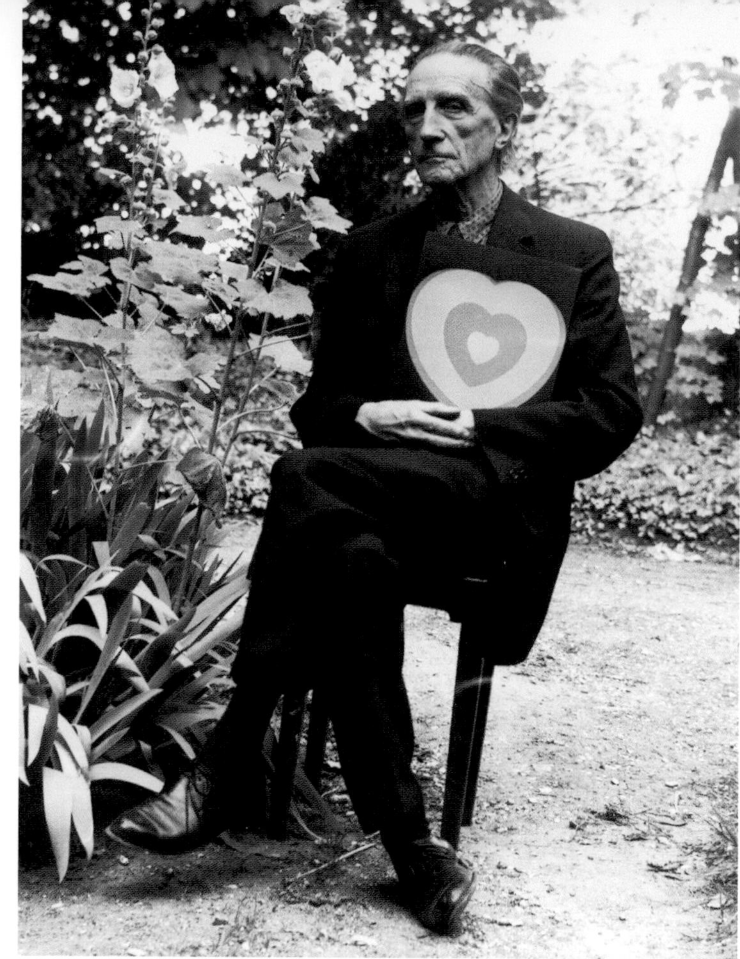

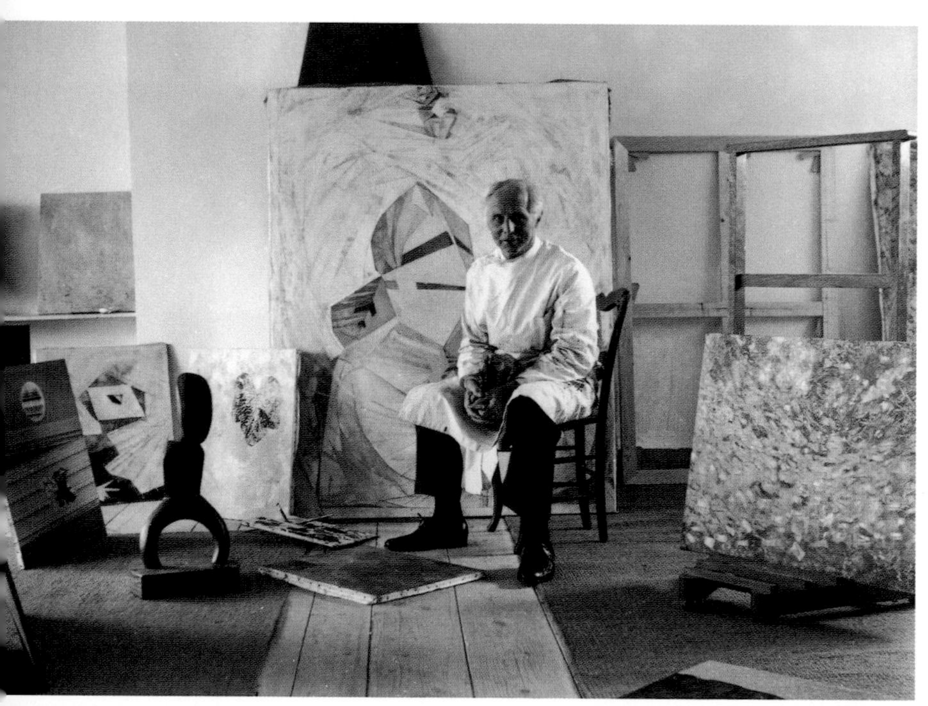

Left: **A brief husband to Peggy Guggenheim, Max Ernst was the artistic force behind her Art of This Century gallery before she broke with the Surrealists and began to champion American painting. This 1952 photograph shows him in his studio on the Impasse Ronsin after his return to Paris from the United States.**

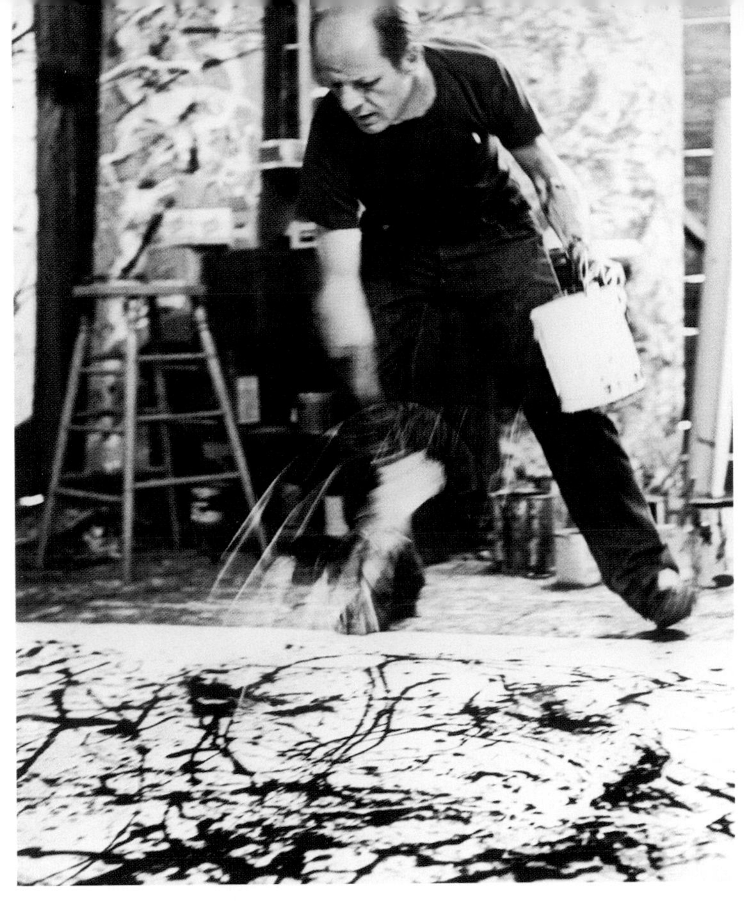

Left: **The photographs and films that Hans Namuth devoted to Jackson Pollock were enough to establish his image as the hero of American painting, perhaps even eclipsing the finished works themselves.**
Below: **Jackson Pollock photographed by Tony Vaccaro in 1953.**

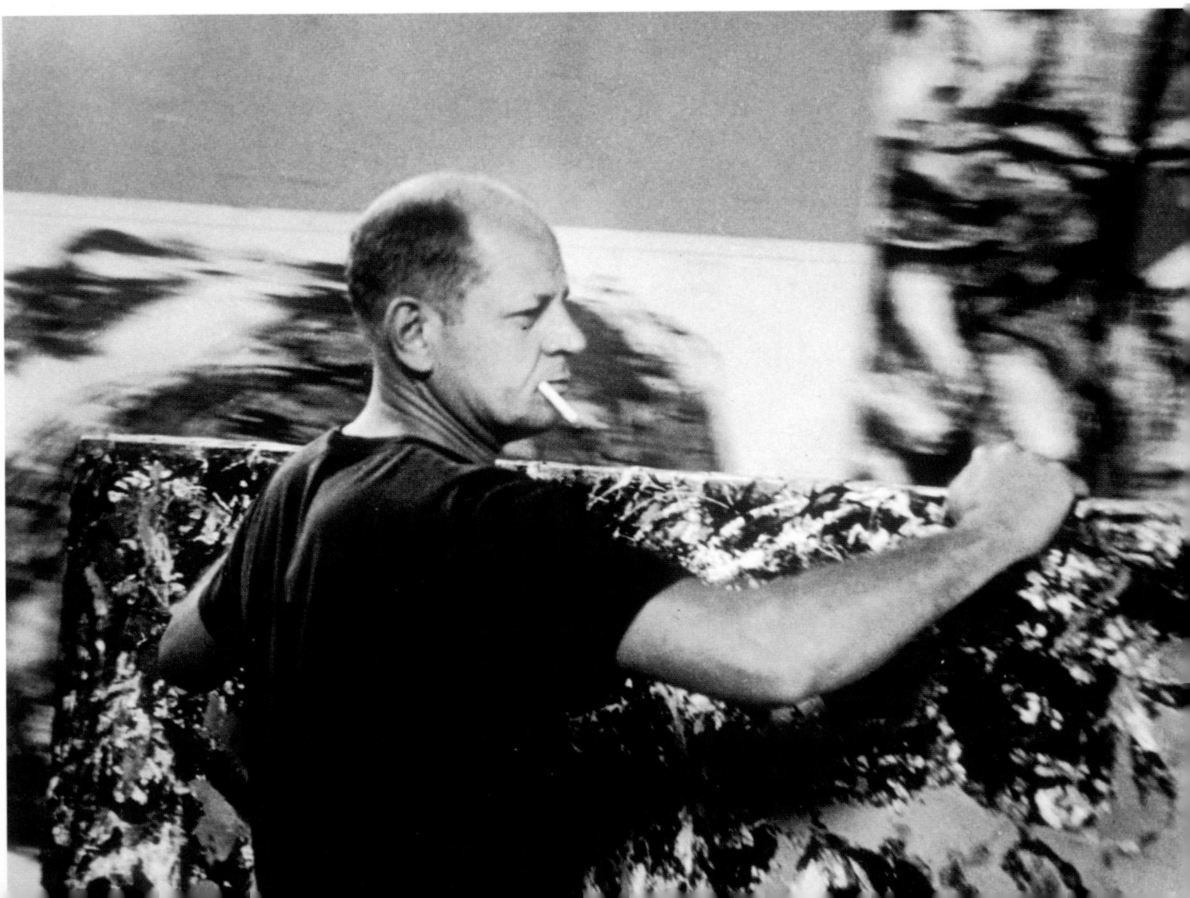

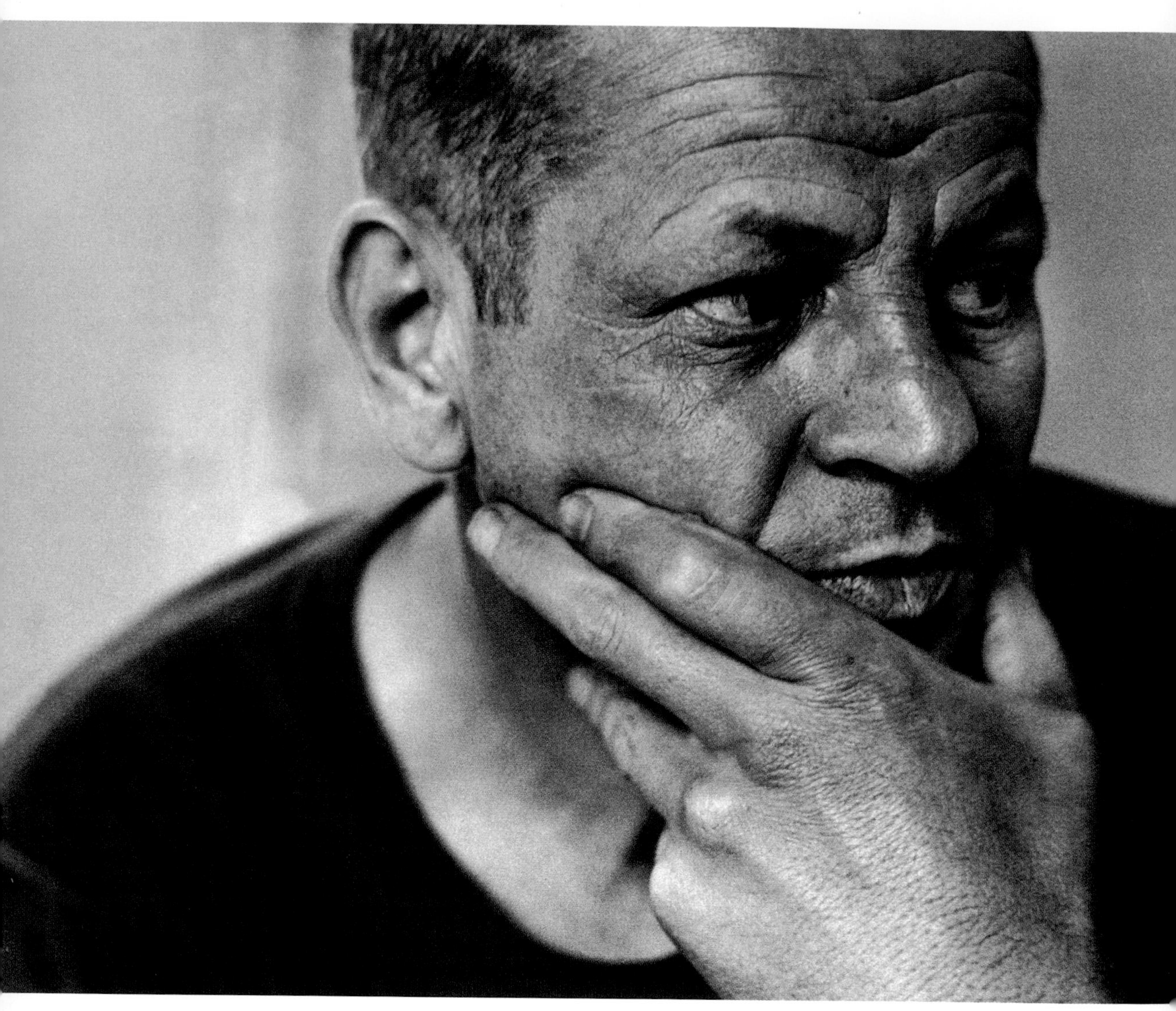

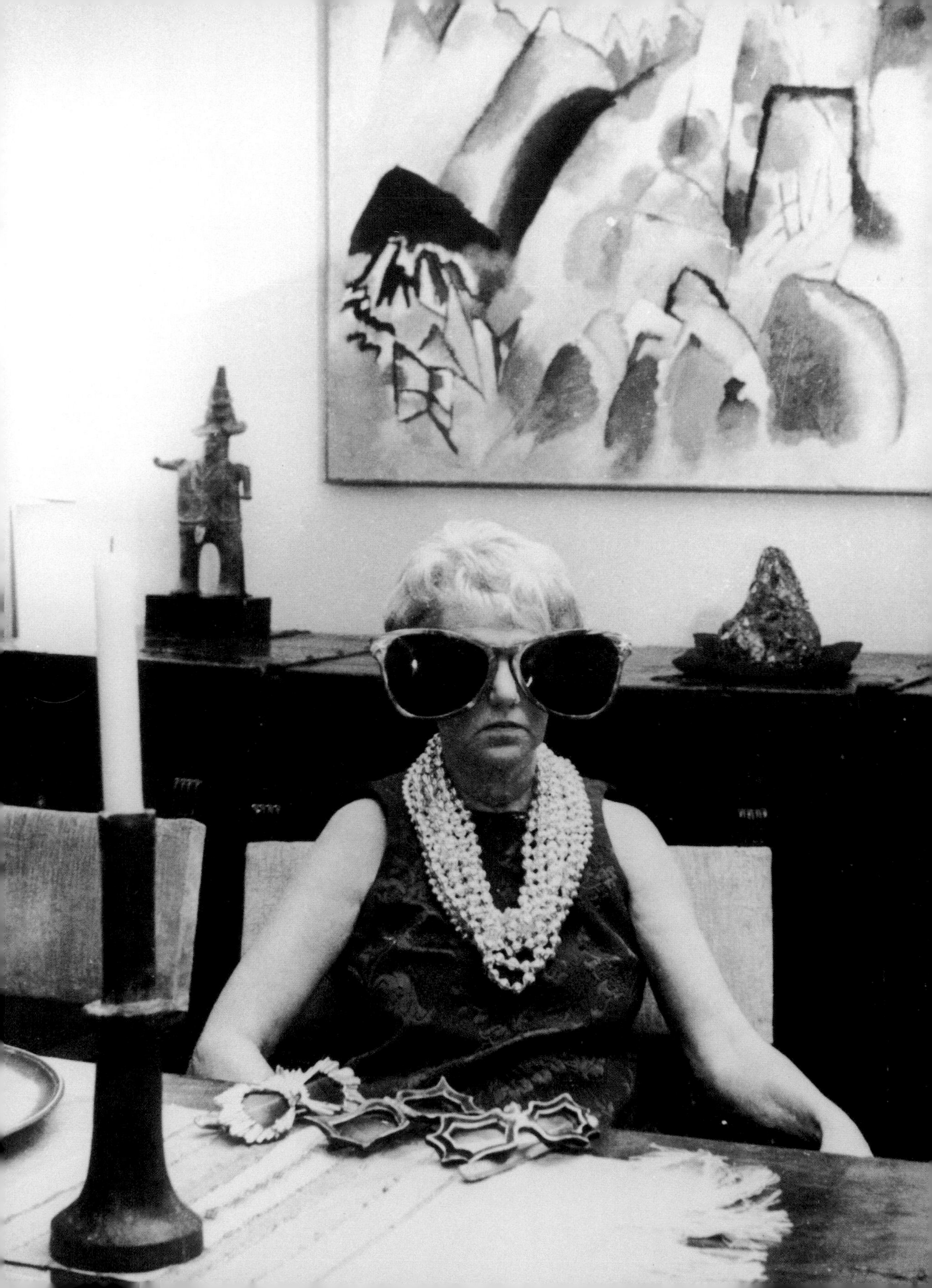

Page 206: **Jackson Pollock in 1953 photographed by Tony Vaccaro. Peggy Guggenheim's departure for Venice in 1947 signified her break with Pollock, who was disappointed by the small financial gains of his success. Withdrawing to his farm studio on Long Island, he became a living legend.**

Page 207: **Ever the eccentric, Peggy Guggenheim loved to pose as she did here in the 1960s with her enormous glasses, surrounded by her fabulous collection brought together in her palazzo on the edge of the Grand Canal in Venice, which has since become her foundation.**

[he had] seen in a long, long time, here or in Europe." But how could such a vehement canvas please him? Peggy wondered. "What I paint and what I think are two different things," replied Mondrian. That was not enough for her. For her only Duchamp would be able to judge this canvas. "Not bad," murmured the inventor of ready-mades when he saw *Stenographic Figure.* That was high praise indeed from this artist known for his laconic judgments.

Pollock would be one of the stars of the salon, and after almost two years of harassment by Sweeney and Putzel, Peggy finally decided to visit his studio. The painter arrived late and dead drunk to this important rendezvous, but being chaperoned by Lee Krasner, he managed to avoid making a very bad impression. Peggy commissioned *Mural* from him for her new duplex, an apartment, she added, that "was so perfect in every respect (except that it had only one kitchen)." Marcel Duchamp wisely advised him to execute it on canvas so that they would eventually be able to move it. "This was a splendid idea and, for the University of Iowa, a most fortunate one," recalled Peggy Guggenheim, "as I gave it to them when I left America. It now hangs there in the students' dining hall." The exhibition took place in November of the same year, her first dedicated to a non-Surrealist, and moreover, a non-European. American art began to command attention.

The Star of the Gallery

"His triumphant canvases lived up to all my hopes," wrote James Johnson Sweeney, who worked to further Pollock's career, in the introduction to the catalogue. "In fact, I always referred to Pollock as our spiritual offspring." Without a declared commercial aim, the gallery became a meeting place for the New York avant-garde about whom Robert Coates, a critic for *The New Yorker* magazine, invented the term "Abstract Expressionism." Pollock was the best among them. "As he required a fixed monthly sum in order to work in peace, I gave him a contract for one year," Peggy said. "I promised him a hundred and fifty dollars a month and a settlement at the end of the year, if I sold more than two thousand seven hundred dollars' worth, allowing one-third to the gallery." From 1943 to 1947, the collector Bill Davis suggested she raise the stipend to three hundred dollars a month in exchange for the totality of his production. This was a heaven-sent chance for Pollock who, for the first time in his life, could envisage living on his painting. The contract was so exceptional, moreover, that when Guggenheim "exhausted by all [her] work in the gallery" left New York in 1947 to create the foundation in Venice, which still exists today, no other gallery would agree to take on his contract. Only one dealer among them, Betty Parsons, offered to organize an exhibition. But relations between Pollock and Peggy had already deteriorated, with the artist believing that the financial renumerations were insufficient for the success he had achieved, and Peggy judging him an ingrate after all that she had done for him. This eternal battle between art dealer and artist was in their case fueled by the patroness's fruitless attempts at sexual relations with a seriously ambivalent Pollock who was ill at ease in his marriage, did not admit his homosexuality, and found refuge in alcohol. And we cannot forget the spectacular contrast between Peggy's fortune and that of her protégés, as well as her need to remark endlessly about how much they were costing her. Friends recalled that she would forbid them from finishing their meals at restaurants because "it was expensive enough as it was." A biography of "Madame Moneybags," a nickname given her by some artists, is chock full of accounts of money loaned, borrowed, returned and not. The money Krasner borrowed from Guggenheim for the purchase of a country house on New York's Long Island was the only way she found to distance Pollock from the New York bars, and it appeared to be money well spent. Pollock withdrew to this farm studio and became a living legend. In 1949 *Life* magazine published a story: "Jackson Pollock: Is he the greatest living painter in the United States?" The question may have been meant as irony but it didn't matter. The photographs and films of the hero of American painting splashing paint on enormous canvases set up on the floor stunned the entire world. Even if her heart was not always there, Peggy Guggenheim was very much at the birth of this era. In later years, while remembering every detail of the contracts that passed between her and Pollock, she could not help herself from writing: "And so now Lee is a millionaire, and I think what a fool I was." In 1956 she learned of Pollock's death in an automobile accident. They had lost contact for some years but, at eighty years old, writing the last words of her autobiography, Peggy Guggenheim addressed the balance sheet of her existence like this: "I launched Pollock. That's enough to justify my efforts."

Bibliography

Gill, Anton. *Art Lover: A Biography of Peggy Guggenheim.* New York: HarperCollins, 2002.

Guggenheim, Peggy. *Out of This Century: Confessions of an Art Addict.* New York: Ecco Press, 1997.

Solomon, Deborah. *Jackson Pollock: A Biography.* New York: Cooper Square Books, 2001.

Tacou-Rumney, Laurence. *Peggy Guggenheim: A Collector's Album.* New York: Rizzoli, 2002.

Misia Sert
Édouard Vuillard

Music and Silence

In the wake of the creative frenzy generated by the journal *La Revue blanche*, the secretive Édouard Vuillard's platonic passion for the exuberant and mysterious Misia gave birth to some of his most beautiful works. From the interiors of Thadée Natanson's Parisian apartment on rue Saint-Florentin to the bucolic scenes of La Grangette or Le Relais, their country houses, Vuillard photographed, drew, and painted his "uncertain and contrary desires."

"One moment, I beg you!" Bending over his camera in the heat of the summer of 1897, the painter Édouard Vuillard had a hard time making himself heard. Misia, his model and his host, the wife of his friend Thadée Natanson, would not stay still while fellow artist Henri de Toulouse-Lautrec, caught in flight, pursued a swarm of wasps to the cries of "Taiaut! Taiaut!" Passionate about the new invention from Kodak, Vuillard practiced photography in a frenzy over several weeks and endlessly asked people to pose. In these images the Natansons played bocce or stretched out on the grass. But more than the Natanson couple, his friend painter Pierre Bonnard, or any other subject, what interested Vuillard most was Misia, with whom he was secretly in love, and he photographed and painted her relentlessly. On December 24, 1896, he noted in his diary: "Thadée and his wife very good moment. Touching desires about work, ambitions, and feelings, returned at 4 a.m., slept till noon. Uncertain and contrary desires. Abundance of memories."

Like a Russian Novel

It was Misia's character that first attracted him. With her well-defined eyebrows and her huge dark eyes, Misia was full of charm without really being beautiful. She was robust and shapely and her unplaceable accent rendered her irresistible. Later her history would fascinate Vuillard. When Misia married Thadée Natanson at twenty-one, she seemed to have already lived several lives. Her birth resembled a fantastic fairy tale with, in the role of the father, Cyprien Godebski, a diabolical husband and a sculptor celebrated in his day, and, in the role of Mother Courage, Sophie, his neglected wife. Eight months pregnant, she traveled across Europe to find her fickle husband in St. Petersburg but, exhausted and humiliated, she died on March 30, 1872, while giving the world Marie Sophie Olga Zenaïde Godebska. The baby, who would quickly be nicknamed Misia, was a burden to her father, who soon took off on new adventures in his ancestral Poland and entrusted his daughter's care to nurses and to a grandmother who lived in Halle, Belgium. In comparison, Vuillard's childhood was very commonplace. We know only that he was born on November 11, 1868, in Cuiseaux, in the Saône-et-Loire region of France, and that he lived a long time in Paris with his omnipresent mother, the reason behind his shy condition.

Misia's gifts as a pianist also seduced Vuillard. As a child she learned the piano on the knees of composer Franz Liszt, who marveled at her talent. Later when her father put an end to her childhood paradise by returning to settle in Paris in the small Polish community near the parc Monceau, she was sent to boarding school but took piano lessons with composer Gabriel Fauré. One day Misia, who had fled her father's house and her evil stepmother, thought of becoming a professional pianist, and while waiting for it to happen tried to earn her living by also giving lessons. It was then that she saw Thadée Natanson again, the son of family friends; she agreed to marry this somewhat dull boy whom she liked well enough and who had just launched *La Revue blanche*.

The idea for the magazine was born in 1889 out of a discussion between the Natanson brothers on the terrace of the café Belle-Vue at the seaside resort of Spa in Belgium. Thadée was twenty-three years old and Alfred was only seventeen. The two young sons of a rich banker imagined a review open to all artistic sensibilities. They decided to name it *La Revue blanche* having recently learned in science class that white was the sum of all colors, and perhaps also as a reference to the famous white page which, according to the poet Stéphane Mallarmé, confronted him; more prosaically, the name distinguished the new journal from *La Revue rose*, which already existed. In fact similar magazines abounded, but Alfred and Thadée, soon aided financially by their father, were sure to play a role in the arts. Their conviction came from the friendships established at the Condorcet school and their future collaborators on the review, contributors who would play key roles in the twentieth century, whether in the fields of literature (Marcel Proust), theater (Aurélien Lugné-Poe), politics (Léon Blum, the future French prime minister from the Popular Front party and future author of incisive literary criticisms and surprising articles on sport), or painting (Maurice Denis, Ker-Xavier Roussel, and the man who would become his brother-in-law, Édouard Vuillard).

In the fourteen years of its existence from 1889 to 1903, the review tackled such subjects as birth control and the place of

Opposite: **Misia painted by Pierre Bonnard in 1895. As the wife of Thadée Natanson, the founder of *La Revue blanche*, a journal dedicated to the avant-garde at the turn of the century, Misia was the central character in the intellectual life of Paris and the great secret love of Édouard Vuillard, who painted her often as did his great friend Bonnard.**

women in society. It published Leo Tolstoy, Ivan Turgenev, Maxim Gorky, Henrik Ibsen, and Oscar Wilde in French for the first time. The French were also well represented. *La Revue blanche* published one of Proust's first texts, *Rêve*, which described the nostalgia of a person, alone in his bed, who begins dreaming of love. Years later in *À La Recherche du Temps Perdu* (*Remembrance of Things Past*), he would be inspired by Misia to create the characters of Madame Verdurin and Princess Youbelieff. But it was the poet Paul Verlaine who enjoyed a veritable cult following among the founders of the magazine, a bias that was not unanimously shared in an era when the novelist Edmond de Goncourt spoke of him as a "pederast assassin." The magazine was not content in merely publishing texts or introducing writers. It commissioned artists and, in the course of the summer of 1893, announced that from that point on, each issue would contain an original unpublished print. Naturally the first artists solicited were Vuillard, Roussel, and Bonnard, whom Thadée Natanson asked to create a poster in 1894. It would be Toulouse-Lautrec's turn the next year, and he would choose to depict the symbol of elegance and Parisian culture: Misia.

By marrying Thadée Natanson on April 25, 1893, Misia became the wife of a publisher of the avant-garde and was adulated by a crowd of artists and writers whom she had the power to invite over to the apartment she renamed the Annex, or to send back to their homes with a definitive cry of "I've had enough!"—a statement that could easily have come straight out of the mouth of Proust's Madame Verdurin. As a model, a friend, or a patroness, Misia did not hesitate to impose her way of living. One day she asked Bonnard to paint a frieze for her new apartment but she found the long right angles of his canvas monotonous and cut them into garlands. Her friends were scandalized. Misia replied superbly: "I don't respect art, I love it."

The Music of Painting

From the beginning Vuillard occupied a special place among the usual crowd. "Of all the reasons to love Vuillard, the sweetest was the conviction that he gave that one was loved by him," wrote Thadée Natanson without malice. Vuillard's ardent supporter, he pushed his cousin Paul Desmarais and then his own brother Alexandre to commission great decorative panels from him for a new home on the avenue du Bois-de-Boulogne, now known as avenue Foch. For the unveiling of the home, the Natansons

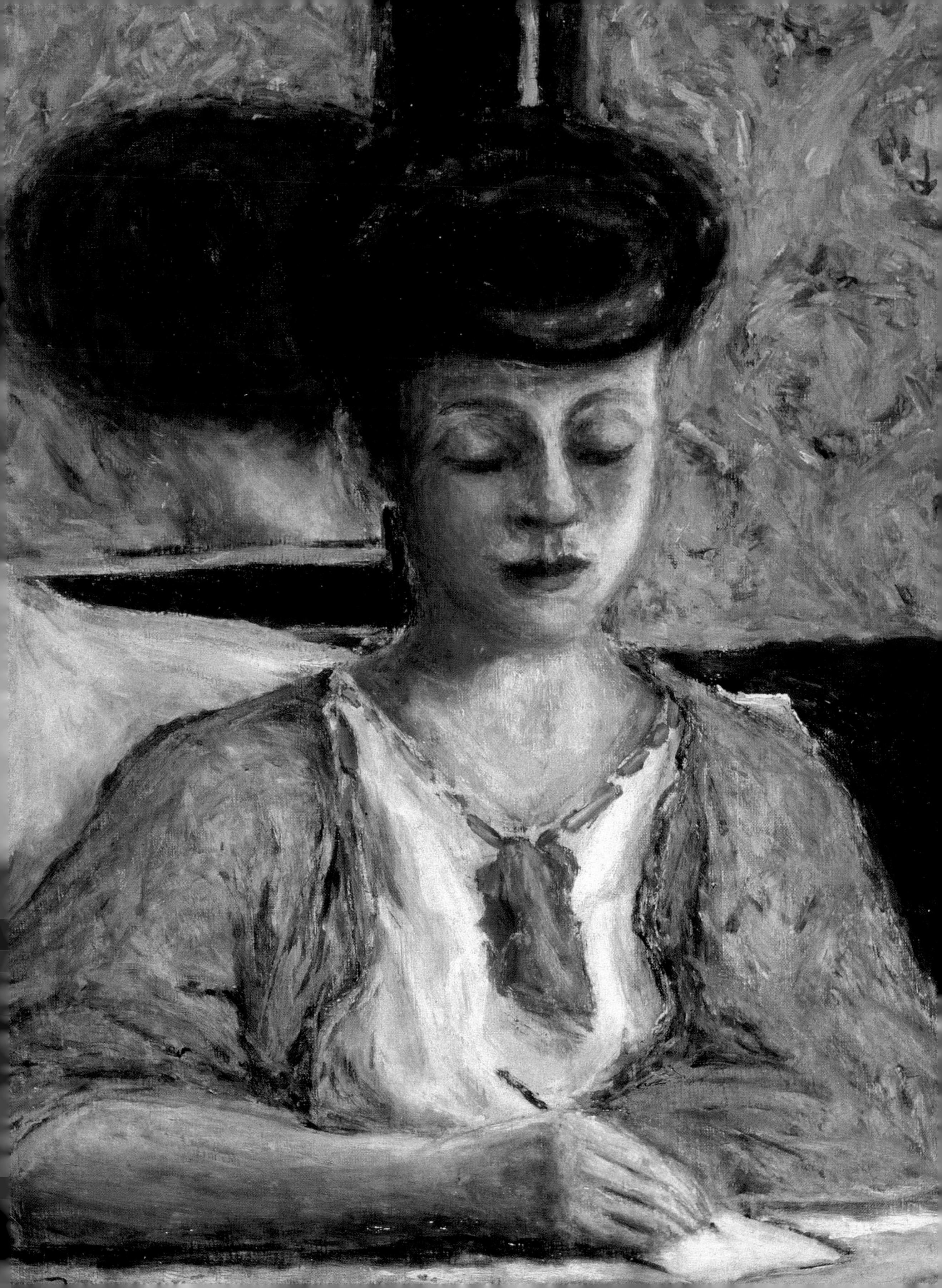

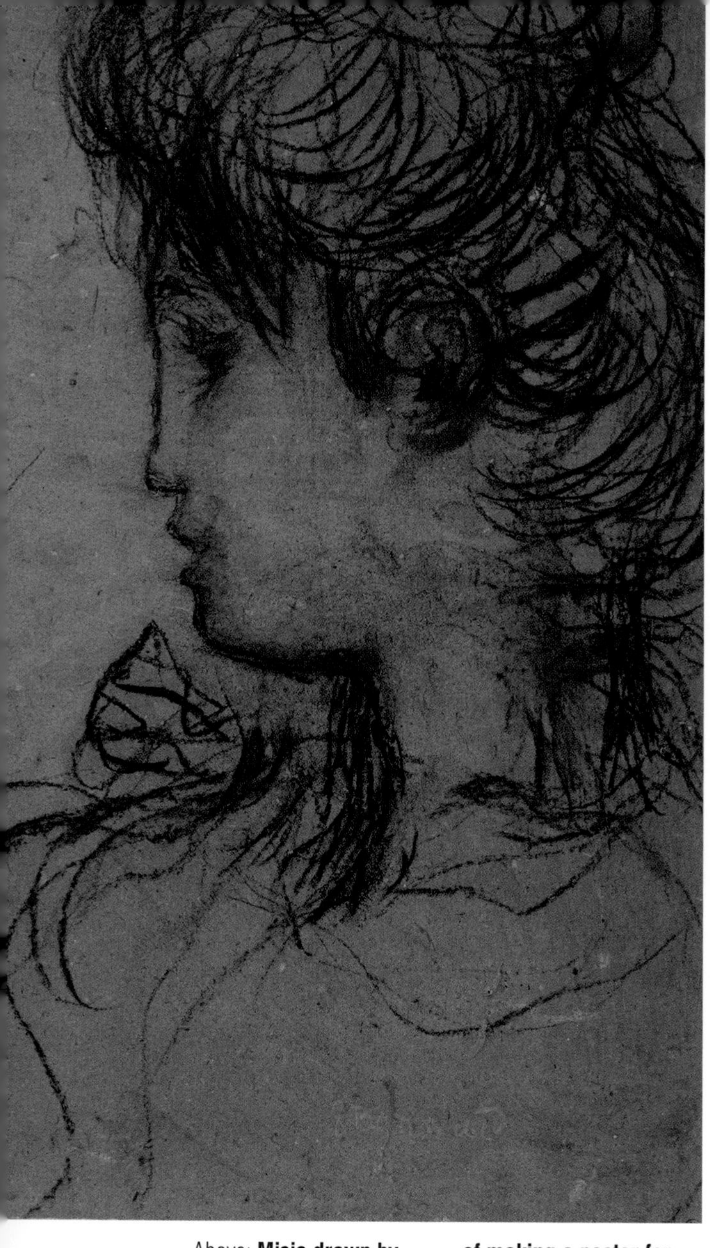

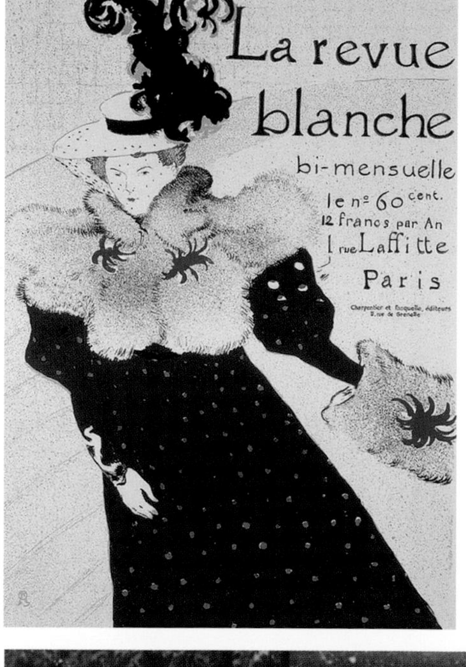

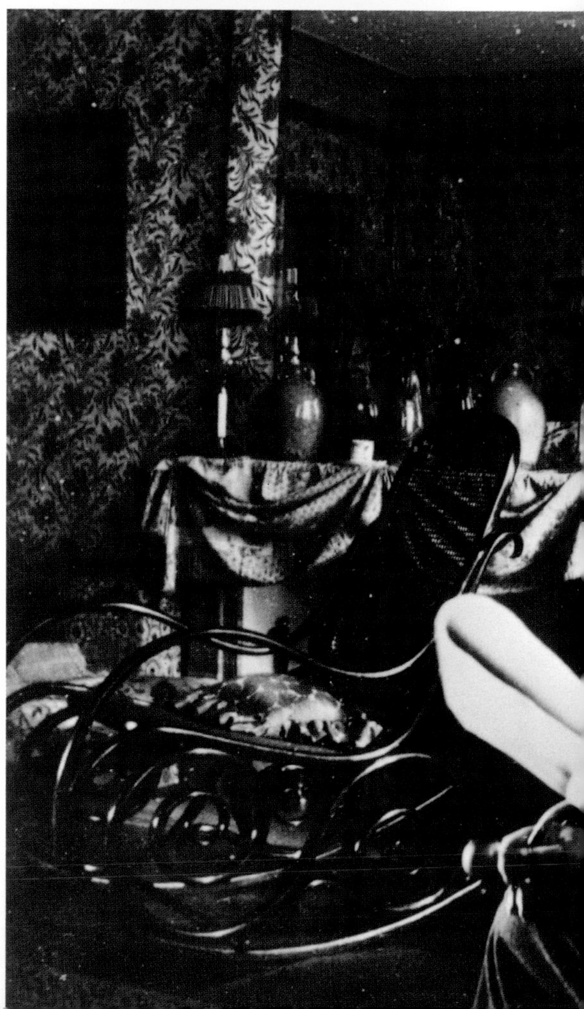

Above: **Misia drawn by Pierre Bonnard around 1895. She can easily be recognized by her straight nose and her hair put up in a bun at the top of her head.** Right, top: **A very close friend of the Natansons, Henri de Toulouse-Lautrec was entrusted with the responsibility of making a poster for *La Revue blanche*. He chose to represent the symbol of Parisian elegance and culture: Misia.** Right, bottom: **Thadée Natanson and Misia in their salon on the rue Saint-Florentin, as photographed by Édouard Vuillard in 1898.**

Right: **Édouard Vuillard, *Misia à Villeneuve-sur-Yonne* (circa 1897). At La Grangette, Misia settled herself into an attic she had converted into a studio for her piano playing. Vuillard spent several months in this small house situated not far from Stéphane Mallarmé's in Valvins.**

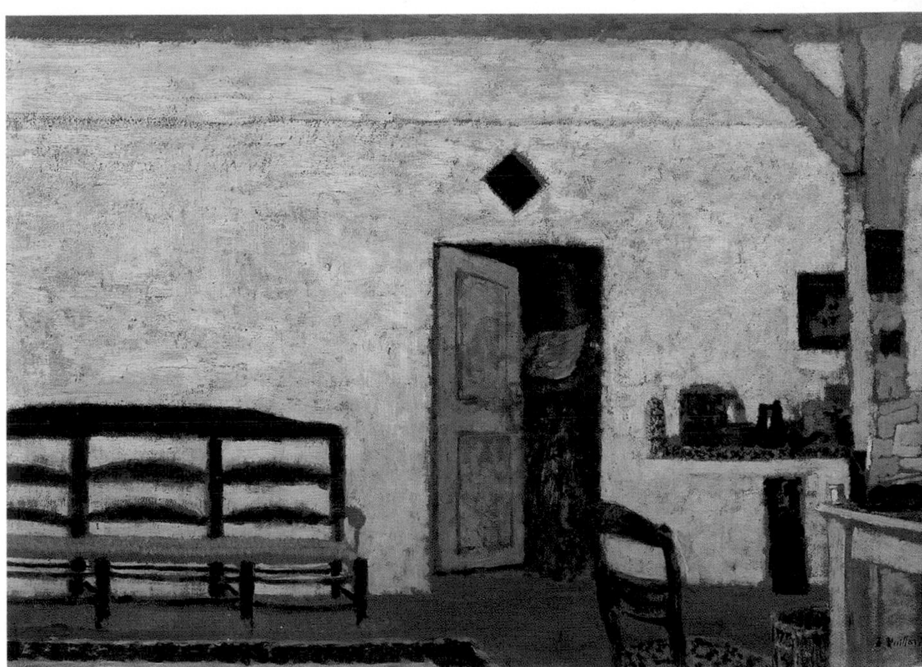

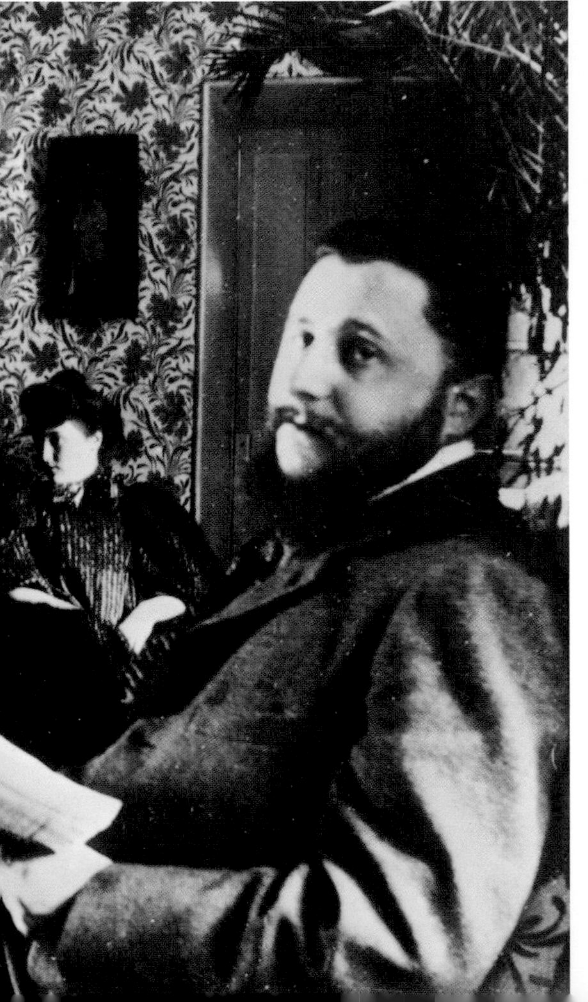

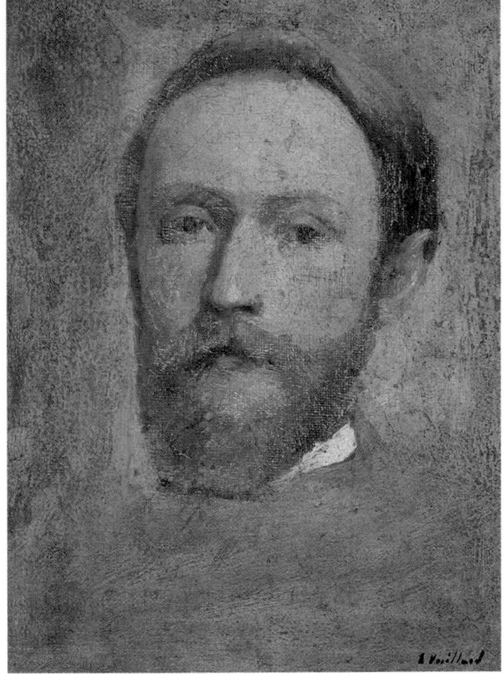

Above: **Édouard Vuillard, *Self-Portrait* (1889). This image of the painter dates from the time of the creation of *La Revue blanche* and the beginning of his unrequited love for Misia.**

organized a party for three hundred people. The invitations were made by Toulouse-Lautrec, who was also charged with tending the bar. A profusion of exuberant cocktails followed, blending colors and tastes, sardines with juniper berries and oysters with cayenne pepper. When Vuillard and Bonnard arrived after a day in the country, they devoured all the mixtures and fell into a semi-coma.

For her part, Misia arranged her apartment on the rue Saint-Florentin like a Vuillard, and Vuillard had only one wish: to paint Misia in its interior. He wrote in his diary in 1894: "There exists a type of emotion particular to a painter. It is in an effect that results from a certain arrangement of colors, of lights, of shadows, etc. It's what one would call the music of the painter." This musicality would be heard in the *Salon aux trois lampes* (*Salon with Three Lamps*) in the decorative lines of the paper that covered the walls, the frames of photographs, the Thonet bentwood rocking chair, the rugs that were strewn on the floor, and Misia's Spanish shawl thrown on the piano. In *Misia et Thadée Natanson*, the mistress of the house, who lies asleep dreaming on a couch, dominates a living room arranged all around her. In the *Peignoir rouge* (*The Red Dressing Gown*), Vuillard finally represents Misia as an odalisque and lets himself loose in romantic contemplation. He paid daily visits to his patrons and, when they bought La Grangette, a little house situated near Mallarmé's in Valvins, Vuillard spent several months there. Misia set up a studio where she played the piano, and Vuillard depicted her under the poster made by the weekend guest, Toulouse-Lautrec. He, in the meantime, never went anywhere without his nutmeg grater to add spice to his port and a mixture of calves' liver with prunes, ragout of squirrel, and roasted legs of lamb for them.

In 1897 La Grangette was not large enough to welcome the many friends of *La Revue blanche*, so Thadée and Misia Natanson moved to a bigger house christened Le Relais in Villeneuve-sur-Yonne. Misia and Vuillard were closer than ever and more than ever the painter suffered from an impossible love. When Thadée left for Paris, Misia noted, "Vuillard serves me as a husband . . . in good and honorable ways naturally"—a somewhat wicked sentence written to the painter Félix Valloton, who was a confidant of his friend's distress. That summer a crucial episode took place during a late afternoon walk, which Misia recalled fifty years later in her *Mémoires*: "I caught my foot on a root and half fell over. Vuillard stopped short to help me regain my equilibrium. Our eyes met abruptly. I could only see his sad eyes shining in the growing darkness. He burst into tears. It was the most beautiful declaration of love that a man had ever made." In the autumn of that same year, Jean Schopfer, a childhood friend of Thadée's and a contributor to *La Revue blanche*, commissioned panels from Vuillard with money he had made winning a tennis tournament. It was Vuillard's last opportunity to capture the special atmosphere of the Natansons' garden. But it seems that the summer storms had subsided. No shadows, just greens and soft reds, Bonnard played with a dog while his companion Marthe read a fashion magazine. Misia smiled, sleeping on the cushion given by Toulouse-Lautrec. Vuillard painted her sleeping and satisfied, with her feet lost in the grass.

Valloton soon introduced Vuillard to Jos and Lucie Hessel, cousins to the dealer of Bernheim canvases. A new relationship began like the one he had maintained with the Natansons but one, without a doubt, in which he had more success with Lucie Hessel. *La Revue blanche* soon ceased publication and, in 1908 Thadée Natanson, a victim of grave financial difficulties, sold a part of his collection, which included twenty-seven Vuillards. After they separated, Misia married the fabulously rich Alfred Edwards before marrying the painter José-Maria Sert. For his part Vuillard never married. He only saw Misia every now and then. One day she sent him a recording of Beethoven with a note assuring him of her eternal friendship. Recalling the times when she had been the muse of *La Revue blanche*, he wrote her: "I was always timid in front of you, but the security and the confidence of a perfect understanding with you lifted every difficulty from me, and nothing was ever lost in being silent."

Bibliography

Gold, Arthur, and Robert Fizdale. *Misia: The Life of Misia Sert*. New York: Vintage, 1993.

Thomson, Belinda. *Vuillard*. London: Phaidon Press, 1997.

Waller, Bret, and Grace Seiberling. *Artists of* La Revue Blanche*: Bonnard, Toulouse-Lautrec, Valloton, Vuillard*. Seattle: University of Washington Press, 1985.

Wynne, Elizabeth Easton. *The Intimate Interiors of Édouard Vuillard*. Washington, D.C.: Smithsonian Institution Press, 1989.

Pannonica de Koenigswarter Thelonious Monk

The Night Butterfly and the Flame

In composing *Pannonica* Thelonious Monk celebrated Pannonica de Koenigswarter, the baroness with the first name of a butterfly. She was born a Rothschild and separated from her diplomat husband to become the leading and eccentric figure of New York jazz after World War II. By restoring to the great pianist the desire and the right to play, she supported for twenty-seven years the man nicknamed "the high priest of bebop."

"Here's the baroness!" No Thelonious Monk concert took place in New York without the regulars keeping an eye open for the arrival of the Baroness Pannonica de Koenigswarter. It was impossible not to notice this tall woman with the wavy brown hair dressed in a mink coat or in a fake panther raincoat, a Chanel bag in her hand. She was a scheming Englishwoman who drew innocent jazzmen to her, according to some American detractors, or a patroness and an inspiration of the greatest musicians, several of whom dedicated their most beautiful pieces to her, according to her admirers. Nica, or "the baroness of jazz" as the jazz players nicknamed her, was at the heart of New York jazz after the war.

New York and jazz. As Laurent de Wilde recounted in his essay on Monk, the two entities were so inseparable to that point that, according to legend, it was jazz musicians who nicknamed the city the "Big Apple" "because when you come there to play, you better be sure you're ready, or you'll feel a lump in your throat you can't swallow, a big Adam's apple. If this story is true, then we need to rename the city. The Big Balls seems more appropriate to me."

A Rare Species of Butterfly

The anxiety of having to play in front of an audience for one's livelihood was not a part of Pannonica de Koenigswarter's world when she arrived in New York. Born a Rothschild on December 10, 1913, in London, the daughter of banker Nathaniel Charles Rothschild, she barely had time to get to know her father, who died when she was nine years old. A passionate entomologist, he had named his daughter Pannonica (*Pannonia*, the Latin name for the region of Hungary) in honor of the rare species of butterfly he had discovered. She could barely recall that her father loved music, and not just the classical variety.

Her brother Victor initiated her into jazz. As the future personal emissary for British prime minister Winston Churchill to president Franklin Roosevelt and a great admirer of the pianist Art Tatum, Victor took advantage of his trips to New York to take piano lessons from Teddy Wilson in Harlem. Pannonica, who was gifted in painting, began to interest herself equally in jazz, and in jazz musicians.

"I told myself that if the jazz music was beautiful, then the soul of the musicians must be as well." At sixteen, however, she was wisely enrolled in school in Paris to round off her education as a young lady. Several basics—like how to put on lipstick—were livened up with classes in literature and philosophy, followed by a year of travel around Germany, Austria, and Italy in the company of her sister Liberty. On their return to London they made their entry into society. Pannonica was presented to the queen and spent several years attending society events and various apprenticeships. Automobiles became her passion, also aviation. She learned how to fly, and it was at the Touquet airport in France that she met Baron Jules de Koenigswarter, who owned his own airplane. She married him several months later, left for a honeymoon in the Far East, and then settled into his château near Dreux, France. When Germany invaded France in 1940, she obeyed the baron's orders and sought refuge first in England and then in the United States. Unable to tolerate the separation from her husband any longer, she entrusted the children to the care of an American family and got involved with the Free French Forces in order to find the baron who had joined up with General Charles de Gaulle in London in June 1940 before he was sent to Africa. She willingly volunteered to carry medicine from New York to Brazzaville in the Congo and just missed being sunk aboard a cargo ship that was attacked by submarines, but she eventually reached her destination safe and sound. She worked for Radio Brazzaville and recorded programs in French that were aimed at the territories under Vichy control. She also decoded and translated messages and then rejoined her husband in the 1st Division of the Free French Forces in Cairo and participated, as a military driver, in the North African, Italian, and French campaigns.

Decorated with the medal of the Liberation at the Armistice, the baron was named as advisor to the French ambassador to Norway and then to Mexico. An orderly life seemed to be on the horizon. From 1949, when they lived in Mexico, Koenigswarter had a hard time tolerating the music his wife listened to all day, and when she was late for receptions, he became so furious that he broke her records. Pannonica had tasted independence during the war and was bored with the regulated life of a diplomat's wife. She began to go on jaunts to New York, and met up with her brother Victor's friend Teddy Wilson, as well as Lionel Hampton and Art Blakey. "One day Teddy told me that I have to listen to *'Round Midnight* by Thelonious Monk. I ran out and bought the record. I put it on, and I missed the plane and stayed in New York three months longer." Soon she would not return to Mexico at all. In 1951 Pannonica left her husband and her youngest children and moved to New York with her oldest daughter.

Jazz, Really

A new life began for Pannonica. She spent her nights at the legendary jazz clubs: the Five Spot, the Village Vanguard, Small's, and Birdland. Continuing to benefit from her considerable family revenues, the flamboyant Pannonica was like a breath of fresh air, described as such by her musician friends who led difficult lives and often drowned themselves in alcohol and drugs. One night in 1955 the radio announced the death of "Bird," the nickname of the saxophonist Charlie Parker, in the apartment of the "baroness" at the Hotel Stanhope. For some time the name of Koenigswarter had been associated with a presumed life of debauchery, and the baron's demand for a divorce was sped up as much as possible.

Indifferent to the malicious gossip, Pannonica lived in the wee hours. A cigarette holder at her lips, and a silver flask often within reach of her mouth, she sped around with her black musician friends in her gray convertible Bentley, also known by the nickname of the silver turtledove. In the afternoons and evenings, they rehearsed in her hotel suite or listened to endless records. "She didn't buy uninteresting records, she only bought records by artists who had something to say," recalled the pianist Horace Silver. Among the albums she kept coming back to was the one that was like the soundtrack to her life, *'Round Midnight.* She had not been able to hear it played live yet. After an episode with drugs in 1951, Thelonious Monk had been deprived of the indispensable "cabaret card" and did not have the right to play clubs in New York. Pannonica finally met him in 1954 in Paris, where he had been invited by Charles Delaunay to appear at his Salon du Jazz. The son of the painters Robert and Sonia Delaunay played the role of jazz ambassador in France, and he brought over this already legendary character about whom it was known that he spoke little, rarely addressed his audience, and wore an increasingly unusual selection of hats. This was Thelonious Monk, and he would turn Pannonica's life upside down. For twenty-seven years, she unfailingly supported the man nicknamed "the high priest of bebop."

Thelonious Sphere Monk was born on October 10, 1917, in Rocky Mount, North Carolina, but grew up in New York in the San Juan Hill neighborhood, which today is the location of Lincoln

Center. At the time, it was an African-American district prefiguring Harlem. As a young boy Monk was well-mannered, active, the firemen's mascot, and in love first with Ruby, his sister's best friend (*Ruby, My Dear*), and then soon after with Nellie, who would become his companion for life. He learned to read notes looking over his sister's shoulder while she played the piano, and from the age of 11, acquired the reputation of a musician. At the St. Cyprien Baptist church, he accompanied his mother on the organ, discovering the play of pedals that would become an integral part of his physical and musical language. At seventeen he left on a two-year tour with an itinerant evangelist and immersed himself in a certain mysticism. Music was not a matter of ego or virtuosity for him, it was the church, the group, the orchestra, a collective work. "Music that speaks. Music that makes people dance. Music that draws the ear to the regions where the soul is elevated, wilder, and too, more serene," Laurent de Wilde states in his superb analysis.

A pianist who would do anything to make a living, he played in a Chinese restaurant in Harlem, in hotel banquet halls, and on dance stages, before appearing at Minton's club, the cradle of bebop. In a few years he became "the high priest of bebop" bringing together what was then a still new combination of bass, drums, and piano to compose atypical pieces for the time, like *'Round Midnight*. Pannonica went to hear him play in public for the first time in 1954.

Monk was then thirty-six years old and his Blue Note and Prestige recordings were still little known. That night in 1954 it was the white saxophonist Gerry Mulligan who was considered the star of the Salon du Jazz. Monk was even booed. Despite this, after the concert he would go on to record eight works of solo piano in Paris that remain today among the most beautiful contributions to music of the twentieth century.

Thanks to his relationship with Pannonica and the support of his manager Harry Colomby, Monk was able to regain his cabaret card and recommence his career in 1957. He had a contract at the Five Spot, a little club on the Lower East Side where he played first in a trio, then in a quartet with Wilbur Ware, Shadow Wilson, and John Coltrane. He stayed there for more than a year. At the end of the year CBS television featured him, along with Billie Holiday and Count Basie, among others, on the successful "The Sound of Jazz" production that was part of their acclaimed "Seven Lively Arts" series.

In 1957 Thelonious was at the point again of being banned from playing. Pannonica was at the wheel of her Bentley driving Monk and the saxophonist Charlie Rouse to a weeklong club date in

Pages 226–27: **Pannonica de Koenigswarter and Thelonious Monk photographed in Washington, D.C., in 1963 by William Claxton.**

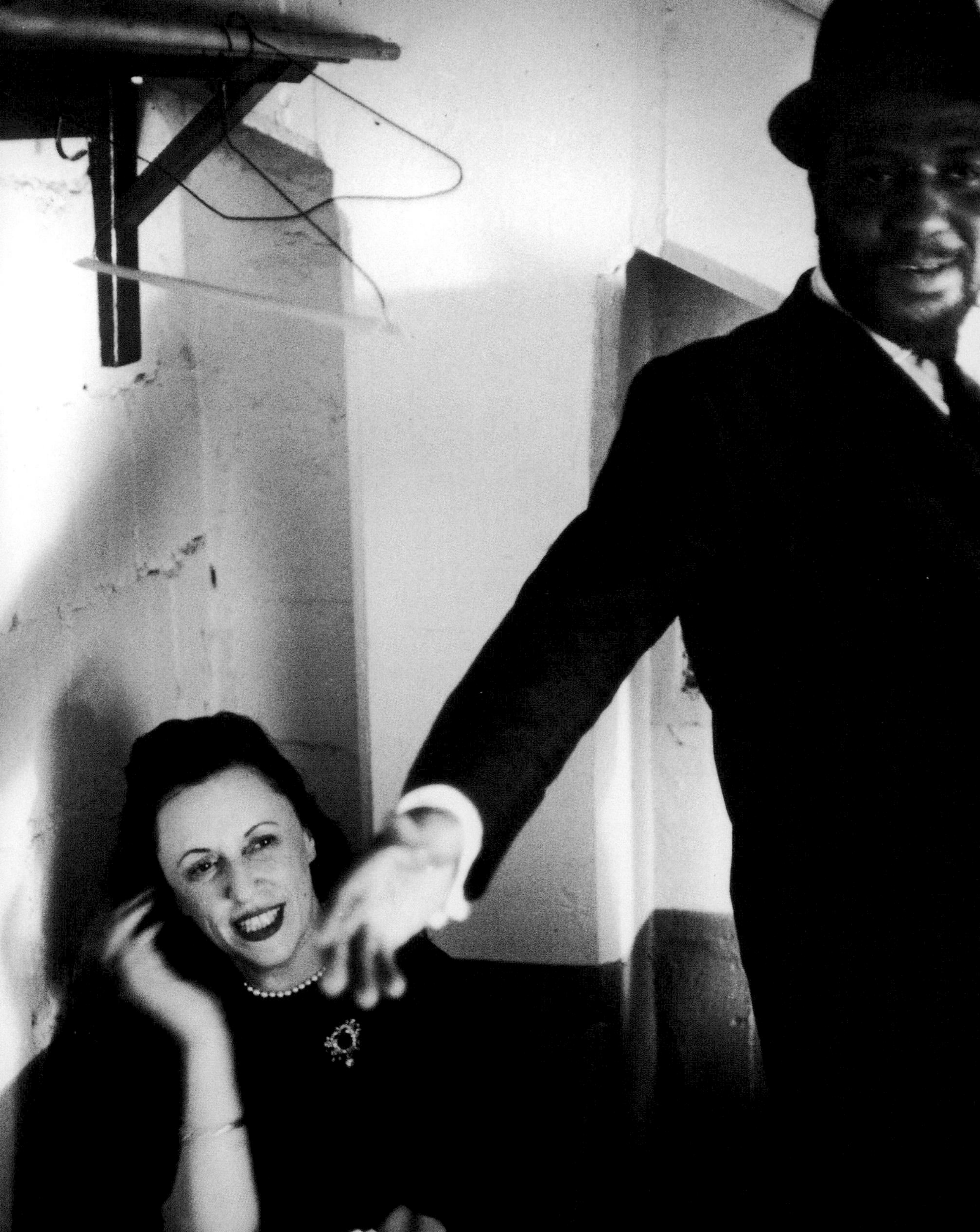

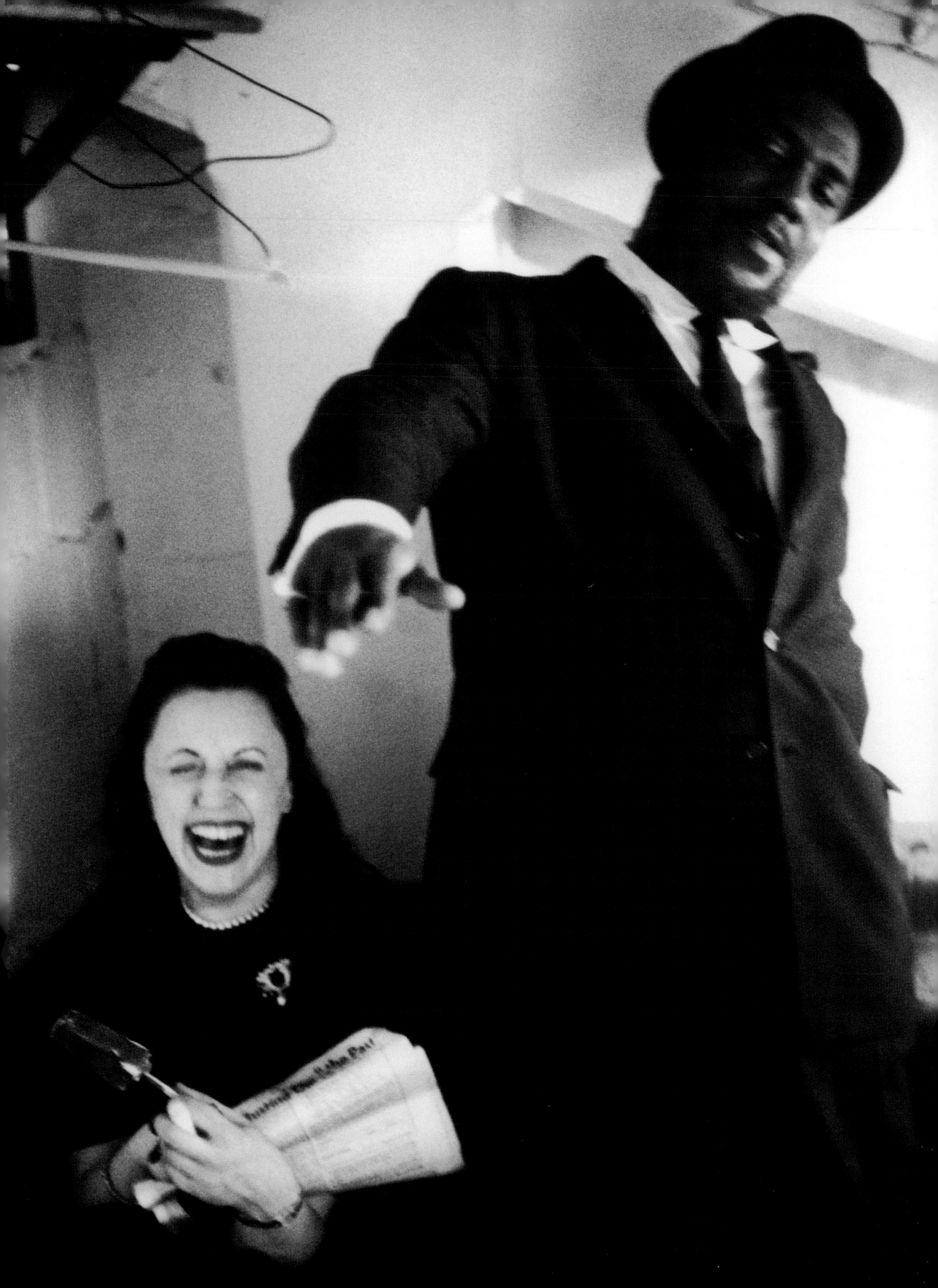

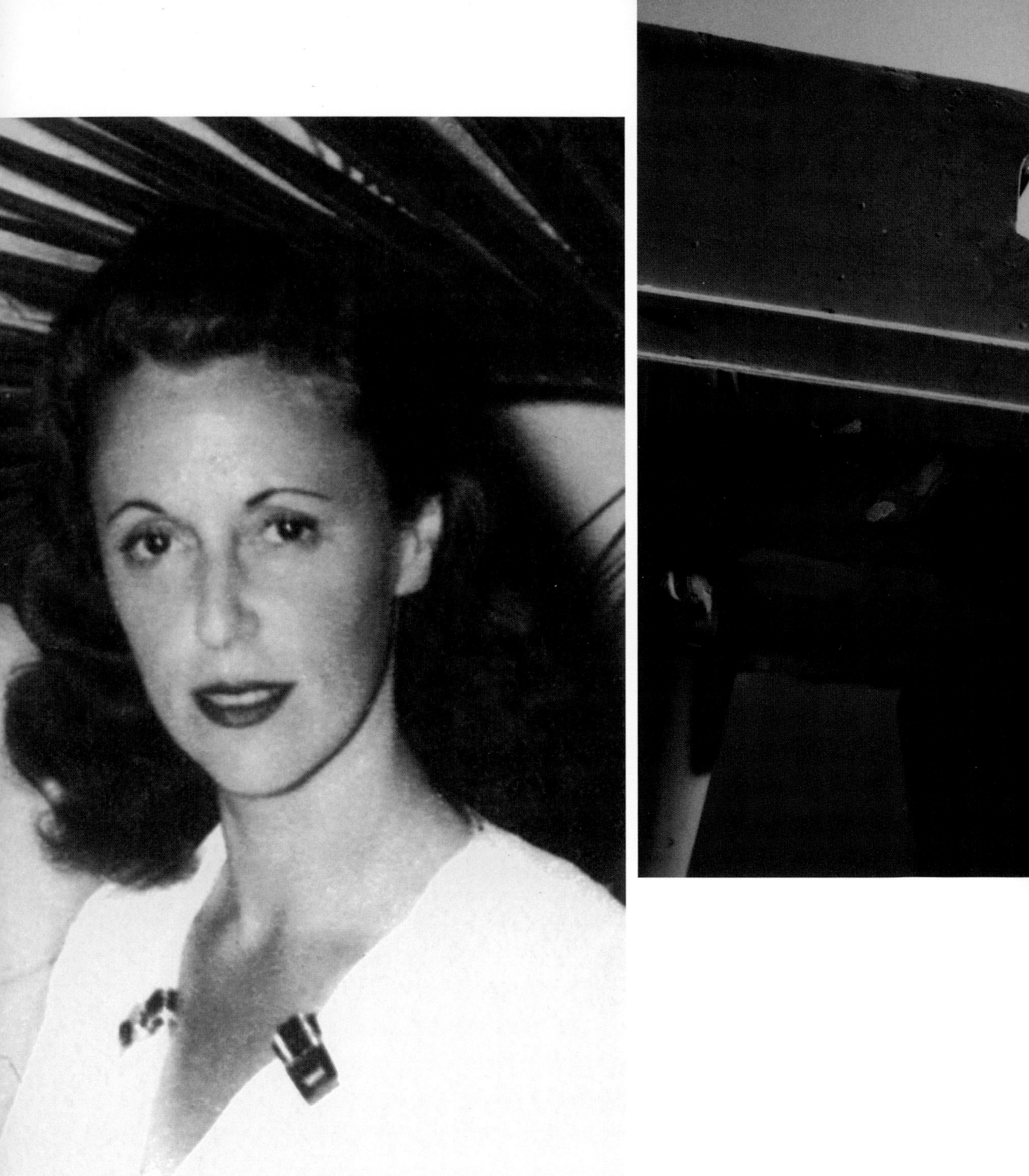

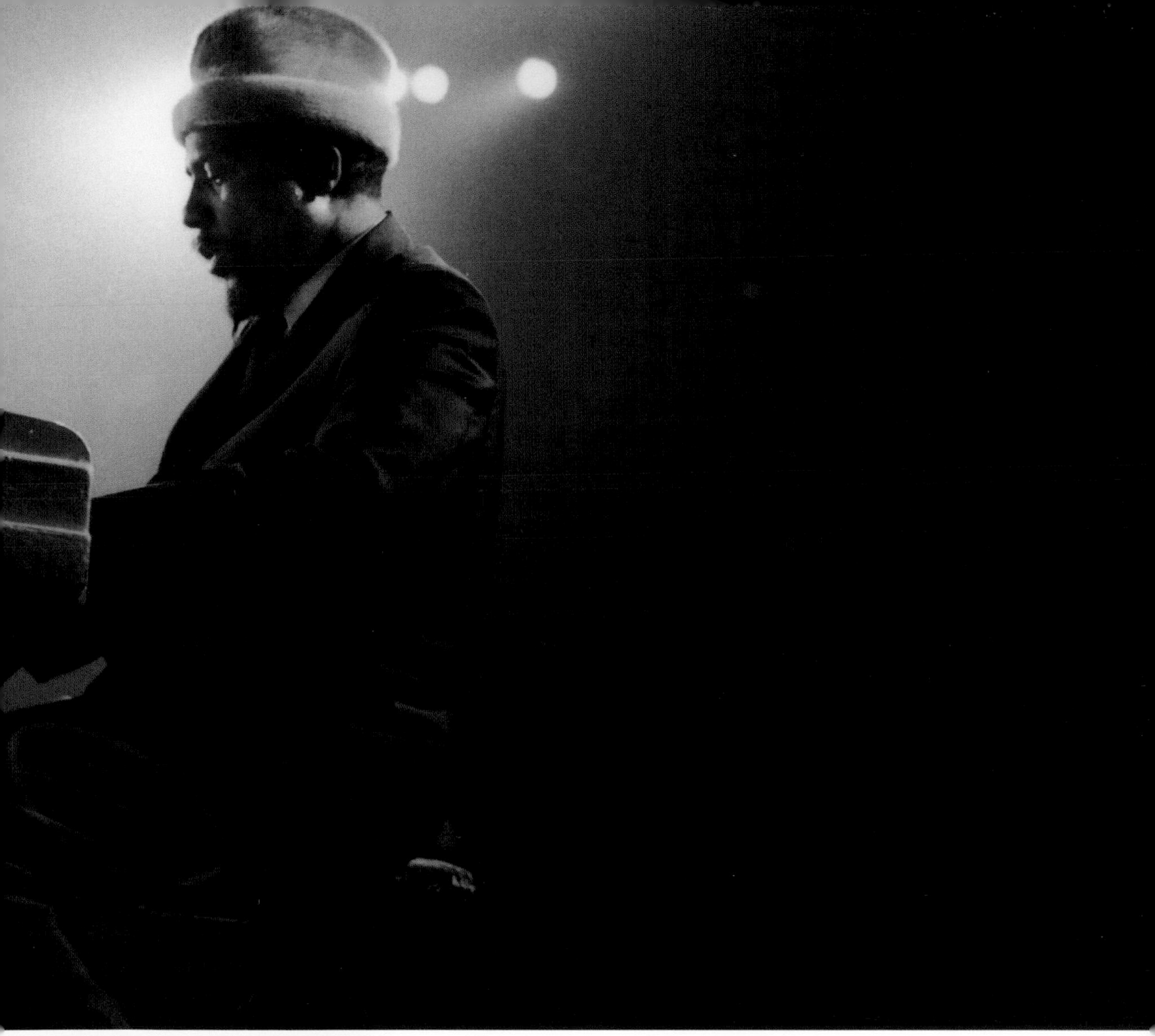

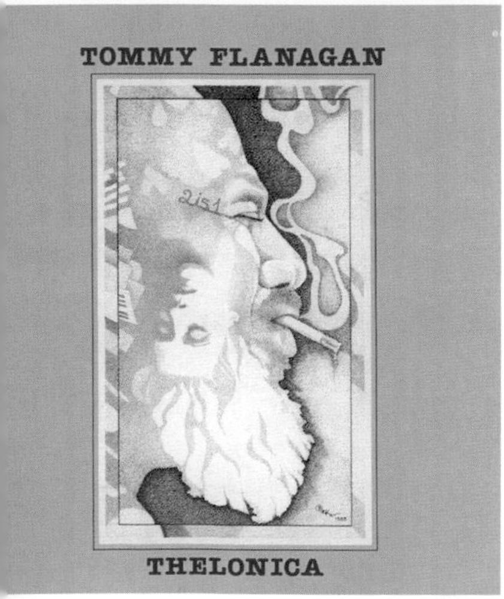

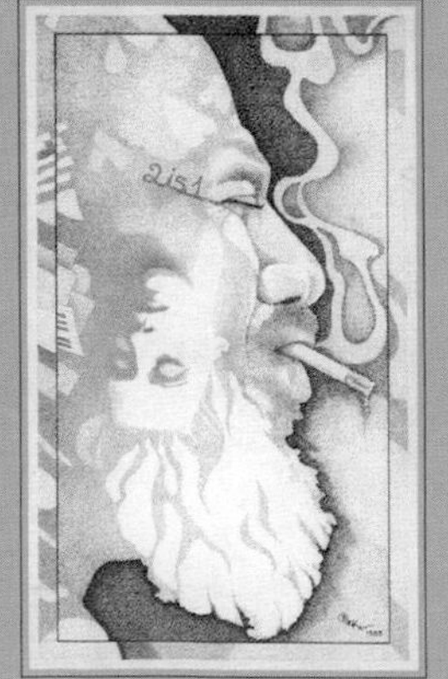

Above: **On February 22, 1964, Thelonious Monk was in Paris for a concert at the Alhambra with his quartet made up of Charlie Rouse, Butch Warren, and Ben Riley. Photograph by Guy Le Querrec.**

Left: **This 1983 Tommy Flanagan album cover celebrated their friendship by interweaving their faces.**

Opposite: **Pannonica de Koenigswarter photographed in Mexico in 1950.**

Maryland when the pianist asked her to stop to get a glass of water on a Baltimore street. Following a misunderstanding, the owner of the bar they stopped in called the police. Monk was roughed up and handcuffed, and Pannonica was arrested after a search of her car yielded some marijuana. She protested that it had come from her garden, but she was sentenced to three years in prison, then released on bail. It took her lawyers three years to dismiss the charges. Monk was once again deprived of his cabaret card and thereby forbidden from playing music in New York clubs. Pannonica gathered medical proof establishing that Monk was not a junkie and should be able to work and regain his cabaret card. Upon his return, he began to play again at the Five Spot with John Coltrane in a series of unforgettable sessions. In 1958 Monk was chosen by the critics of *Down Beat* magazine as the Musician of the Year. He was then forty years old, with money, an agent, and a protector. The following year he was at the head of a large band and his compositions, *Ruby, My Dear*, *Off Minor*, *Blue Monk*, and *'Round Midnight* had become classics. In 1959 he played the West Coast for the first time, followed by his tours of Europe and Japan. At the 1962 Newport Jazz Festival, the great Duke Ellington composed *Frère Monk* in his honor. In Baltimore a crowd protested against the closing of the club where he was performing with cries of "We want Monk, We want Monk, We want. . . ." He was soon pictured on the cover of *Time* magazine in 1964. For several years he was under contract with the prestigious Columbia label, for which he recorded no less than thirty sessions. The title of his last album sums up the era: *It's Monk's Time*. But the competition from pop music was making itself felt more and more, and Columbia did not renew his contract. After a memorable benefit with his own son in 1975 in the course of which he completely eclipsed the young rising star Keith Jarrett, Monk performed for one last time at Carnegie Hall in 1976, his final public appearance, of which there remains no recording. Little by little he retired from the world. His years of glory had not only been given rhythm by the drums of his different bands ("Make the drummer sound good," according to one of his laconic expressions). Something was sapping him. From 1959 he collapsed more often and his stays in psychiatric hospitals multiplied. But Pannonica watched over him and in 1973 moved him into her home.

Coming on the Hudson

In 1958 the baroness had moved to Weehawken, New Jersey, on the other side of the Hudson River, to a house constructed ten years earlier by the director Joseph von Sternberg. She lived there surrounded by so many felines that she would nickname the place "The Cat House." A tireless member of the Musicians Union, she campaigned against and ended up abolishing the "cabaret card" system. She actively occupied herself with Monk's interests and agreed to provide permanent shelter for him, as she had done already for her friend Barry Harris. The baroness set up a huge room on the first floor filled with records and books. Between the bedroom and the kitchen was a living room with a ping-pong table, another of her favorite pastimes. Upstairs was a music room with a Steinway grand piano, a fireplace, and walls covered with portraits of her jazz musician friends. It was here that Monk composed *Coming on the Hudson* and *Jackie-ing* while taking in the magnificent view of Manhattan. It was a peaceful harbor far from all the everyday problems.

Thelonious Monk sank more and more into his silence. He stayed alone in his bedroom in the Cat House, receiving a few rare visitors to whom he said nothing. He no longer touched the piano. "He has never said that he won't play the piano again," Nica recalled in 1986. "He suddenly went into this, so maybe he'll suddenly come out." But he did not come out of it. A few weeks before his death, for his birthday on October 10, 1981, Barry Harris called him from Bradley's, a club in Greenwich Village, and played *'Round Midnight*. On the other side of the phone, Monk could not see the tears that fell down the pianist's cheeks. Monk died on February 17, 1982. The baroness retreated into her home surrounded by 129 cats.

Pannonica de Koenigswarter died on December 1, 1988. At her funeral at St. Peter's Lutheran Church, where most of the giants of jazz were immortalized, Barry Harris played *Just As Though You Were Here*, one of the fifteen pieces composed in her honor. "Music," said the great lady of New York jazz, "is the music that moved me. It was a desire for freedom. And in all my life, I never met anyone who warmed me as much by their friendship as the jazz musicians I knew." But only Thelonious possessed this strange quality that Pannonica described so marvelously: "He could make you hear the music on the inside of the music . . . to infinity."

Bibliography

Gourse, Leslie. *Straight, No Chaser: The Life and Genius of Thelonious Monk.* New York: Schirmer Books, 1997.

Wilde, Laurent de. *Monk*. New York: Marlowe & Co., 1997.

Mirror Image

If in mythology the beautiful Narcissus died of love pining for the unattainable reflection of his own image, real history is often less tragic. The meeting of two artists, one playing the role of the perfect image for the other, can generate not one but two fruitful bodies of work. What is more natural for a photographer than to enter into a creative game of mirrors with his companion when she also happens to be a photographer? The affair between Tina Modotti and Edward Weston is well on its way to becoming a legend, for all the ingredients of romantic drama are joined there. Moreover, this mirror image seems to be the innovative element in the twentieth-century relationships between the artist and the muse. In their treatment of the same subjects, whether on canvas or in photographs, or the interpretation by one partner of songs written by the other, these muses succeeded in creating their own autonomous works while inspiring—to different degrees—their companions, husbands, and lovers. Painters, singers, writers, from Frida Kahlo to Georgia O'Keeffe, their stories are examples of the creative game of mirrors to which these artists dedicated their lives.

Frida Kahlo
Diego Rivera
The Dove and the Elephant

Mexico, love, death. For many years the wildly romantic life of the most famous couple in Mexican painting concealed the game of mirrors played by this creative pair. From the beginning of their marriage, there was a pointed contrast between Frida Kahlo, the dove, and Diego Rivera, the elephant, two nicknames affectionately given to them by the father of the young bride.

In April 1953, one year before her death at the age of forty-seven, Frida Kahlo opened her first retrospective in her native Mexico. Taken to the Galería de Arte Contemporáneo by ambulance, she lay stretched out on a bed surrounded by her husband, Diego Rivera, and photographs of her political heroes, Georgy Malenkov and Joseph Stalin, to receive the tributes from her innumerable friends and admirers.

More than ever Frida the dove and Diego the elephant were as stunning as they were dissimilar. Frail, thinned by months in the hospital and by the amputation of her leg, Frida was but a shadow of herself. With his three hundred and thirty pounds (150 kilograms) and his ferocious energy, Diego, even though twenty years older, seemed ever young and brimming with health.

Meeting on the Scaffold

The legend goes that they met on a scaffold. She below, a young student from the National Preparatory School of Mexico, he above, an already famous painter commissioned by the Mexican government to create a fresco at the school. He was then thirty-six years old, already known around the world, and still carrying his reputation as a child prodigy (which he had been, painting from the age of 8) and as a revolutionary (which he was not really, having received a scholarship to study in Europe from the hands of a strike-breaking governor). Also his love of women was as legendary as his taste for words. In France, where he lived for several years, he had left two wives: Angelina and Marevna. He had had a child with each—Dieguito, a boy who died a year after his birth, and Marika, a girl he never met. On his return to Mexico, he married the beautiful and joyous Lupe Marin with whom he had two children, but he could not resist other women. Nor could he resist the pleasure of endless conversation, all while painting away, wearing his ever-present Stetson hat, a pair of huge miners' shoes, and a large belt barely able to hold up his oversized pants.

At the outset Frida did not have as many things going for her. Born July 6, 1907, in Coyoacán, a suburb of Mexico City, she was breastfed by an Indian woman, her mother being too ill to give her milk; Frida would always be very proud of this wet nurse, a living symbol of her Mexican and working-class connections. Nicknamed Frida *pata de palo* (Frida wooden leg) after an attack of polio, she followed courses at the preparatory school with the aim of becoming a doctor and drew occasionally without ever dreaming of becoming an artist. But on September 17, 1925, her life changed radically. The victim of a bus accident that broke her spinal column, her legs, several ribs, and her pelvis, she spent weeks in the hospital. The pain from those injuries would increase all her life, despite roughly thirty-two operations. Several months after her accident, for the lack of anything better to do, she began to paint in her sick bed. The first painting she finished, at the end of the summer of 1926, was a self-portrait dedicated to her lover at the time, Alejandro, whom she had met at school. Painting, love, and Frida: from the outset, the three inseparable components of her work were united. The legend goes that Diego and Frida would see each other next at the home of the photographer and revolutionary Tina Modotti, a mutual friend and eventually Frida's lover, unless it's true that Frida called out to him again that day on the scaffolding, as Diego describes the story in his autobiography. Frida used to say that Diego was already the star painter of Mexico, crowned by his stay in Europe where he rubbed shoulders with the greatest artists—Foujita, Georges Braque, Pablo Picasso, among others—and a symbol of Mexican cultural renewal. To mark the new postrevolutionary era, the government commissioned him, as well as other artists also known as muralists, to create enormous frescoes celebrating the glory of the people and the country. Apparently Rivera's glory did not impress this young woman. "I was in the middle of finishing a fresco at the Ministry of Education when a girl cried out to me, 'Diego, get down from there. I have something important to discuss with you.' She was a girl of about eighteen, with a slim body topped by a delicate face. Her hair was long, her thick black eyebrows met above her nose." She wanted to know for sure. In seeking professional advice on the quality of her first paintings and drawings, Frida wanted to show her work to the greatest living painter in Mexico. His favorable reaction did not impress Frida, however, who suspected that he wanted to pick her up. But Diego was truly enthusiastic about the honesty of the work and the temperament of the young girl. "You must continue to paint," he said to her peremptorily. Frida dreamed that when her time came she would also make frescoes, which seemed to her to be the highest expression of contemporary Mexican art. Diego advised her against it: "You must find your own means of expression." For some time Frida searched for the meaning of her work and groped about painting "Rivera-esque" pictures, like her portraits of Cristina Kahlo and of Agustin M. Olmedo. They were large-scale works with broad fields of blue, simple backgrounds, and few small details. In 1929 she painted *The Bus*, a populist work in which a housewife, a worker, a peasant, an employee, and she, a young middle-class girl, travel in front of an industrial and rural background under the gaze of a curious boy—a subject that could have addressed Diego. Sensing Frida's strong personality, the painter did not encourage her on this political path and refused to teach her. Slowly his stylistic influence faded. Her drawing was more naïve than Diego's and she did not seek, as he had upon his return from Europe, to Mexicanize her subjects. While Rivera painted large-scale frescoes portraying history and Mexican society and, later on, American life, Kahlo painted in smaller formats, depicting her friends, her animals, Diego, and above all, herself.

American Upheaval

Their marriage on August 22, 1929, was a media event that the Mexican newspaper *La Prensa* covered without mentioning that the bride went home that night to her parents's house, terrified by a drunken Rivera who beat up several guests.

Their political commitment was also public. Named director of the Academy of San Marcos the same year, Rivera had radical plans for the overhaul of the school's curriculum, and conservative and communist students alike were shocked to learn that the artist had just been expelled from the Communist Party, which Kahlo then quit in solidarity. The party reproached Rivera for accepting money and support from Dwight Morrow, the American ambassador to Mexico for the painting of a mural at the Cortès Palace in Cuernavaca. The turmoil aroused by his departure prompted him to accept a proposal to create a mural in San Francisco. The couple left Mexico in November 1929. For four years they lived principally in the United States where Frida, more isolated than in Mexico, consecrated herself entirely to her painting. A euphoric Rivera secured several commissions and then tackled twenty-seven panels at the Detroit Institute of Arts at the request of Edsel Ford, the embodiment of capitalism if there ever was one. For her part Frida suffered a miscarriage and drew imaginary sequences crowded with incongruous objects, like self-portraits dreaming of Diego in which organs transform into roots, or *Bed Flying* (1932), in which her naked body is lying in a puddle of blood. In an article in 1943, Rivera was the first

Opposite: **Frida Kahlo's studio in 1945. *The Two Fridas*, a painting from 1939, hangs in the background.**

Page 240: **Diego Rivera photographed by Edward Weston in 1923.**
Page 241: **Frida Kahlo, a photograph from October 16, 1932.**

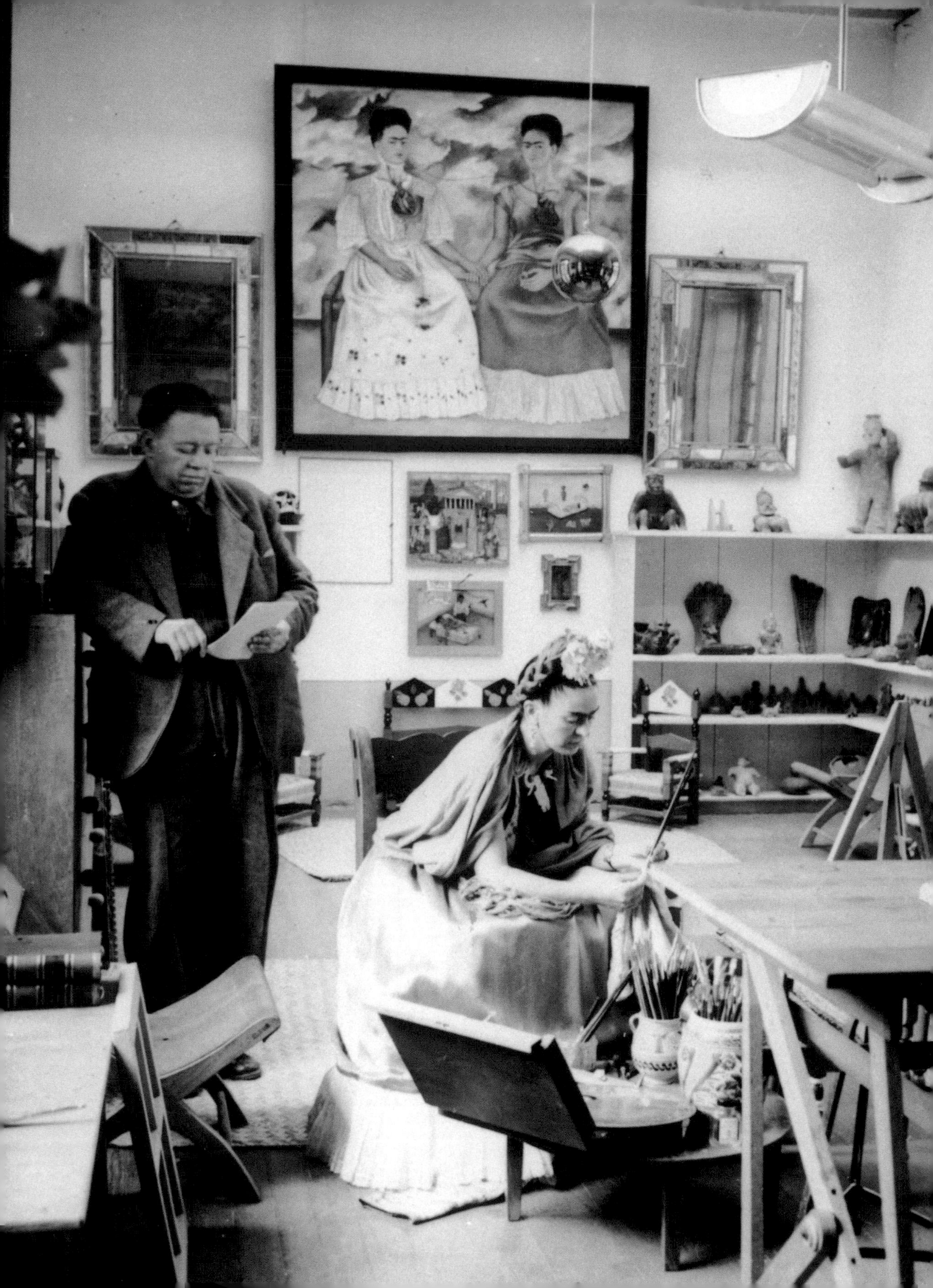

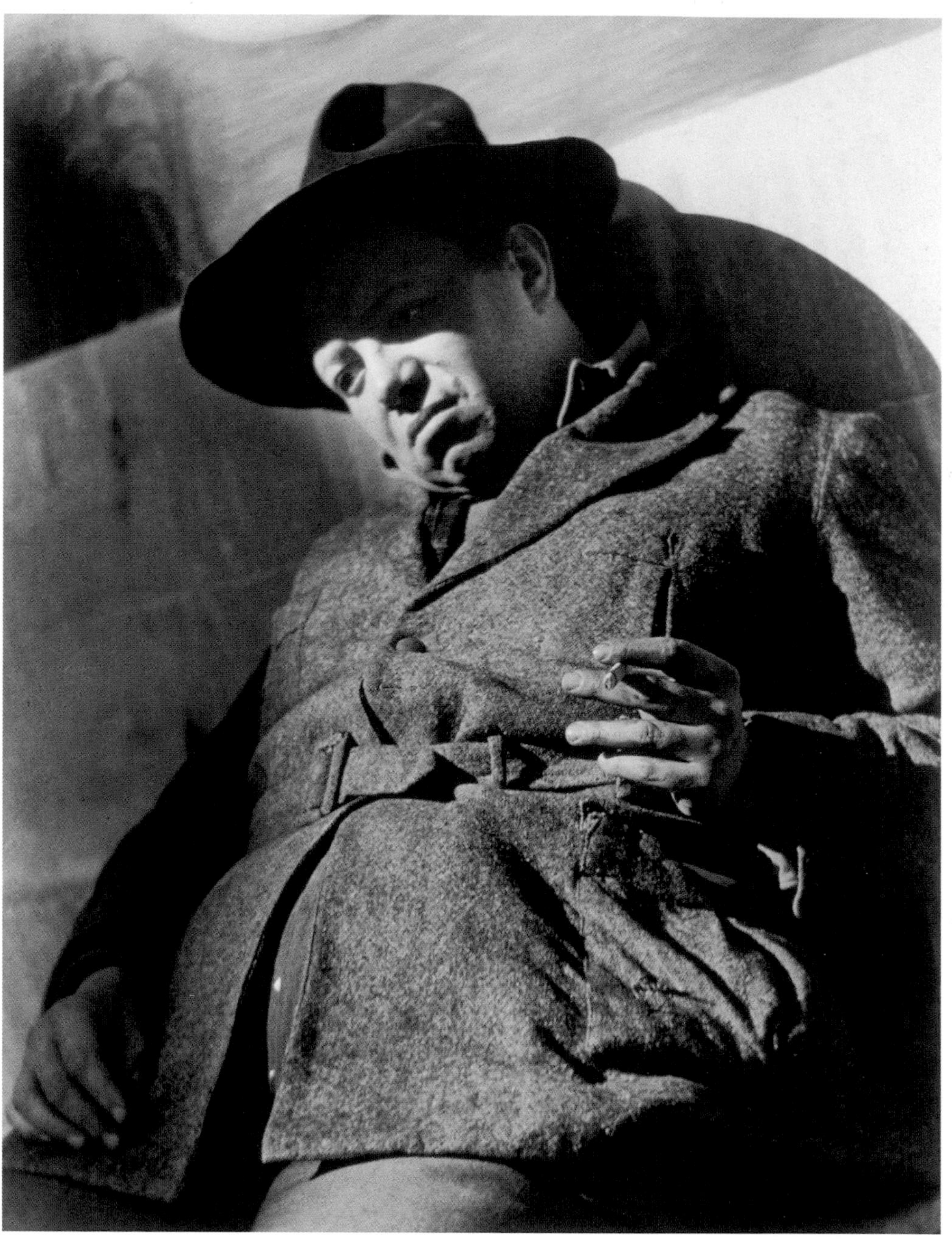

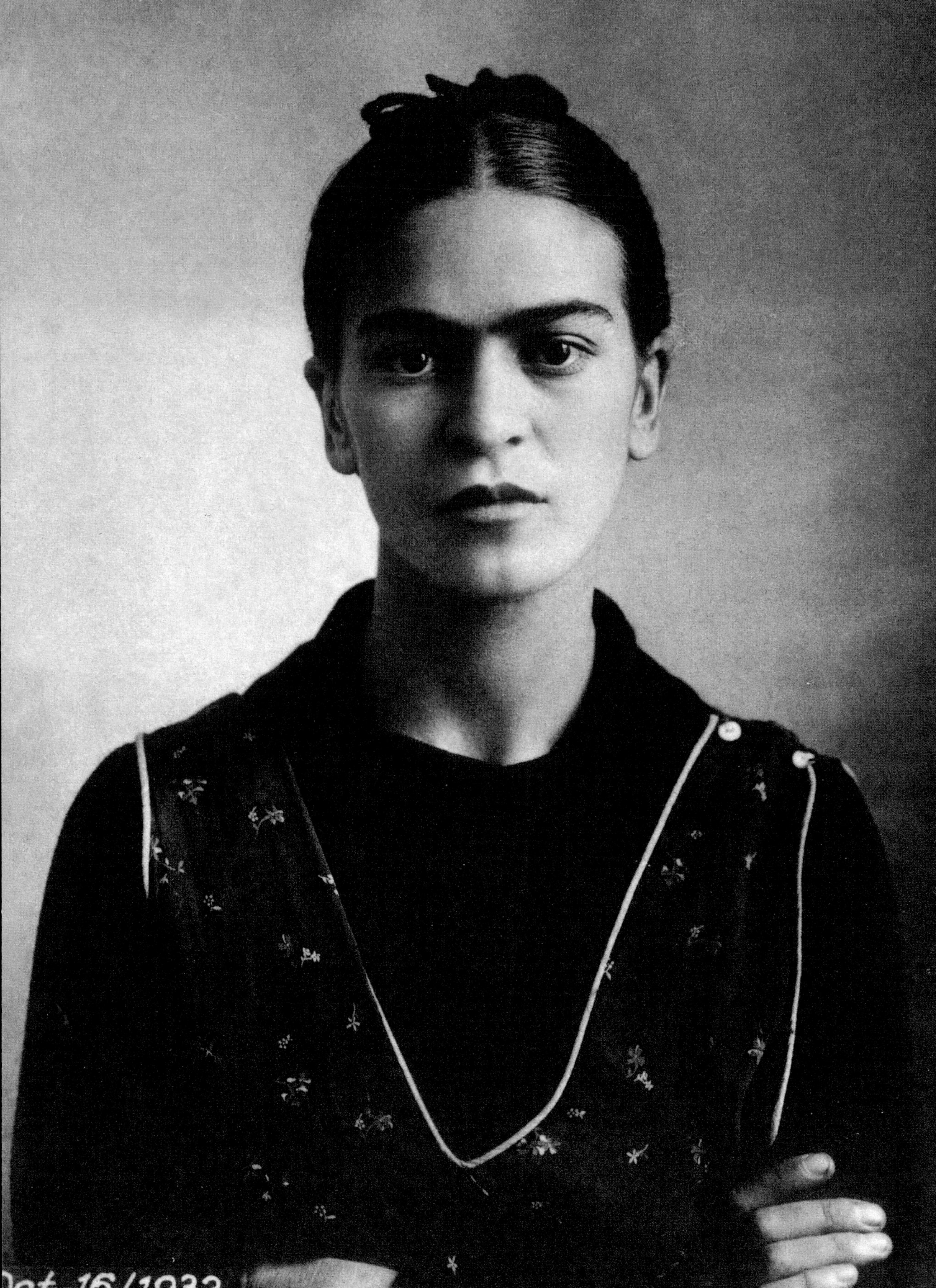

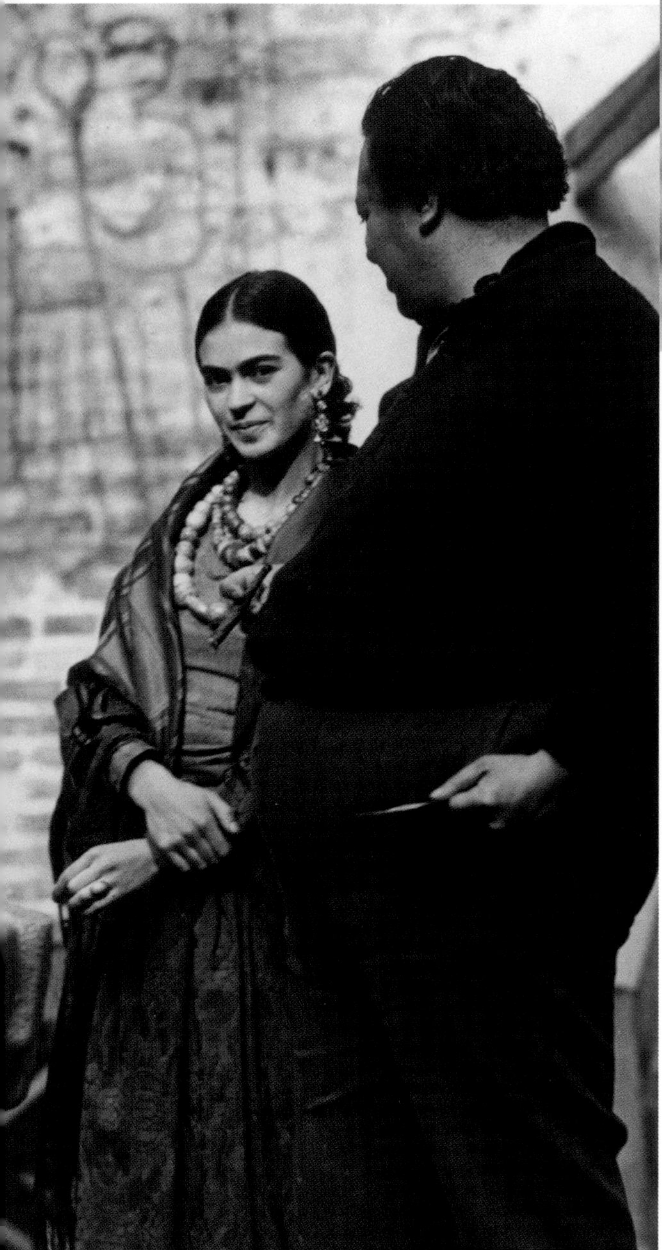

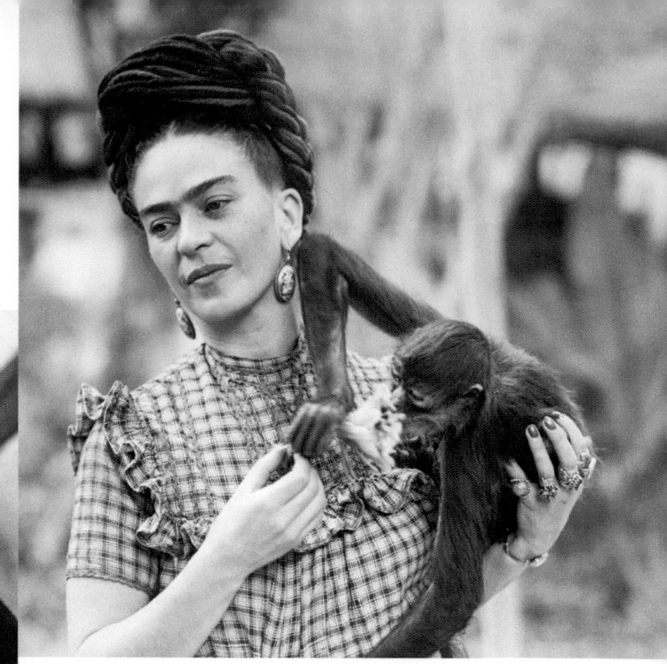

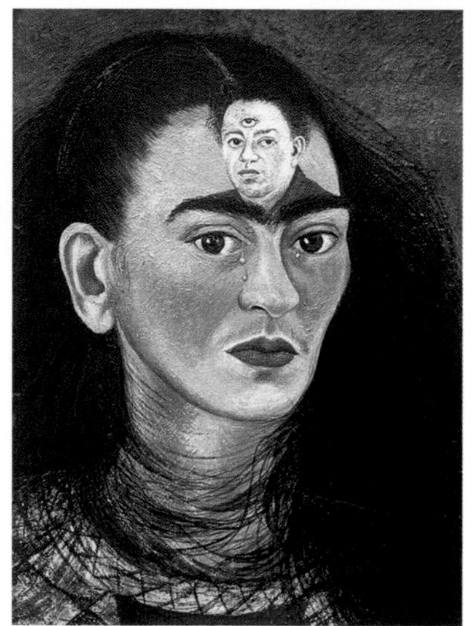

Left: **Dressed in a Mexican costume, Frida Kahlo made a sensation in 1930 walking the streets of San Francisco with an elephantine Diego Rivera.**
Above: **Frida Kahlo never stopped painting beside or—in the case of *Diego and Me*—in total fusion with Diego Rivera. This time Diego is her third eye, but her despairing expression, the flowing tears, and Diego's distant demeanor, speak to the suffering of a marriage that was wearing thin.**
Top: **Frida Kahlo in 1944 with a pet monkey.**

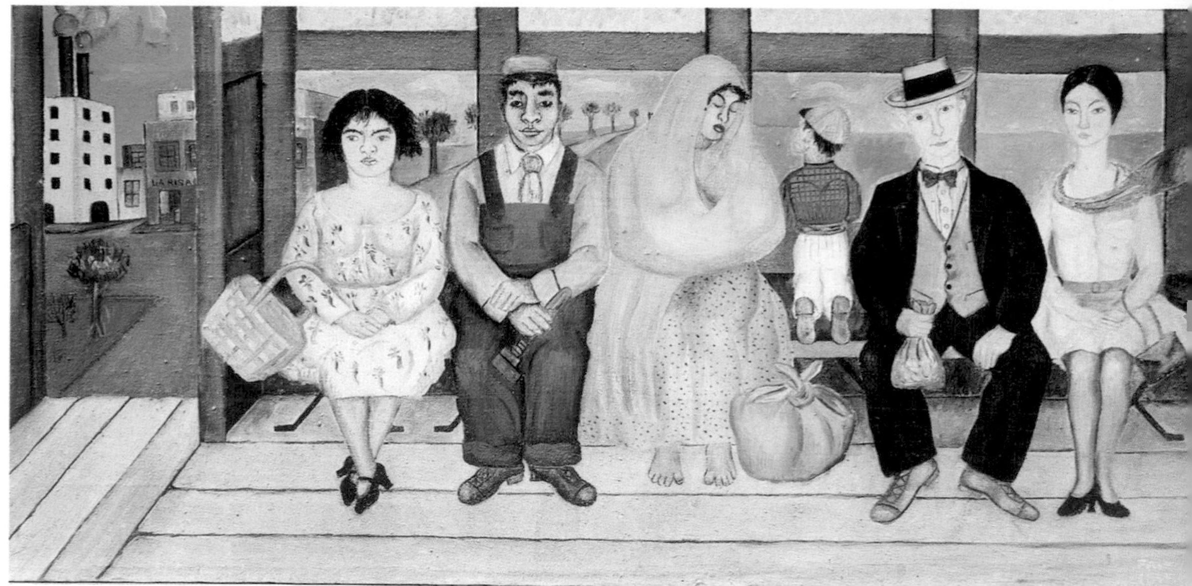

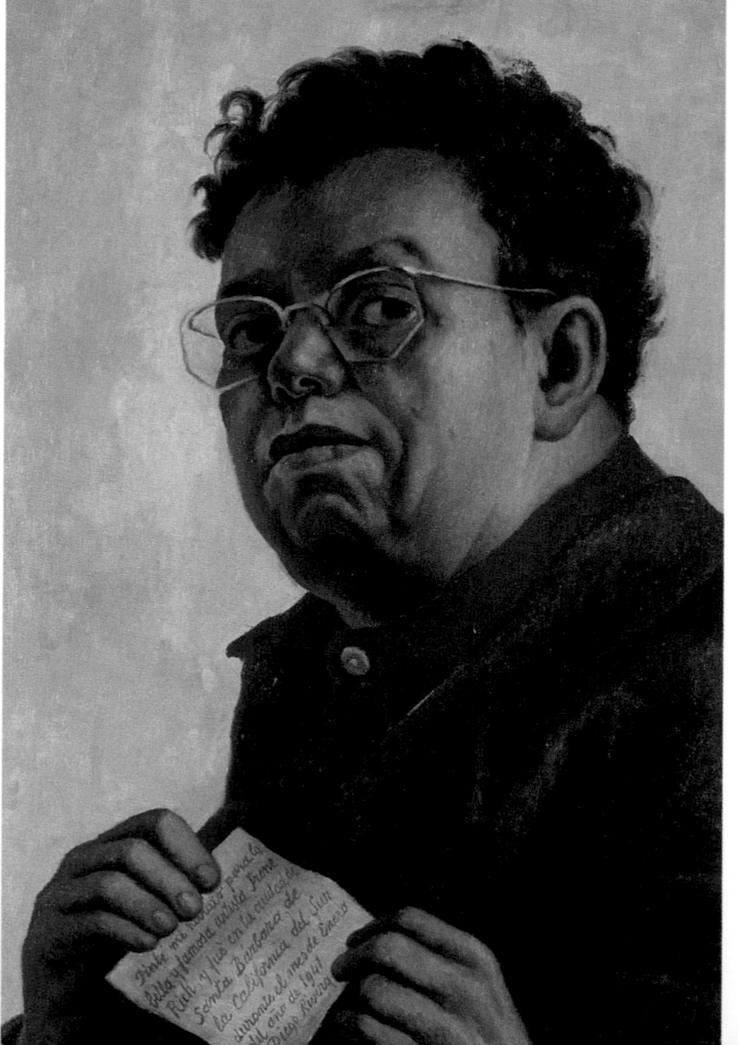

Above: **In the spirit of Diego Rivera's frescoes, Frida Kahlo brought together in *The Bus* all the stereotypical elements of Mexican society: the housewife with her shopping basket, the worker, the peasant woman, the young middle-class woman, and the dreaming boy. This populist painting is full of humor and the bar *La Risa* (the laugh) appears in the background.**

Left: **A candid *Self-Portrait* by Diego Rivera, painted several months after his remarriage to Frida Kahlo in late 1940.**

to outline the evolution of Kahlo's painting and connected her to the traditional and popular arts of Mexico. "In Mexico there exists a little-known style of painting, humble in its physical scale and its content. These are the small metal or wooden plaques on which are painted miracles committed by the saints, the Virgin, or God . . . the only painter who possesses a close connection . . . to this pure folk art tradition is Frida Kahlo." Rivera went on to describe what made Kahlo's works unique. "This is the first time in the history of art that a woman has expressed with an absolute and uncompromising honesty, one might even say with impassive cruelty, the general and specific themes that exclusively affect women."

Eventful from the first day, their tumultuous marriage was punctuated by their mutual infidelities. In response to the innumerable romances of Diego's, who flaunted his liaisons—including one with his wife's sister—Frida replied with both homosexual and heterosexual affairs. Rivera exhibited a fierce jealousy that would have unforeseen consequences when, after the fact, he discovered Frida's liaison with the Soviet political fugitive Leon Trotsky, whom he had sheltered during his exile. Diego punished Trotsky by forcing him to move to another less well-guarded house. In May 1940 Trotsky and his wife, Natalia, escaped assassins sent by Joseph Stalin, but in August, Ramón Mercader, who had established a friendship with Frida, killed Trotsky with an ice pick. Diego, who was anti-Stalinist before the war—after having been excluded from the Communist Party for his work at the service of American capitalism—changed sides at the end of World War II. To rejoin the party—flush now with Stalin's victory over Adolf Hitler—Diego claimed that he had only received Trotsky in order to eliminate him more easily. Frida experienced the same reversal of political opinion and wrote in her diary on March 4, 1953: "The WORLD MEXICO THE WHOLE UNIVERSE has lost its balance with the loss (the passing) of STALIN."

"Diego = Me"

Punctuated by a divorce in December 1939 and a remarriage in December 1940, their tormented union became one of the major subjects in Frida Kahlo's painting. Much less prolific than Rivera, she expressed the states of her soul in her self-portraits, transforming herself into a Mexican icon to please Diego, cutting her hair to affirm her independence, and above all painting herself torn apart by her suffering, her desire for children, her grief at having lost a baby, and her sadness at being betrayed. She seemed to reach a point of not being able to separate herself from him, as in *Diego and*

Me, a painting from 1949, in which the muralist's face adorns her forehead while tears run down her cheeks, or again in her diary when she wrote the poem, "Diego my child . . . Diego my mother, Diego my father . . . Diego = me." Was this fusion reciprocal?

Although less intimate and autobiographical, Rivera's paintings nevertheless placed great emphasis on his companion's face. There are several nudes, the first of which, painted in 1930, portrays Kahlo wearing only a necklace and a pair of high-heeled shoes. But especially in *Distributing Arms* (1928), the last panel painted for the Ministry of Education, he positioned her near the photographer Tina Modotti taking part in the proletarian revolution, weapons in their hands. In imaginary scenes like the one in *The Nightmare of War and the Dream of Peace* (1952), Frida was represented seated in a wheelchair in the street, collecting signatures against the war. Two years later, Frida actually did demonstrate in the street in her wheelchair to the cries of "Gringo assassins, out of Guatemala," to protest against the overthrow of the democratic government of Jacobo Arbenz Guzmán fomented by the United States. But for Rivera, Kahlo was not just a wife, a model, or an inspiration, she was above all an artist whose career he had taken in hand, presenting her to patrons and collectors and always referring to her as "the best Mexican painter." When André Breton arrived in Mexico in 1938 he went to see Diego but, to his great surprise, it was Frida's paintings that impressed him the most. He said to her solemnly, "You are a Surrealist." Frida was amused by such seriousness but was disappointed later when she stayed at his home in Paris. "You have no idea of the filth in which people live nor the kind of food they eat," she wrote to a friend. As for the enflamed discussions between Parisian artists on café terraces, she saw only the activity "of parasites wasting their time in pseudo-intellectual malicious gossip." The romantic charms of artistic Paris had no effect on the artist who felt in her creative element only in Mexico. In *The Two Fridas*, a key work from 1939, she placed herself on the left wearing a European outfit and on the right in Mexican dress. From that point on, Frida the dove took the side of Mexico and, for comfort and support, she clasped in her hand a little cameo on which Diego the elephant appears.

Bibliography

Hamill, Pete. *Diego Rivera*. New York: Harry N. Abrams, Inc., 2000.

Herrara, Hayden. *Frida: A Biography of Frida Kahlo*. New York: Harper & Row, 1983.

Lowe, Sarah M., and Carlos Fuentes. *The Diary of Frida Kahlo: An Intimate Self-Portrait*. New York: Abradale Press, 2001.

Marnham, Patrick. *Diego Rivera: Le Rêveur éveillé, biographie*. Paris: Le Seuil, coll. "Fiction et Cie," 2000.

Tina Modotti
Edward Weston

Life in Black and White

In the Hollywood of the 1920s, Tina Modotti was a beautiful, hot-blooded Italian actress. In Mexico in the 1930s, she was a dangerous activist accused of wanting to assassinate the country's president. In New York in 1991, a platinum photographic print of her *Roses* broke all auction records at the time at Sotheby's at $165,000. A magnificent photographer and militant revolutionary, Modotti developed her style in Mexico alongside Edward Weston, one of the great American photographers, to whom she had been both mistress and inspiration.

"I hope, Edward, that you laughed when you learned that I was accused of having participated in an attempt to assassinate President Ortiz Rubio. Who would have suspected it, huh? Such a nice young girl who takes such pretty photos of flowers and children!" So Tina Modotti wrote to her former lover Edward Weston. It is February 1930 in Mexico, and the nice young woman accused of having participated in the attempt to assassinate the new president of the republic would be expelled from the country shortly thereafter. In order to dedicate herself entirely to activism and the revolution, she would even abandon photography, persuaded to continue the battle for equality and justice by other means. Sixty years later, when the Sotheby's auctioneer's hammer in New York made her *Roses* the most expensive photograph in the world at $165,000—a record that has since been broken—the myth of Tina Modotti was born. All the ingredients were brought together: a beauty who struck everyone who knew her and an adventurous life traveling from Italy to the United States, from Mexico to Berlin and Moscow, then again to Mexico, where she died suddenly in a taxi in 1942. Add to this the Rimbaudian aura of an artist, who like the poet of *Bâteau Ivre*, decided one day to forsake her art. Tina Modotti was a photographer for just ten years—ten years that were sufficient to change at least the history of photography, if not, as she had hoped, the face of the world.

Tina was born in 1896 in Udine in the north of Italy to poor parents—her mother was a dressmaker, her father a mechanic and carpenter—who never had enough to feed the family. Tina never forgot her miserable childhood, the emigration first to Austria and then to the United States. A good student, Tina was forced from the age of 12 to work in order to help the family survive. Perhaps out of nostalgia for her studies, she always had an autodidact's appetite for knowledge. She frequented exhibitions, and acted in the theater in Little Italy in Los Angeles. At the Pacific-Panama International Exposition of 1915–1917, she met the painter and poet Roubaix de l'Abrie Richey, nicknamed Robo by his friends, whom she married in 1917. A photograph from that era presents the image of a sensible young woman sewing while her artist husband paints in front of her, but it is a most deceptive picture; this twenty-five-year-old woman already had a career as a Hollywood actress behind her, but she had grown tired of roles as "the pretty Italian girl with fiery eyes clenching a knife between her teeth" that the directors wanted her to play. And, above all, the sensible spouse had discovered love: in April 1921 she wrote to her lover, the photographer Edward Weston, that she was "intoxicated with the memory of last night and overwhelmed by the beauty and madness of it."

Twelve years older than she, Edward most likely met Tina through photographing her. He was one of the most sought-after portrait photographers in Los Angeles, an activity that he deemed purely commercial. He had developed his artistic career as a photographer of a very distinctive aesthetic of pictorialism, a style whose slightly blurry imagery gave his shots an Impressionistic charm. Edward was married and led a very middle-class life. He had wed Flora, a teacher and his sister's best friend, and he already had four sons. But his friendship with the photographer Margrethe Mather led him to discover another Los Angeles and the bohemian gatherings at Robo's studio.

In 1922 Tina and Edward's more or less clandestine affair took on another dimension when Robo died of smallpox in Mexico, where he had been invited as an artist. Before dying Robo had sent several enthusiastic letters describing the country to his wife and to Edward.

In the days after the revolutionary adventures of Pancho Villa and Emiliano Zapata, Mexico experienced a veritable renaissance. Álvaro Obregón's presidency and José Vasconcelos's presence at the Ministry of Public Education created a paradise for the arts. Everything was done to facilitate the work of artists and to create a specifically Mexican art that would take its inspiration as much from the Pre-Columbian tradition as from the European avant-garde. At the center of this renaissance were the *murales*, the painters of the great frescoes: the enormous Diego Rivera, who had participated in France in the adventure of Cubism, as well as David Alfaro Siqueiros and José Clemente Orozco. All three were members of the Mexican Communist Party and founders of its cultural organ, the magazine *El Machete*. This was the country that Tina Modotti discovered when she went to bury her husband. She brought along with her photographs by Edward Weston, whose exhibition there would achieve a notable success, while in the

United States his latest works—strongly geometric, almost Cubist interiors and nudes that weren't in the least ethereal—were seen as oddities. Weston was at a turning point in his career. Modotti's rich personality and the magic of Mexico would transform this respected pictorialist photographer into one of the greatest artists of the century. Edward had been seduced by Tina's extraordinary beauty; she was described by one of her friends as: "not very large, with a supple and well-made body, smooth curves, a very expressive face, ardent black eyes, a sensual mouth, auburn hair, a large forehead, fine and delicate hands." In the course of their tumultuous love affair, the artist never stopped celebrating her body, photographing not an academic model but flesh that was full of life. Photography, he discovered through Tina, must record life, "the very substance and quintessence of the *thing itself*, whether it be polished steel or palpitating flesh."

"Black and white, never gray"

Upon their return to the United States, Tina had but one desire—to move to Mexico with Edward. Their love affair was already over but there would be a simple agreement between him, an already recognized artist, and her, a student whose artistic ascension would be dazzling. Edward would teach her photographic techniques while Tina would assist in running the studio and act as interpreter, since Weston did not speak Spanish.

In July 1923 Tina, Edward, and Chandler, the oldest of his four sons, embarked for Mexico. From his contacts with this new land, Weston's photography was turned completely upside down. "Later, exploring the city streets at night," he wrote in the diary that he kept throughout his Mexican adventure, "we found life both gay and sad—sharp clashes of contrasting extremes, but always life—vital, intense, black and white, never gray."

Weston opened a studio and discovered a much more enlightened clientele than in the United States, one that did not demand endless retouching to make the sitters look younger. In his personal work, he found what he named the "heroic pose," with the camera's lens oriented slightly above a model posed against the background of the sky. This is how he photographed Lupe, Diego Rivera's fiery wife; Mexican senator Manuel Hernandez Galvan firing a pistol, "a portrait of Mexico" according to Diego; a palm tree; an Aztec pyramid, renamed "the pyramid of the sun"; and of course Tina, beautiful and melancholy on the balcony of their house. Edward related an episode in his diary on July 9, 1924:

"My eyes and thoughts were heavenward indeed—until, glancing down, I saw Tina lying naked on the azotea taking a sun-bath. My cloud-sitting was ended, my camera turned down toward a more earthly theme, and a series of interesting negatives was obtained. Having just examined them again, I am enthusiastic and feel that this is the best series of nudes I have done of Tina." Tina was not content to recite poems, and she learned photography with stunning rapidity. In a shot dated from 1923, she captured Edward behind his large Graflex camera. Although one senses the influence of her teacher here, this is not a copy of one of his famous "heroic poses." In November 1924, when she exhibited her photographs for the first time next to Edward's, the latter remarked proudly: "The photographs lost nothing in comparison to mine—they are her own expression."

Tina Modotti's "expression" was her empathy with her subject, whether it was the walls of the convent of Tepotzotlan, two geraniums, her henceforth legendary roses, or a portrait of Elisa, a Mexican friend. Out of her difficult childhood, Tina always maintained a humane vision of people, of flowers, and things. From the beginning, she believed that photography deserved to play a role in the "social revolution," as she called it. While Weston would increasingly explore the encounter between an individual and the harmony of the world, the beauty of a pepper shaped like a human body or a cabbage leaf with the allure of a dress, for Tina, photography had a social role. She photographed the frescoes of Gabriel Orozco and Diego Rivera at work. She also posed for the latter, in the nude for his allegories or as a militant distributing rifles to Mexican revolutionaries.

If the purposes to which they dedicated their art distinguished Tina and Edward, it was the same for their lives. They both increased the number of their affairs and, despite the presence of his oldest son, Chandler, Edward felt the absence of his three other sons more and more severely. And yet they did not stop loving each other but took a more ironic stance regarding their romantic partnership. One day, Edward recorded in his journal, they passed by the shop windows of a neighborhood photographer who made the "most ridiculous portraits that [they had] ever seen in Mexico." Tina had the idea of having the photographer take their portrait, and pretended in front of the photographer that it was their first wedding anniversary. "El señor is a true believer," specified Tina. "Perhaps you could place us against the background of a church." This rare shot uniting two of the greatest

Page 252, top: **Edward Weston photographed in Mexico in 1923 by Tina Modotti.**
Page 252, bottom: **A letter from Edward Weston to Tina Modotti dated January 11, 1928.**
Page 253: **Tina Modotti in Hollywood in 1920.**

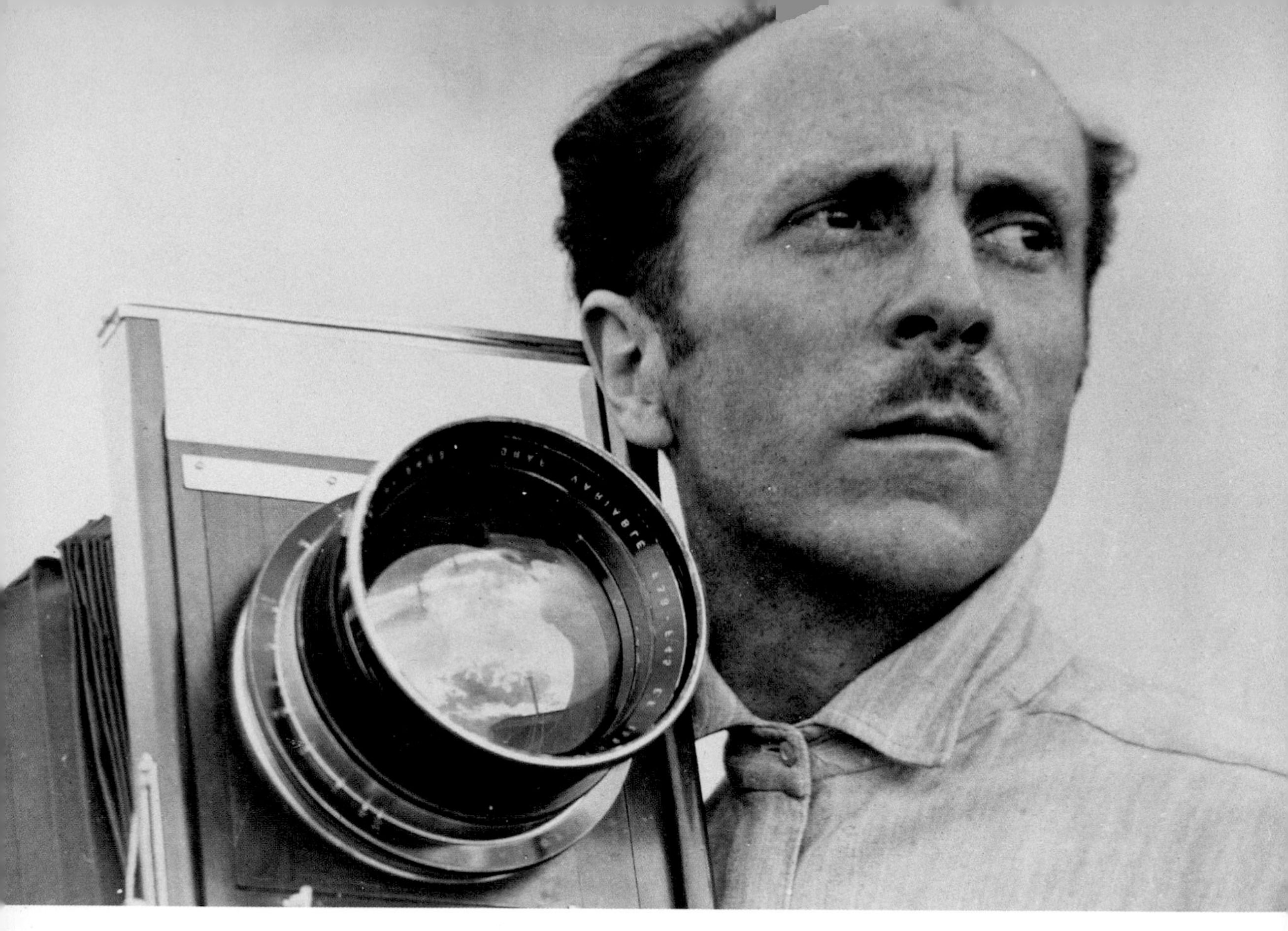

Tina dear, if I have been an important factor in your life, you have certainly been in mine. What you have given me in beauty and fineness is a permanent part of me, and goes with me no matter where life leads. This thought needs no elaboration! My love goes out to you always---

Edward-

1-11-1928-

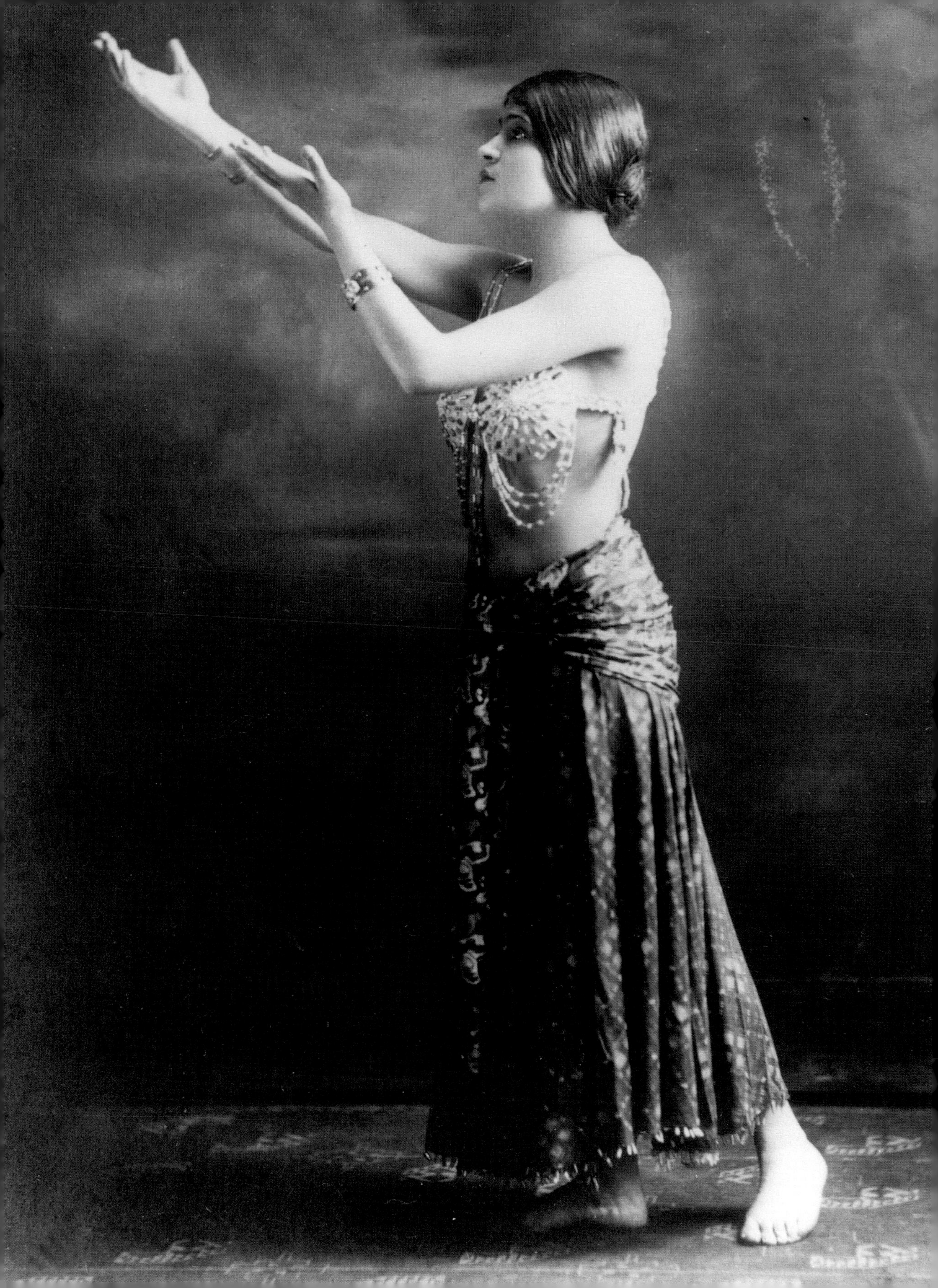

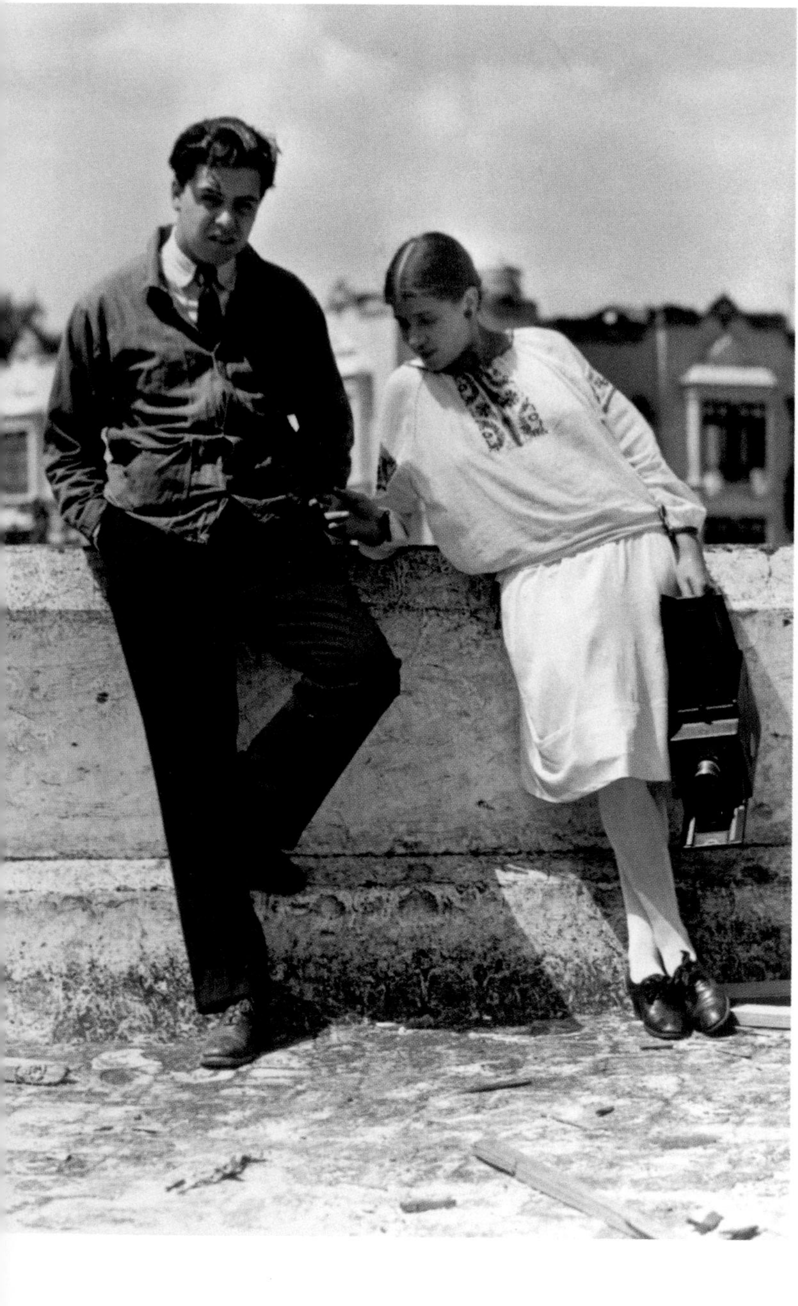

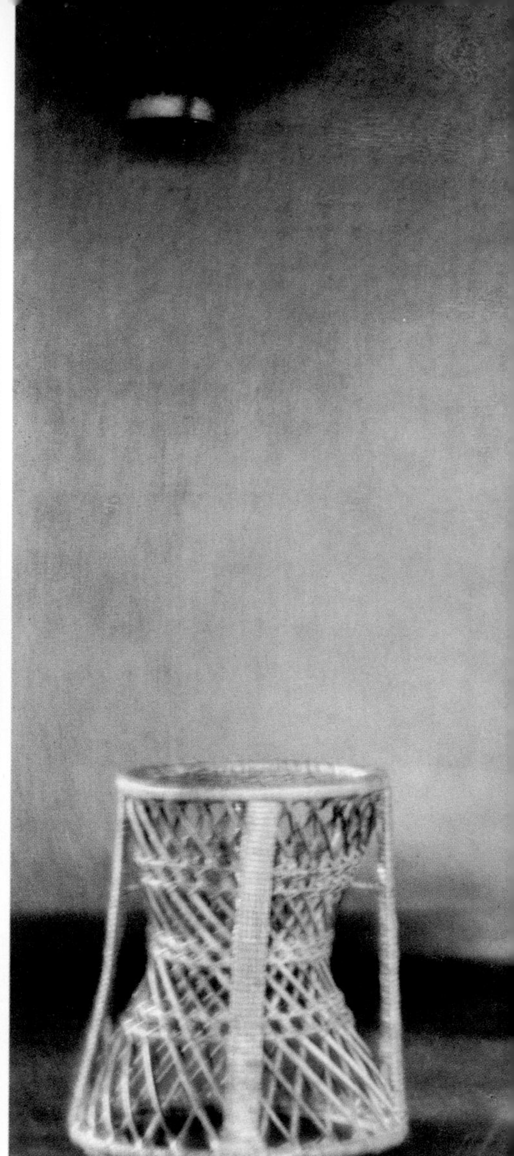

Left: **Tina Modotti became a professional photographer in Mexico, which she visited for the first time in 1922. In this 1924 shot taken there, Modotti poses, under Edward Weston's attentive gaze, next to the illustrator Miguel Covarrubias.**

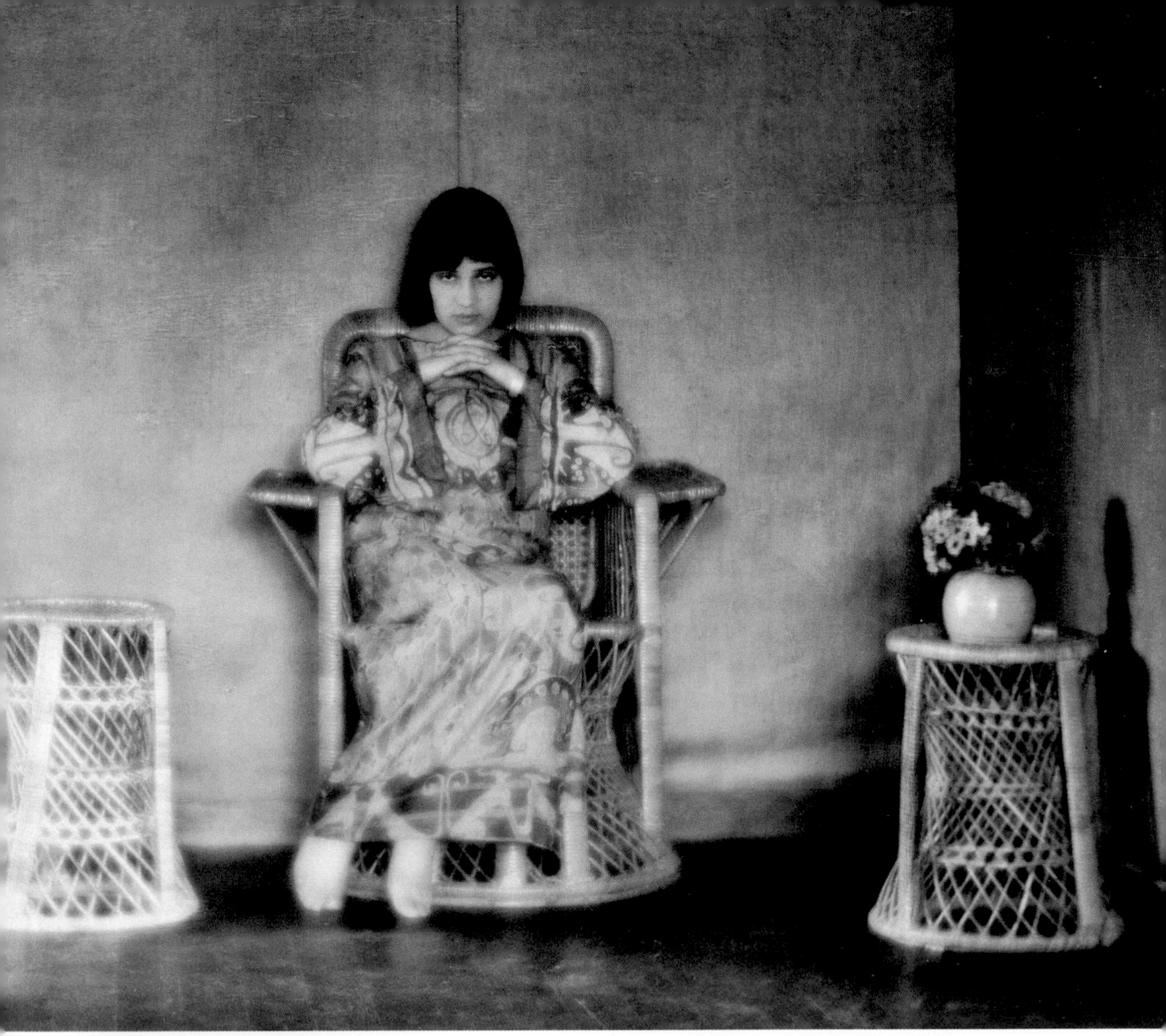

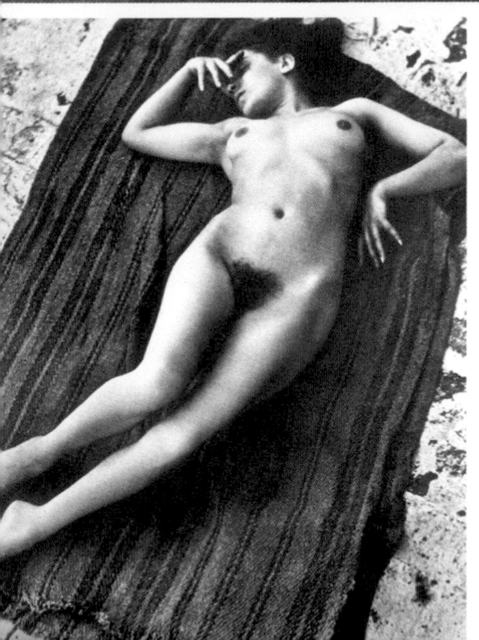

Left: **This 1924 photograph of a nude on a towel was a tribute to the beauty of Tina Modotti's body whose "smooth curves" inspired Edward Weston.** Above: **One of the first portraits of Tina Modotti taken by Edward Weston in Los Angeles, where they met in 1921. Like the mood created by the vaguely Asian furniture, her oriental dress and bare feet suggest the exoticism of a woman who, at the time, had dedicated herself to a career as an actress.**

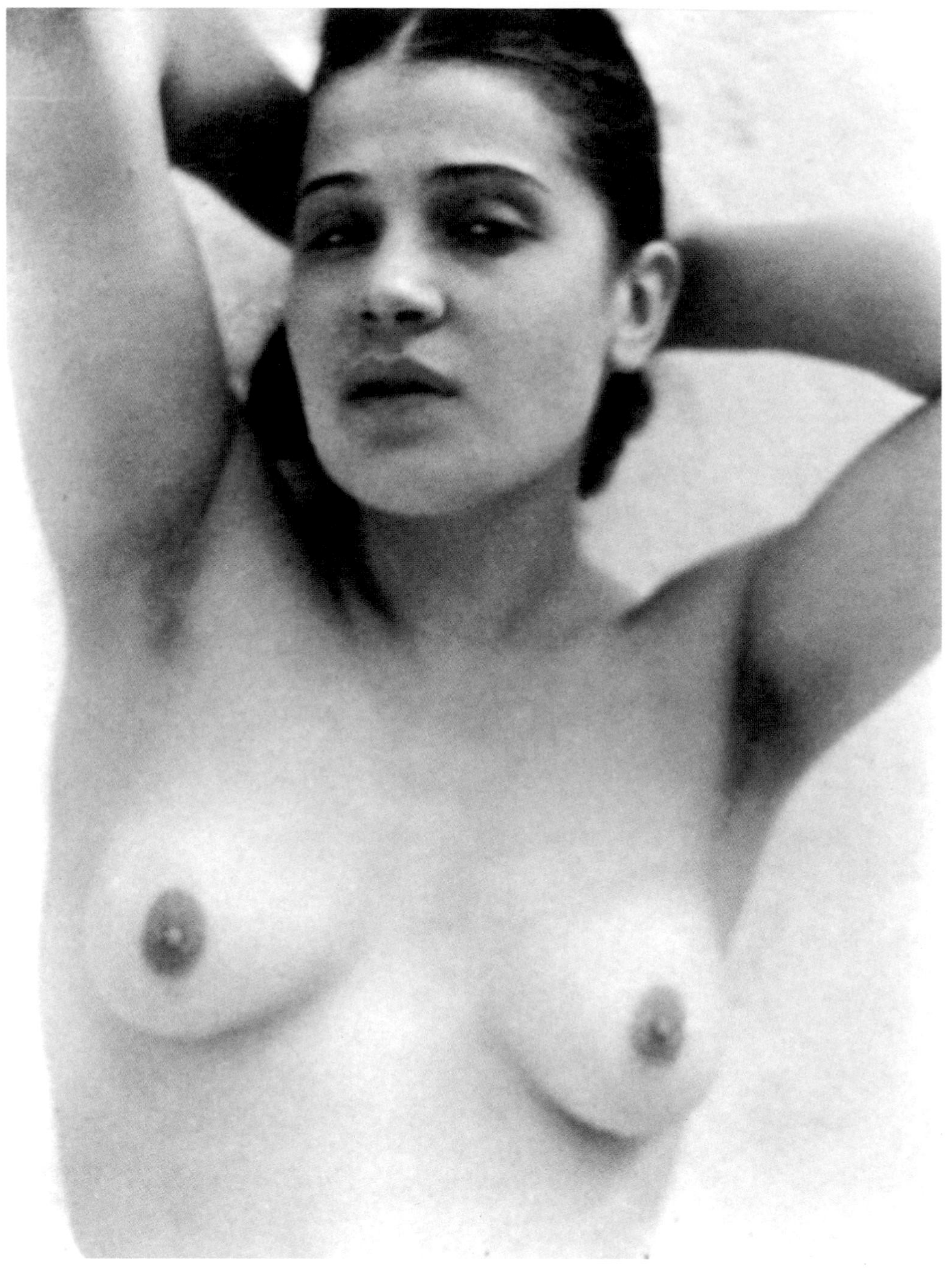

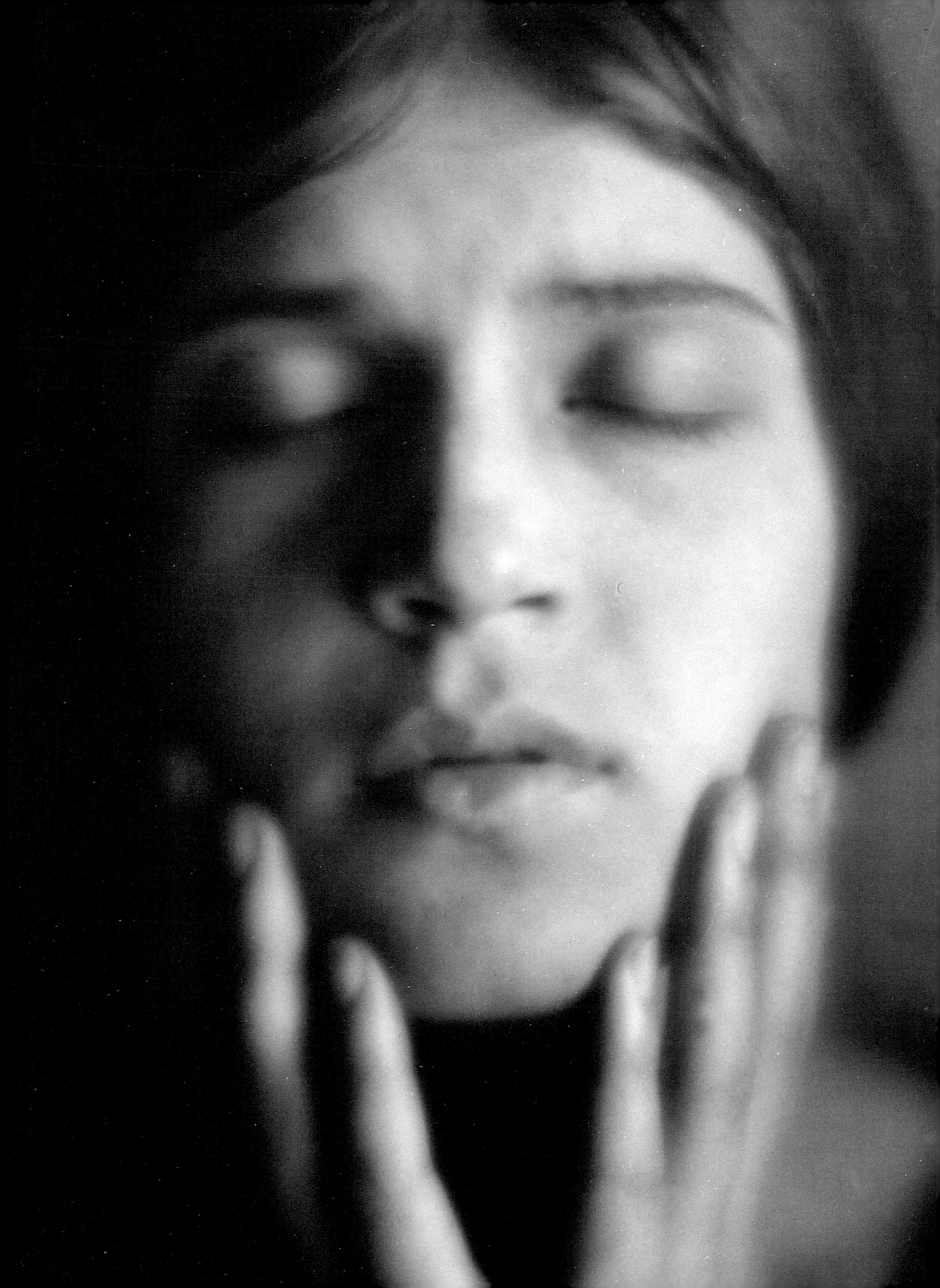

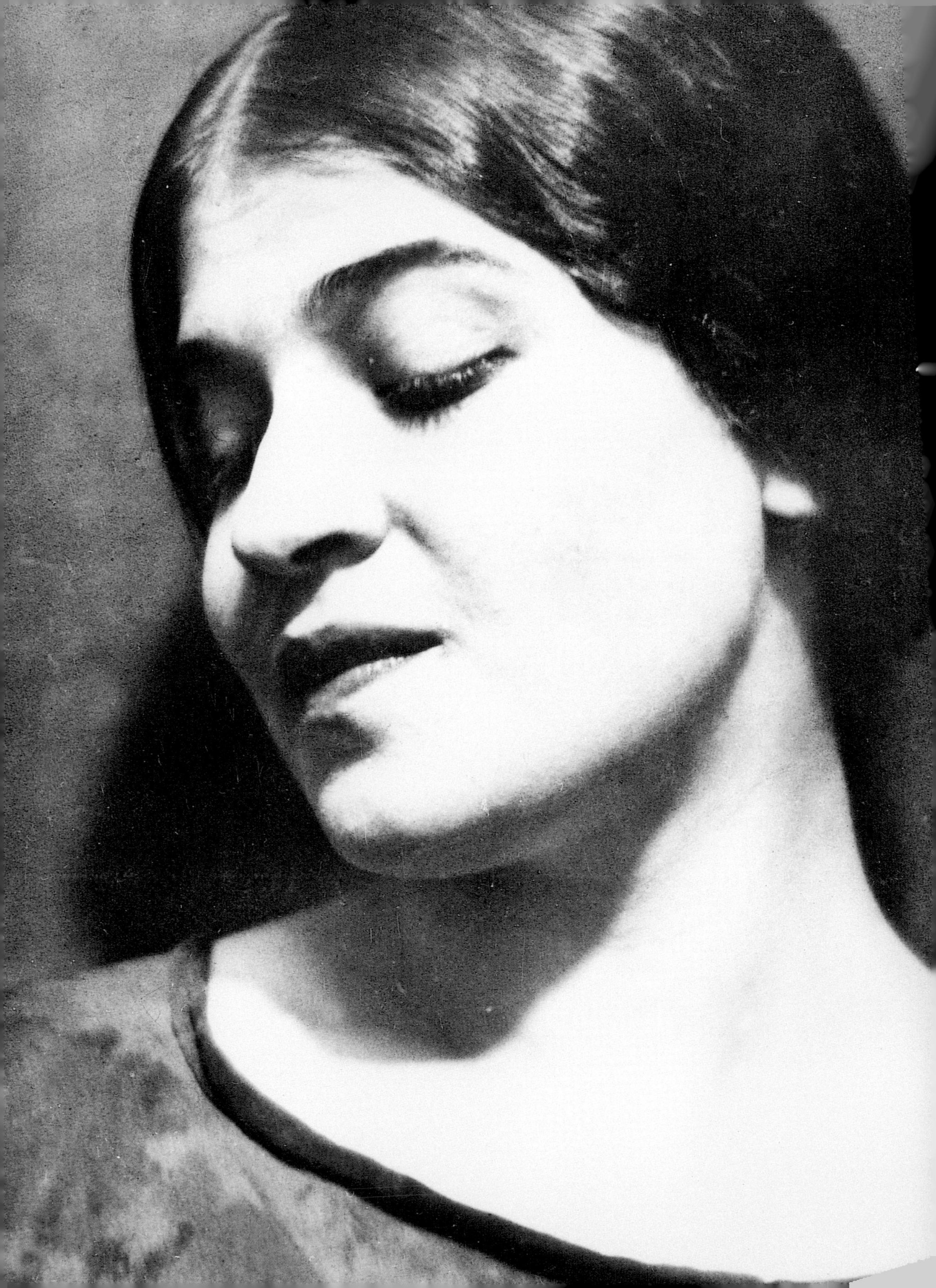

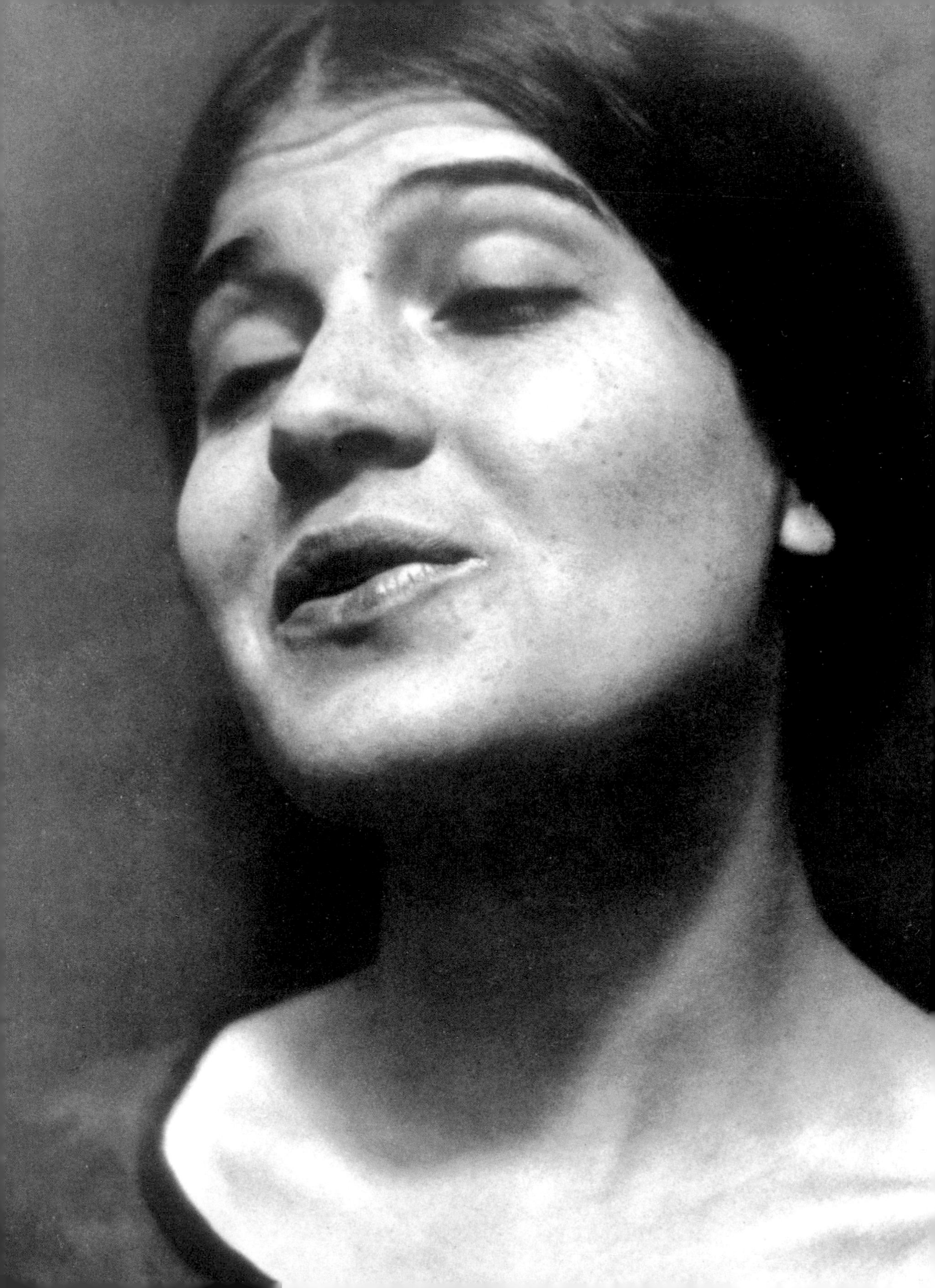

Pages 256–59: **Tina Modotti photographed by Edward Weston in 1924.**

photographers of the century immortalized them, she holding in her hand a dusty bouquet of roses, and he—in a pose that suggests nothing of the heroic—seated quite stiffly against the painted backdrop of a church interior and a statue of Christ.

In December 1924 Edward left for the United States. Tina had a hard time working during this separation. In a letter to Edward she described the painful conflict that troubled her and that led her one day to abandon photography. "Life is always struggling to predominate and art naturally suffers. . . . I put too much of my art into *life*—too much energy—and consequently I have not much left to give art." Edward Weston returned for a final visit to Mexico in August 1925. He set out with Tina on a trip to the center of the country to shoot photographs for *Idols Behind Altars*, a book by Anita Brenner, but their amorous relationship deteriorated further. Tina had begun a liaison with the Mexican revolutionary Xavier Guerrero that was more serious than her other affairs. When he departed in November 1926 Weston knew that he had left Mexico and Tina Modotti forever.

The Photo, the Hammer, and the Sickle

Permanently separated from an Edward who was little preoccupied by political problems, Tina now joined the Mexican Communist Party in 1927, and her life and her art reached a moment of rare accord. The divide between the intentions declared by the Mexican regime and the social reality became flagrant. Tina depicted it in her photographs. Here were beautiful and miserable children, the calloused hands of workers and worn hands of washerwomen, men proudly bearing immense burdens, the women of Tehuantepec carrying painted gourds filled with fruit and flowers on their heads—women whose photographs she had difficulty taking because their rapid step blurred the camera exposures. There were photographs full of hope, of electric wires heralding progress, and there were the directly activist photographs: union meetings of peasants, a worker reading *El Machete*, a woman carrying the huge red flag, the still life of the sickle, guitar, and cartridge belt. There were so many works. They became the subject of a manifesto-exhibition in December 1929 at the University of Mexico and she was a great popular success. But the political situation changed and Tina suddenly became an undesirable. At the beginning of this same year, she was basely attacked in the press after the assassination of her new great love, the Cuban opposition leader Julio Antonio Mella, targeted by killers hired by the

Cuban dictator Gerardo Machado. To sully her reputation, nude photographs were published to show her low morals, and she was accused of being a party to the crime while the real killers escaped. Tina was arrested, imprisoned, and expelled, left with only a passport from Fascist Italy, where she had a price on her head. After an interminable voyage on a Dutch freighter, she found refuge in Berlin, a city then full of artistic effervescence. She exhibited in photographer Lotte Jacobi's studio, but in the correspondence that she continued to exchange with Weston, she revealed the difficulties in pursuing her work. "My usual manner of working, in minutely determining my surroundings, has not adapted well. . . . When I succeed in finding the composition and the expression at the right moment, the image has already disappeared. I tell myself that I want to do the impossible, then I do nothing."

She was in Moscow in October 1930 when she presented her photographs for the last time, and then abandoned photography to consecrate herself to her work as an activist for the International Red Aid. Until 1935 she lived between Moscow, Warsaw, Vienna, Madrid, and Paris. In July 1936 the Spanish Civil War exploded. Tina and Vittorio Vidali, her companion since her Mexican misadventures, left for Madrid. They would go on to play a decisive role there under the names of Maria and Carlos. Then they returned to Mexico where the new president had offered them clemency. Despite a difficult existence, the couple met numerous intellectuals who had also taken refuge in this land of asylum. It was while going out to dinner one evening with Hannes Mayer, the last director of the Bauhaus—the legendary German design school that flourished between the wars—that she died of cardiac arrest in a taxi. Once again rumors circulated about the sudden death of the woman better known as Maria, La Passionaria, who had always been afraid of not being revolutionary enough.

Bibliography

Albers, Patricia. *Shadows, Fire, Snow: The Life of Tina Modotti.* Berkeley: University of California Press, 2002.

Cacucci, Pino. *Tina Modotti: A Life*. New York: St. Martin's Press, 1999.

Constantine, Mildred. *Tina Modotti: A Fragile Life*. San Francisco: Chronicle Books, 1993.

Hooks, Margaret. *Tina Modotti: Radical Photographer*. New York: Da Capo Press, 2000.

Lowe, Sarah M. *Tina Modotti: Photographs*. New York: Harry N. Abrams, Inc., 1998.

Mora, Gilles, ed. *Edward Weston: Forms of Passion*. New York: Harry N. Abrams, Inc., 1995.

Newhall, Beaumont, and Nancy Newhall, eds. *The Daybooks of Edward Weston: Mexico California*. New York: Aperture, 1996.

Rivera, Diego. *My Art, My Life: An Autobiography*. New York: Dover Publications, 1992.

Stark, Amy, ed. *The Letters from Tina Modotti to Edward Weston*. Tucson, Arizona: Center for Creative Photography, 1986.

Eva Hesse
Sol LeWitt
and the American
Minimalists

The Ick and the Cool

In the heart of the "cool '60s" of American art—a decade in which the Minimalists Sol LeWitt and Donald Judd developed a cold, almost sterile approach to art in contrast to the expressive paintings of Jackson Pollock or Willem de Kooning—Eva Hesse, a young woman who had moved to New York after fleeing Nazi Germany, would become a painter, sculptor, and inventor of ick art—a "disgusting" art, according to her own terms, which would fascinate the great minimalist artists of the era.

At the beginning of the 1960s, they were called the Bowery Boys, named after the avenue they lived on in New York's Lower Manhattan. They made their living with minor jobs at The Museum of Modern Art, working in the library, at the bookstore, and even as guards. They had descended on the art scene at the end of the "hot" years, those made famous by Pollock's drippings and de Kooning's splashes, paintings made with intensity and without fear of getting dirty. Art to the new generation was resolutely impersonal, almost sterile. "Cool" describes the spirit of the era. Robert Ryman composed his white squares, Robert Mangold his geometric figures with their staggered lines and, above all, there were the Minimalists Carl Andre, Sol LeWitt, Dan Flavin, and the most theoretical among them, Donald Judd. They steered clear of all expression to the point of refusing to create their artworks themselves. For these artists there was nothing beyond the painting or the sculpture, and the life of the creator had no importance. "What you see is what you see," said the painter Frank Stella. A drawing on a wall, a box, four neon lights in the corner of a room—that's all.

It was in this Manhattan neighborhood that a young woman of twenty-seven, already a painter and soon to be a sculptor, would join up with the Bowery Boys one day in 1963. Her name was Eva Hesse and she would become the common thread among all these artists. Contrary to all the declarations made by the Minimalists and their friends, Hesse was not scared of declaring that "art and life are inseparable," and she was not afraid of sullying herself with her paintings. Worst of all, her art was only that—a dirty mark.

"The only word that she ever used to describe her art to me was 'ick,'" declared LeWitt one day. The ick was in herself and in her work "because it's not pure, it's not simple, it's not beautiful," added the Minimalist sculptor. Against the purity of immaculate surfaces in the works of LeWitt or Judd were contrasted the soft and disturbing ones of Hesse. Works of sweat, of spit, and of tears, of papier-mâché, inflated shapes, latex, and surgical tubes. In one of her pieces medical bandages are wrapped around an empty frame from which extends a long steel wire. She named it *Hang Up* (1962–63). It was her favorite work because it was "the most absurd, as absurd as life." It was as absurd as her life. Her "ick" art sounded like "*ich,*" or "I," in German. Eva had been born in Germany, fled it, and on returning there came into her own artistically, before coming back to the United States to be greeted as "one of the most accomplished and promising artists of her generation." Then in May 1970 she was struck down by a brain tumor "at the outset of a brilliant career," according to the press. She was thirty-three.

Eva Hesse was born in 1936 in Hamburg to a Jewish family who sought refuge in the United States in 1939. Shortly after their arrival, her parents divorced and her mother committed suicide. Eva always lived in fear of having inherited her mother's instability. As an eighteen-year-old student at the Art Students League in New York, she published a series of illustrations accompanied by this text: "I paint what I see and I feel like expressing life with all its reality and impulses." She then attended the School of Art and Architecture at Yale University where her professor was Josef Albers, a historic figure from the Bauhaus, the legendary German art and design school in the era between the wars. She was "his little colorist," and they got along well, though he hated her painting. All her life she had to "fight to be a painter. Fight to be healthy. Fight to be strong," she wrote in 1960 in the diary she kept regularly.

"The most contemporary and proficient"

Eva Hesse was in frail health and had numerous hospital stays. Add to this the psychoses arising from her childhood and permanent feelings of guilt and fear resulting from her mother's suicide and the Holocaust. So she noted in her diary in the beginning of 1960: "Received $1300 from grandparents' stay in concentration camp. I will make use of the money wisely." Her encounter in April 1961 with the sculptor Tom Doyle, whom she married in November that same year, made her hope for a certain stability for herself, even though she was beginning to get some recognition during this period for her art. "The most contemporary and proficient," wrote Judd, then an influential critic, about her work in a group exhibition in 1961. In 1963 Tom and Eva moved to the Bowery. The apparent happiness of her marriage interrupted her diary entries for three years, but when she resumed in January 1964, it was to write: "I cannot be so many things . . . woman, beautiful, artist, wife, housekeeper, cook, saleslady, all these things." And

Right: **The tragic destiny of Eva Hesse, dead at thirty-four of brain cancer, made her a veritable legend. But even during her life, she was recognized as one of the greatest artists at the end of the twentieth century.**

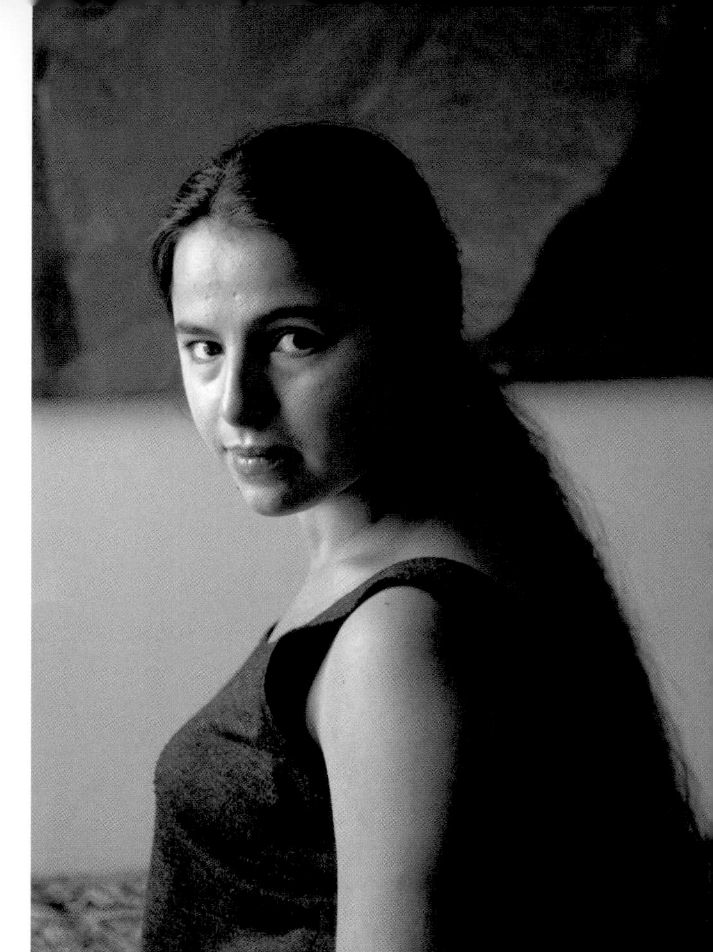

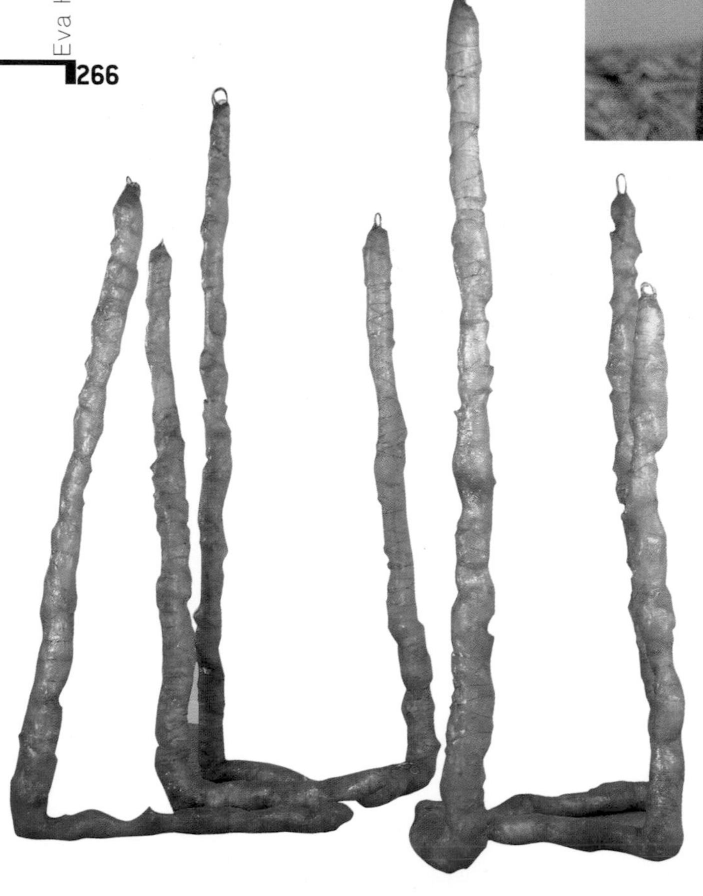

Left: **Eva Hesse*, Untitled. Seven Poles* (1970). In one of Hesse's last sculptures, the geometric forms stand heroically just at the point of falling. She put human feeling back into art, blending absurdity and eroticism.**

Below: **Sol LeWitt, *Open Cubes in the Form of a Cross* (1966–69). With his art founded on a rigorous geometric system, LeWitt seemed to be the opposite of Eva Hesse. He was, however, one of her closest confidants.**

Bottom: **Eva Hesse with her husband, the sculptor Tom Doyle, in 1965.**

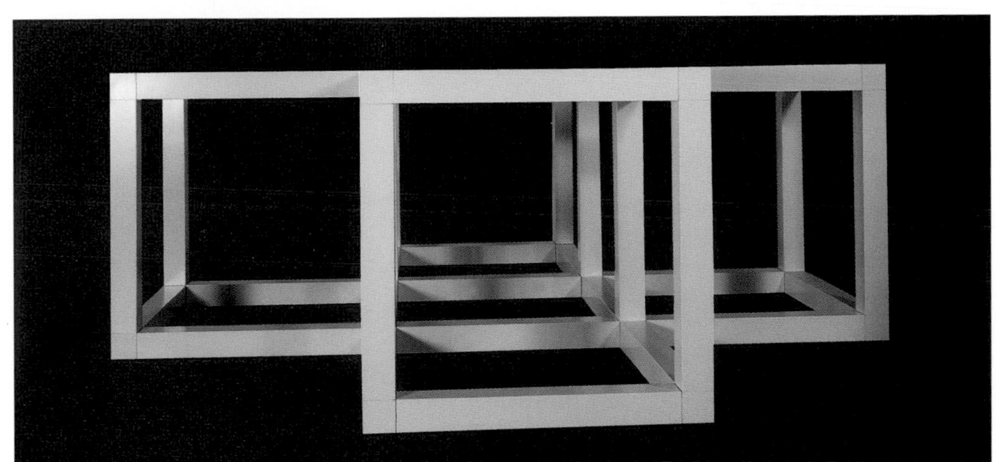

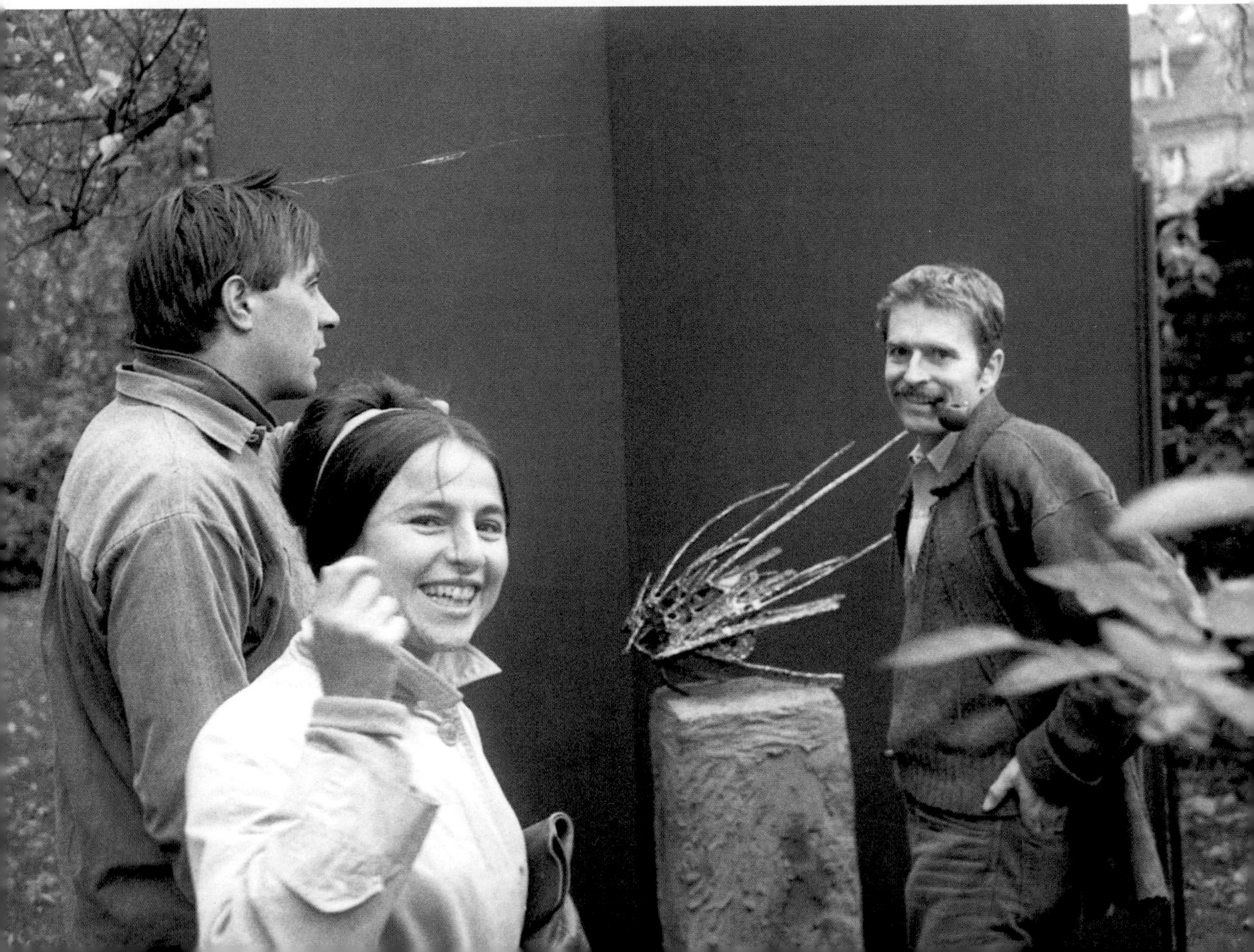

several days later: "Our marriage is over, a farce now." It was at this moment of great distress that an event intervened that would turn her life upside down. In April 1964 Friedrich Arnhard Scheidt, a collector of Tom's sculpture, invited them to work for a year in one of his empty factories in Kettwig-am-Ruhr near Düsseldorf. In photographs she stands laughing beside Tom or next to the sculptor Arman during the installation of paintings and reliefs. This period could have been grueling for Eva, but instead of coming out of it crushed and overwhelmed, she developed into a key artist of the end of the twentieth century.

During this year Tom and Eva worked together but were in fact separated. Eva suffered another trauma when she returned to Hamburg to visit her childhood home but the new owners refused her entry. Nights of insomnia and nightmares followed. She questioned her art, caught between painting and sculpture. "If painting poses too many problems for you, tell it to fuck off!" she confided in her diary.

"Do the wrong thing"

She opened herself up to an artist she had met five years earlier, her stylistic opposite and her closest confidant, Sol LeWitt. "It's you I want to talk to when things are bothering me," she wrote to him. "You understand me a little, me and my non-art art." "Do the wrong thing," LeWitt advised. Then she made her ick sculptures. Forms attached to the wall and hanging from it: three balls of papier-mâché stuffed with three filaments or two long tubes, always in papier-mâché, always hanging. She named them the "LeWitt balloon." LeWitt always kept this "ick" sculpture near him, and he explicitly attributed to Hesse the direct inspiration for several of his pieces, such as his 1970 *Wall Drawing #46 (Vertical Lines, not straight, not touching . . .)*.

Upon her return to the United States, Hesse became the center of the New York art world, a point of convergence for the diverse group of artists whom she had a way of understanding intimately. And so she wrote regarding the metal squares positioned on the ground by the Minimalist sculptor Carl Andre: "I feel very close to Carl Andre. I feel, let's say, emotionally connected to his work. It does something to my insides. His metal plates were the concentration camps for me. They were those showers where they put on the gas."

In August 1966 her father died. She wrote, "I am overcome. . . . I have to work even harder now to be strong, to be a happy Being.

I have grown so this year. Last August 28, we came back to America. Since then in fact I have lost my husband (because of our separation) and my father through death. . . . My only weapon is art, my friends." She exhibited her drawings with the Minimalist and Conceptual artists, but her art, which she qualified herself as "independent but intimately personal," soon saw its originality recognized.

"Sexy Minimalist"

Lucy Lippard, one of the greatest art critics of the 1960s and Hesse's neighbor on the Bowery, invited her to participate in the *Eccentric Abstraction* exhibition alongside Louise Bourgeois and Bruce Nauman, which marked the birth of an art supplanting the chilliness of the "cool" years. Eva then met Richard Serra in 1968, and this time it would be the philosopher and art historian Rosalind Krauss who connected their works under the title of "Process Art," an approach that brought to light the manipulations necessary for the fabrication of a work. Serra dedicated *Splashing with Four Moulds, to Eva Hesse* (1969) to her, a piece consisting of a spattering of lead against a wall—these splatters seemed the opposite of the neutral forms of Minimalism. It was Hesse, however, who spoke to the cool movement with her *Box*, a fiberglass cube pierced by many plastic tubes (an allusion to the boxes made by the Minimalist Donald Judd and a play on the word "box" which is slang for "vagina"). It earned her the nickname of the "sexy Minimalist." A *Life* magazine article entitled "Drip Art" made her the heir of Pollock's heroic painting style. William S. Rubin, the director of The Museum of Modern Art in New York, saw her at the origin of a "primitive approach" that marked art at the end of the twentieth century. Far from the "Eva Hesse myth" of an ignored and misunderstood artist that some have built up around her, her central role is unanimously recognized as that of one who persevered "in doing the wrong thing." "We were all influenced by her," said her friend Mel Bochner. "She marked the final point of the 1960s. The end of the beginning." And the beginning of a new art.

Bibliography

Lippard, Lucy R. *Eva Hesse*. New York: Da Capo Press, 1992.

Sandler, Irving. *The Triumph of American Art: A History of Abstract Expressionism*. New York: Icon, 1999.

Sussman, Elisabeth, et al. *Eva Hesse*. Exhibition catalogue. San Francisco Museum of Modern Art. New Haven, Conn.: Yale University Press, 2002.

Georgia O'Keeffe
Alfred Stieglitz
The Flower and the Gardener

Georgia O'Keeffe, a Midwest native, was first seduced by paintings introduced by Alfred Stieglitz, the undisputed master of New York photography and the owner of an avant-garde gallery. A romantic and creative relationship developed between the two that brought new life to the photographer, liberated the work of the painter and, for the first time, imposed on the art world the vision of an American woman and painter.

"I have not been in Europe. I prefer to live in a room as bare as possible. I have been much photographed." Georgia O'Keeffe had a curious way of summarizing her life in 1922. However, looking a little closer, this self-portrait in three parts (America, asceticism, and the photography of Alfred Stieglitz) was actually quite eloquent. Contrary to the then well-established tradition that held that all young American artists make their first trip to Europe via London, Paris, and Rome, Georgia O'Keeffe assumed an exclusively American education and inspiration from the outset. At an age when other students were frequenting Montparnasse and the great European museums, she was already earning her living as a teacher of drawing in a remote Texas town, calmly helping in the settling of scores the *O.K. Corral* way, and delighting in the vision of immense deserts. Born into a family whose ruin would inexorably accompany her adolescence, O'Keeffe drew an unexpected strength from privation.

The voyage to Europe was financially unthinkable, so it became intellectually useless. As for her taste for empty rooms, it reflected the sole preoccupation from which she could not be distracted: painting. And finally, photography. Without naming him she referred to Stieglitz, who not only made her famous from one day to the next by photographing her but who also encouraged her to paint and exhibited her work in his gallery next to that of Paul Cézanne and Pablo Picasso. Her self-portrait was no less accurate because it was concise. The photographs that revealed O'Keeffe to her contemporaries revealed her first of all to herself. Leaving the exhibition of the first images produced by her new lover, Georgia wrote to a friend: "I was always amazed to find out what I looked like. You see I'd never known what I looked like or thought much about it. I was amazed to find my face was lean and structured. I'd always thought it was round. Now I can see myself and that will help me say what I want to say in painting."

Georgia was born on November 15, 1887, on a farm in Wisconsin. The first newspaper to mention her name was the *Sun Prairie Countryman*, a journal that delighted in noting even the smallest events concerning this community of immigrants. In the family of Ida and Francis (Frank) O'Keeffe, Georgia's parents, the women had to learn how to handle the brush and to paint flowers and still lifes, which would then decorate the walls of the farm. Singing was also a family discipline and for a long time Georgia said that she would have preferred to sing but, not being very gifted, she did not insist on this. On the other hand, she was aware early on of her talent for drawing and color and sought to confirm her hopes with her successive teachers. From her schoolteacher to her drawing professor at a Virginia college, all insisted on the necessity of nourishing and developing her exceptional gifts. But her academic training was abridged for the lack of sufficient financial means. Several months of university studies at The Art Institute of Chicago, several more months in 1907 at the Art Students League on 57th Street in New York, that was it. The great attraction that winter for the students of the fine arts school was Alfred Stieglitz's gallery at 291 Fifth Avenue. He was exhibiting the drawings of Auguste Rodin, which were deemed scandalous by the academic professors. Georgia and her friends went there in a group on January 2, 1908. Hair disheveled, photographs dripping from his hand, the art dealer-photographer welcomed them without ceremony and launched into an enflamed discourse justifying the exhibition. Georgia O'Keeffe was stupefied by the force of his comments and backed away, intimidated by this character. Several years would pass before they were in each other's presence again.

A Woman on Paper

Over several years Georgia earned her keep with advertising jobs and commercial design that left her no time to paint. In 1912 a girlfriend informed her that the position of professor had opened up in a school in Amarillo, Texas. She was soon hired and there discovered cowboys who ate three meals at one sitting and adultery dealt with in the street by gunfire, with the law on the side of the killer, but above all, she walked for hours in the countryside through "terrible winds and a grand emptiness." For years after having left Amarillo, she dreamt of returning to this landscape. At twenty-seven, she returned to New York in 1914 with just enough money in her pockets to follow a semester of courses at Columbia University Teacher's College. More than ever there was talk about Stieglitz who had had the audacity to exhibit the European avant-garde: Picasso, Cézanne, and *Nude Descending a Stair-*

case by Marcel Duchamp, *the* scandal of the great Armory exhibition the year before. Stieglitz was equally famous for his vehement defense of freedom in art and his diatribes regarding the creation of an American art that would finally ignore the lessons of the Europeans. The young visitors listened to him fascinated, and the monologue would often continue in the café at the bottom of the gallery where Stieglitz, then married to a rich brewery heiress, regaled everyone. Although the gallery did not provide its director with much money, at least it allowed young artists to consecrate themselves entirely to their work. It was a valuable lesson for Georgia.

At a teaching post in a South Carolina college she began working in black and white, with charcoal on large pieces of paper. She was a subscriber to *Camera Work*, a review run by Stieglitz and she considered it the absolute authority on matters of contemporary art. If she had to show her work to someone, it would be to him. When Stieglitz eventually did unfurl the charcoal rolls in his gallery at the end of a dreary day in January 1916, it was not O'Keeffe who had brought them to him but her friend Anita Pollitzer who lived in New York. The legend says that Stieglitz's face then lit up: "Finally, a woman on paper." Regarding these abstract and sensual drawings that had been realized in alternately euphoric and desperate states, Stieglitz declared, "they were the purest finest sincerest things that have entered 291 in a long time," and expressed the desire to exhibit them one day.

An intense correspondence followed that would last until the end of Stieglitz's life, reaching the astronomical number of three thousand four hundred letters and telegrams exchanged between them. The letters were not enough and O'Keeffe decided to come to New York. Upon her arrival she discovered that her exhibition had begun in 1916 without Stieglitz informing her. Her drawings were a sensation, like all her works that would be exhibited over the years, but O'Keeffe was enraged at not having been consulted. Stieglitz tried to bypass her anger by insisting that he felt very attracted by this young woman, young enough to be his daughter. He was fifty-four—the same age as O'Keeffe's mother who had just died in a state of complete destitution. His hair was long and gray and his moustache white. He had been married for twenty-four years and had an eighteen-year-old daughter. O'Keeffe was young, very thin but, above all, she was at the beginning of her creative life while Stieglitz felt at the end of his own. He had not worked as a photographer for years, refusing all commissions. He preferred to show the work of others and to talk to his visitors.

On Equal Footing with Europe

The following year, 1917, he organized a proper exhibition of Georgia O'Keeffe works. She received several positive critical responses, but three days later America entered into World War I and any public interest in contemporary art dissipated. Stieglitz's gallery closed. He consoled himself by proclaiming simply: "I gave the world a woman." In 1918 O'Keeffe settled in New York and the two became lovers. In his family's country house on Lake George in upstate New York, Alfred photographed her from every angle for the composite portraits that would occupy him over the next twenty years. Her hands, her breasts, her shoulders, Georgia painting, reading, walking, Georgia nude, Georgia in bed, Georgia in a sweater. It was a work that was created in collaboration with O'Keeffe, who decided on the poses. Stieglitz chose the shots for the exhibition. In looking at these photos and the paintings by O'Keeffe, a banker friend said to Stieglitz, "I never imagined that a love between a man and a woman could mutually inspire them to this degree."

With his nudes of O'Keeffe and his series on clouds, *Equivalents* (1923–31), which he pursued simultaneously, Stieglitz got back in touch with photography and creativity. He also served as O'Keeffe's "eye," the one to whom she showed her paintings first and foremost. It allowed her to pursue her work without worrying about the reactions or moods of a gallery owner.

With the war now over, Stieglitz exhibited the nude photographs in his new gallery and O'Keeffe became a celebrity. But when they proposed to only exhibit these works, he imposed O'Keeffe's paintings. Whoever wanted to buy or exhibit O'Keeffe had to address themselves to Stieglitz. Passing through New York, the sculptor Constantin Brancusi discovered her work and what he observed filled Stieglitz with joy: "There's none of the European limit in her. . . . It's a force, a liberating free force." America was now on equal footing with Europe in matters of contemporary art.

In 1924 at age 36, O'Keeffe married Stieglitz and decided against having children. Stieglitz considered himself too old and the worries he had had with his psychologically fragile daughter, Kitty, did not encourage him to take on a second fatherhood. From now on O'Keeffe's life was mapped out; she would devote herself entirely to her art.

Page 276: **Alfred Stieglitz, *Georgia O'Keeffe: A Portrait (Hands)* (1918).**
Page 277: **Alfred Stieglitz, *Georgia O'Keeffe: A Portrait (Neck)* (1921).**

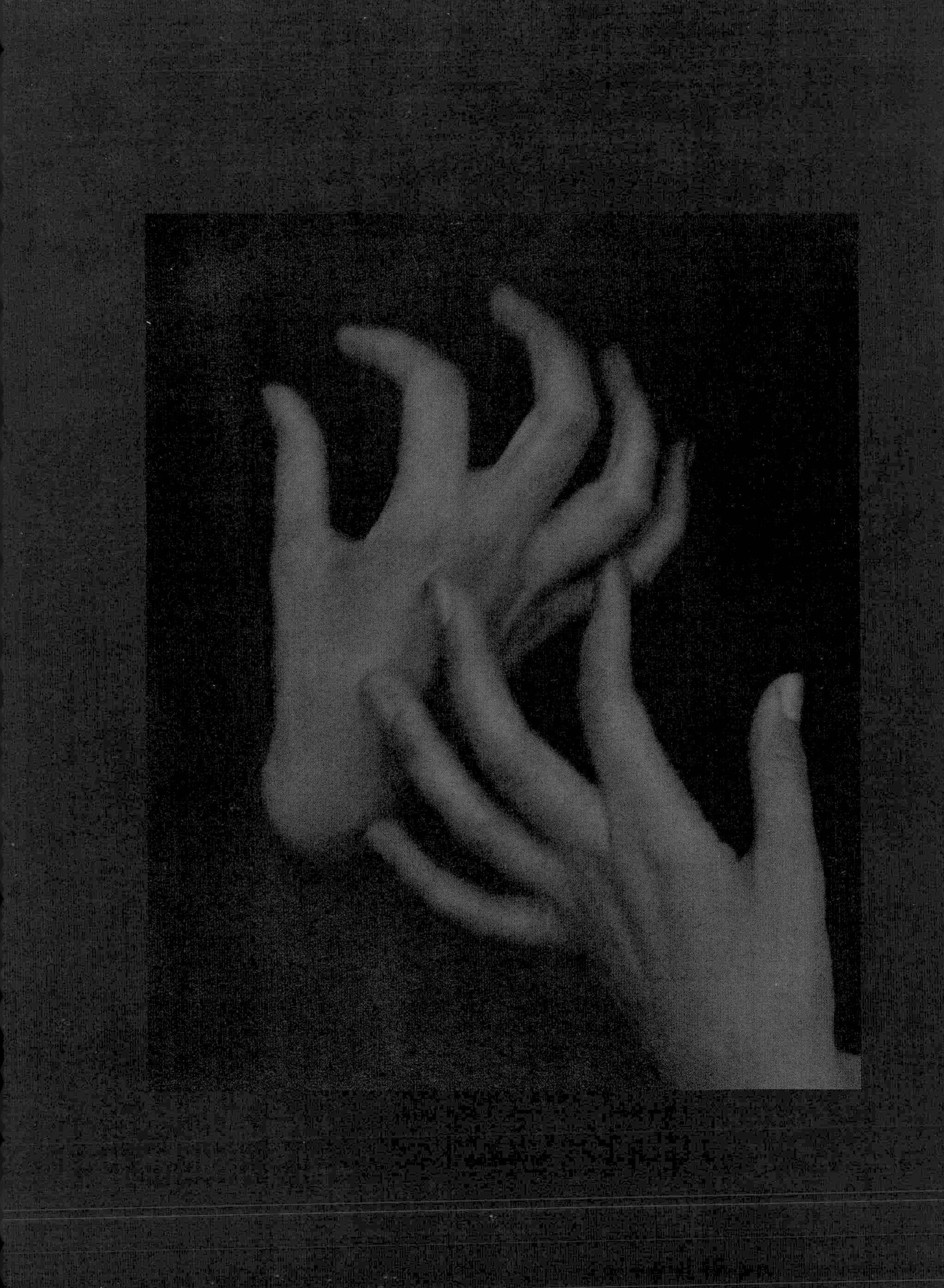

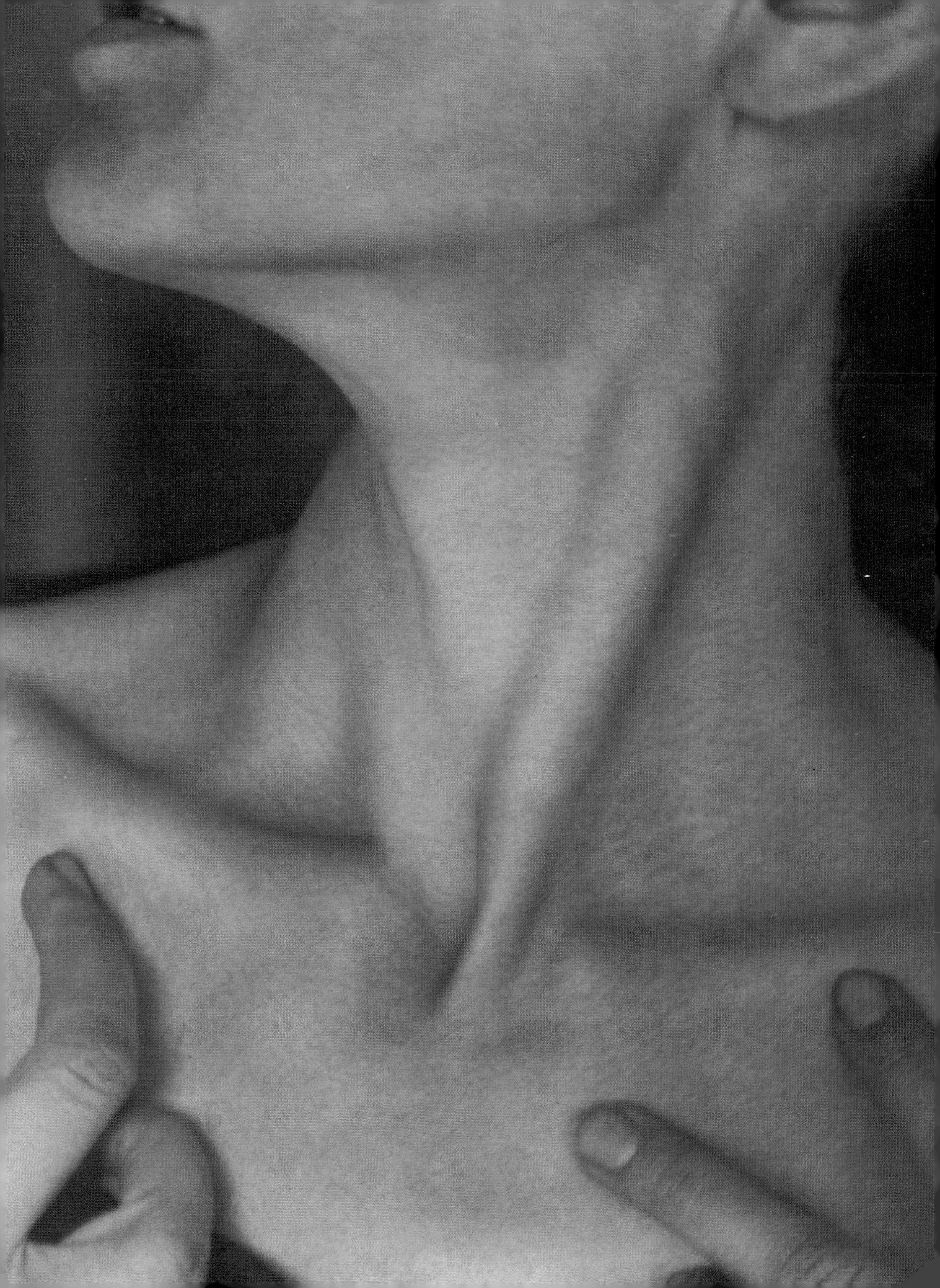

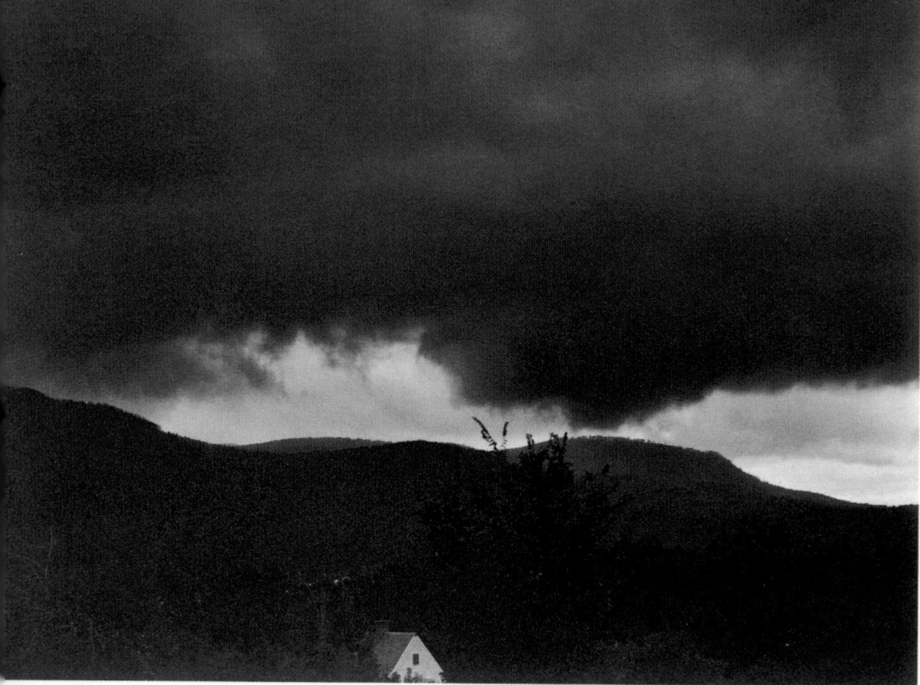

Opposite: **Georgia O'Keeffe and Alfred Stieglitz photographed in 1942 by Arnold Newman, in a pose that suggests their de facto separation.**

Above: **While Georgia O'Keeffe painted landscapes with cloudy skies, Alfred Stieglitz got back in touch with creative photography and in 1922 composed a series entitled *Music: A Sequence of Ten Cloud Photographs* (pictured here is *No. 1*). Later, he named these works *Equivalents*.**

Right: **Alfred Stieglitz tirelessly photographed Georgia O'Keeffe, revealing to her all the beauty of her body. For twenty years, her hands, her breasts, her shoulders, her neck, her chest, tightly framed, came together to form composite portraits, *Georgia O'Keeffe: A Portrait (Profile)* (1920).**

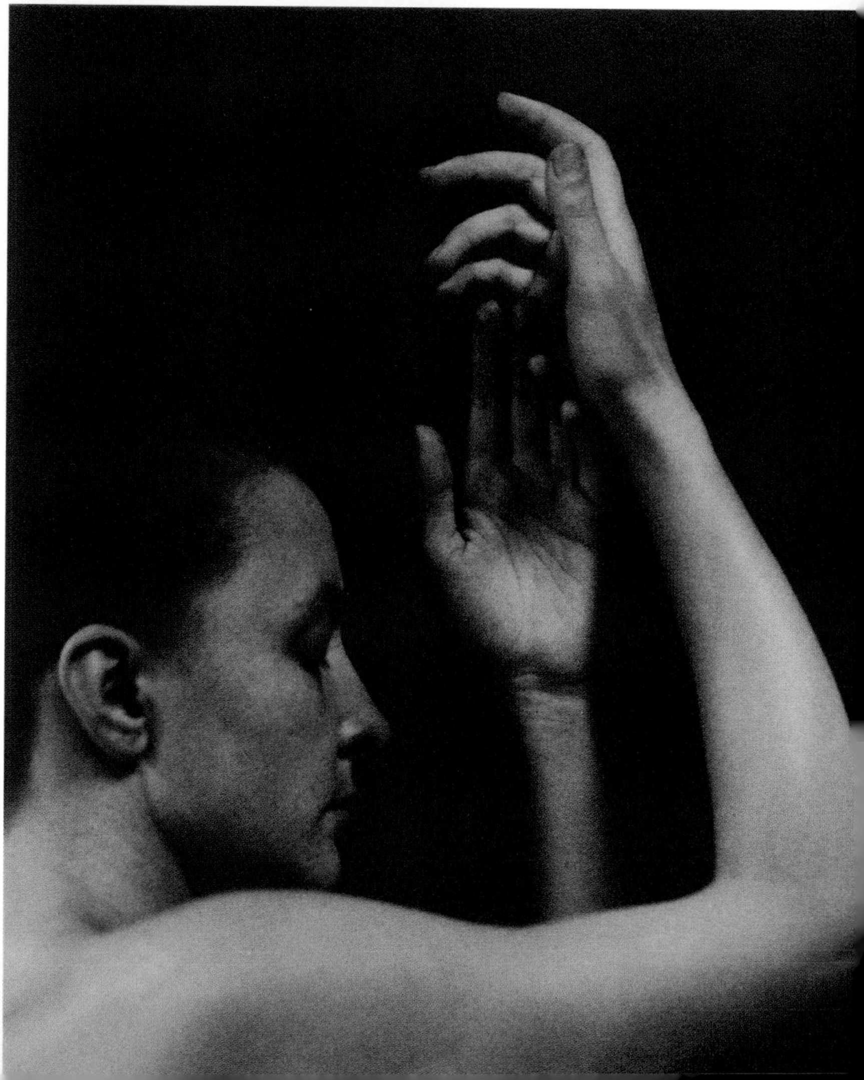

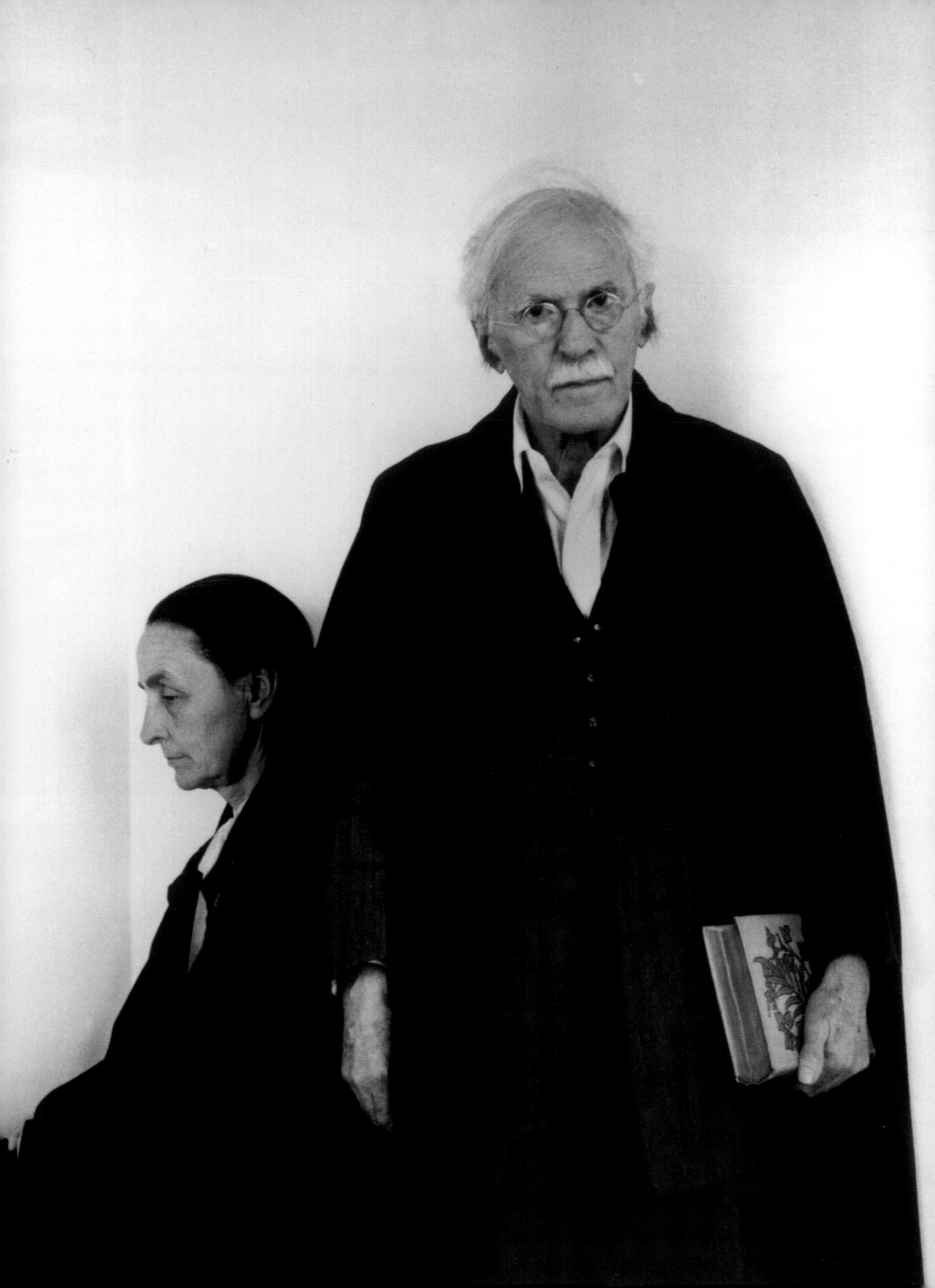

Right: **Georgia O'Keeffe, New Mexico, 1960. In this period, O'Keeffe crisscrossed the United States in her car, always returning to the desert landscape of New Mexico. Photograph by Tony Vaccaro.**
Below: **Georgia O'Keeffe, *East River, No. 3* (1926). From the twenty-eighth floor of a New York high-rise, O'Keeffe began to love the urban landscape with its geometric forms.**
Opposite: **Georgia O'Keeffe, *Cow's Skull with Calico Roses* (1931–32). In this painting, O'Keeffe blends the desert and death with the voluptuous gentleness of blooming roses.**

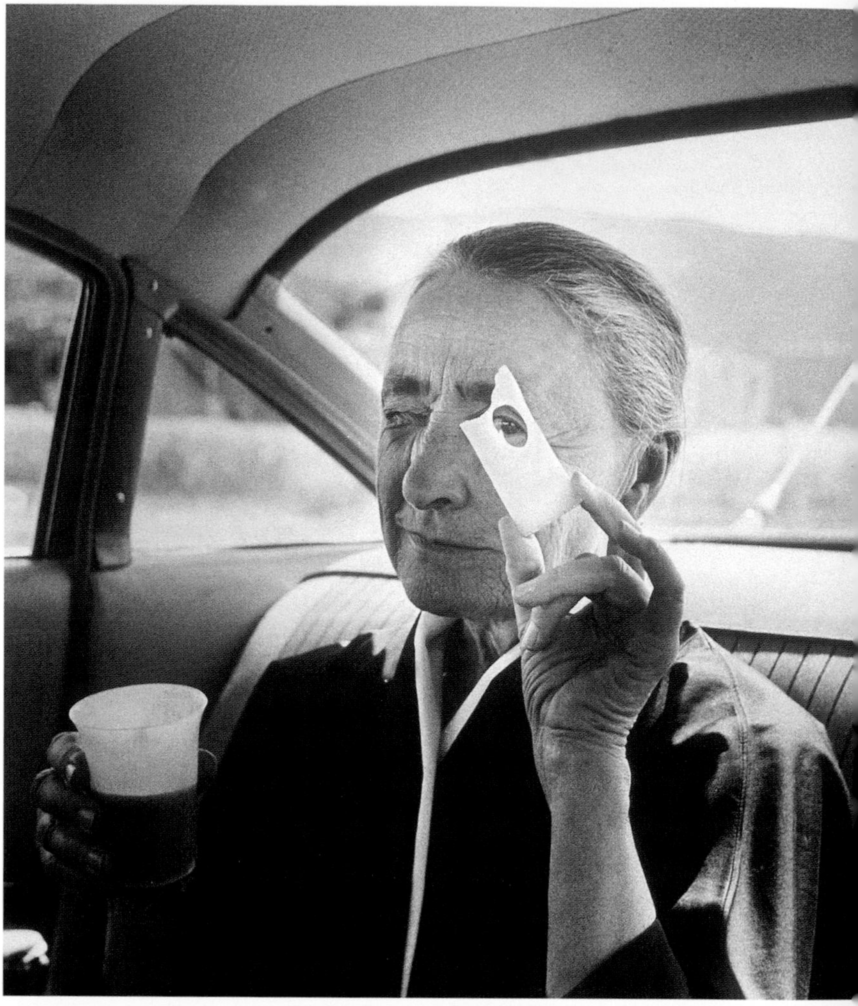

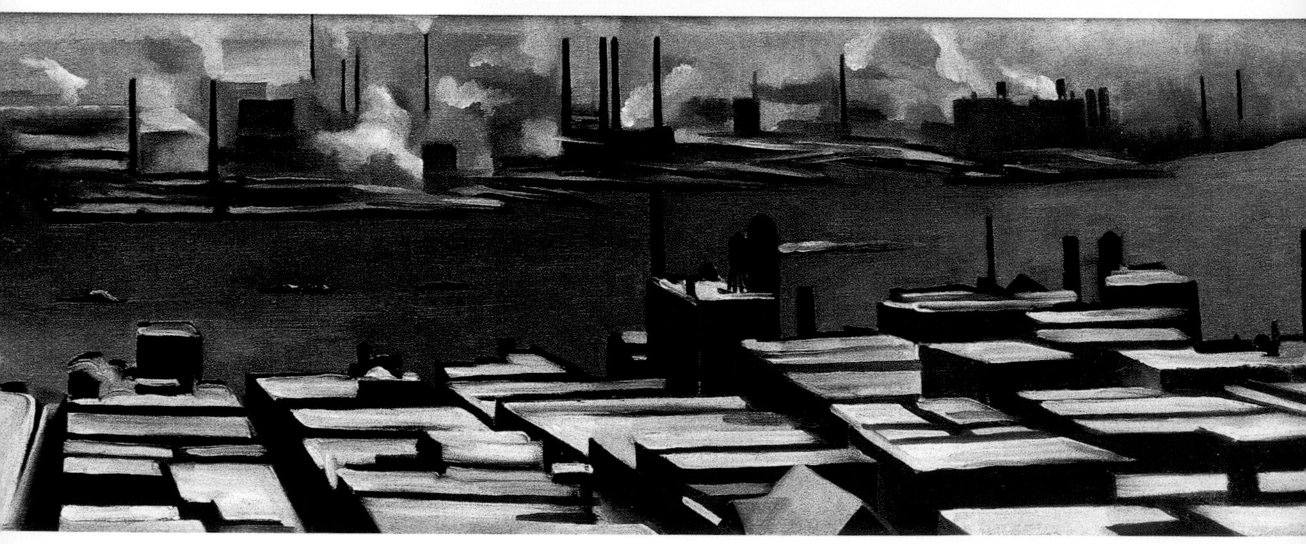

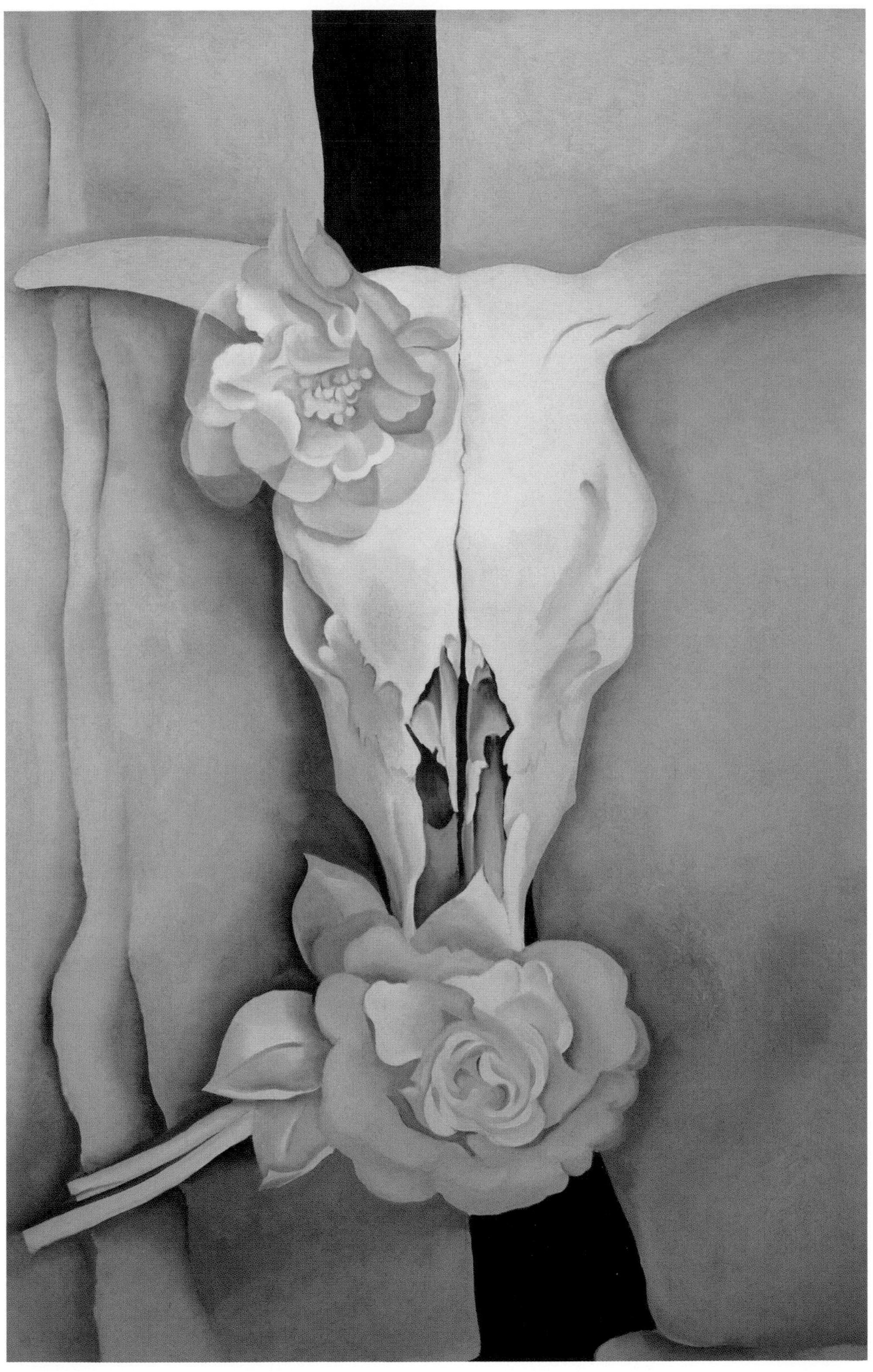

In his new gallery The Room (officially called the Intimate Gallery), Stieglitz reigned as the guide for a small group of American artists, always cloaked in a black cape, a cane in his hand, with a hat perched on his head. As the last arrival to this group, O'Keeffe had to prove herself so that she would not be considered as just the art dealer's wife. When they called her "Mrs. Stieglitz," she coldly corrected them. "It's Georgia O'Keeffe." While she may have listened to Stieglitz's advice, she was firmly set on pursuing her work in an independent manner. When she showed him for the first time one of her immense and colorful flowers, which would become her trademark, an annoyed Stieglitz said to her: "I wonder what you think you're going to do with that?" Huge subjects painted frontally—which in a certain way recall the equally head-on photos by Stieglitz—these flowers would give rise to endless discussions about the sexuality they expressed, to the greatest irritation of their creator who kept on painting them. Dismissing all easy interpretations, O'Keeffe maintained, "I hate flowers—I paint them because they're cheaper than models and they don't move."

Settled into the twenty-eighth floor of a New York high-rise, O'Keeffe found herself falling in love with the views of the city and the play of light on the buildings, but the couple's accommodations remained quite basic. There was no kitchen so they would never have to make a meal; they ate at the café downstairs. There was very little decoration so as not to encumber themselves and give free rein to her painting. Her reputation grew year by year and in 1927, when an anonymous French collector bought six small paintings for the astronomical sum of $25,000, she felt reassured about her ability to live on her work. Stieglitz, who made the sale, had committed a masterstroke by setting this price provocatively high to avoid selling six paintings to the same buyer but, to his great surprise, the collector agreed without hesitation. For this advocate of the superiority of American art, such a sale to a European collector was a great reward.

Fly with Your Own Wings

Over the years, however, their art began to divide them. While Stieglitz pursued his work as a photographer, whether in the country or in New York, O'Keeffe felt the need to change her surroundings and to discover new spaces. In December 1929 in a new gallery significantly named An American Place, O'Keeffe exhibited some paintings inspired by a recent trip to Santa Fe,

New Mexico. Stieglitz understood that she needed to leave New York in order to renew her inspiration. From then on each time he photographed her, she was no longer the inspiring nude but an austere woman, dressed in costumes or wearing Navajo jewelry, often with a far-off gaze, or seated in her car, one hand on the steering wheel.

While O'Keeffe distanced herself from her mentor, Stieglitz found new inspiration in Dorothy Norman, a young woman with whom he had begun a love affair. From now on their creative life diverged. O'Keeffe spent more and more time in New Mexico where she had rented a house at Ghost Ranch, an artists' community near Santa Fe, before buying one not far away in Abiquiu. Stieglitz stayed more often in New York. They would meet in the summers at the house on Lake George, and O'Keeffe crossed the United States by car—her new passion—alone or accompanied. She slept under the stars or in inexpensive motels, and each year changed the itinerary to vary the scenery. At the age of ninety, she prided herself on knowing America's smallest nooks and crannies.

When Stieglitz died in July 1946, O'Keeffe had become so famous that the *New York Times* obituary announced the death of "Georgia O'Keeffe's husband." Nothing could keep her on the East Coast any longer and until her death in 1986, O'Keeffe alternated her stays in New Mexico with voyages around the world. At sixty-five, she went to Europe for the first time and returned disappointed. She found Paris interesting but declined an invitation to meet Picasso. She did not speak French, so why meet an artist with whom she could not speak? Rome seemed deadening to her. Only Spain was a delight. Frequent voyages to Asia and South America would follow, but she would always return to the desert landscapes of New Mexico. Asked once when she was over ninety about her fear of death, O'Keeffe, who had always nourished an unquenchable passion for music, said simply, "I would like to come back as a blonde soprano who could sing high clear notes without fear."

Bibliography

Eisler, Benita. *O'Keeffe and Stieglitz: An American Romance*. New York: Penguin Books, 1992.

Robinson, Roxane. *Georgia O'Keeffe: A Life*. Hanover, N.H.: University Press of New England, 1989.

Nico
Andy Warhol
The Singer and the Master

As a Warhol superstar, the leading actress of his film *Chelsea Girls*, the psychedelic singer of the Velvet Underground, and a living model for the master of the Factory, the blonde Nico, with her androgynous physique and her raspy voice, embodied Andy Warhol's dream at the end of the 1960s, in which painting, music, and cinema were all integral parts of the Pop art movement.

NICO—Hi, Andy!
ANDY—Oh, hi!
Silence. A moment later:
NICO—Andy?
ANDY—Hmmm.
NICO—I . . .
Silence.
ANDY—You said?
NICO—I . . . thought that . . .
Silence.
ANDY—What?
NICO— . . . that . . . no, nothing

This exchange between the king of Pop art and the freshly promoted Warhol superstar may seem terse, but in fact everything was fine. On this November 9, 1966, the Abraham & Straus department store in Brooklyn, New York, had asked Andy Warhol to create a promotion for a two-dollar paper dress kit, complete with outfit and paint. In front of a crowd of onlookers who pressed against the glass, Warhol poured red paint onto a silkscreen framework, which his assistant Gerard Malanga placed on Nico's chest and then her back. Ari, Nico's young son, spray-painted his mother's stockings with green paint while the word "Fragile" was being screened on her dress. In the street Nico's monotone voice could be heard over the loudspeakers singing "All Tomorrow's Parties." Warhol then feebly pronounced: "Nico is the first psychedelic singer in the Velvet Underground." Suspense was at its height. Putting the finishing touches on the performance, he took several plastic bananas out of his pocket and stuck them randomly on his model's dress. A store employee closed the spectacle explaining, "The dress that Mr. Warhol has just created will be offered to the Brooklyn Museum." The onlookers dispersed.

Ten years after one of his drawings appeared in his first group exhibition at The Museum of Modern Art in New York, Warhol had become the figurehead of the New York art and social scene. It was a spectacular triumph for little Andy Warhola, born August 6,

1928, in Pittsburgh, the third son of Ondrej (Andrew) and Julia Zavacky Warhola, Slovak peasants from the Carpathian Mountains and first-generation immigrants. He was famous around the world for his series of paintings of Coca-Cola bottles, Campbell's Soup cans, and disasters; his portraits of such stars as Elvis, Marilyn Monroe, Marlon Brando, and Jackie Kennedy; his provocative advertising campaigns; and his avant-garde films. In choosing objects of daily consumption or advertising as the subjects of his paintings, he proclaimed, "What's great about this country is that America started the tradition where the richest consumers buy essentially the same things as the poorest." Warhol also filmed the actions of daily life. After 1963's *Sleep*, a six-hour film of John Giorno resting—a work described by one critic as "the first film to sleep by"—*Eat* and *Blow Job* (both 1964) followed.

The Time of the Counterculture

They came from near and far to take the freight elevator that led directly into the Factory, Warhol's fourth-floor studio located at 231 East 47th Street in New York. In this loft, whose walls were covered in aluminum foil or sprayed with silvery paint, models, photographers, musicians, and singers all wanted to spend time with Warhol, to watch him work or wander about apparently indifferent to those around him. Warhol printed miles of paintings, elevated the silkscreen and the multiple to the level of art, and caused a scandal by exhibiting *Brillo Boxes*, his silkscreened replicas of the well-known brand of cleaning pads. But he always found the time to move about the Factory with a recording device in his hand to capture the most innocuous conversations and turn them into theater. Warhol never dismissed anyone, but he occasionally marked his disapproval with a few murmurs that were quickly interpreted by his longtime assistant Gerard Malanga, who had become head of the household in this new temple of counterculture. If the Factory became a true factory for filming and painting, it owed a great deal to the personality of Malanga, the curly-haired poet converted into a talent scout. It was he who spotted young unknown beauties in magazines or at parties and invited them to a screen test at the Factory, where they met famous artists or soon became famous themselves. "It was a constant open house," Warhol said. "Like the format of a children's TV program—you just hung around and characters you knew dropped in." Nico, a young blonde model who was trying to break into singing, seized her chance. Her real name was Christa

Paffgen, and she was born in Cologne but grew up in Berlin, then lived in Paris and in Rome, where she played a small role in Federico Fellini's film *La Dolce Vita* (1960). When she arrived in New York in January 1966, she was twenty-three years old, with a lanky silhouette, fine features, and straight hair that fell to her shoulders. For Warhol she was a "moon goddess" who had to become a superstar. He worked hard to re-create her and to present her to the world as a singer, model, and actress.

The Superstar of the Velvet Underground

Fascinated for several years by pop music and by the success of the Rolling Stones, the Beatles, and the Beach Boys, Warhol dreamed of working with a rock group. At the end of 1965 Malanga brought him to the Café Bizarre, a cabaret in Greenwich Village, to see the Velvet Underground, which had evolved around the singer Lou Reed. The tie between his films and their music was blindingly obvious. Warhol suggested to them that they add a new member, a beautiful girl capable of electrifying the public. He suggested Nico, and while some of them found her too cold and others disliked her voice, Warhol forced her on the group.

One of the first stage appearances by Warhol's updated Velvet Underground took place at Delmonico's Hotel on the occasion of the meeting of the New York Society for Clinical Psychiatry. Warhol presented two films and introduced Nico, who began to sing while a group of fake journalists launched into savage interviews posing embarrassing questions to the attendees. Abandoning their plates of roast beef, the psychiatrists left. The next day a headline in the *Herald Tribune* read "Psychiatrists Flee Warhol," setting up an ironic portrait of the artist as a perverse terrorist, capable of putting specialists in the field into flight.

The Velvet Underground took a malevolent delight in unsettling their public, determinedly turning their backs on them, or changing the rhythm as soon as the audience began to dance. Despite Warhol's efforts, there would never be perfect harmony between the American group and the German singer. Moreover, the critics were not very kind to Nico. They compared her voice to "an amplified moose" or the sound of the "wind in a drainpipe," when it was not described as "a Bedouin woman singing a funeral dirge in Arabic while accompanied by an off-key air raid siren." Warhol was not discouraged; he had raised Nico to the firmament of superstars and planned to keep her there for a while. He designed the cover of their new album entitled *The Velvet Underground and*

Opposite: **Nico in Jacques Poitrenaud's 1963 film *Strip-tease*.**

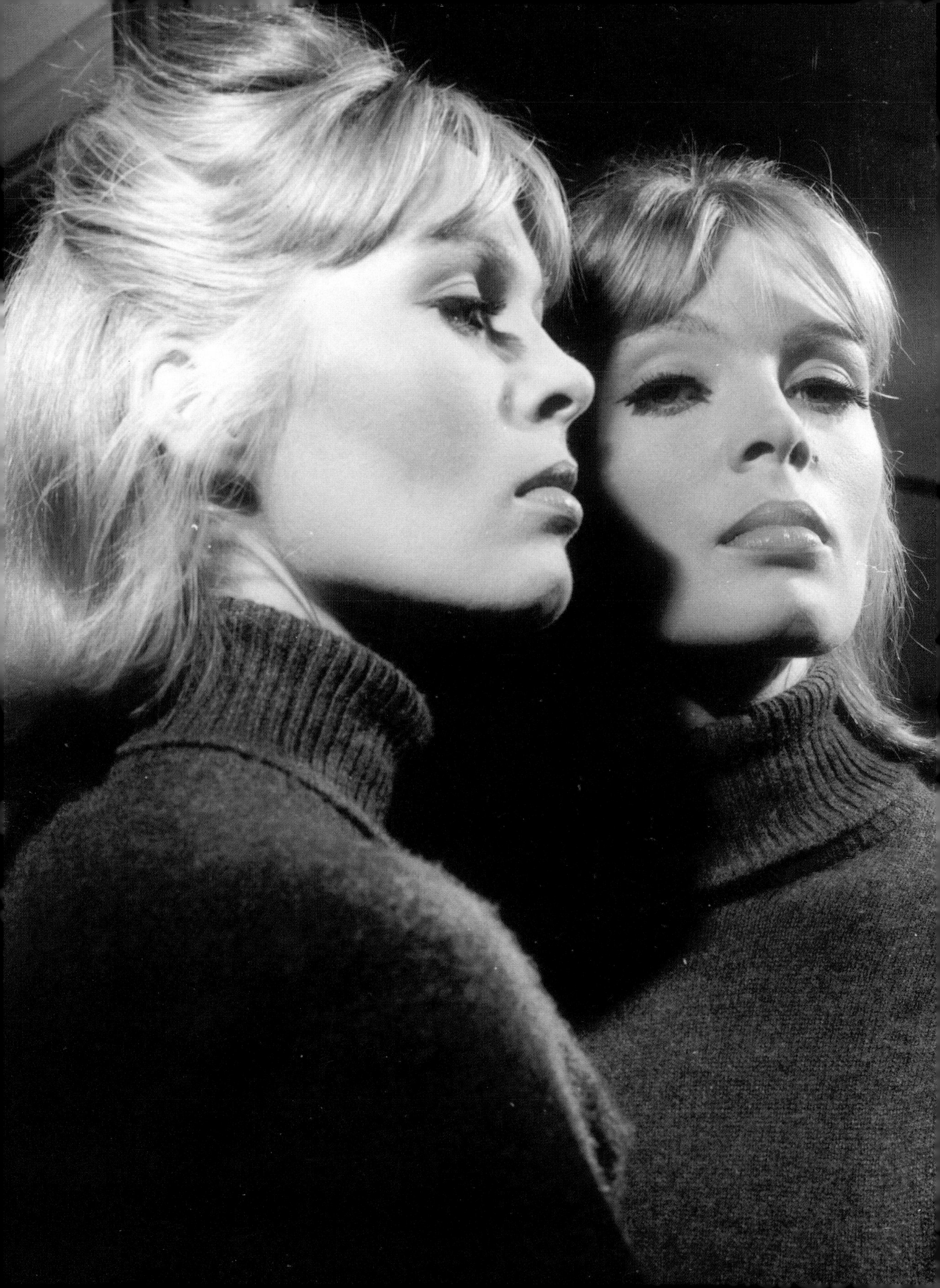

Poor Richard

— PRESENTS —

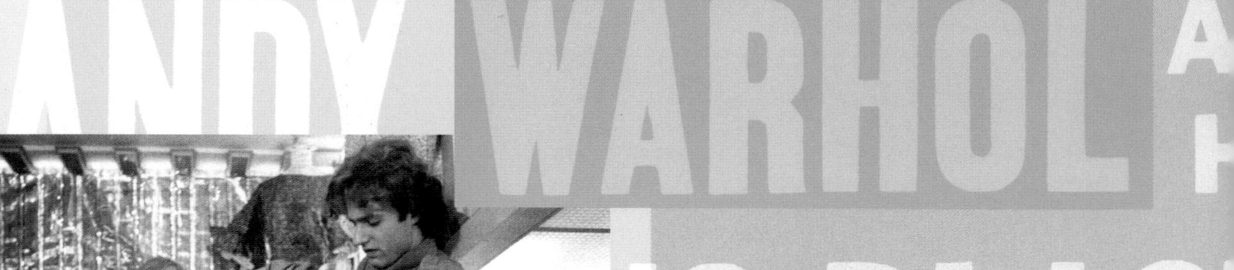

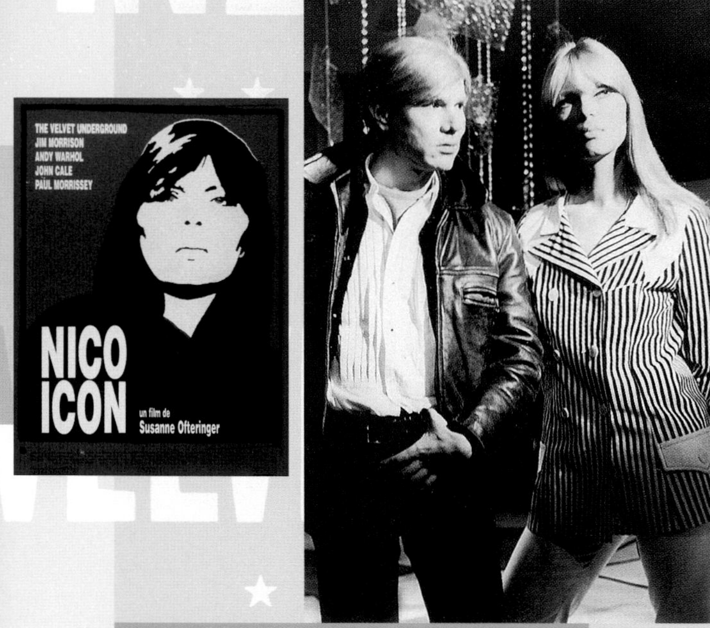

NICO - Pop Girl of

Newly arrived in 1966, Nico became the Warhol superstar. Top, left: **She is wearing a paper dress decorated by Andy Warhol and Gerard Malanga. Nico also filmed a television series with Warhol called *Late Night Horrors*, which was shown in Boston.** Above: **Andy Warhol in 1975.**

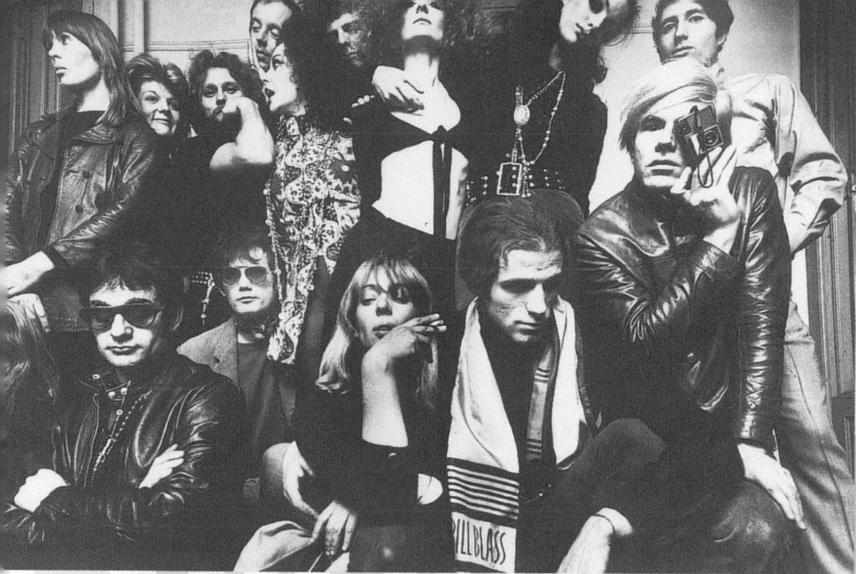

Below: **Top model Nico wishes the readers of *Elle* a Happy New Year in 1963.**

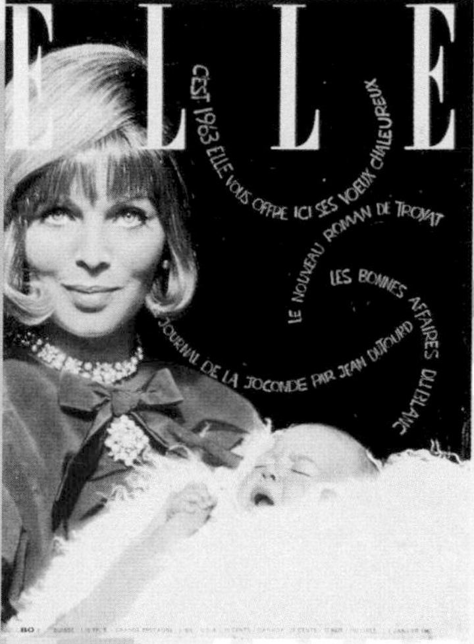

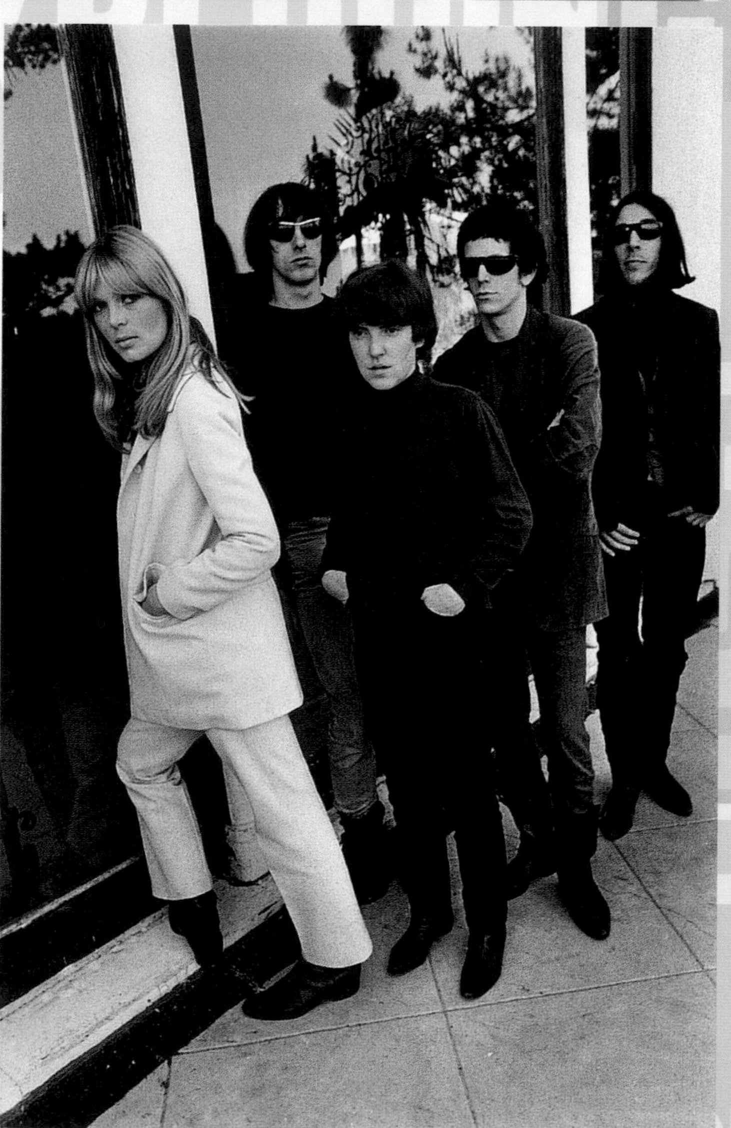

Left: **By forcing Nico on the Velvet Underground's four musicians, Andy Warhol made each appearance by the group an event, as in this shot taken in the Hollywood Hills in 1966. The singer and the band could never reach an understanding. Photograph by Gerard Malanga.**

Top, left: **A scene from daily life at the Factory in 1968. In the top row at left, Nico has a distracted air about her while, at right, Andy Warhol hides himself behind a camera. Photograph by Gerard Malanga.**

Right: **Nico becomes a brunette again and wears an air of mystery. Cigarette in hand, leaning lightly against a cemetery cross, Nico is no longer the ethereal Chelsea Girl of the 1960s but a woman battling with her demons.**

Opposite: **Silkscreened by Andy Warhol, Nico had a lost look and a mysterious air that fascinated him from their first meeting. She was a "moon goddess" that he wanted to turn into the 1966 Girl of the Year. Photograph by Gerard Malanga.**

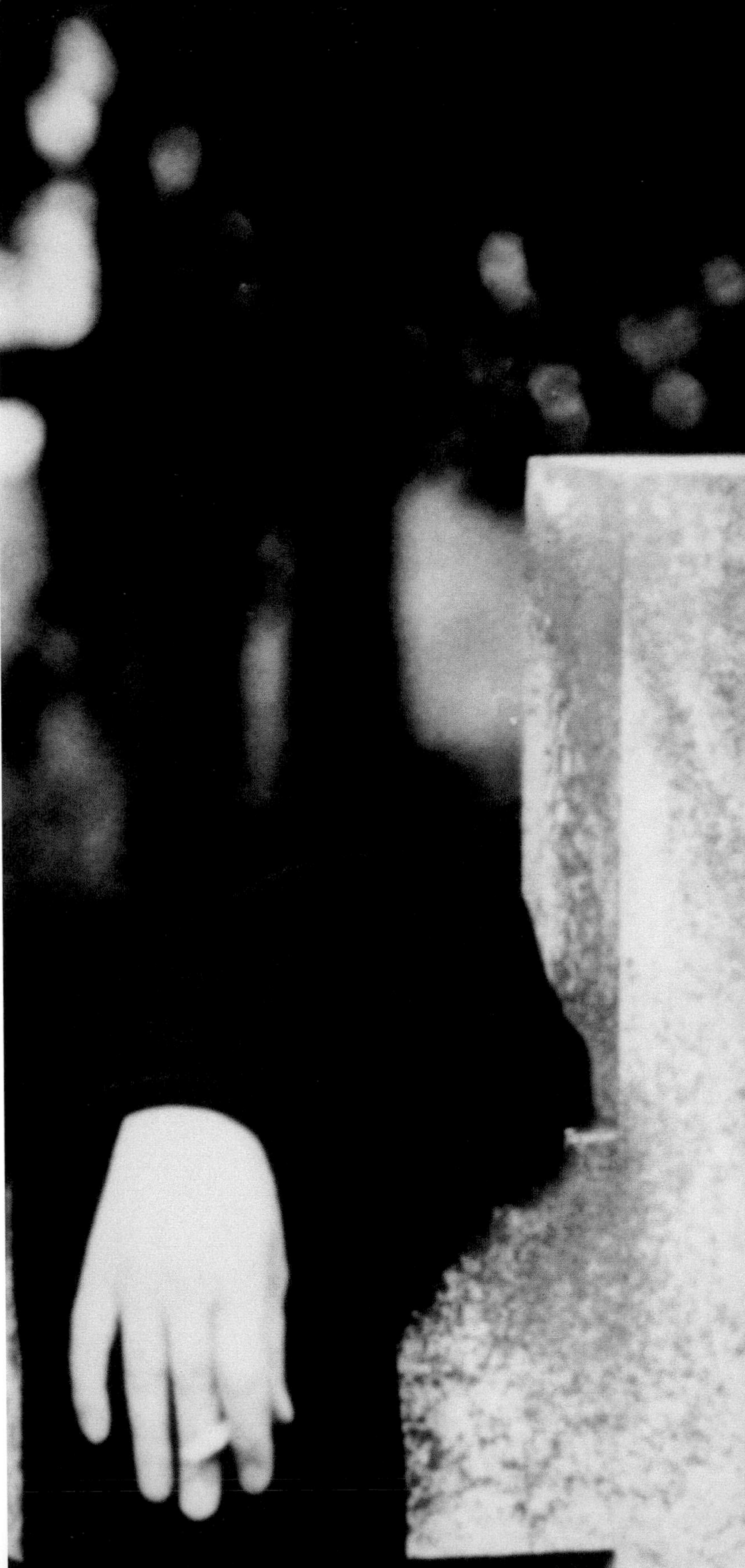

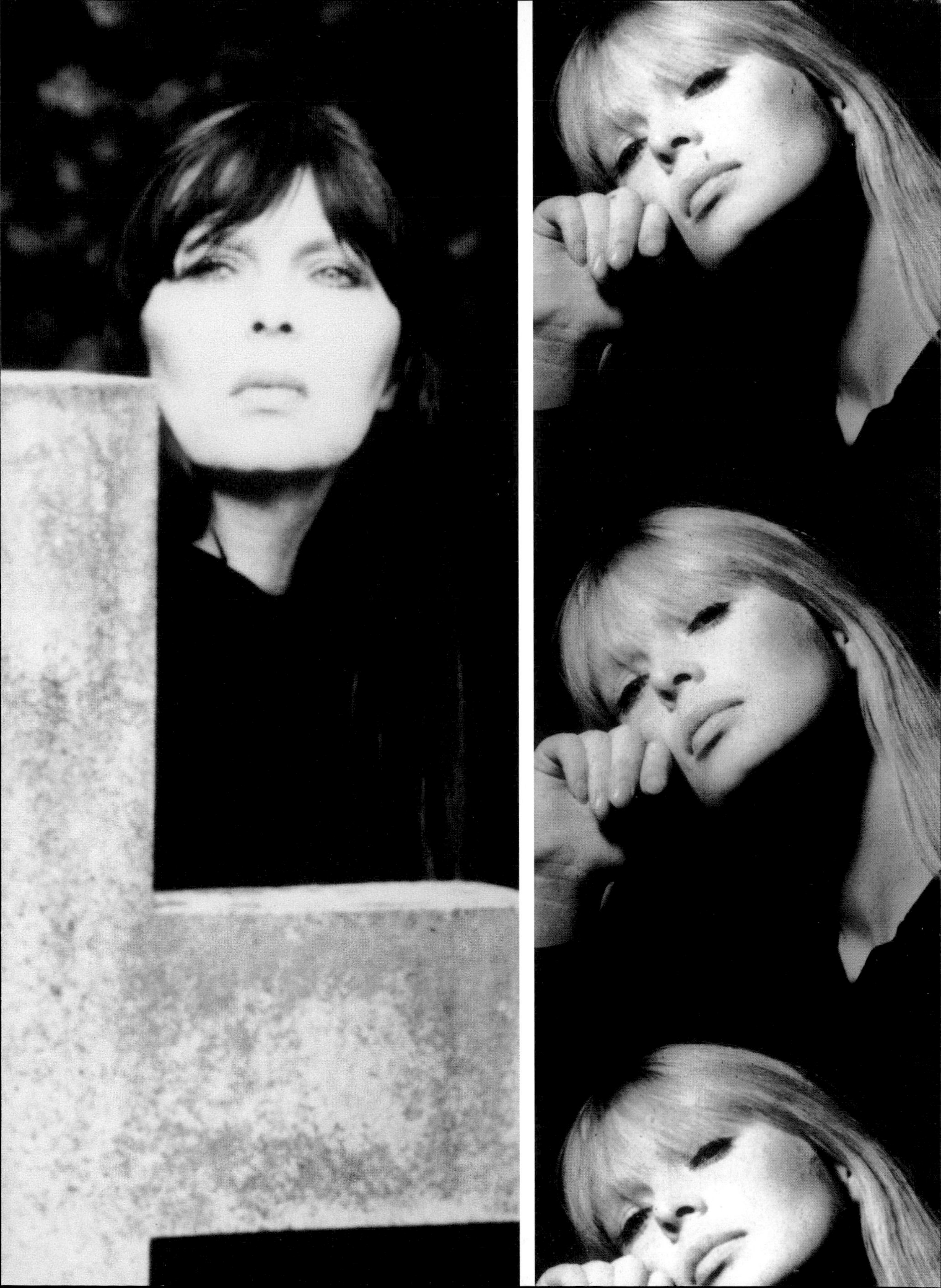

Nico (1966) and silkscreened a banana whose skin could be peeled away to expose the bare fruit. On tour the audience found themselves confronted with images of the singer: "Nico's face, Nico's mouth, Nico sideways, backwards, superimposed, on the walls, the ceiling, on Nico herself as she stands onstage impassively singing," recalled a spectator. Warhol worked hard in 1966 to make her the Girl of the Year. To support his campaign, he bought a half-page ad in the *Village Voice* and invited the public to enjoy themselves at the Exploding Plastic Inevitable. It was a wild name for an eclectic group that combined the Velvet Underground, Warhol himself, and Malanga, who performed sadomasochistic dances on stage. The event was produced at a huge dance hall located in the Polski Dom Narodowy (the Polish National Home) in the heart of the East Village. A mixed crowd of fashion people, middle-class partyers, criminals, and drug addicts of every kind lined up for a month to get into the center of cruising and drugs.

Returning to the Factory, Warhol had more and more difficulty working. Malanga tried to regulate the premises by posting a sign that read: "Please telephone or confirm visits, appointments, etc. No drop-ins. The Factory. ALL JUNK OUT." Wishful thinking.

Chelsea Girl

Among the habitués of the Factory, many lived in the Chelsea Hotel on West 23rd Street in New York. Warhol decided to take his cameras there in 1966 to film eight rooms in twelve reels and juxtapose the stories on the screen. Scenes in the bathrooms, stripteases, drugs, all the falseness of the Factory was displayed in the light of day. At the head of the cast was Nico, who would prove her charisma as a superstar on the screen. In the first sequence she cuts her bangs wordlessly. A masculine voice is heard in the background, then the sound of a child crying "Mommy." It's Ari, Nico's son, who played his own role. Nico responds to him in French. The camera zooms in on a cabinet. Nico brushes her hair, all the while looking at herself in the mirror. A grotesque vision of a happy family, *Chelsea Girls* provides a mournful view of America, of the quagmire in Vietnam, the fascination with drugs, with sexual liberty, the demand for equal opportunity, and the liberalization of marijuana. In an era when the United States was aiming for the moon, Warhol filmed Americans in a dreary hotel who seemed to live lives unconnected to the outside world. Three hours and fifteen minutes long, *Chelsea Girls* became a film legend. This underground movie was being shown at the biggest theaters in Manhattan and was a sensation on university campuses. The following spring, the whole group traveled to the Cannes Film Festival, dressed in pants, black leather boots, and sunglasses of the same color, and were the main attraction on La Croisette, stealing the scene from Brigitte Bardot. But the film, judged scandalous, was not shown, further increasing its wild reputation.

Warhol's dream of being the king of rock and roll, however, misfired. His tours ran out of steam the more he struggled to impose Nico on the Velvet Underground. The singer recorded her first solo album, *Chelsea Girl,* in July 1967, and the Velvet Underground, abandoned by Warhol, soon disappeared from the New York scene. Nico would lead a rocky existence, alternating periods of drugs and detox. When she died in a hospital in Ibiza, Spain, on July 18, 1988, after a fall from a motorcycle, the medical examiner simply noted in his report that the cause of death was cerebral hemorrhage. The year before on April 1, 1987, Nico did not attend a memorial service for Warhol at St. Patrick's Cathedral in New York. The music chosen for her last rites was neither the Velvet Underground nor Nico but *Louange à l'immortalité de Jésus* by Olivier Messiaen. By way of obituary, Serge Daney wrote in the French newspaper *Libération*: "Nico was broke the greater part of her life, she made few concessions, she loved Goethe and, each morning, she sang her whole repertoire, very loudly, and the neighbors never complained."

Bibliography

Bourdon, David. *Warhol*. New York: Harry N. Abrams, Inc., 1989.

Nico Icon. Documentary directed by Susanne Ofteringer, 1995.

Ultra Violet. *Famous for 15 Minutes: My Years with Andy Warhol*. New York: Avon Books, 1990.

From the Beyond

The spirit of Captain Gregg, dictating his memoirs to Lucy in *The Ghost and Mrs. Muir*, the 1947 film by Joseph L. Mankiewicz, has become the archetype of an artist inspired daily by the familiar presence of a person who has died. Certain people can continue to be a muse even after their passing. The death of the brother to whom all his work was dedicated did not prevent the artist Joseph Cornell from pursuing a dialogue with him, and the loss of Aoki Yoko, the wife of the photographer Araki Nobuyoshi, seemed to act as additional artistic incentive, prolonging in both cases the creative processes that had begun during their lifetimes.

Robert Cornell
Joseph Cornell

The Brother and the Box

The first American artist to be recognized in Europe, Joseph Cornell rarely left his house on Utopia Parkway in Flushing, Queens, New York. It was there, near his invalid brother, that Cornell created the boxes that enclosed the small universes he designed for Robert. His brother's death would not interrupt their dialogue. By becoming Joseph's "angel," Robert continued to inspire him after his death.

In 1910 Joseph Cornell was nearly seven years old when his brother Robert was born, a small child almost without words and gestures who would spend his life in a wheelchair due to cerebral palsy. He possessed, they said, "just enough body to house his soul." But to Joseph, Robert's eyes spoke of the eternal childhood into which he was plunged. Confined indoors, Robert lived as if outside of time, and his brother Joseph brought the world to him. He crafted a kaleidoscope with a fragmented view of the stars, into which Robert could travel without end, as well as an enormous model to play with—a landscape complete with hills, waterfalls, and villages that could light up. Robert was connected to the world through his love of radio and his drawings; he sketched animals in a naïve style, especially innocent and kind rabbits, to whom he gave varied names: the white rabbit, Prince Pince, and, referring to his brother Joseph's boxes, Kepler Rabbit and Ravel-Rabbit. Joseph worked close by. After the first toys created for his brother, he moved on to collages and then to boxes in which he obsessively built worlds using objects, photos, and old books he found in Manhattan.

Celebrating Eternal Childhood

His boxes would quickly render him famous. Joseph Cornell was the first American artist internationally recognized at a time when the two terms—artist and American—were seldom linked. He was known as the American Surrealist, and his creations were regularly presented in group exhibitions, even in Europe. In 1937 Cornell's *Glass Bell* (1932), a glass bell jar positioned over a mannequin's hand holding a collage of a rose containing an eye, was reproduced in the Surrealist review *Le Minotaure*. "As long as he is alive and working, Europe cannot treat our country's art with disdain," said Robert Motherwell of Joseph Cornell.

And yet it was almost by accident that Joseph Cornell became such a recognized artist. The man who would celebrate eternal childhood was born into a well-off family on December 24, 1903, the oldest son of four children: himself, his brother Robert, and two sisters. They lived in a large house in Nyack, north of New York

City, on the Hudson River. But in 1917 his father, a textile designer and fabric salesman for men's clothing, was struck down by leukemia. "He loved life and luxuries and left nothing behind him but debts," said Diane Waldman, Joseph Cornell's biographer, of the father. The family had to find more modest accommodations and moved into a succession of houses in Queens before settling down at 37-08 Utopia Parkway. Joseph was studying the natural sciences and romance languages—Spanish, French, and Latin—but abandoned them in 1921 to assume financial responsibility for the family by working in the textile industry. He was employed in Manhattan, and his journey there each day was a constant source of inspiration. He discovered the cinema and ballet, frequented used bookstores near Times Square, and bought records—principally Debussy, Ravel, and Satie. He also began to collect "Americana" as well as colored Sandwich glass. He never returned to Utopia Parkway later than 8:30 pm. When he saw his brother, his face would light up. It brought him great happiness to see him smile and he marveled at Robert's cheerfulness.

The stock market crash of 1929 would upset this routine. Cornell lost his job in 1931 and took on a series of part-time jobs to survive. It was in the course of his rounds that he discovered the works of Max Ernst, Salvador Dalí, and other Surrealists exhibited in Julian Levy's new gallery on Madison Avenue. Cornell showed the dealer his collages, which, like those by Max Ernst, reworked end-of-the-century engravings. Levy encouraged him and the following year began to exhibit the objects and boxes that would make Cornell famous.

These works were usually glass-fronted shadow boxes, which Cornell fabricated out of wood. Sometimes they were painted in white or blue tones, the colors of his house on Utopia Parkway. Occasionally he glued old texts printed in French, Latin, or Greek on the edges of the frames or on the back. Sometime the boxes resembled little pharmaceutical cabinets filled with bottles containing images, shells, folded paper, or butterfly wings. Other times they were like mini stages featuring silhouettes or images of children's heads cut out from copies of Renaissance paintings, or they displayed old-fashioned advertisements. Mirror fragments and bits of colored glass refracted these strange universes, in which the viewer encountered birds, compasses, wooden and glass balls, marbles, soap bubble pipes, and more. Of these endless and infinitely small worlds, Joseph Cornell was both a creator and an explorer.

Right: **A rare photograph reuniting all the Cornell children. Born in 1903, Joseph was the oldest. After him came his two sisters and then Robert, his invalid brother for whom he began to create the boxes that would earn him the moniker "American Surrealist."**
Below: **A horse drawn by Robert Cornell enclosed in a box by Joseph Cornell. Shortly after the death of his brother, Joseph exhibited constructions and collages that incorporated Robert's drawings.**

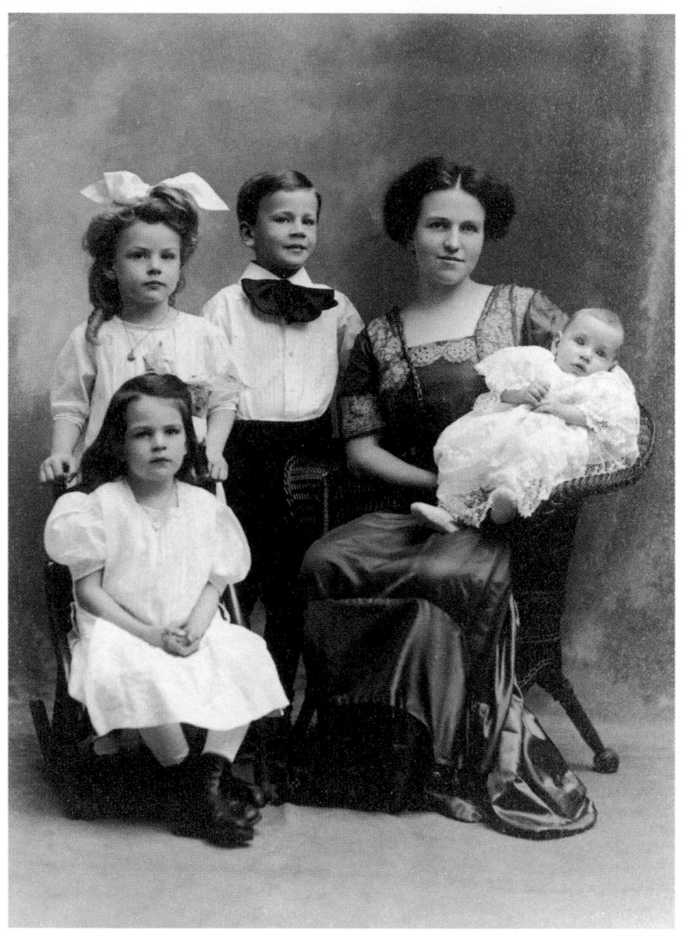

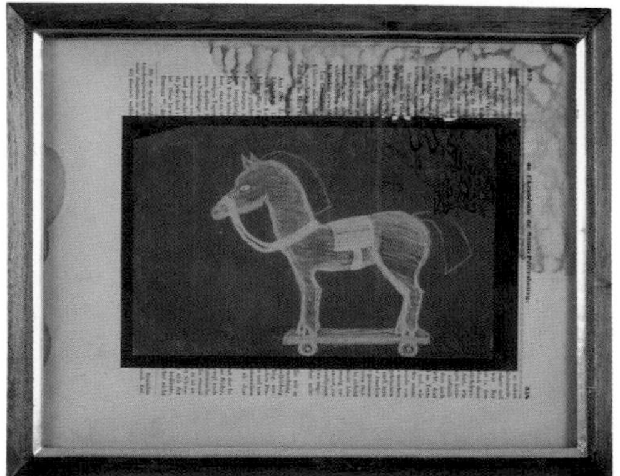

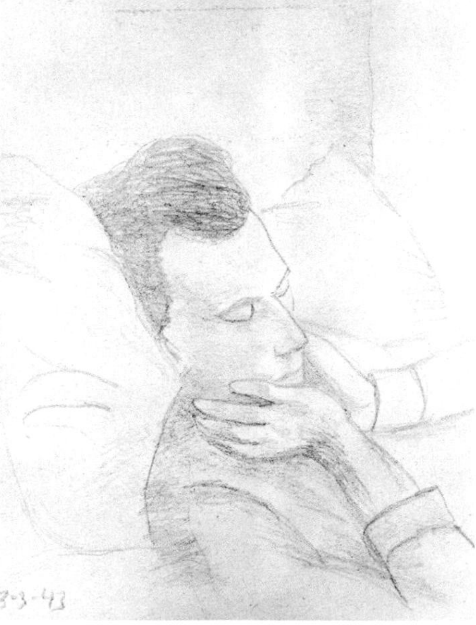

Right: **Joseph Cornell drawn by Robert Cornell in March 1943. The creator of the famous boxes considered his brother to be an artist in his own right.**
Opposite: **Joseph Cornell in front of his *Garbo: The Crystal Mask*, c. 1939.**

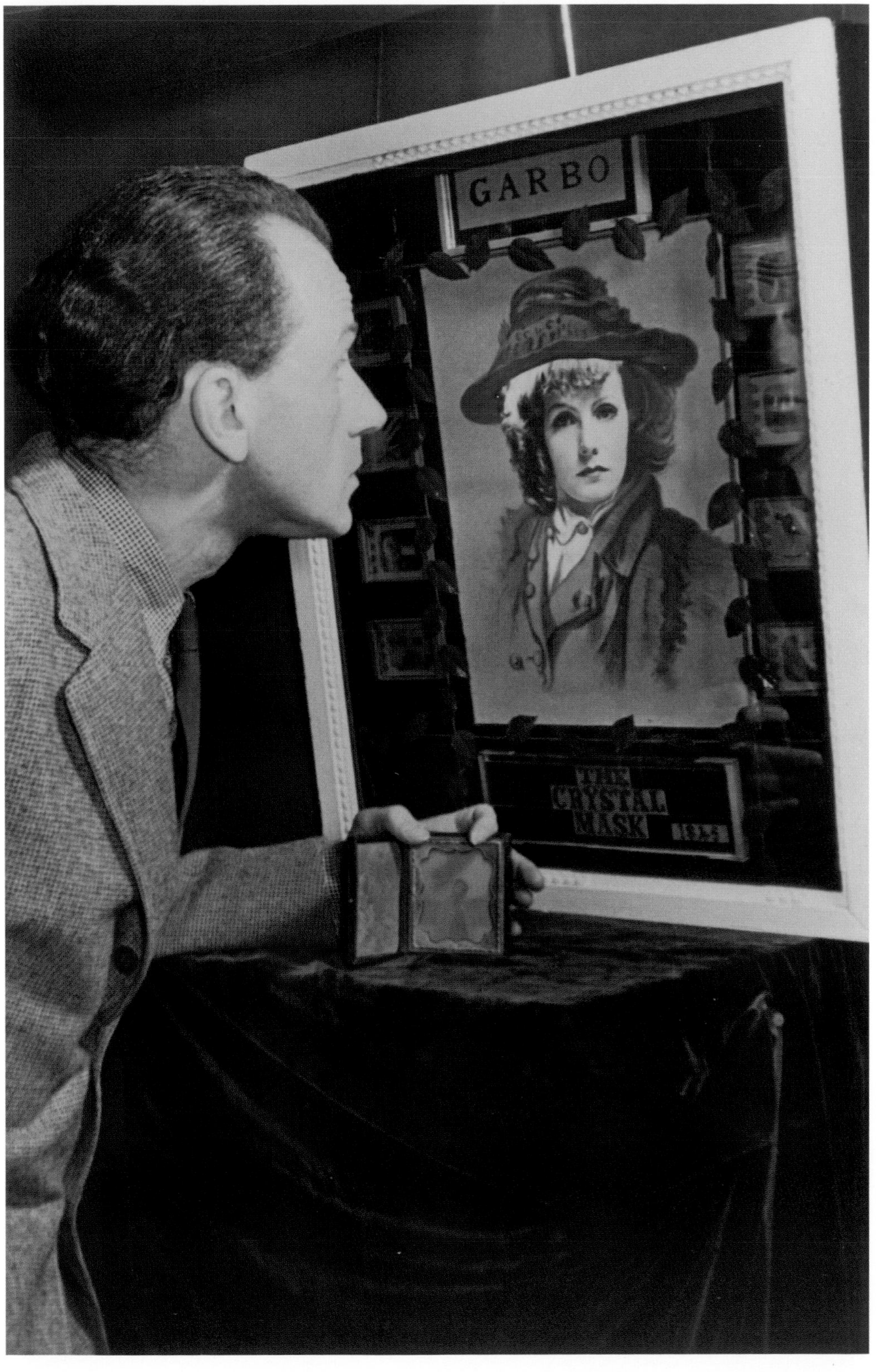
GARBO
THE
CRYSTAL
MASK

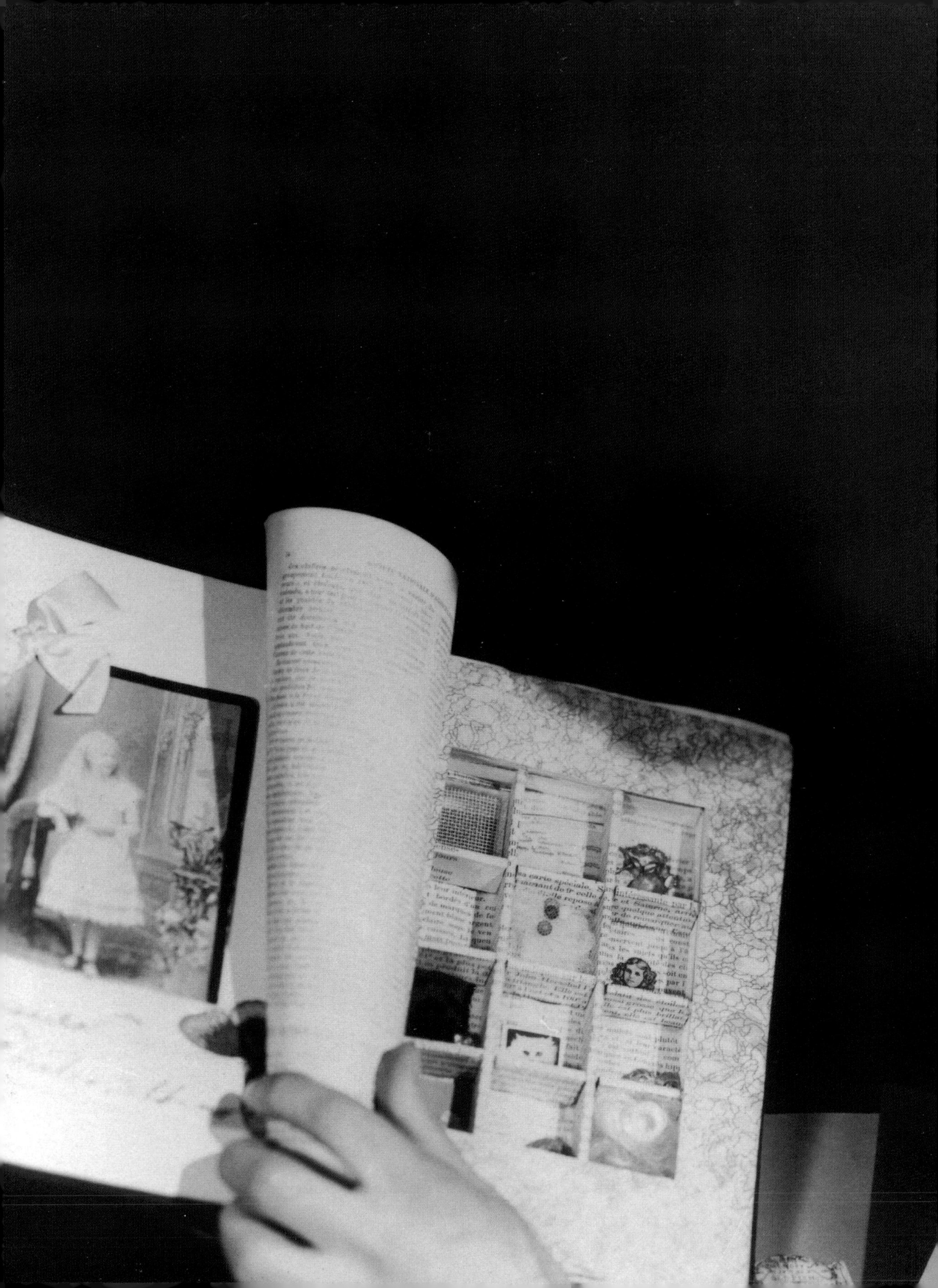

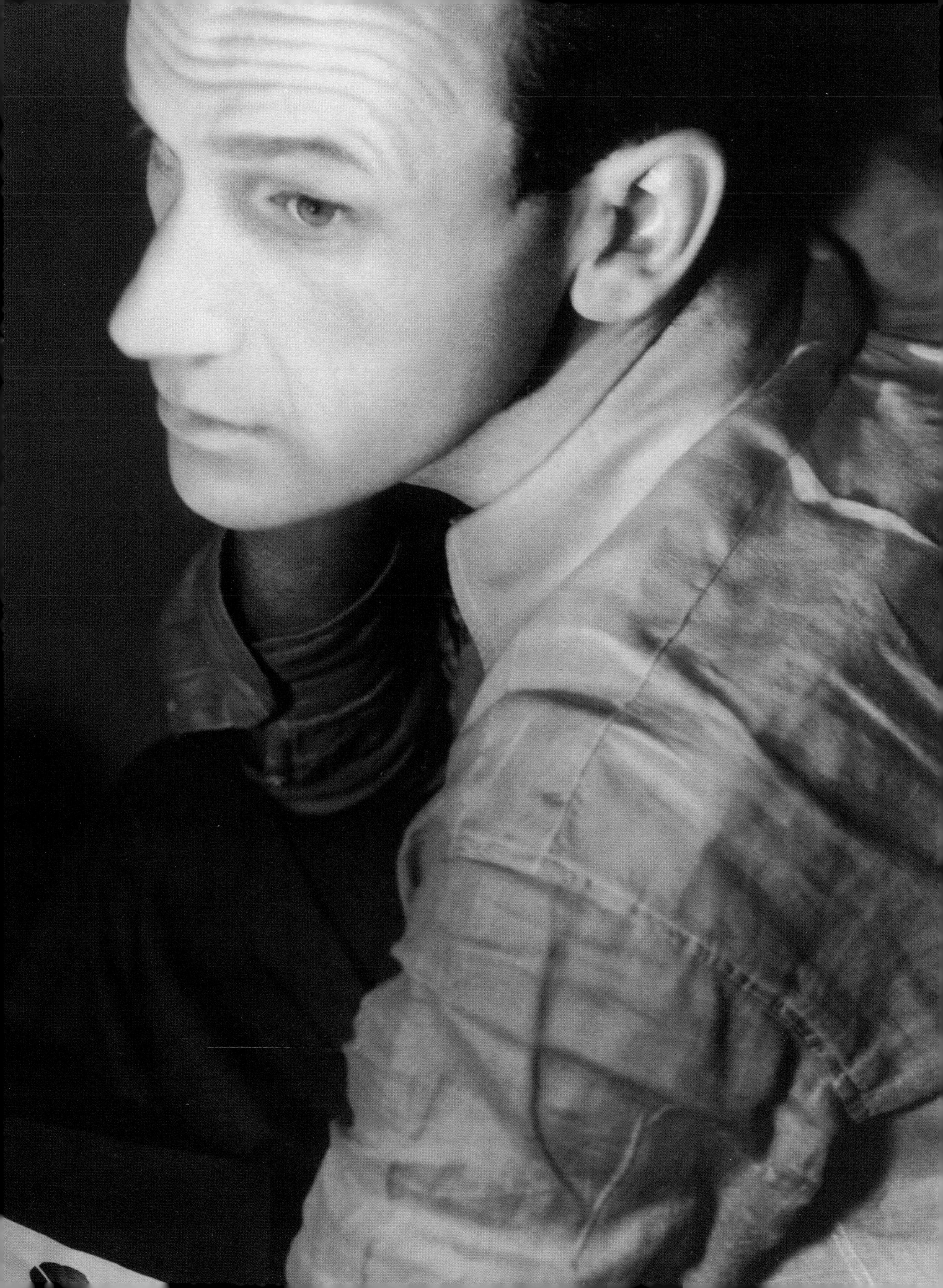

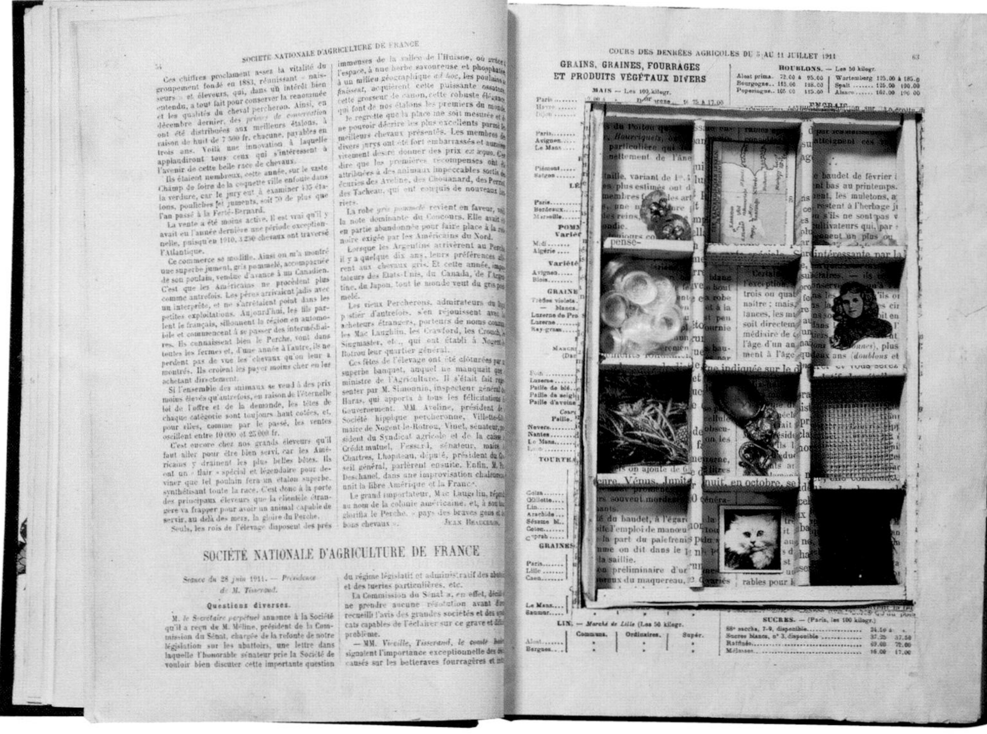
SOCIÉTÉ NATIONALE D'AGRICULTURE DE FRANCE
COURS DES DENRÉES AGRICOLES DU 5 AU 11 JUILLET 1911
GRAINS, GRAINES, FOURRAGES ET PRODUITS VÉGÉTAUX DIVERS

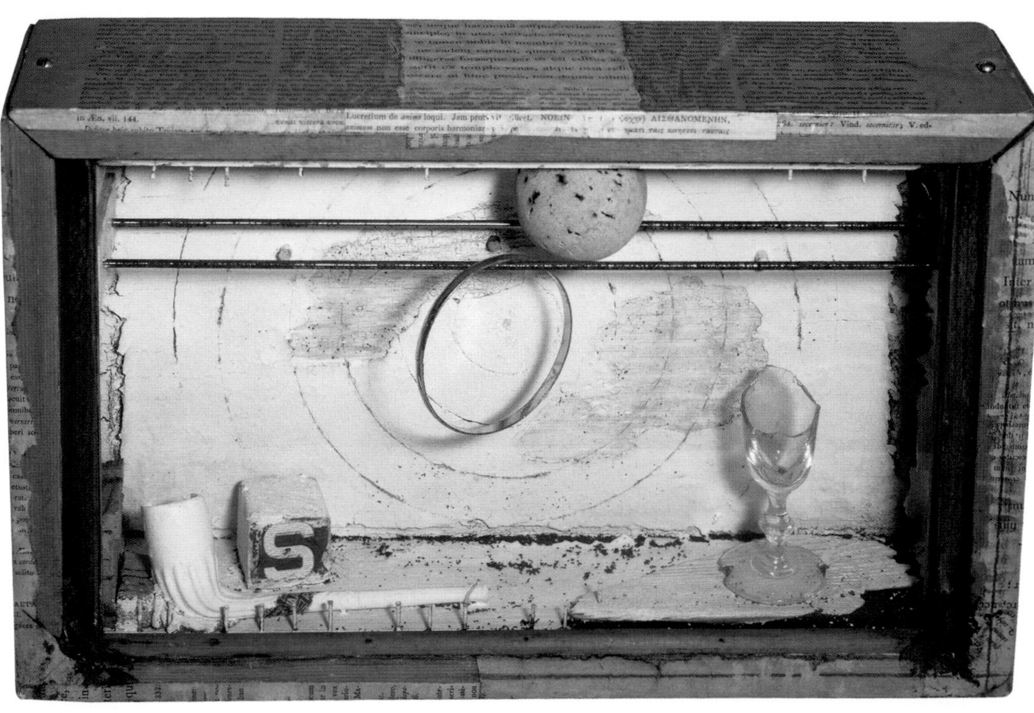
S

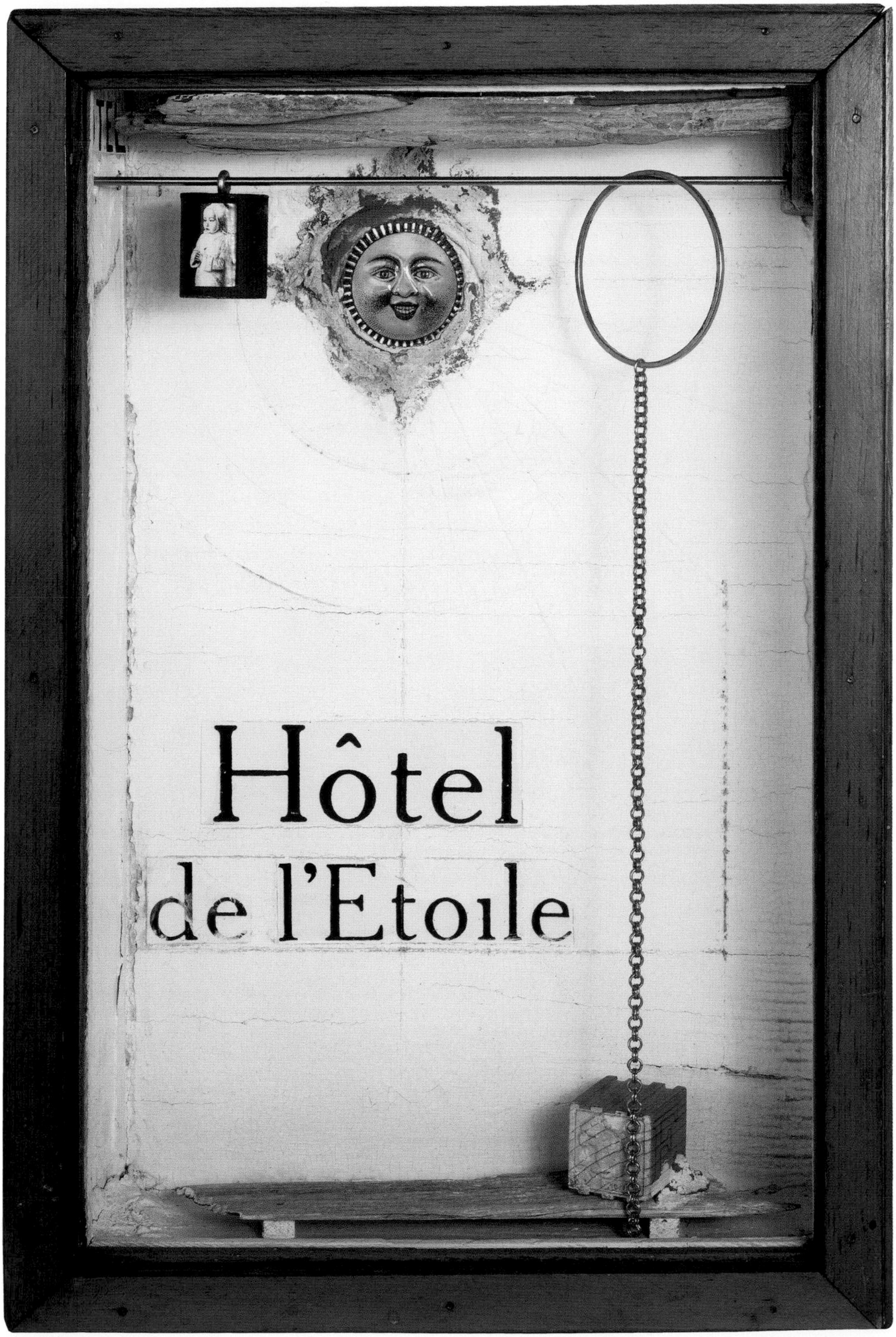

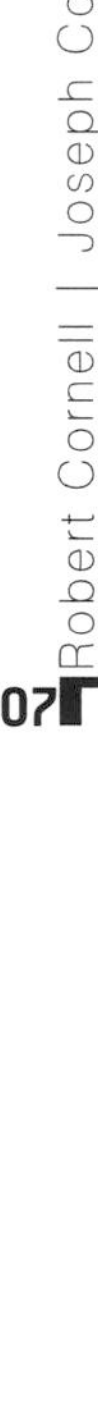

Pages 304–05: **Joseph Cornell posing with one of his works.**

Page 306, top: **Joseph Cornell, *Untitled ("To Marguerita Blachas")* (before 1940). One of the strangest works by Cornell, it features a collection of small boxes fitted into a volume from the Société nationale d'agriculture de France (The National Agricultural Society of France).**

Page 306, bottom: **Joseph Cornell, *Untitled (Liber Tertius)* (1966). Cornell often covered his boxes with Latin and Greek texts so that the voyage into space was combined with a voyage in time.**

Page 307: **Joseph Cornell, *Untitled (Hôtel de l'Étoile)* (circa 1956). In the course of his imaginary travels through his boxes, Cornell often wound up at the Hôtel de l'Étoile, whose name evokes the heavens and Paris simultaneously.**

For a man who never left the state of New York, Joseph Cornell was a great traveler. His boxes contain traces of imaginary visits to Mozambique, from which he brought back a stamp, or to the Grand Hotel in the imaginary Golden Islands, or to hotels in Paris. Was this nostalgia for his studies or a consequence of his association with Surrealists? More than anything, Cornell was obsessed with France; his diary and his correspondence, published under the lovely title *Theater of the Mind*, are written half in French, and fragments of the *Bulletin de la Société française d'agriculture* and mementos of the Hôtel des Grands Hommes, where André Breton met the mysterious Nadja, can be found in his constructions.

A Store Full of Holiday Toys

Cornell's imaginary voyages led him to the edge of the universe; his works are filled with smiling suns, star charts, city maps, and starfish. Like an absent-minded professor, everything was collected, classified, and arranged with the seriousness of a child at play. These works, so carefully conserved by museums and found in the most prestigious art collections today, were originally toys destined to be manipulated by his brother—with balls that would roll and rings that would slide along a metal bar. Cornell's oeuvre, wrote a journalist in the *Herald Tribune*, was "a store full of holiday toys for the delight of intellectuals."

"How," asked Robert Motherwell, "could he have created this work in the conditions in which he created it?" Joseph's magic universe was not limited only to boxes. He and his brother shared a fascination with the films of Charlie Chaplin and Georges Méliès, which Joseph showed during family parties, as well as *Un Chien andalou*, the avant-garde film by Luis Buñuel and Dalí, and this led Cornell to create his own films. Just as personal as his constructions, these movies were often created from bits of film stock glued end to end. In the 1950s and 1960s a new generation of American artists would be filled with enthusiasm for these short films, claiming that they represented Pop art or Minimalism.

In addition, Cornell, who lived alone with his infirm brother and deaf mother, was often infatuated with young working girls and movie stars. In his diary he expressed his emotions at having walked by Marlene Dietrich on a New York street and made artwork inspired by Lauren Bacall, by the French actress Mylène Demongeot, and even by a ballerina once loved by the nineteenth-century children's author Hans Christian Andersen. Cornell also fell in love with the dancer—as if he had lived in another era, as in a dream. The artist's romantic life was as mysterious as his work. There was a brief liaison in 1964 with the great Japanese artist Yayoi Kusama, whose life was always balanced on the edge of madness, and a passion for a certain Joyce Hunter, whom Cornell liked to call Tina, a cashier at the Ripley's Believe It or Not Museum in Manhattan. Hunter would go on to live with him, like a new incarnation of his brother's eternal innocence. Hunter would steal a number of the artist's boxes, but Cornell—usually so careful with his works—could not bring himself to deal with her harshly and continued the relationship.

In December 1964 Tina was killed by a policeman. Her death, followed by Robert's two months later and his mother's in October 1967, while devastating to Joseph, would open a new world for him peopled by those whom he called "angels." At his brother's death, he exclaimed: "Rabbit, darling rabbit!" and recorded in his diary: "The road is mapped out for me."

The following year he prepared an exhibition of collages that integrated his brother's drawings. Robert had not really left him. He heard his voice and saw him transformed into a little girl. He bought him a book by the poet T.S. Eliot which he dedicated equally to his other angel, Tina, and recopied into his diary this citation by Marcel Proust: "We have learned from Chardin that a pear is as alive as a woman, that ordinary pottery is as beautiful as a precious stone. The painter has proclaimed the divine equality of all things in the mind and before the light that embellishes them." Joseph continued to fabricate his boxes, so that after his death Robert would not stop dreaming before them.

Bibliography

Caws, Mary Ann, ed. *Joseph Cornell's Theater of the Mind: Selected diaries, letters and files.* New York: Thames and Hudson, 2000.

Solomon, Diane. *Utopia Parkway: The Life and Work of Joseph Cornell*. New York: Noonday Press/Farrar, Straus and Giroux, 1997.

Waldman, Diane. *Joseph Cornell*. New York: George Braziller Inc., 1977.

———. *Joseph Cornell: Master of Dreams*. New York: Harry N. Abrams, Inc., 2002.

Aoki Yoko
Araki Nobuyoshi

Love and Bondage

The heroine of Araki Nobuyoshi's photographic novel since their encounter in 1968, their marriage, and their honeymoon, Aoki Yoko remained the key figure in Araki's life and work after her death in 1990, alongside the bound women who brought fame to the Japanese photographer.

A candle beneath the portrait of a woman. Next page. Flowers everywhere and a passing cat. An urn and the photo of the same woman with the shapely mouth. A coffin ready for the crematory oven. A hearse in the early morning street. A body laid out. A gown for the dead. The face of a woman and the hands of a man on the edge of a coffin. An abandoned bicycle. A meal, a city unaware of this death, factories, a large turning wheel. A hospital, a hand sticking out of a bed. A waiting cat. The woman from the portrait smiling and eating soup. A still smiling woman standing in an empty hotel room. A woman preparing to take a bath and caressing the cat. A woman brushing her teeth, laying in bed as if after love-making, posing half nude in the countryside, posing completely nude in her bedroom. A woman with a sad expression seated on a train looking at the empty place beside her. A photo of a marriage. Yoko and Araki. She, a brunette of no great beauty. He, a short fellow, half samurai, half monk. They met in 1968 at the Dentsu advertising agency where they both worked. He was twenty-three, she was twenty; From then on, Araki's photographic universe revolved around her. Or rather around the "I novel" of which Araki claimed to be the author. In this photographic story, which followed the formula set by writer Alain Jouffroy, Araki focused on everyday life: the 1971 marriage, the honeymoon on the islands of Okinawa, bathrooms, a meal, an unmade bed. These snapshots were published quickly under the title *Sentimental Journey*. At the same time Araki took his first bondage shots, images of bound women which he refused to qualify as pornography but which he published from 1979 in the very "specialized" magazine, *S & M Sniper*. With these photos of pubic areas, naked bound women, pregnant bodies, twisted forms, Araki instantly acquired a reputation as a wild photographer. When a year after Yoko died Araki published *Sentimental Journey, Winter Journey*, the scandal brought his work to light. His friend Kishin Shinoyama initiated a debate with him through the intermediary of newspapers, accusing him of profiting from the death of his wife to gain publicity and make money, all while seeking to obtain the public's pity. The photos do great harm, said the friend. They are honest, replied Araki. With this death Araki proved something that he had felt for a long time: photography and death are closely related. "When you stop something that moves, it is a kind of death," he declared to the American photographer Nan Goldin, with whom he worked in 1994 on an illustrated book called *Tokyo Love*. "The camera, the photographic image have always suggested the idea of death. And I think about death when I take photos."

Against Death: Binding Life

Of Yoko, we know nothing, or almost nothing. In 1984 as an anniversary present, Araki published at his own expense a short story by Yoko entitled *Novel* and the following year *Love Life*. Together they collaborated on several illustrated books, the last of which, *Beautiful Tokyo Days*, was interrupted by her illness and then death. Yoko existed, since Araki photographed her—or did she exist because he photographed her? Was this absolute love also a poetic invention? "Perhaps I had only the relationship of photographer with her, not partner," Araki intimated. Did her death change Araki's photography? From then on his models were perpetually changed and his photographic novel seemed to be enlarged to include all of Tokyo.

Curiously we also know very little about Araki. He was born on May 25, 1940, in Minowa, a working class area of Tokyo, into a family of clog makers. His father, an amateur photographer, gave him his first camera, a Baby Pearl, with which he took his first snapshots during vacations. He collected odds and ends, miniature animals, scale models, snakes, lizards, dragons, dinosaurs, and crocodiles. "The little animals I collected represented my desires. Through them I penetrated the female body," he admitted readily. At the center of his photography, therefore, was the female body: women wearing make-up, often with cheerful expressions, nude or clad in open kimonos, usually tied up, and offering their sex to the viewer. Condemned several times for his "bondage" shots—these bound women who made him famous—he defended himself against the charge of providing degrading images of woman, insisting on their consent, on their pleasure at posing, at playing even, since it was for him a kind of theater, complete with actors and lighting. Between Araki and his model a kind of choreography was improvised each time Araki moved, spoke, directed, requested, or leaned on the camera, initiating a duel or a kind of dance with his actress, who in her turn, suggested new poses. A veritable pop star for more than twenty years in

Japan, his first solo exhibition in the West took place in Graz, Austria, in 1992, soon followed by innumerable shows in Europe. Sought by the world's great museums, selling images in the best galleries—at prices lower than shots by the greatest photographers, however, since Araki did not want to enter into the Western system of limited editions—he has changed nothing about his way of life. He seldom leaves Tokyo, and when he travels to Europe for an exhibition it is so that he can also work there, like in Amsterdam where he surveyed and photographed the red-light district. He lives at night, surrounded by a flock of fans, always accompanied by his assistant and manager, who also acts as an interpreter for foreign visitors. In the street girls greet him and ask him to take a turn at karaoke. There's a party every night, but he is working, strolling around with several cameras to capture everything that's happening. Araki also creates in the studio with a lighting person and a make-up artist meticulously arranging the models who line up to be photographed. What is most shocking for many in the West are the bound bodies that evoke torture and submission. But this interpretation is contrary to the artist's aim, according to Jean-Claude Amman, an expert on Japan and the author of several studies on Araki. "In Japan binding is an expression of auto-eroticism which transcends smallness. Binding is a great art in which blood must not be let and which must be executed by a master." The bound bodies evoke the typically Japanese art of bonsai—dwarf trees whose roots are pruned and compressed, their stalks tied up. Is he shaping the living to give it a new life? This is Araki's gamble: "With Yoko's death, the love that was closest to me disappeared. From that experience, I am moving again toward life. Today I want to show the joy of life." Now every woman who enters into Araki's dance is a substitute for Yoko, perfectly interchangeable with any other model posing under Tokyo skies, whose clouds he photographed during the months after Yoko's death. Today when one of his models sends him a thank you note with the message: "It was a happy day for me," he is happy too.

Opposite: **In 1991, one year after the death of Yoko, Araki published this photograph in *Colorscapes*. By holding a portrait of his wife, he reunites them one last time.**

Bibliography

Nobuyoshi, Araki. *Nobuyoshi Araki: Shino*. Tokyo: Graphic-Sha Pub. Co., 2001.

Ito, Hiromi, et al. *Nobuyoshi Araki: Akt-Tokyo: 1971-1991*. New York: Distributed Art Publishers, 1993.

Sans, Jerome. *Araki by Araki*. New York: Taschen, 2002.

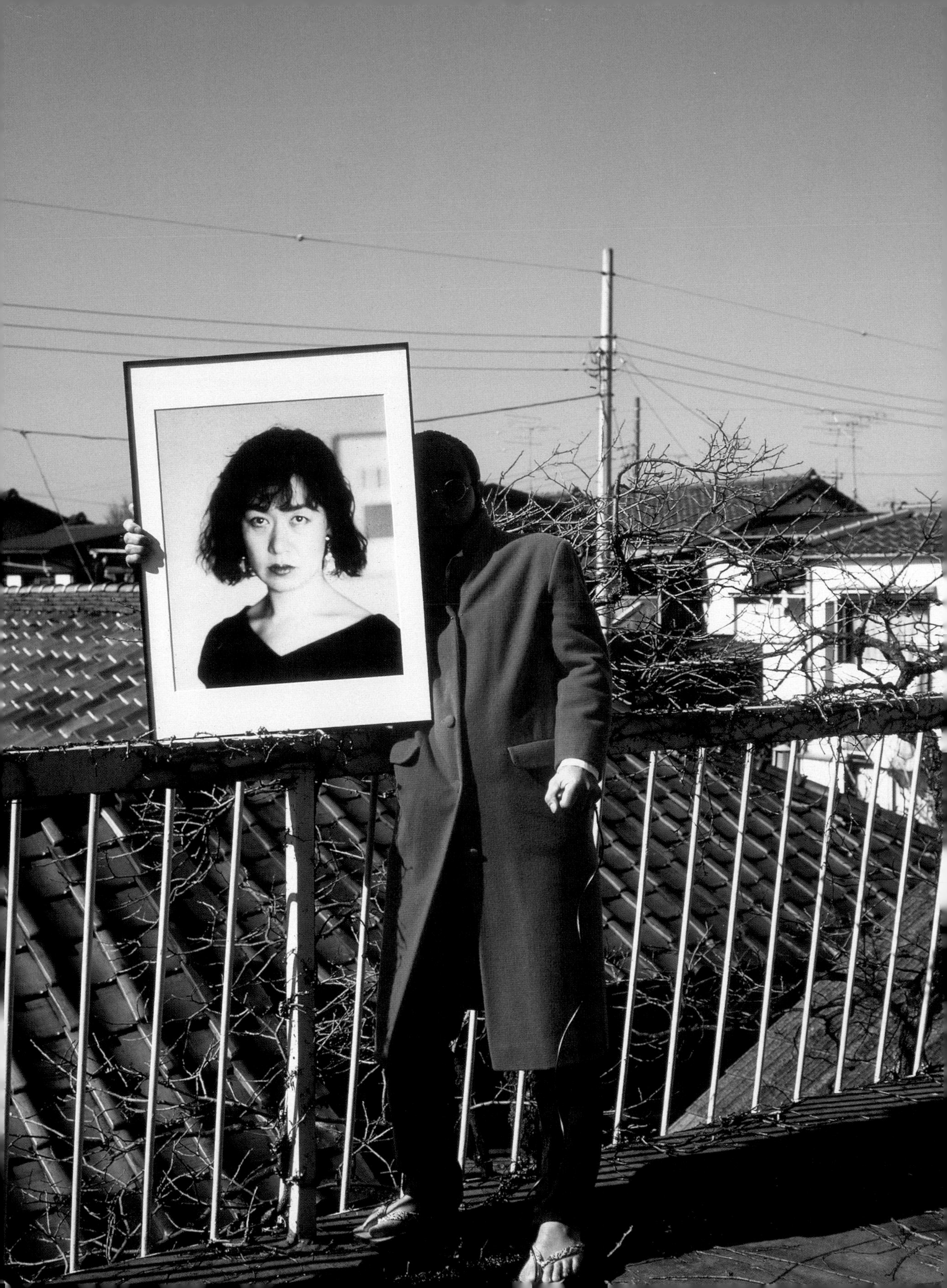

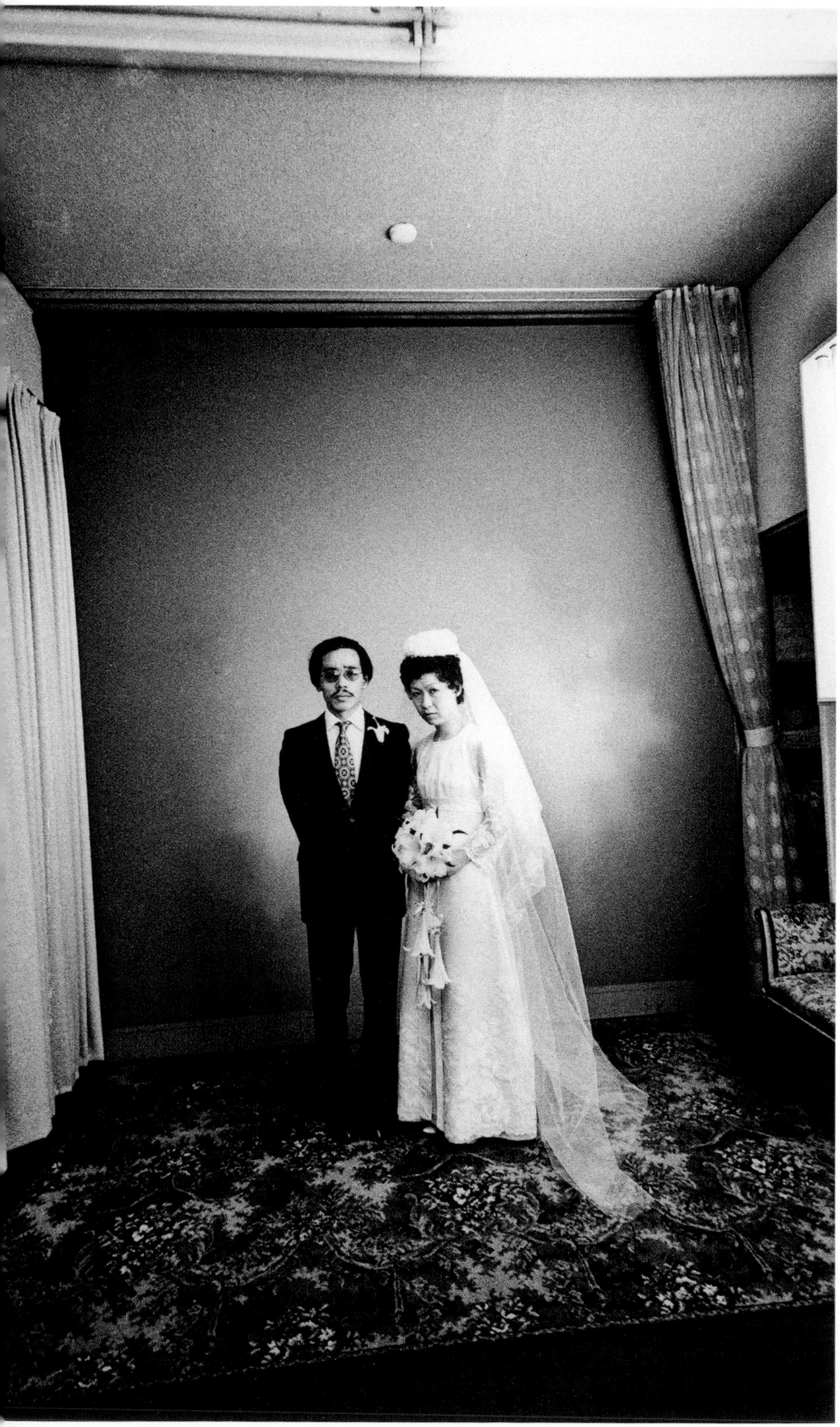

Left: **The official marriage photograph of Araki and Yoko, before they left on their honeymoon to the islands of Okinawa.**
Opposite, top: **Yoko on a bed, part of *Sentimental Journey, Winter Journey*, which Araki printed and published after the death of his wife.**
Below: **Araki and Yoko's hands joined together on a hospital bed.**

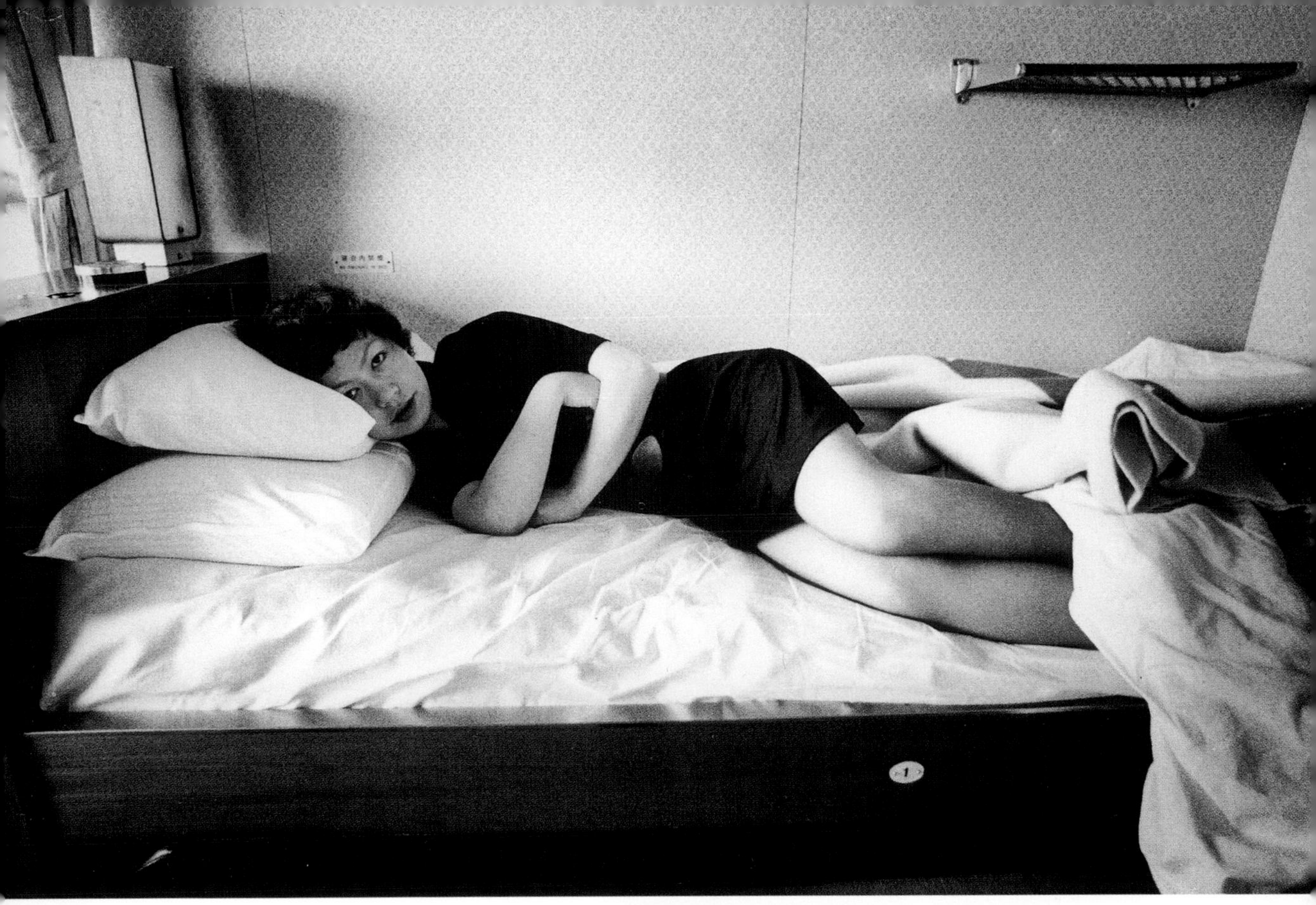

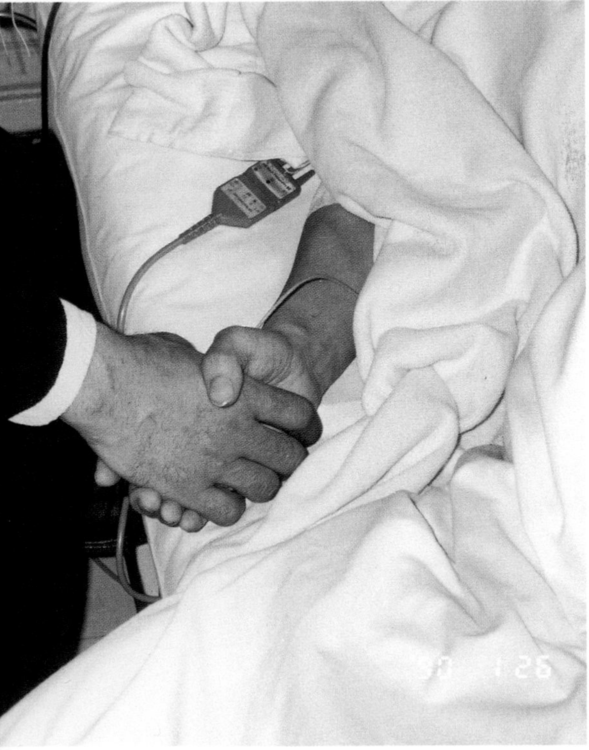

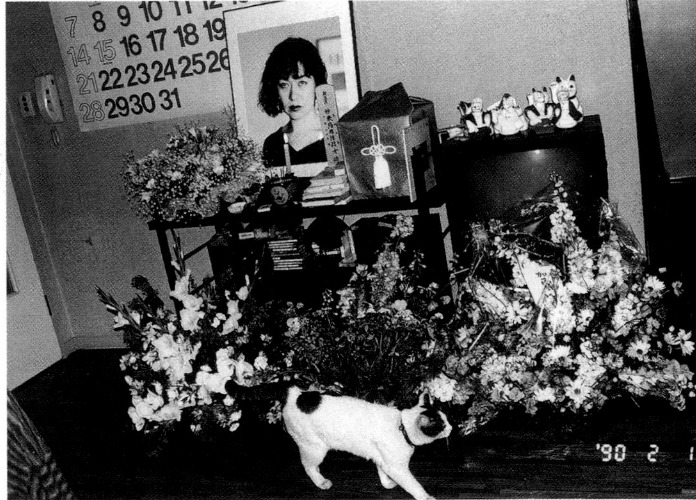

Above: **Their cat—the main witness to their joint adventure—passes in front of the altar set up by Araki as tribute to his wife.**

Pages 318–19: **The butterfly and the flower, the artist's ultimate homage to his muse.**

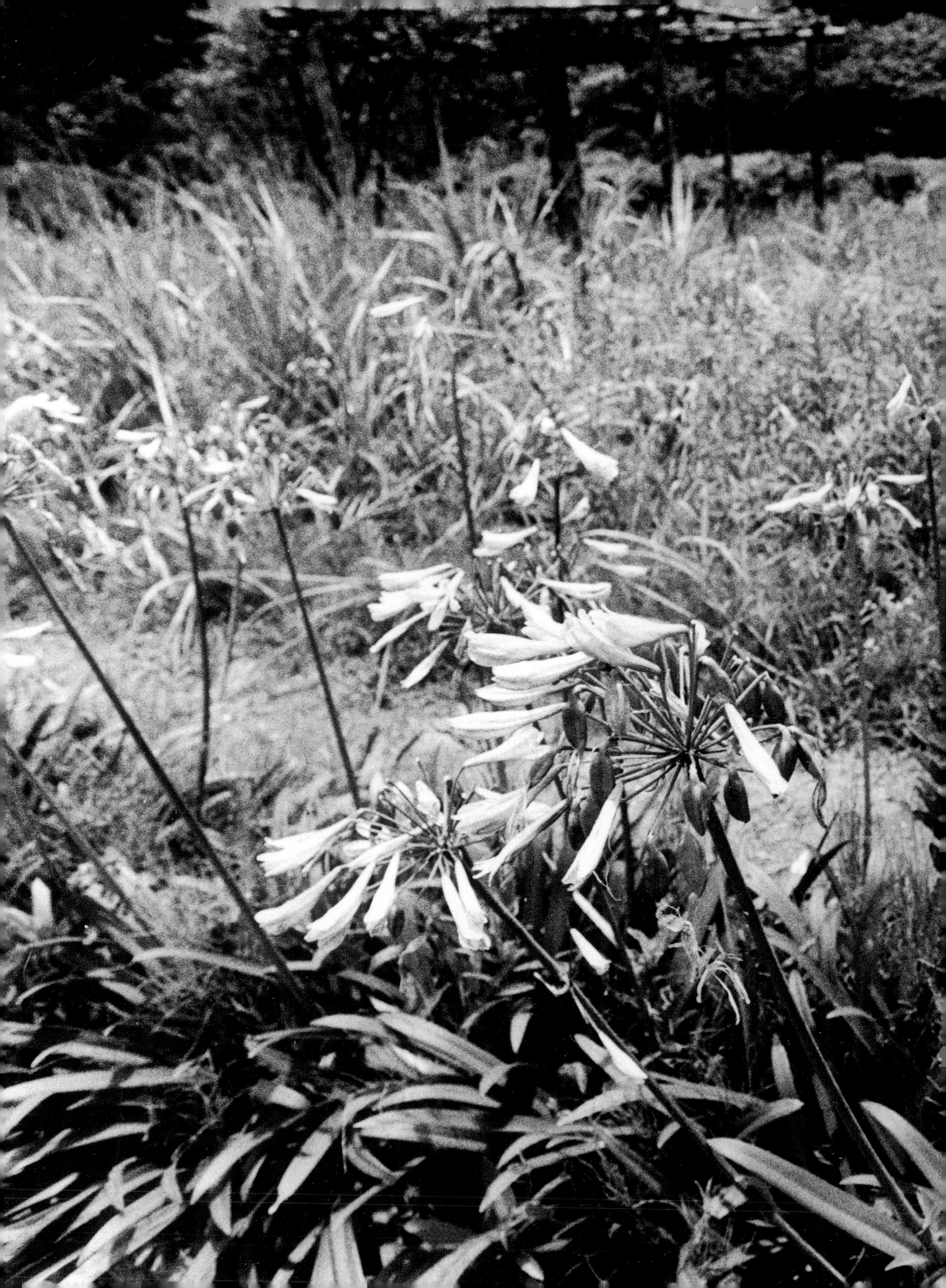